Early Praise for *A Common-Sense Guide to Data Structures and Algorithms in Python, Volume 1*

Students and programmers everywhere are told how important algorithms and data structures are for creating quality software—not to mention getting hired at the best companies—and, yet, there are so few resources that bring actual clarity to the topic. This book does! The combination of Python's simplicity and Jay's ability to drill down on what you need to know is a winning formula. Reading this book is a worthwhile investment for any software engineer.

➤ **Lyndon Purcell**
Software Developer, OK200

A Common Sense Guide to Data Structures and Algorithms in Python is one of those rare books that both unravels the sometimes impenetrable algorithmic content and keeps the reader engaged with a direct and approachable writing style. I highly recommend this book to anyone that wants to dig into algorithms to improve their programming skills.

➤ **Terry Peppers**
Vice President of Engineering, LogicGate

As a beginner to coding, I have read many books on algorithms and Jay's book is the only one which doesn't assume the reader is a math genius nor does it treat you in a condescending manner. From the start of the book he encourages your learning and understanding as a mentor and a friend.

➤ **Katy Douglas**
Student, The Open University

The book serves as an exceptional reference for individuals seeking to grasp the fundamental concepts in data structures and algorithms (DSA) and an ideal entry point to the realm of DSA, particularly for those with limited or no prior background in computer science. It excels in explaining the complex algorithms by using clever illustrations and examples, making the book a fascinating read.

➤ **Ahmad Shahba**
   Lead Software Engineer, Science Systems and Applications, Inc.

The easy-to-digest and approachable content makes the rather obtuse and math-heavy jargon field of data structures and algorithms quite approachable to all. If you don't like switching contexts whilst studying, this special edition is for you, as it uses only Python to demonstrate concepts. You can't go wrong with this book!

➤ **Paa JAKE**
   Software and Test Engineer

A Common-Sense Guide to Data Structures and Algorithms in Python, Volume 1

Level Up Your Core Programming Skills

Jay Wengrow

The Pragmatic Bookshelf

Dallas, Texas

Many of the designations used by manufacturers and sellers to distinguish their products are claimed as trademarks. Where those designations appear in this book, and The Pragmatic Programmers, LLC was aware of a trademark claim, the designations have been printed in initial capital letters or in all capitals. The Pragmatic Starter Kit, The Pragmatic Programmer, Pragmatic Programming, Pragmatic Bookshelf, PragProg and the linking *g* device are trademarks of The Pragmatic Programmers, LLC.

Every precaution was taken in the preparation of this book. However, the publisher assumes no responsibility for errors or omissions, or for damages that may result from the use of information (including program listings) contained herein.

For our complete catalog of hands-on, practical, and Pragmatic content for software developers, please visit *https://pragprog.com*.

The team that produced this book includes:

Publisher: Dave Thomas
COO: Janet Furlow
Managing Editor: Tammy Coron
Development Editor: Katharine Dvorak
Copy Editor: L. Sakhi MacMillan
Indexing: Potomac Indexing, LLC
Layout: Gilson Graphics

For sales, volume licensing, and support, please contact *support@pragprog.com*.

For international rights, please contact *rights@pragprog.com*.

ISBN-13: 979-8-88865-035-6
Book version: P1.0—December 2023

Contents

Preface

Data structures and algorithms are more than abstract concepts. Mastering them enables you to write code that is *efficient*, leading to software that runs faster and consumes less memory. This is a big deal for today's software applications, which exist on increasingly mobile platforms and handle increasingly greater amounts of data.

The problem with most resources on these subjects, though, is that they are...well...obtuse. Most texts go heavy on the math jargon, and if you're not a mathematician, it can be difficult to grasp what on earth is going on. Even books that claim to make algorithms "easy" seem to assume that the reader has an advanced math degree. Because of this, too many people shy away from these concepts feeling that they're not "smart" enough to understand them.

The truth, though, is that everything about data structures and algorithms boils down to common sense. Mathematical notation itself is simply a particular language, and everything in math can also be explained with common-sense terminology. In this book, I use that common-sense language (plus a lot of diagrams!) to explain these concepts in simple and, dare I say, enjoyable ways.

Once you understand these concepts, you'll be equipped to write code that is efficient, fast, and elegant. You'll be able to weigh the pros and cons of various code alternatives and be able to make educated decisions as to which code is best for the given situation.

In this book, I go out of my way to make these concepts real and practical with ideas that you can make use of *today*. Sure, you'll learn some really cool computer science along the way. But this book is about taking that seemingly abstract stuff and making it directly practical. You'll be writing better code and faster software by the time you're done reading this book.

Who Is This Book For?

This book is ideal for several audiences:

- You're a computer science student who wants a text that explains data structures and algorithms in plain English. This book can serve as a supplement to whatever "classic" textbook you happen to be using.

- You're a beginning developer who knows basic programming but wants to learn the fundamentals of computer science to write better code and increase your programming knowledge and skills.

- You're a self-taught developer who has never studied formal computer science (or a developer who did but forgot everything!) and wants to leverage the power of data structures and algorithms to write more scalable and elegant code.

Whoever you may be, I tried to write this book so that it can be accessed and enjoyed by people of all skill levels.

The Python Edition

Pythonistas, rejoice! All the code in this book is written in Python. The original edition of this book, *A Common-Sense Guide to Data Structures and Algorithms* (the second edition of which was published in 2020), was language-agnostic; it was written using multiple programming languages. The idea behind this was that we didn't want to imply that the book would only be helpful for one language, given that data structures and algorithms are concepts that apply across all of computing in general.

Over the years, I received feedback from readers who expressed that they would love to see language-specific editions of the book. After all, if you're working with one particular programming language, wouldn't it be nice to have a book in which all of the code is in that language?

Accordingly, I set out to create new single-language versions of *A Common-Sense Guide to Data Structures and Algorithms*. The first of these is the Python version and is what you're reading now! And because there's so much to say about data structures and algorithms, this is the first volume in a progression of books. In this volume, I lay the foundation for these concepts and cover the most common data structures and algorithms. In the next volume, I'll build upon this knowledge to level up further with more advanced ideas and techniques.

A Note About the Code

I strived to follow PEP 8 standards (for the most part) and write the code in such a way so that it runs equivalently in both Python Version 2 and Python Version 3. You can now enjoy reading the code samples in your language of choice.

That being said, I still want to emphasize that the concepts in this book apply to virtually all coding languages, and I expect that some people not as familiar with Python will be reading this book. Because of this, sometimes I have avoided certain Python idioms where I thought that this would utterly confuse people coming from other languages. It's a tricky balance to keep the code Pythonic while also being welcoming to non-Python coders, but I hope that I've maintained an equilibrium that satisfies most readers.

Virtually all the code in this book can be downloaded online from the book's web page.[1] This code repository contains automated tests too! I encourage you to check that out since the tests don't appear in the actual book.

You'll find some longer code snippets under the headings that read "Code Implementation." I certainly encourage you to study these code samples, but you don't necessarily have to understand every last line to proceed to the next section of the book. If these long pieces of code are bogging you down, just skim (or skip) them for now.

Finally, it's important to note that the code in this book is not "production ready." My greatest focus has been to clarify the concept at hand, and while I did also try to make the code generally complete, I have not accounted for every edge case. There's certainly room for you to optimize the code further—so feel free to go crazy with that.

What's in This Book?

As you may have guessed, this book talks quite a bit about data structures and algorithms. More specifically, the book is laid out as follows:

In *Why Data Structures Matter* and *Why Algorithms Matter*, I explain what data structures and algorithms are and explore the concept of time complexity—which is used to determine how fast an algorithm is. In the process, I also talk a great deal about arrays, sets, and binary search.

---

1. https://pragprog.com/titles/jwpython

In *O Yes! Big O Notation*, I unveil Big O notation and explain it in terms that are easy to understand. We use this notation throughout the book, so this chapter is pretty important.

In *Speeding Up Your Code with Big O*, *Optimizing Code With and Without Big O*, and *Optimizing for Optimistic Scenarios*, we delve further into Big O notation and use it to make our day-to-day code faster. Along the way, I cover various sorting algorithms, including Bubble Sort, Selection Sort, and Insertion Sort.

In *Big O in Everyday Code*, you apply all that you learned about Big O notation and analyze the efficiency of code from the real world.

In *Blazing Fast Lookup with Hash Tables* and *Crafting Elegant Code*, I discuss a few additional data structures, including hash tables, stacks, and queues. I show how they impact the speed and elegance of our code and how we can use them to solve real-world problems.

Recursively Recurse with Recursion introduces recursion, an anchor concept in the world of computer science. We break it down in this chapter and see how it can be a great tool for certain situations. *Learning to Write in Recursive* teaches you how to write recursive code, which can be confusing if you're not familiar with it.

Dynamic Programming shows you how to optimize recursive code and prevent it from spiraling out of control. And *Recursive Algorithms for Speed* shows you how to use recursion as the foundation for turbo-fast algorithms like Quicksort and Quickselect, and then it takes your algorithm-development skills up a few notches.

The following chapters, *Node-Based Data Structures*, *Speeding Up All the Things*, *Keeping Your Priorities Straight with Heaps*, *It Doesn't Hurt to Trie*, and *Connecting Everything with Graphs*, explore node-based data structures including the linked list, the binary tree, the heap, the trie, and the graph and show how each is ideal for various applications.

Dealing with Space Constraints explores space complexity, which is important when programming for devices with relatively small amounts of disk space or when dealing with big data.

The final chapter, *Techniques for Code Optimization*, walks you through various practical techniques for optimizing the efficiency of code and gives you new ideas for improving the code you write every day.

How to Read This Book

You've got to read this book in order. In some books out there you can read each chapter independently and skip around a bit, but *this isn't one of them.* Each chapter assumes you've read the previous ones, and the book is carefully constructed so you can ramp up your understanding as you proceed.

That being said, there are certain chapters in the latter half of the book that don't depend entirely on each other. The diagram below depicts which chapters are prerequisites for other chapters.

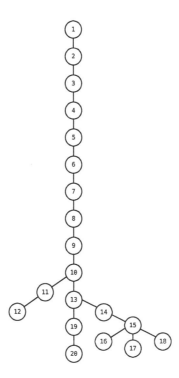

For example, you could technically skip from Chapter 10 to Chapter 13 if you wanted to. (Oh! And this diagram is based on a data structure called a *tree.* You're going to learn about it in Chapter 15.)

Another important note: to make this book easy to understand, I don't always reveal everything about a particular concept when I first introduce it. Sometimes, the best way to break down a complex concept is to reveal a small piece of it and only reveal the next piece once the first piece has sunk in. If I define a particular term as such-and-such, don't take that to be the textbook definition until you've completed the entire section on that topic.

It's a trade-off: to make the book digestible, I've chosen to oversimplify certain concepts at first and clarify them over time rather than ensure that every sentence is completely, academically, accurate. But don't worry too much, because by the end, you'll see the entire accurate picture.

Online Resources

This book has its own web page[2] on pragprog.com where you can find more information about the book, download the source code for the code examples, and help improve the book by reporting errata, typos, and content suggestions.

Additionally, I post updates about my writing at my website.[3] There you can find more information about my books as well as video tutorials made by my colleagues and me in which we use the "common-sense" approach to explaining all sorts of technologies and concepts. We can also train your employees! We cover all sorts of topics regarding code efficiency and leveling up their software development skills, including:

- Writing maintainable code
- Refactoring
- Unit testing
- And of course, writing efficient code!

My colleagues and I teach a variety of technologies, and we always develop curriculum using the "common-sense" way of explaining things. You can find more information at the aforementioned website.[4]

Connecting

I enjoy connecting with my readers and invite you to find me on LinkedIn.[5] I'd gladly accept your connection request—just send a message that you're a reader of this book. I look forward to hearing from you!

Jay Wengrow
December 2023

---

2.   https://pragprog.com/titles/jwpython
3.   https://commonsensedev.com
4.   https://commonsensedev.com
5.   https://www.linkedin.com/in/jaywengrow

Acknowledgments

While the task of writing a book may seem like a solitary one, this book simply could not have happened without the *many* people who have supported me in my journey writing it. I'd like to personally thank *all* of you.

To my wonderful wife, Rena—thank you for the time and emotional support you've given to me. You took care of everything while I hunkered down like a recluse and wrote. To my adorable kids, Tuvi, Leah, Shaya, Rami, and Yechiel—thank you for your patience as I wrote my book on "algorizms." And yes—it's finally done.

To my parents, Mr. and Mrs. Howard and Debbie Wengrow—thank you for initially sparking my interest in computer programming and helping me pursue it. Little did you know that getting me a computer tutor for my ninth birthday would set the foundation for my career—and now this book.

To my wife's parents, Mr. and Mrs. Paul and Kreindel Pinkus—thank you for your continued support of my family and me. Your wisdom and warmth mean so much to me.

When I first submitted my manuscript to the Pragmatic Bookshelf, I thought it was good. However, through the expertise, suggestions, and demands of all the wonderful people who work there, the book has become something much, much better than I could have written on my own.

Firstly, I'd like to thank my editor, Katharine Dvorak, for helping get this Python edition to the finish line quickly while also improving the book's quality at the same time.

I'd also like to thank Tammy Coron, managing editor of the Pragmatic Bookshelf, for overseeing this project. (And thanks for generating all of the Python-specific images!)

Thank you to Dave Rankin, CEO of the Pragmatic Bookshelf, for leading the best publishing company to write for as well as for supporting and sharing my vision for creating the language-specific editions of this book.

To Brian MacDonald, the editor of the original editions—thank you for showing me how a book like this should be written. This book has your imprint all over it.

To the extremely talented software developer and artist, Colleen McGuckin—thank you for taking my chicken scratch and transforming it into beautiful digital imagery. This book would be nothing without the spectacular visuals you've created with such skill and attention to detail.

I've been fortunate that so many experts have reviewed this book. Your feedback has been extremely helpful and has made sure that this book can be as accurate as possible. I'd like to thank all of you for your contributions.

The reviewers of the original editions were: Alessandro Bahgat, Ivo Balbaert, Rinaldo Bonazzo, Alberto Boschetti, Mike Browne, Craig Castelaz, Jacob Chae, Javier Collado, Zulfikar Dharmawan, Ashish Dixit, Dan Dybas, Emily Ekhdal, Mohamed Fouad, Derek Graham, Neil Hainer, Peter Hampton, Rod Hilton, Jeff Holland, Jessica Janiuk, Aaron Kalair, Stephan Kämper, Grant Kazan, Arun S. Kumar, Sean Lindsay, Nigel Lowry, Joy McCaffrey, Dary Merckens, Nouran Mhmoud, Kevin Mitchell, Daivid Morgan, Brent Morris, Jasdeep Narang, Emanuele Origgi, Stephen Orr, Kenneth Parekh, Jason Pike, Sam Rose, Ayon Roy, Frank Ruiz, Brian Schau, Tibor Simic, Matteo Vaccari, Mitchell Volk, Stephen Wolff, and Peter W. A. Wood.

The reviewers of this Python edition are: Connor Baskin, Katy Douglas, Tzvi Friedman, Joey Gallotta, Rod Hilton, Paa JAKE, Patrick Nikolaus, Nathan Pena, Terry Peppers, Lyndon Purcell, Cody Rutt, Brian Schau, Ahmad Shahba, and Joe Yakich.

In addition to the official reviewers, I'd also like to thank all the beta book readers who provided feedback as I continued to write and edit the book. Your suggestions, comments, and questions have been invaluable.

I'd also like to thank all the staff, students, and alumni at Actualize for your support. This book was originally an Actualize project, and you've all contributed in various ways. I'd like to particularly thank Luke Evans for giving me the idea to write this book.

Thank you all for making this book a reality.

CHAPTER 1

Why Data Structures Matter

When people first learn to code, their focus is—and *should* be—on getting their code to run properly. Their code is measured using one simple metric: does the code actually work?

As software engineers gain more experience, though, they begin to learn about additional layers and nuances regarding the *quality* of their code. They learn that there can be two snippets of code that both accomplish the same task, but that one snippet is *better* than the other.

There are numerous measures of code quality. One important measure is code maintainability. Maintainability of code involves aspects such as the readability, organization, and modularity of one's code.

However, another aspect of high-quality code is code *efficiency*. For example, you can have two code snippets that both achieve the same goal, but one *runs faster than the other*.

Take a look at these two functions, both of which print all the even numbers from 2 to 100:

```python
def print_numbers_version_one():
    number = 2

    while number <= 100:
        # If number is even, print it:
        if number % 2 == 0:
            print(number)

        number += 1
```

```
def print_numbers_version_two():
    number = 2

    while number <= 100:
        print(number)

        # Increase number by 2, which, by definition,
        # is the next even number:
        number += 2
```

Which of these functions do you think runs faster?

If you said Version 2, you're right. This is because Version 1 ends up looping 100 times, while Version 2 only loops 50 times. The first version then, takes twice as many steps as the second version.

This book is about writing *efficient* code. Having the ability to write code that runs quickly is an important aspect of becoming a better software developer.

The first step in writing fast code is to understand what data structures are and how different data structures can affect the speed of our code. So let's dive in.

Data Structures

Let's talk about data.

Data is a broad term that refers to all types of information, down to the most basic numbers and strings. In the simple but classic "Hello World!" program, the string "Hello World!" is a piece of data. In fact, even the most complex pieces of data usually break down into a bunch of numbers and strings.

Data structures refer to how data is *organized.* You're going to learn how the same data can be organized in a variety of ways.

Let's look at the following code:

```
x = "Hello! "
y = "How are you "
z = "today?"

print(x + y + z)
```

This simple program deals with three pieces of data, outputting three strings to make one coherent message. If we were to describe how the data is organized in this program, we'd say that we have three independent strings, each contained within a single variable.

However, this same data can also be stored in an array:

```
array = ["Hello! ", "How are you ", "today?"]
print(array[0] + array[1] + array[2])
```

You're going to learn in this book that the organization of data doesn't just matter for organization's sake, but can significantly impact *how fast your code runs.* Depending on how you choose to organize your data, your program may run faster or slower by orders of magnitude. And if you're building a program that needs to deal with lots of data, or a web app used by thousands of people simultaneously, the data structures you select may affect whether your software runs at all or simply conks out because it can't handle the load.

When you have a solid grasp on data structures' performance implications on the software you're creating, you'll have the keys to write fast and elegant code, and your expertise as a software engineer will be greatly enhanced.

In this chapter, we're going to begin our analysis of two data structures: arrays and sets. While the two data structures may seem almost identical, you're going to learn the tools to analyze the performance implications of each choice.

The Array: The Foundational Data Structure

The *array* is one of the most basic data structures in computer science. (In Python, the built-in array-like data structure is called a *list,* but I'll refer to them as arrays, keeping in line with the more general computer science term.) I assume you've worked with arrays before, so you're aware that an array is a list of data elements. The array is versatile and can serve as a useful tool in many situations, but let's take a look at one quick example.

If you're looking at the source code for an application that allows users to create and use shopping lists for the grocery store, you might find code like this:

```
array = ["apples", "bananas", "cucumbers", "dates", "elderberries"]
```

This array happens to contain five strings, each representing something that I might buy at the supermarket. (You've *got* to try elderberries.)

Arrays come with their own technical jargon.

The *size* of an array is how many data elements the array holds. Our grocery list array has a size of 5 since it contains five values.

The *index* of an array is the number that identifies where a piece of data lives inside the array.

In most programming languages, we begin counting the index at 0. So for our example array, "apples" is at index 0, and "elderberries" is at index 4, like this:

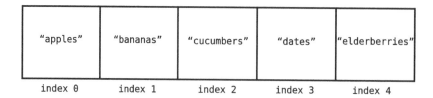

Data Structure Operations

To understand the performance of any data structure—such as the array—we need to analyze the common ways our code might interact with that data structure.

Many data structures are used in four basic ways, which we refer to as *operations*. These operations are:

- *Read*: Reading refers to looking something up at a particular spot within the data structure. With an array, this means looking up a value at a particular index. For example, looking up which grocery item is located at index 2 would be *reading* from the array.

- *Search*: Searching refers to looking for a particular value within a data structure. With an array, this means looking to see if a particular value exists within the array and, if so, at which index. For example, looking up the index of "dates" in our grocery list would be *searching* the array.

- *Insert*: Insertion refers to adding a new value to our data structure. With an array, this means adding a new value to an additional slot within the array. If we were to add "figs" to our shopping list, we'd be *inserting* a new value into the array.

- *Delete*: Deletion refers to removing a value from our data structure. With an array, this means removing one of the values from the array. For example, if we removed "bananas" from our grocery list, this value would be *deleted* from the array.

In this chapter, we'll analyze how fast each of these operations is when applied to an array.

Measuring Speed

So how do we measure the speed of an operation?

If you take away just one thing from this book, let it be this: when we measure how "fast" an operation is, we do not refer to how fast the operation takes in terms of pure *time*, but instead in how many *steps* it takes.

We've actually seen this earlier in the context of printing the even numbers from 2 to 100. The second version of that function was faster because it took half as many steps as the first version did.

Why do we measure code's speed in terms of steps?

We do this because we can never say definitively that any operation takes, say, five seconds. While a piece of code may take five seconds on a particular computer, that same piece of code may take longer on an older piece of hardware. For that matter, that same code might run much faster on the supercomputers of tomorrow. Measuring the speed of an operation in terms of time is undependable, since the time will always change depending on the hardware it's run on.

However, we *can* measure the speed of an operation in terms of how many computational *steps* it takes. If Operation A takes 5 steps, and Operation B takes 500 steps, we can assume that Operation A will always be faster than Operation B on *all* pieces of hardware. Measuring the number of steps is, therefore, the key to analyzing the speed of an operation.

Measuring the speed of an operation is also known as measuring its *time complexity*. Throughout this book, I'll use the terms *speed*, *time complexity*, *efficiency*, *performance*, and *runtime* interchangeably. They all refer to the number of steps a given operation takes.

Let's jump into the four operations of an array and determine how many steps each one takes.

Reading

The first operation we'll look at is *reading*, which looks up what value is contained at a particular index inside the array.

A computer can read from an array in just one step. This is because the computer has the ability to jump to any particular index in the array and peer inside. In our example of ["apples", "bananas", "cucumbers", "dates", "elderberries"], if we looked up index 2, the computer would jump right to index 2 and report that it contains the value "cucumbers".

How is the computer able to look up an array's index in just one step? Let's see how.

A computer's memory can be viewed as a giant collection of cells. In the following diagram, you can see a grid of cells in which some are empty and some contain bits of data:

		9			16				"a"
		100							
					"hi"				
	22								
							"woah"		

While this visual is a simplification of how computer memory works under the hood, it represents the essential idea.

When a program declares an array, it allocates a contiguous set of empty cells for use in the program. So if you were creating an array meant to hold five elements, your computer would find a group of five empty cells in a row and designate it to serve as your array:

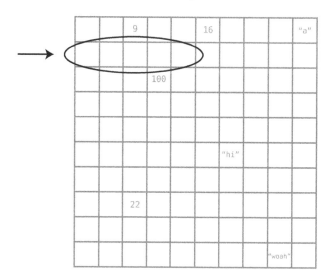

Now, every cell in a computer's memory has a specific address. It's sort of like a street address (for example, 123 Main St.), except that it's represented with a number. Each cell's memory address is one number greater than the previous cell's address. Here's a visual that shows each cell's memory address:

1000	1001	1002	1003	1004	1005	1006	1007	1008	1009
1010	1011	1012	1013	1014	1015	1016	1017	1018	1019
1020	1021	1022	1023	1024	1025	1026	1027	1028	1029
1030	1031	1032	1033	1034	1035	1036	1037	1038	1039
1040	1041	1042	1043	1044	1045	1046	1047	1048	1049
1050	1051	1052	1053	1054	1055	1056	1057	1058	1059
1060	1061	1062	1063	1064	1065	1066	1067	1068	1069
1070	1071	1072	1073	1074	1075	1076	1077	1078	1079
1080	1081	1082	1083	1084	1085	1086	1087	1088	1089
1090	1091	1092	1093	1094	1095	1096	1097	1098	1099

In the next diagram, you can see our shopping list array with its indexes and memory addresses:

"apples"	"bananas"	"cucumbers"	"dates"	"elderberries"

memory address:	1010	1011	1012	1013	1014
index:	0	1	2	3	4

When the computer reads a value at a particular index of an array, it can jump straight to that index because of the combination of the following facts about computers:

1. A computer can jump to any *memory address* in one step. For example, if you asked a computer to inspect whatever's at memory address 1063, it can access that without having to perform any search process. As an analogy, if I ask you to raise your right pinky finger, you wouldn't have to search all your fingers to find which one is your right pinky. You'd be able to identify it immediately.

2. Whenever a computer allocates an array, it also makes note at which memory address the array *begins*. So if we asked the computer to find the first element of the array, it would be able to instantly jump to the appropriate memory address to find it.

Now, these facts explain how the computer can find the *first* value of an array in a single step. However, a computer can also find the value at *any* index by performing simple addition. If we asked the computer to find the value at index 3, the computer would simply take the memory address at index 0 and add 3. (Memory addresses are sequential, after all.)

Let's apply this to our grocery list array. Our example array begins at memory address 1010. So, if we told the computer to read the value at index 3, the computer would go through the following thought process:

1. The array begins with index 0, which is at memory address 1010.
2. Index 3 will be exactly three slots past index 0.
3. By logical extension, index 3 would be located at memory address 1013, since 1010 + 3 is 1013.

Once the computer knows that index 3 is at memory address 1013, it can jump right there and see that it contains the value "dates".

Reading from an array is, therefore, an efficient operation, since the computer can read any index by jumping to any memory address in one step. Although I described the computer's thought process by breaking it down into three parts, we are currently focusing on the main step of the computer jumping to a memory address. (In later chapters, we'll explore how to know which steps are the ones worth focusing on.)

Naturally, an operation that takes just one step is the fastest type of operation. Besides being a foundational data structure, arrays are also a very powerful data structure because we can read from them with such speed.

Now, what if instead of asking the computer what value is contained at index 3, we flipped the question around and asked at what index "dates" can be found? That's the search operation, and we'll explore that next.

Searching

As I stated previously, *searching* an array means looking to see whether a particular value exists within an array and if so, at which index it's located.

In a sense, it's the inverse of reading. Reading means providing the computer an *index* and asking it to return the value contained there. Searching, on the other hand, means providing the computer a *value* and asking it to return the index of that value's location.

While these two operations sound similar, there's a world of difference between them when it comes to efficiency. Reading from an index is fast, since a computer can jump immediately to any index and discover the value contained there. Searching, though, is tedious since the computer has no way to jump to a particular value.

This is an important fact about computers: a computer has immediate access to all of its memory addresses, but it has no idea offhand what *values* are contained at each memory address.

Let's take our earlier array of fruits and veggies, for example. The computer can't immediately see the actual contents of each cell. To the computer, the array looks something like this:

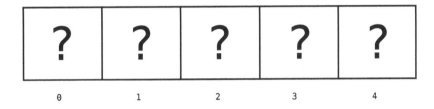

To search for a fruit within the array, the computer has no choice but to inspect each cell, one at a time.

The following diagrams demonstrate the process the computer would use to search for "dates" within our array.

First, the computer checks index 0:

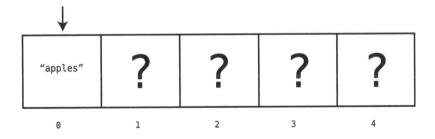

Since the value at index 0 is "apples", and not the "dates" we're looking for, the computer moves on to the next index, as shown in the diagram on page 10.

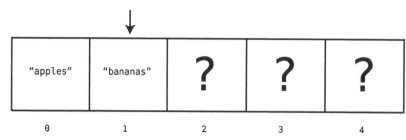

Since index 1 doesn't contain the "dates" we're looking for either, the computer moves on to index 2:

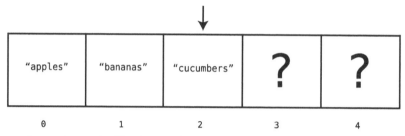

Once again, we're out of luck, so the computer moves to the next cell:

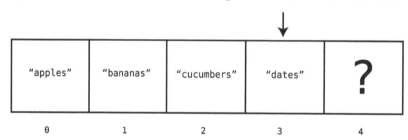

Aha! We've found the elusive "dates" and now know that the "dates" are found at index 3. At this point, the computer doesn't need to move on to the next cell of the array, since it already found what we're looking for.

In this example, because the computer had to check four different cells until it found the value we were searching for, we'd say that this particular operation took a total of four steps.

In Chapter 2, Why Algorithms Matter, on page 21, you'll learn about another way to search an array, but this basic search operation—in which the computer checks each cell one at a time—is known as *linear search*.

Now, what is the *maximum* number of steps a computer would need to perform to conduct a linear search on an array?

If the value we're seeking happens to be in the final cell in the array (like "elderberries"), then the computer would end up searching through *every* cell of the array until it finally finds the value it's looking for. Also, if the value we're looking for doesn't occur in the array at all, the computer likewise would have to search every cell so that it can be sure the value doesn't exist within the array.

So it turns out that for an array of 5 cells, the maximum number of steps linear search would take is 5. For an array of 500 cells, the maximum number of steps linear search would take is 500.

Another way of saying this is that for N cells in an array, linear search would take a maximum of N steps. In this context, N is just a variable that can be replaced by any number.

In any case, it's clear that searching is less efficient than reading, since searching can take many steps, while reading always takes just one step, no matter the size of the array.

Next, we'll analyze the operation of insertion.

Insertion

The efficiency of inserting a new piece of data into an array depends on *where* within the array you're inserting it.

Let's say we want to add "figs" to the end of our shopping list. Such an insertion takes just one step.

This is true due to another fact about computers: when allocating an array, the computer always keeps track of the array's size.

When we couple this with the fact that the computer also knows at which memory address the array begins, computing the memory address of the last item of the array is a cinch: if the array begins at memory address 1010 and is of size 5, that means its final memory address is 1014. So to insert an item beyond that would mean adding it to the *next* memory address, which is 1015.

Once the computer calculates which memory address to insert the new value into, it can do so in one step.

This is what inserting "figs" at the end of the array looks like:

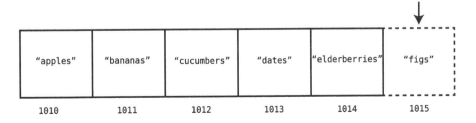

But there's one hitch. Because the computer initially allocated only five cells in memory for the array, and now we're adding a sixth element, the computer may have to allocate additional cells toward this array. In many programming languages, this is done under the hood automatically, but each language handles this differently, so I won't get into the details of it.

We've dealt with insertions at the end of an array, but inserting a new piece of data at the *beginning* or in the *middle* of an array is a different story. In these cases, we need to *shift* pieces of data to make room for what we're inserting, leading to additional steps.

For example, let's say we want to add "figs" to index 2 within the array. Take a look at the following diagram:

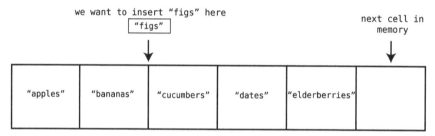

To do this, we need to move "cucumbers", "dates", and "elderberries" to the right to make room for "figs". This takes multiple steps, since we need to first move "elderberries" one cell to the right to make room to move "dates". We then need to move "dates" to make room for "cucumbers". Let's walk through this process.

Step 1: We move "elderberries" to the right:

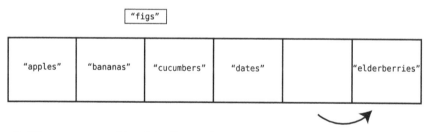

Step 2: We now move "dates" to the right:

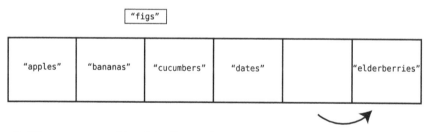

Step 3: We now move "cucumbers" to the right:

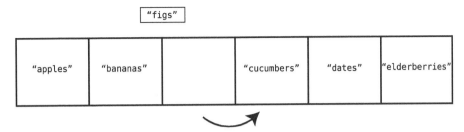

Step 4: Finally, we can insert "figs" into index 2:

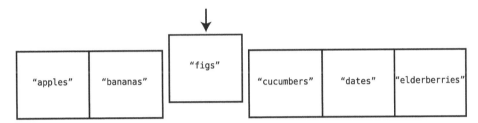

Notice that in the preceding example, insertion took four steps. Three of the steps involved shifting data to the right, while one step involved the actual insertion of the new value.

The worst-case scenario for insertion into an array—that is, the scenario in which insertion takes the most steps—is when we insert data at the *beginning* of the array. This is because when inserting at the beginning of the array, we have to move *all* the other values one cell to the right.

We can say that insertion in a worst-case scenario can take *N + 1 steps* for an array containing N elements. This is because we need to shift all N elements over, and then finally execute the actual insertion step.

Now that we've covered insertion, we're up to the array's final operation: deletion.

Deletion

Deletion from an array is the process of eliminating the value at a particular index.

Let's return to our original example array and delete the value at index 2. In our example, this value is "cucumbers".

Step 1: We delete "cucumbers" from the array:

"apples"	"bananas"		"dates"	"elderberries"

While the actual deletion of "cucumbers" technically took just one step, we now have a problem: we have an empty cell sitting smack in the middle of our array. An array isn't effective when there are gaps in the middle of it, so to resolve this issue, we need to shift "dates" and "elderberries" to the left. This means our deletion process requires additional steps.

Step 2: We shift "dates" to the left:

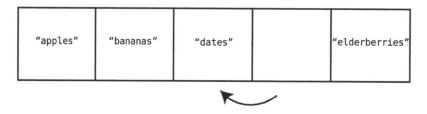

Step 3: We shift "elderberries" to the left:

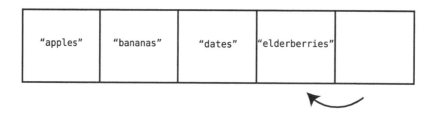

It turns out that for this deletion, the entire operation took three steps. The first step involved the actual deletion, and the other two steps involved data shifts to close the gap.

Like insertion, the worst-case scenario of deleting an element is deleting the very first element of the array. This is because index 0 would become empty, and we'd have to shift *all* the remaining elements to the left to fill the gap.

For an array of 5 elements, we'd spend 1 step deleting the first element and 4 steps shifting the 4 remaining elements. For an array of 500 elements, we'd spend 1 step deleting the first element, and 499 steps shifting the remaining data. We can say then, that for an array containing N elements, the maximum number of steps that deletion would take is N steps.

Congratulations! We've analyzed the time complexity of our first data structure. Now that you've learned how to analyze a data structure's efficiency, you can now discover how different data structures have different efficiencies. This is crucial, because choosing the correct data structure for your code can have serious ramifications on your software's performance.

The next data structure—the *set*—seems so similar to the array at first glance. However, you'll see that the operations performed on arrays and sets have different efficiencies.

Sets: How a Single Rule Can Affect Efficiency

Let's explore this other data structure: the *set*. A set is a data structure that does not allow duplicate values to be contained within it.

Sets are of different types, but for this discussion, I'll talk about an *array-based set*. This set is just like an array—it's a simple list of values. The only difference between this set and a classic array is that the set never allows duplicate values to be inserted into it.

For example, if you had the set ["a", "b", "c"] and tried to add another "b", the computer just wouldn't allow it, since a "b" already exists within the set.

Sets are useful when you need to ensure that you don't have duplicate data.

For instance, if you're creating an online phone book, you don't want the same phone number appearing twice. In fact, I'm currently suffering from this with my local phone book: my home phone number is not just listed for me but is also listed erroneously as the phone number for some family named Zirkind. (Yes, this is a true story.) Let me tell you—it's annoying to receive phone calls and voicemail from people looking for the Zirkinds. For that matter, I'm sure the Zirkinds are also wondering why no one ever calls them. And when I call the Zirkinds to let them know about the error, my wife picks up the phone because I've called my own number. (Okay, that last part never happened.) If only the program that produced the phone book had used a set...

In any case, an array-based set is an array with one additional constraint of barring duplicates. While not allowing duplicates is a useful feature, this simple constraint also causes the set to have a *different efficiency* for one of the four primary operations.

Let's analyze the reading, searching, insertion, and deletion operations in the context of an array-based set.

Reading from a set is exactly the same as reading from an array—it takes just one step for the computer to look up what's contained within a particular index. As I described earlier, this is because the computer can jump to any index within the set since it can easily calculate and jump to its memory address.

Searching a set also turns out to be no different than searching an array—it takes up to N steps to search for a value within a set. And deletion is also identical between a set and an array—it takes up to N steps to delete a value and move data to the left to close the gap.

Insertion, however, is where arrays and sets diverge. Let's first explore inserting a value at the *end* of a set, which was a best-case scenario for an array. We saw that with an array, the computer can insert a value at its end in a single step.

With a set, however, the computer first needs to determine that this value doesn't already exist in this set—because that's what sets do: they prevent duplicate data from being inserted into them.

Now, how will the computer ensure that the new data isn't already contained in the set? Remember, a computer doesn't know offhand what values are contained within the cells of an array or set. Because of this, the computer will first need to *search* the set to see whether the value we want to insert is already there. Only if the set does not yet contain our new value will the computer allow the insertion to take place.

So, every insertion into a set *first requires a search*.

Let's see this in action with an example. Imagine our grocery list from earlier was stored as a set—which would be a decent choice since we don't want to buy the same thing twice, after all. If our current set is ["apples", "bananas", "cucumbers", "dates", "elderberries"], and we want to insert "figs" into the set, the computer must execute the following steps, beginning with a search for "figs".

Step 1: Search index 0 for "figs":

| "apples" | "bananas" | "cucumbers" | "dates" | "elderberries" |

It's not there, but it might be somewhere else in the set. We need to make sure "figs" doesn't exist anywhere before we can insert it.

Step 2: Search index 1:

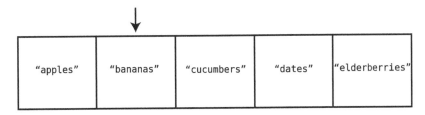

Step 3: Search index 2:

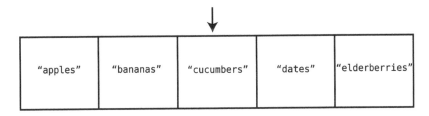

Step 4: Search index 3:

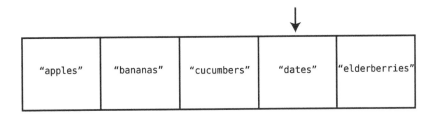

Step 5: Search index 4:

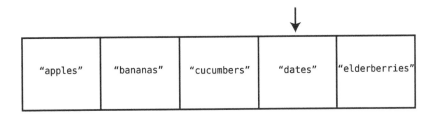

Now that we've searched the entire set, we know with certainty that it doesn't already contain "figs". At this point, it's safe to complete the insertion. And that brings us to our final step:

Step 6: Insert "figs" at the end of the set:

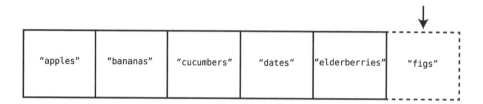

Inserting a value at the end of a set is the best-case scenario, but we still had to perform six steps for a set originally containing five elements. That is, we had to search all five elements before performing the final insertion step.

Said another way: insertion into the end of a set will take up to N + 1 steps for N elements. This is because there are N steps of search to ensure that the value doesn't already exist within the set, and then one step for the actual insertion. Contrast this with the regular array, in which such an insertion takes a grand total of one step.

In the worst-case scenario, where we're inserting a value at the *beginning* of a set, the computer needs to search N cells to ensure that the set doesn't already contain that value, another N steps to shift all the data to the right, and another final step to insert the new value. That's a total of 2N + 1 steps. Contrast this to insertion into the beginning of a regular array, which only takes N + 1 steps.

Now, does this mean you should avoid sets just because insertion is slower for sets than regular arrays? Absolutely not. Sets are important when you need to ensure that there's no duplicate data. (Hopefully, one day my phone book will be fixed.) But when you don't have such a need, an array may be preferable, since insertions for arrays are more efficient than insertions for sets. You must analyze the needs of your own application and decide which data structure is a better fit.

Wrapping Up

Analyzing the number of steps an operation takes is the heart of understanding the performance of data structures. Choosing the right data structure for your program can spell the difference between bearing a heavy load versus collapsing under it. In this chapter, you've learned to use this analysis to weigh whether an array or a set might be the appropriate choice for a given application.

Now that you've begun to learn how to think about the time complexity of data structures, we can use the same analysis to compare competing algorithms (even within the *same* data structure) to ensure the ultimate speed and performance of our code. And that's exactly what the next chapter is about.

Exercises

The following exercises provide you with the opportunity to practice with arrays. The solutions to these exercises are found in the section Chapter 1, on page 435.

1. For an array containing 100 elements, provide the number of steps the following operations would take:
    a. Reading
    b. Searching for a value not contained within the array
    c. Insertion at the beginning of the array
    d. Insertion at the end of the array
    e. Deletion at the beginning of the array
    f. Deletion at the end of the array

2. For an array-based set containing 100 elements, provide the number of steps the following operations would take:
    a. Reading
    b. Searching for a value not contained within the set
    c. Insertion of a new value at the beginning of the set
    d. Insertion of a new value at the end of the set
    e. Deletion at the beginning of the set
    f. Deletion at the end of the set

3. Normally the search operation in an array looks for the first instance of a given value. But sometimes we may want to look for *every* instance of a given value. For example, say we want to count how many times the value "apple" is found inside an array. How many steps would it take to find all the "apple"s? Give your answer in terms of N.

CHAPTER 2

Why Algorithms Matter

In the previous chapter, we took a look at our first data structures and saw how choosing the right data structure can affect the performance of our code. Even two data structures that seem so similar, such as the array and the set, can have very different levels of efficiency.

In this chapter, we're going to discover that even if we decide on a particular data structure, another major factor can affect the efficiency of our code: the proper selection of which *algorithm* to use.

Although the word *algorithm* sounds like something complex, it really isn't. An algorithm is simply *a set of instructions for completing a specific task.*

Even a process as simple as preparing a bowl of cereal is technically an algorithm, as it involves following a defined set of steps to achieve the task at hand. The cereal-preparation algorithm follows these four steps (for me, at least):

1. Grab a bowl.
2. Pour cereal into the bowl.
3. Pour milk into the bowl.
4. Dip a spoon into the bowl.

By following these steps in this particular order, we can now enjoy our breakfast.

When applied to computing, an algorithm refers to the set of instructions given to a computer to achieve a particular task. When we write any code, then, we're creating algorithms for the computer to follow and execute.

We can also express algorithms using plain English to set out the details of the instructions we plan on providing the computer. Throughout this book, I'll use both plain English as well as code to show how various algorithms work.

Sometimes, it's possible to have two different algorithms that accomplish the same task. We saw an example of this at the beginning of Chapter 1, Why Data Structures Matter, on page 1, where we had two different approaches for printing out even numbers. In that case, one algorithm had twice as many steps as the other.

In this chapter, we'll encounter another two algorithms that solve the same problem. In this case, though, one algorithm will be faster than the other by *orders of magnitude*.

To explore these new algorithms, we'll need to take a look at a new data structure.

Ordered Arrays

The *ordered array* is almost identical to the classic array we saw in the previous chapter. The only difference is that ordered arrays require that the values are always kept—you guessed it—*in order*; that is, every time a value is added, it gets placed in the proper cell so that the values in the array remain sorted.

For example, let's take the array [3, 17, 80, 202]:

Assume we want to insert the value 75 into the array. If this array were a classic array, we could insert the 75 at the end, as follows:

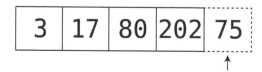

As we saw in the previous chapter, the computer can accomplish this in a single step.

On the other hand, if this were an *ordered array*, we'd have no choice but to insert the 75 in the proper spot so that the values remain in ascending order:

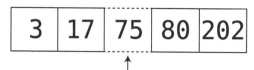

Now, this is easier said than done. The computer cannot simply drop the 75 into the right slot in a single step, because it first has to *find* the right place to insert the 75 and then shift the other values to make room for it. Let's break down this process step by step.

Let's start again with our original ordered array:

3	17	80	202

Step 1: We check the value at index 0 to determine whether the value we want to insert—the 75—should go to its left or to its right:

Because 75 is greater than 3, we know that the 75 will be inserted somewhere to its right. However, we don't know yet exactly which cell it should be inserted into, so we need to check the next cell.

We'll call this type of step a *comparison*, where we compare the value we're inserting to a number already present in the ordered array.

Step 2: We inspect the value at the next cell:

3	17	80	202

Since 75 is greater than 17, we need to move on.

Step 3: We check the value at the next cell:

3	17	80	202

We've encountered the value 80, which is *greater* than the 75 we wish to insert. Since we've reached the first value that is greater than 75, we can conclude that the 75 must be placed immediately to the left of this 80 to maintain the order of this ordered array. To do this, we need to shift data to make room for the 75.

Step 4: Move the final value to the right:

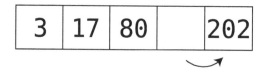

Step 5: Move the next-to-last value to the right:

Step 6: We can finally insert the 75 into its correct spot:

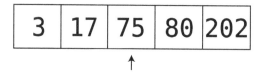

It emerges that when inserting into an ordered array, we need to always conduct a search before the actual insertion to determine the correct spot for the insertion. This is one difference in performance between a classic array and an ordered array.

We can see in this example that there were initially four elements and that insertion took six steps. In terms of N, we'd say that for N elements in an ordered array, the insertion took N + 2 steps in total.

Interestingly, the number of steps for insertion remains similar no matter where in the ordered array our new value ends up. If our value ends up toward the beginning of the ordered array, we have fewer comparisons and more shifts. If our value ends up toward the end, we get more comparisons but fewer shifts. The fewest steps occur when the new value winds up at the very end, since no shifts are necessary. In this case, we take N steps to compare the new value with all N existing values, plus one step for the insertion itself, yielding a total of N + 1 steps.

While insertion is less efficient for an ordered array than for a classic array, the ordered array has a secret superpower when it comes to searching.

Searching an Ordered Array

In the previous chapter, I described the process for searching for a particular value within a classic array: we check each cell one at a time—from left to right—until we find the value we're looking for. I noted that this process is referred to as linear search.

Let's see how linear search differs between a classic and an ordered array.

Say we have a regular array of [17, 3, 75, 202, 80]. If we were to search for the value 22—which happens to be nonexistent in this array—we would need to search each and every element because the 22 could potentially be anywhere in the array. The only time we could stop our search before we reach the array's end is if we happen to find the value we're looking for before we reach the end.

With an ordered array, however, we can stop a search early even if the value isn't contained within the array. Let's say we're searching for a 22 within an ordered array of [3, 17, 75, 80, 202]. We can stop the search as soon as we reach the 75, since it's impossible for the 22 to be anywhere to the right of it.

Here's a Python implementation of linear search on an ordered array:

```python
def linear_search(array, search_value):

    for index, element in enumerate(array):

        if element == search_value:
            return index
        elif element > search_value:
            break

    return None
```

This method accepts two arguments: array is the ordered array we're searching, and search_value is the value we're searching for.

Here's how to use this function to find the 22 in our example array:

```python
print(linear_search([3, 17, 75, 80, 202], 22))
```

As you can see, this linear_search method iterates over every element of the array, looking for the search_value. The search stops as soon as the element it's iterating over is greater than the search_value, since we know that the search_value will not be found further within the array.

In this light, linear search can take fewer steps in an ordered array than in a classic array in certain situations. That being said, if we're searching for a value that happens to be the final value or not within the array at all, we'll still end up searching each and every cell.

At first glance, then, standard arrays and ordered arrays don't have tremendous differences in efficiency, or at least not in worst-case scenarios. For both kinds of arrays, if they contain N elements, linear search can take up to N steps.

But we're about to unleash an algorithm that is so powerful that it'll leave linear search in the dust.

We've been assuming until now that the only way to search for a value within an ordered array is linear search. The truth, however, is that linear search is only *one possible algorithm* for searching for a value. It's not the *only* algorithm we can use.

The big advantage of an ordered array over a classic array is that an ordered array allows for an alternative searching algorithm. This algorithm is known as *binary search*, and it is a much, *much* faster algorithm than linear search.

Binary Search

You've probably played this guessing game as a child: I'm thinking of a number between 1 and 100. Keep guessing which number I'm thinking of, and I'll let you know whether you need to guess higher or lower.

You may know intuitively how to play this game. You wouldn't begin by guessing number 1. Instead, you'd probably start with 50, which is smack in the middle. Why? Because by selecting 50, no matter whether I tell you to guess higher or lower, you've automatically eliminated half the possible numbers!

If you guess 50 and I tell you to guess higher, you'd then pick 75, to eliminate half of the *remaining* numbers. If after guessing 75, I told you to guess lower, you'd pick 62 or 63. You'd keep on choosing the halfway mark to keep eliminating half of the remaining numbers.

Let's visualize this process where we're told to guess a number between 1 and 10, as shown in the image on page 27.

This, in a nutshell, is binary search.

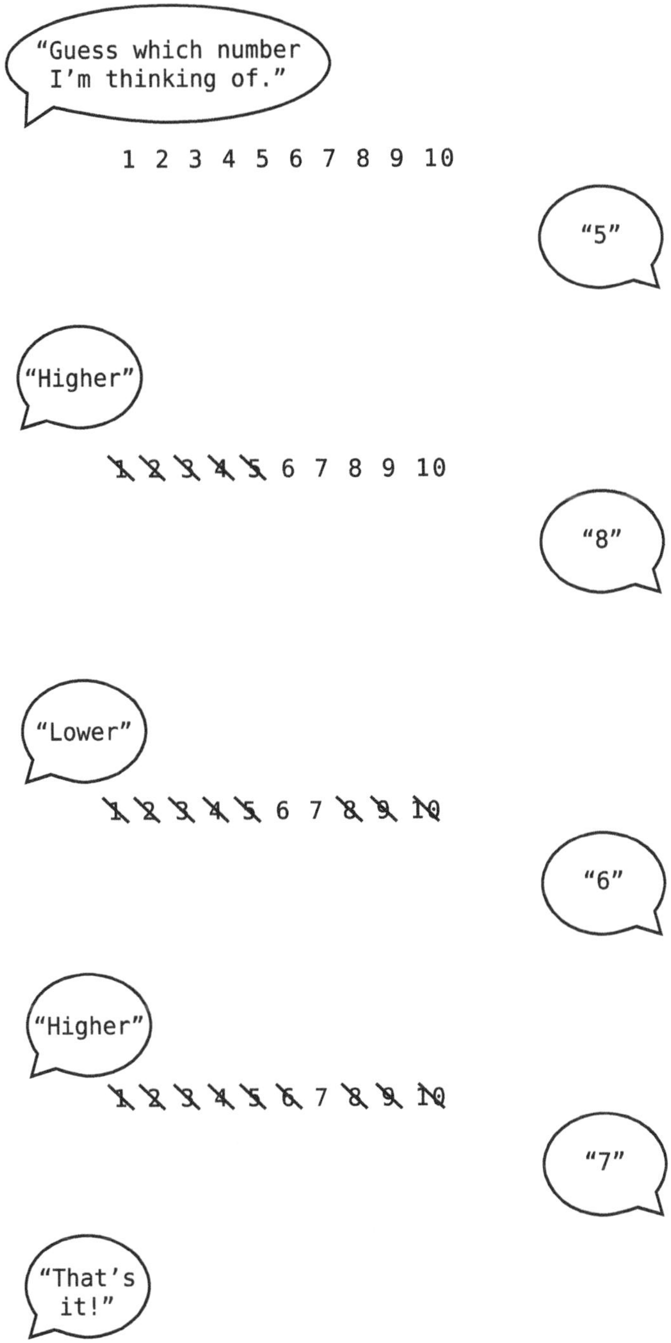

Let's see how binary search is applied to an ordered array. Say we have an ordered array containing nine elements. The computer doesn't know offhand what value each cell contains, so we'll portray the array like this:

Say we'd like to search for the value 7 inside this ordered array. Here's how binary search would work:

Step 1: We begin our search from the central cell. We can immediately jump to this cell, since we can calculate its index by taking the array's length and dividing it by 2. We check the value at this cell:

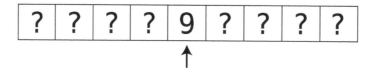

Because the value uncovered is a 9, we can conclude that the 7 is somewhere to its left. We've just successfully eliminated half of the array's cells—that is, all the cells to the right of the 9 (and the 9 itself):

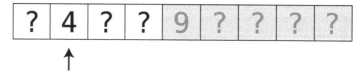

Step 2: Among the cells to the left of the 9, we inspect the middlemost value. There are two middlemost values, so we arbitrarily choose the left one:

It's a 4, so the 7 must be somewhere to its right. We can eliminate the 4 and the cell to its left:

Step 3: There are two more cells where the 7 can be. We arbitrarily choose the left one, as shown in the image on page 29.

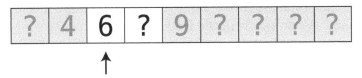

Step 4: We inspect the final remaining cell. (If it's not there, that means there is no 7 within this ordered array.)

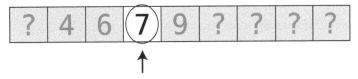

We found the 7 in four steps. In this example this is the same number of steps linear search would have taken, but we'll take a look shortly at another example to see the power of binary search.

Note that binary search is only possible within an ordered array. With a classic array, values can be in any order and we'd never know whether to look to the left or right of any given value. This is one of the advantages of ordered arrays: we have the option of binary search.

Code Implementation: Binary Search

Here's an implementation of binary search in Python:

```python
def binary_search(array, search_value):
    lower_bound = 0
    upper_bound = len(array) - 1

    while lower_bound <= upper_bound:

        midpoint = (upper_bound + lower_bound) // 2
        value_at_midpoint = array[midpoint]

        if search_value == value_at_midpoint:
            return midpoint
        elif search_value < value_at_midpoint:
            upper_bound = midpoint - 1
        elif search_value > value_at_midpoint:
            lower_bound = midpoint + 1

    return None
```

Let's break this down. As with the linear_search method, binary_search accepts the array and the search_value as arguments.

Here's an example of how to call this method:

```python
print(binary_search([3, 17, 75, 80, 202], 22))
```

The method first establishes the range of indexes in which the search_value might be found. We do this with the following code:

```
lower_bound = 0
upper_bound = len(array) - 1
```

Because when starting our search, the search_value might be found anywhere within the entire array, we establish the lower_bound as the first index and the upper_bound as the last index.

The essence of the search takes place within the while loop:

```
while lower_bound <= upper_bound:
```

This loop runs while we still have a range of elements in which the search_value may lie. As we'll see shortly, our algorithm will keep narrowing this range as we go. The clause lower_bound <= upper_bound will no longer hold true once there's no more range left, and we can conclude that the search_value is not present in the array.

Within the loop, our code inspects the value at the midpoint of the range. The following code accomplishes this:

```
midpoint = (upper_bound + lower_bound) // 2
value_at_midpoint = array[midpoint]
```

The value_at_midpoint is the item found at the center of the range.

Now, if the value_at_midpoint is the search_value we're looking for, we've struck gold and can return the index in which the search_value is found:

```
if search_value == value_at_midpoint:
    return midpoint
```

If the search_value is less than the value_at_midpoint, it means the search_value must be found somewhere earlier in the array. We can then narrow the range of our search by making the upper_bound the index to the left of the midpoint, since the search_value cannot possibly be found anywhere further than that:

```
elif search_value < value_at_midpoint:
    upper_bound = midpoint - 1
```

Conversely, if the search_value is greater than the value_at_midpoint, it means the search_value can only be found somewhere to the right of the midpoint, so we raise the lower_bound appropriately:

```
elif search_value > value_at_midpoint:
    lower_bound = midpoint + 1
```

We return None once the range has been narrowed down to 0 elements, and we know with certainty that the search_value doesn't exist within the array.

Binary Search vs. Linear Search

With ordered arrays of a small size, the algorithm of binary search doesn't have much of an advantage over linear search. But let's see what happens with larger arrays.

With an array containing 100 values, here are the maximum number of steps each type of search would take:

- Linear search: 100 steps
- Binary search: 7 steps

With linear search, if the value we're searching for is in the final cell or is greater than the value in the final cell, we have to inspect each and every element. For an array of size 100, this would take 100 steps.

When we use binary search, however, each guess we make eliminates half of the possible cells we'd have to search. In our very first guess, we get to eliminate a whopping fifty cells.

Let's look at this another way, and we'll see a pattern emerge.

With an array of size 3, binary search would take a maximum of two steps.

If we double the number of cells in the array (and add one more to keep the number odd for simplicity's sake), there are seven cells. For such an array, the maximum number of steps to find something using binary search is three.

If we double it again (and add one) so that the ordered array contains fifteen elements, the maximum number of steps for binary search is four.

The pattern that emerges is that for each time we double the size of the ordered array, the number of steps needed for binary search increases by one. This makes sense, as each lookup eliminates half of the elements from the search.

This pattern is unusually efficient: each time we double the data, the binary search algorithm adds *just one more step*.

Contrast this with linear search. If you had 3 elements, you'd need up to 3 steps. For 7 elements, you'd need a maximum of 3 steps. For 100 values, you'd need up to 100 steps. With linear search, then, *there are as many steps as there are items*. So for linear search, each time we double the size of the array, we *double* the number of steps of our search. For binary search, though, each time we double the size of the array, we only need to add *one more step*.

Let's see how this plays out for larger arrays. With an array of 10,000 elements, linear search can take up to 10,000 steps, while binary search takes up to a maximum of just 13 steps. For an array of size one million, linear search would take up to one million steps, while binary search would take up to just *20 steps*.

We can visualize the difference in performance between linear and binary search with this graph:

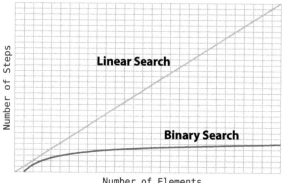

We'll be analyzing a bunch of graphs that look like this, so let's take a moment to digest what's going on. The x-axis represents the number of elements inside the array. That is, as we move from left to right, we're dealing with an increasing amount of data.

The y-axis represents how many steps the algorithm takes. As we move up the graph, we're looking at a greater number of steps.

If you look at the line representing linear search, you'll see that as an array has more elements, linear search takes a proportionally increasing number of steps. Essentially, for each additional element in the array, linear search takes one additional step. This produces a straight diagonal line.

With binary search, on the other hand, you'll see that as the data increases, the algorithm's steps only increase marginally. This makes perfect sense with what we know: you have to double the amount of data just to add one additional step to binary search.

Keep in mind that ordered arrays aren't faster in every respect. As you've seen, insertion in ordered arrays is slower than in standard arrays. But here's the trade-off: by using an ordered array, you have somewhat slower insertion but much faster search. Again, you must always analyze your application to see which is a better fit. Will your software be doing many insertions? Will searching be a significant feature of the app you're building?

Pop Quiz

I find the following pop quiz question really forces one to grasp the efficiency of binary search. Cover the answer and see if you get it right.

The question: We said that for an ordered array with 100 elements, binary search takes seven steps. How many steps would binary search take on an ordered array containing *200* elements?

The answer: Eight steps.

The intuitive answer I often hear is fourteen steps, but this is incorrect. The whole beauty of binary search is that each inspection eliminates half of the remaining elements. Therefore, each time we *double* the amount of data, we add only one step. After all, this doubling of data gets totally eliminated with the first inspection!

It's worth noting that now that we've added binary search to our toolkit, insertion within an ordered array can become faster as well. Insertion requires a search before the actual insertion, but we can now upgrade that search from a linear search to a binary search. However, insertion within an ordered array still remains slower than within a regular array, as the regular array's insertion doesn't require a search at all.

Wrapping Up

Often there's more than one way to achieve a particular computing goal, and the algorithm you choose can seriously affect the speed of your code.

It's also important to realize that there usually isn't a single data structure or algorithm that is perfect for every situation. For example, just because ordered arrays allow for binary search doesn't mean you should always use ordered arrays. In situations where you don't anticipate the need to search the data much but, instead, to add data, standard arrays may be a better choice because their insertion is faster.

As we've seen, the way to analyze competing algorithms is to count the number of steps each one takes. In the next chapter, we're going to look at a formalized way of expressing the time complexity of competing data structures and algorithms. Having this common language will give us clearer information that will allow us to make better decisions about which algorithms we choose.

Exercises

The following exercises provide you with the opportunity to practice with binary search. The solutions to these exercises are found in the section Chapter 2, on page 436.

1. How many steps would it take to perform a linear search for the number 8 in the ordered array [2, 4, 6, 8, 10, 12, 13]?

2. How many steps would binary search take for the previous example?

3. What is the maximum number of steps it would take to perform a binary search on an array of size 100,000?

CHAPTER 3

O Yes! Big O Notation

We've seen in the preceding chapters that the primary factor in determining an algorithm's efficiency is the number of steps it takes.

However, we can't simply label one algorithm a "22-step algorithm" and another a "400-step algorithm." This is because the number of steps an algorithm takes cannot be pinned down to a single number. Let's take linear search, for example. The number of steps linear search takes varies, as it takes as many steps as there are elements in the array. If the array contains 22 elements, linear search takes 22 steps. If the array contains 400 elements, however, linear search takes 400 steps.

The more effective way, then, to quantify the efficiency of linear search is to say that linear search takes *N steps* for *N elements in the array*; that is, if an array has N elements, linear search takes N steps. Now, this is a pretty wordy way of expressing this concept.

To help ease communication regarding time complexity, computer scientists have borrowed a concept from the world of mathematics to describe a concise and consistent language around the efficiency of data structures and algorithms. Known as Big O notation, this formalized expression of these concepts allows us to easily categorize the efficiency of a given algorithm and convey it to others.

Once you understand Big O notation, you'll have the tools to analyze each algorithm going forward in a consistent and concise way—it's the way the pros do it.

While Big O notation comes from the math world, I'm going to leave out all the mathematical jargon and explain it as it relates to computer science. Additionally, I'm going to begin by explaining Big O notation in simple terms and then continue to refine it as we proceed through this chapter and the next three chapters. It's not a difficult concept, but it'll be made even easier if I explain it in chunks over multiple chapters.

Big O: How Many Steps Relative to N Elements?

Big O achieves consistency by focusing on the number of steps an algorithm takes, but in a specific way. Let's start off by applying Big O to the algorithm of linear search.

In a worst-case scenario, linear search will take as many steps as there are elements in the array. As we've previously phrased it: for N elements in the array, linear search can take up to N steps. The appropriate way to express this in Big O notation is:

O(N)

Some pronounce this as "Big Oh of N." Others call it "Order of N." My personal preference, however, is "Oh of N."

Here's what the notation means. It expresses the answer to what we'll call the *key question*. The key question is this: *if there are N data elements, how many steps will the algorithm take?* Go ahead and read that sentence again. Then, emblazon it on your forehead, as this is the definition of Big O notation that we'll be using throughout the rest of this book.

The answer to the key question lies within the *parentheses* of our Big O expression. O(N) says that the answer to the key question is that *the algorithm will take N steps.*

Let's quickly review the thought process for expressing time complexity with Big O notation, again using the example of linear search. First, we ask the key question: if there are N data elements in an array, how many steps will linear search take? Because the answer to this question is that linear search will take N steps, we express this as O(N). For the record, an algorithm that is O(N) is also known as having *linear time*.

Let's contrast this with how Big O would express the efficiency of *reading* from a standard array. As you learned in Chapter 1, Why Data Structures Matter, on page 1, reading from an array takes just one step, no matter how large the array is. To figure out how to express this in Big O terms, we're going to again ask the key question: if there are N data elements, how many steps will reading from an array take? The answer is that reading takes just one step. So we express this as O(1), which I pronounce "Oh of 1."

O(1) is interesting, since although our key question revolves around N ("If there are N data elements, how many steps will the algorithm take?"), the answer has nothing to do with N. And that's actually the whole point: *no matter how many elements* an array has, reading from the array *always* takes one step.

And this is why O(1) is considered the "fastest" kind of algorithm. Even as the data increases, an O(1) algorithm doesn't take any additional steps. The algorithm always takes a constant number of steps no matter what N is. In fact, an O(1) algorithm can also be referred to as having *constant time*.

So, Where's the Math?

As I mentioned earlier in this book, I'm taking an easy-to-understand approach to the topic of Big O. That's not the only way to do it; if you were to take a traditional college course on algorithms, you'd probably be introduced to Big O from a mathematical perspective. Big O is originally a concept from mathematics, and therefore, it's often described in mathematical terms. For example, one way of describing Big O is that it describes the upper bound of the growth rate of a function, or that if a function g(x) grows no faster than a function f(x), then g is said to be a member of O(f). Depending on your mathematics background, that either makes sense or doesn't help very much. I've written this book so that you don't need as much math to understand the concept.

If you want to dig further into the math behind Big O, check out *Introduction to Algorithms* by Thomas H. Cormen, Charles E. Leiserson, Ronald L. Rivest, and Clifford Stein (MIT Press, 2009) for a full mathematical explanation. Justin Abrahms also provides a pretty good definition in his article: https://justin.abrah.ms/computer-science/understanding-big-o-formal-definition.html.

The Soul of Big O

Now that we've encountered O(N) and O(1), we begin to see that Big O notation does more than simply describe the number of steps an algorithm takes, such as with a hard number like 22 or 400. Rather, it's an answer to that key question on your forehead: if there are N data elements, how many steps will the algorithm take?

While that key question is indeed the strict definition of Big O, there's actually more to Big O than meets the eye.

Let's say we have an algorithm that always takes three steps no matter how much data there is. That is, for N elements, the algorithm always takes three steps. How would you express that in terms of Big O?

Based on everything you've learned up to this point, you'd probably say that it's O(3).

However, it's actually O(1). And that's because of the next layer of understanding Big O, which I will reveal now.

While Big O is an expression of the number of an algorithm's steps relative to N data elements, that alone misses the deeper *why* behind Big O, what I dub the "soul of Big O."

The soul of Big O is what Big O is truly concerned about: how will an algorithm's performance *change as the data increases*?

This is the soul of Big O. Big O doesn't want to simply tell you how many steps an algorithm takes. It wants to tell you the story of how the number of steps increases as the data *changes*.

Viewed with this lens, we don't care very much whether an algorithm is O(1) or O(3). Because both algorithms are the type that aren't affected by increased data, as their number of steps remains constant, they're essentially the same kind of algorithm. They're both algorithms whose steps remain constant irrespective of the data, and we don't care to make a distinction between the two.

An algorithm that is O(N), on the other hand, is a different type of algorithm. It's an algorithm whose performance *is* affected as we increase the data. More specifically, it's the kind of algorithm whose steps increase in direct proportion to the data as the data increases. This is the story O(N) tells. It tells you about the proportional relationship between the data and the algorithm's efficiency. It describes exactly how the number of steps increases as the data increases.

Look at how these two types of algorithms are plotted on a graph:

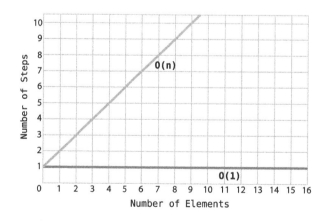

Notice that O(N) makes a perfect diagonal line. This is because for every additional piece of data, the algorithm takes one additional step. Accordingly, the more data, the more steps the algorithm will take.

Contrast this with O(1), which is a perfect horizontal line. No matter how much data there is, the number of steps remains constant.

Deeper into the Soul of Big O

To see why the soul of Big O is so important, let's go one level deeper. Say we had an algorithm of constant time that always took 100 steps no matter how much data there was. Would you consider that to be more or less performant than an algorithm that is O(N)?

Take a look at the following graph:

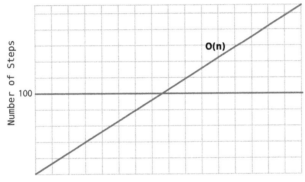

As the graph depicts, for a data set that is fewer than 100 elements, an O(N) algorithm takes fewer steps than the O(1) 100-step algorithm. At exactly 100 elements, the lines cross, meaning the two algorithms take the same number of steps, namely 100. But here's the key point: for *all arrays greater than 100*, the O(N) algorithm takes more steps.

Because there will always be *some* amount of data at which the tides turn, and O(N) takes more steps from that point until infinity, O(N) is considered to be, on the whole, less efficient than O(1) no matter how many steps the O(1) algorithm actually takes.

The same is true even for an O(1) algorithm that always takes one million steps. As the data increases, there will inevitably reach a point at which O(N) becomes less efficient than the O(1) algorithm and will remain so up toward an infinite amount of data.

Same Algorithm, Different Scenarios

As you learned in the previous chapters, linear search isn't *always* O(N). It's true that if the item we're looking for is in the final cell of the array, it will take N steps to find it. But when the item we're searching for is found in the *first* cell of the array, linear search will find the item in just one step. So this case of linear search would be described as O(1). If we were to describe the efficiency of linear search in its totality, we'd say that linear search is O(1) in a *best-case* scenario and O(N) in a *worst-case* scenario.

While Big O effectively describes both the best- and worst-case scenarios of a given algorithm, Big O notation generally refers to the *worst-case scenario* unless specified otherwise. This is why most references will describe linear search as being O(N) even though it *can* be O(1) in a best-case scenario.

This is because a "pessimistic" approach can be a useful tool: knowing exactly how inefficient an algorithm can get in a worst-case scenario prepares us for the worst and may have a strong impact on our choices.

An Algorithm of the Third Kind

In the previous chapter, you learned that binary search on an ordered array is much faster than linear search on the same array. Let's now look at how to describe binary search in terms of Big O notation.

We can't describe binary search as being O(1), because the number of steps increases as the data increases. It also doesn't fit into the category of O(N), since the number of steps is much fewer than the N data elements. As we have seen, binary search takes only seven steps for an array containing 100 elements.

Binary search, then, seems to fall somewhere *in between* O(1) and O(N). So what is it?

In Big O terms, we describe binary search as having a time complexity of:

O(log N)

I pronounce this as "Oh of log N." This type of algorithm is also known as having a time complexity of *log time*.

Simply put, O(log N) is the Big O way of describing an algorithm that *increases one step each time the data is doubled*. As you learned in the previous chapter, binary search does just that. You'll see momentarily *why* this is expressed as O(log N), but let's first summarize what you've learned so far.

The three types of algorithms you've learned about so far can be sorted from most efficient to least efficient as follows:

O(1)

O(log N)

O(N)

Let's look at a graph that compares the three types:

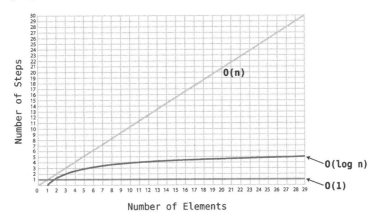

Note how O(log N) curves ever so slightly upward, making it less efficient than O(1) but much more efficient than O(N).

To understand why this algorithm is called O(log N), you need to first understand what *logarithms* are. If you're already familiar with this mathematical concept, feel free to skip the next section.

Logarithms

Let's examine why algorithms such as binary search are described as O(log N). What is a log, anyway?

Log is shorthand for *logarithm*. The first thing to note is that logarithms have nothing to do with algorithms, even though the two words look and sound so similar.

Logarithms are the inverse of *exponents*. Here's a quick refresher on what exponents are:

2^3 is the equivalent of:

$2 * 2 * 2$

This just happens to be 8.

Now, $\log_2 8$ is the converse. It means: how many times do you have to multiply 2 by itself to get a result of 8?

Because you have to multiply 2 by itself 3 times to get 8, $\log_2 8 = 3$.

Here's another example:

2^6 translates to:

$2 * 2 * 2 * 2 * 2 * 2 = 64$

Because we had to multiply 2 by itself six times to get 64, we have, therefore:

$\log_2 64 = 6$.

While the preceding explanation is the "textbook" definition of logarithms, I like to use an alternative way of describing the same concept because many people find that they can wrap their heads around it more easily, especially when it comes to Big O notation.

Another way of explaining $\log_2 8$ is this: if we kept *dividing* 8 by 2 until we ended up with 1, how many 2s would we have in our equation?

$8 / 2 / 2 / 2 = 1$

In other words, how many times do we need to halve 8 until we end up with 1? In this example, it takes us three times. Therefore,

$\log_2 8 = 3$.

Similarly, we could explain $\log_2 64$ as: how many times do we need to halve 64 until we end up with 1?

$64 / 2 / 2 / 2 / 2 / 2 / 2 = 1$

Since there are six 2s, $\log_2 64 = 6$.

Now that you understand what logarithms are, the meaning behind O(log N) will become clear.

O(log N) Explained

Let's bring this all back to Big O notation. In computer science, whenever we say O(log N), it's actually shorthand for saying O($\log_2$ N). We just omit that small 2 for convenience.

Recall that Big O notation resolves the key question: if there are N data elements, how many steps will the algorithm take?

O(log N) means that for N data elements, the algorithm would take log_2 N *steps*. If there are 8 elements, the algorithm would take three steps, since log_2 8 = 3.

Said another way, if we keep dividing the 8 elements in half, it would take us three steps until we end up with 1 element.

This is *exactly* what happens with binary search. As we search for a particular item, we keep dividing the array's cells in half until we narrow it down to the correct number.

Said simply: *O(log N) means the algorithm takes as many steps as it takes to keep halving the data elements until we remain with 1.*

The following table demonstrates a striking difference between the efficiencies of O(N) and O(log N):

N Elements	O(N)	O(log N)
8	8	3
16	16	4
32	32	5
64	64	6
128	128	7
256	256	8
512	512	9
1024	1024	10

While the O(N) algorithm takes as many steps as there are data elements, the O(log N) algorithm takes just one additional step each time the data is doubled.

In future chapters, you'll encounter algorithms that fall under categories of Big O notation other than the three you've learned about so far. But in the meantime, let's apply these concepts to some examples of everyday code.

Practical Examples

Here's some typical Python code that prints all the items from a list:

```python
things = ['apples', 'baboons', 'cribs', 'dulcimers']

for thing in things:
    print("Here's a thing: " + thing)
```

How would we describe the efficiency of this algorithm in Big O notation?

The first thing to realize is that this is an example of an algorithm. While it may not be fancy, any code that does anything at all is technically an algorithm—it's a particular process for solving a problem. In this case, the problem is that we want to print all the items from a list. The algorithm we use to solve this problem is a for loop containing a print statement.

To break this down, we need to analyze how many steps this algorithm takes. In this case, the main part of the algorithm—the for loop—takes four steps. In this example, there are four things in the list, and we print each one out a single time.

However, the number of steps isn't constant. If the list contained ten elements, the for loop would take ten steps. Since this for loop takes as many steps as there are elements, we'd say that this algorithm has an efficiency of O(N).

The next example is a simple Python-based algorithm for determining whether a number is prime:

```python
def is_prime(number):
    for i in range(2, number):
        if number % i == 0:
            return False

    return True
```

The preceding code accepts a number as an argument and begins a for loop in which we divide the number by every integer from 2 up to (but not including) that number and see if there's a remainder. If there's no remainder, we know that the number is not prime and we immediately return False. If we make it all the way up to the number and always find a remainder, then we know that the number is prime and we return True.

In this case, the key question is slightly different than in the previous examples. In the previous examples, our key question asked how many steps the algorithm would take if there were N data elements in an array. Here, we're not dealing with an array, but we *are* dealing with a number that we pass into this function. Depending on the number we pass in, this will affect how many times the function's loop runs.

In this case, then, our key question will be: when passing in the number N, how many steps will the algorithm take?

If we pass the number 7 into is_prime, the for loop runs about 7 times. (It technically runs 5 times, since it starts at 2 and ends right before the actual number.) For the number 101, the loop runs about 101 times. Because the number of steps increases in lockstep with the number passed into the function, this is a classic example of O(N).

Again, the key question here dealt with a different kind of N, since our primary piece of data was a number rather than an array. We'll get more practice in identifying our Ns as we progress through the future chapters.

Wrapping Up

With Big O notation, we have a consistent system that allows us to compare any two algorithms. With it, we'll be able to examine real-life scenarios and choose between competing data structures and algorithms to make our code faster and able to handle heavier loads.

In the next chapter, we'll encounter a real-life example in which we use Big O notation to speed up our code significantly.

Exercises

The following exercises provide you with the opportunity to practice with Big O notation. The solutions to these exercises are found in the section Chapter 3, on page 437.

1. Use Big O notation to describe the time complexity of the following function that determines whether a given year is a leap year:

    ```
    def is_leap_year(year):

        if year % 100 == 0:
            if year % 400 == 0:
                return False
            else:
                return True

        return year % 4 == 0
    ```

2. Use Big O notation to describe the time complexity of the following function that sums up all the numbers from a given array:

    ```
    def array_sum(array):
        sum = 0

        for number in array:
            sum += number

        return sum
    ```

3. The following function is based on the age-old analogy used to describe the power of compounding interest:

    Imagine you have a chessboard, and put a single grain of rice on one square. On the second square, you put two grains of rice, since that is double the amount of rice on the previous square. On the third square, you put four grains. On the fourth square, you put eight grains, and on the fifth square, you put sixteen grains, and so on.

The following function calculates which square you'll need to place a certain number of rice grains. For example, for sixteen grains, the function will return 5, since you will place the sixteen grains on the fifth square.

Use Big O notation to describe the time complexity of this function, which is below:

```python
def chessboard_space(number_of_grains):
    chessboard_spaces = 1
    placed_grains = 1

    while placed_grains < number_of_grains:
        placed_grains *= 2
        chessboard_spaces += 1

    return chessboard_spaces
```

4. The following function accepts an array of strings and returns a new array that only contains the strings that start with the character "a". Use Big O notation to describe the time complexity of the function:

```python
def select_a_strings(array):
    new_array = []

    for string in array:
        if string[0] == "a":
            new_array.append(string)

    return new_array
```

5. The following function calculates the median from an *ordered* array. Describe its time complexity in terms of Big O notation:

```python
def median(array):
    if not array:
        return None

    middle = len(array) // 2

    # If array has even amount of numbers:
    if len(array) % 2 == 0:
        return (array[middle - 1] + array[middle]) / 2.0
    else:  # If array has odd amount of numbers:
        return array[middle]
```

CHAPTER 4

Speeding Up Your Code with Big O

Big O notation is a great tool for expressing the efficiency of an algorithm. We've already been able to use it to quantify the difference between binary search vs. linear search, as binary search is O(log N)—a much faster algorithm than linear search, which is O(N).

With Big O, you also have the opportunity to compare your algorithm to *general algorithms out there in the world*, and you can say to yourself, "Is this a fast or slow algorithm as far as algorithms generally go?"

If you find that Big O labels your algorithm as a slow one, you can now take a step back and try to figure out if there's a way to optimize it by trying to get it to fall under a faster category of Big O. This may not always be possible, of course, but it's certainly worth thinking about.

In this chapter, we'll write some code to solve a practical problem and then measure our algorithm using Big O. We'll then see if we might be able to modify the algorithm to give it a nice efficiency bump. (Spoiler: we will.)

Bubble Sort

Before jumping into our practical problem, though, we need to first look at a new category of algorithmic efficiency in the world of Big O. To demonstrate it, we'll get to use one of the classic algorithms of computer-science lore.

Sorting algorithms have been the subject of extensive research in computer science, and tens of such algorithms have been developed over the years. They all solve the following problem:

Given an array of unsorted values, how can we sort them so that they end up in ascending order?

In this chapter and those following, we're going to encounter a number of these sorting algorithms. Some of the first ones you'll learn about are known as *simple sorts*, in that they are easy to understand but are not as efficient as some of the faster sorting algorithms out there.

Bubble Sort is a basic sorting algorithm and follows these steps:

1. Point to two consecutive values in the array. (Initially, we start by pointing to the array's first two values.) Compare the first item with the second one:

    | 2 | 1 | 3 | 5 |

2. If the two items are out of order (in other words, the left value is greater than the right value), swap them (if they already happen to be in the correct order, do nothing for this step):

    | 2 | 1 | 3 | 5 |

    | 1 | 2 | 3 | 5 |

3. Move the "pointers" one cell to the right:

    | 1 | 2 | 3 | 5 |

4. Repeat Steps 1 through 3 until we reach the end of the array, or if we reach the values that have already been sorted. (This will make more sense in the walk-through that follows.) At this point, we've completed our first *pass-through* of the array—we "passed through" the array by pointing to each of its values until we reached the end.

5. We then move the two pointers back to the first two values of the array and execute another pass-through of the array by running Steps 1 through 4 again. We keep on executing these pass-throughs until we have a pass-through in which we did not perform any swaps. When this happens, it means our array is fully sorted and our work is done.

Bubble Sort in Action

Let's walk through a complete example of Bubble Sort.

Assume we want to sort the array [4, 2, 7, 1, 3]. It's currently out of order, and we want to produce an array that contains the same values in ascending order.

Let's begin the first pass-through:

This is our starting array:

$$4\ 2\ 7\ 1\ 3$$

Step 1: First, we compare the 4 and the 2:

$$4\ 2\ 7\ 1\ 3$$

Step 2: They're out of order, so we swap them:

$$4\ 2\ 7\ 1\ 3$$

$$2\ 4\ 7\ 1\ 3$$

Step 3: Next, we compare the 4 and the 7:

$$2\ 4\ 7\ 1\ 3$$

They're in the correct order, so we don't need to perform a swap.

Step 4: We now compare the 7 and the 1:

$$2\ 4\ 7\ 1\ 3$$

Step 5: They're out of order, so we swap them:

$$2\ 4\ 7\ 1\ 3$$

$$2\ 4\ 1\ 7\ 3$$

Step 6: We compare the 7 and the 3:

$$2\ 4\ 1\ 7\ 3$$

Step 7: They're out of order, so we swap them:

$$2\ 4\ 1\ \begin{array}{c}7\\3\end{array}$$

$$\boxed{2\ 4\ 1\ 3\ 7}$$

We now know for a fact that the 7 is in its correct position within the array because we kept moving it along to the right until it reached its proper place. The previous diagram has little lines surrounding the 7 to indicate that the 7 is officially in its correct position.

This is actually the reason why this algorithm is called *Bubble* Sort: in each pass-through, the highest unsorted value "bubbles" up to its correct position.

Because we made at least one swap during this pass-through, we need to conduct another pass-through.

We begin the second pass-through:

Step 8: We compare the 2 and the 4:

$$\boxed{2\ 4\ 1\ 3\ 7}$$

They're in the correct order, so we can move on.

Step 9: We compare the 4 and the 1:

$$\boxed{2\ 4\ 1\ 3\ 7}$$

Step 10: They're out of order, so we swap them:

$$2\ \begin{array}{c}4\\1\end{array}\ 3\ 7$$

$$\boxed{2\ 1\ 4\ 3\ 7}$$

Step 11: We compare the 4 and the 3:

$$\boxed{2\ 1\ 4\ 3\ 7}$$

Step 12: They're out of order, so we swap them:

We don't have to compare the 4 and the 7 because we know that the 7 is already in its correct position from the previous pass-through. And now we also know that the 4 has bubbled up to its correct position as well. This concludes our second pass-through.

Because we made at least one swap during this pass-through, we need to conduct another pass-through.

We begin the third pass-through:

Step 13: We compare the 2 and the 1:

Step 14: They're out of order, so we swap them:

Step 15: We compare the 2 and the 3:

They're in the correct order, so we don't need to swap them.

We now know that the 3 has bubbled up to its correct spot:

Since we made at least one swap during this pass-through, we need to perform another one.

And so begins the fourth pass-through:

Step 16: We compare the 1 and the 2:

Because they're in order, we don't need to swap. We can end this pass-through, since all the remaining values are already correctly sorted.

Now that we've made a pass-through that didn't require any swaps, we know that our array is completely sorted:

Code Implementation: Bubble Sort

Here's an implementation of Bubble Sort in Python:

```python
def bubble_sort(array):
    unsorted_until_index = len(array) - 1
    sorted = False

    while not sorted:
        sorted = True
        for i in range(unsorted_until_index):
            if array[i] > array[i+1]:
                array[i], array[i+1] = array[i+1], array[i]
                sorted = False
        unsorted_until_index -= 1

    return array
```

To use this function, we can pass an unsorted array to it, like so:

```python
print(bubble_sort([65, 55, 45, 35, 25, 15, 10]))
```

This function will then return the sorted array.

Let's break the function down line by line to see how it works. I'll explain each line by first providing the explanation, followed by the line of code itself.

The first thing we do is create a variable called unsorted_until_index. This keeps track of the rightmost index of the array that has *not* yet been sorted. When we first start the algorithm, the array is completely unsorted, so we initialize this variable to be the final index in the array:

```
unsorted_until_index = len(array) - 1
```

We also create a variable called sorted that will keep track of whether the array is fully sorted. Of course, when our code first runs, it isn't, so we set it to False:

```
sorted = False
```

We begin a while loop that continues to run as long as the array is not sorted. Each round of this loop represents a pass-through of the array:

```
while not sorted:
```

Next, we preliminarily establish sorted to be True:

```
sorted = True
```

The approach here is that in each pass-through, we'll assume the array is sorted until we encounter a swap, in which case we'll change the variable back to False. If we get through an entire pass-through without having to make any swaps, sorted will remain True, and we'll know that the array is completely sorted.

Within the while loop, we begin a for loop in which we point to each pair of values in the array. We use the variable i as our first pointer, and it starts from the beginning of the array and goes until the index that hasn't yet been sorted:

```
for i in range(unsorted_until_index):
```

Within this loop, we compare each pair of adjacent values and swap those values if they're out of order. We also change sorted to False if we have to make a swap:

```
for i in range(unsorted_until_index):
    if array[i] > array[i+1]:
        array[i], array[i+1] = array[i+1], array[i]
        sorted = False
```

At the end of each pass-through, we know that the value we bubbled up all the way to the right is now in its correct position. Because of this, we decrement the unsorted_until_index by 1, since the index it was already pointing to is now sorted:

```
unsorted_until_index -= 1
```

The while loop ends once sorted is True, meaning the array is completely sorted. Once this is the case, we return the sorted array:

```
return array
```

The Efficiency of Bubble Sort

The Bubble Sort algorithm contains two significant kinds of steps:

- *Comparisons*: two numbers are compared with one another to determine which is greater.

- *Swaps*: two numbers are swapped with one another to sort them.

Let's start by determining how many *comparisons* take place in Bubble Sort.

Our example array has five elements. Looking back, you can see that in our first pass-through, we had to make four comparisons between sets of two numbers.

In our second pass-through, we only had to make three comparisons. This is because we didn't have to compare the final two numbers, since we knew that the final number was in the correct spot due to the first pass-through.

In our third pass-through, we made two comparisons, and in our fourth pass-through, we made just one comparison.

So that's:

4 + 3 + 2 + 1 = 10 comparisons.

To put this in a way that would hold true for arrays of all sizes, we'd say that for N elements, we make

(N - 1) + (N - 2) + (N - 3) ... + 1 comparisons.

Now that we've analyzed the number of comparisons that take place in Bubble Sort, let's analyze the *swaps*.

In a worst-case scenario, where the array is sorted in descending order (the exact opposite of what we want), we'd actually need a swap for each comparison. So we'd have 10 comparisons and 10 swaps in such a scenario for a grand total of 20 steps.

Let's look at the big picture. With an array containing five values in reverse order, we make 4 + 3 + 2 + 1 = 10 comparisons. Along with the 10 comparisons, we also have 10 swaps, totaling 20 steps.

For such an array with 10 values, we get 9 + 8 + 7 + 6 + 5 + 4 + 3 + 2 + 1 = 45 comparisons, and another 45 swaps. That's a total of 90 steps.

With an array containing *20* values, we'd have:

19 + 18 + 17 + 16 + 15 + 14 + 13 + 12 + 11 + 10 + 9 + 8 + 7 + 6 + 5 + 4 + 3 + 2 + 1 = *190* comparisons, and approximately 190 swaps, for a total of 380 steps.

Notice the inefficiency here. As the number of elements increases, the number of steps grows *exponentially*. (In technical math terms, we'd actually say that it grows quadratically.) We can see this clearly in the following table:

N Data Elements	Max # of Steps
5	20
10	90
20	380
40	1560
80	6320

If you look at the growth of steps as N increases, you'll see that it's growing by approximately N^2. Take a look at the following table:

N Data Elements	# of Bubble Sort Steps	N^2
5	20	25
10	90	100
20	380	400
40	1560	1600
80	6320	6400

Let's express the time complexity of Bubble Sort with Big O notation. Remember, Big O always answers the key question: if there are N data elements, how many steps will the algorithm take?

Because for N values, Bubble Sort takes N^2 steps, in Big O we say that Bubble Sort has an efficiency of $O(N^2)$.

$O(N^2)$ is considered to be a relatively inefficient algorithm, since as the data increases, the steps increase dramatically. Look at this graph, which compares $O(N^2)$ against the faster $O(N)$:

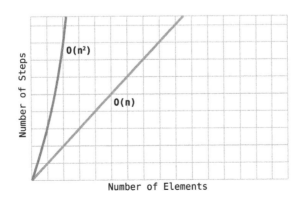

Note how $O(N^2)$ curves sharply upward in terms of number of steps as the data grows. Compare this with O(N), which plots along a simple, diagonal line.

One last note: $O(N^2)$ is also referred to as *quadratic time.*

A Quadratic Problem

Here's a practical example of where we can replace a slow $O(N^2)$ algorithm with a speedy O(N) one.

Let's say you're working on a Python application that analyzes the ratings people give to products, where users leave ratings from 0 to 10. Specifically, you're writing a function that checks whether an array of ratings contains any duplicate numbers. This will be used in more complex calculations in other parts of the software.

For example, the array [1, 5, 3, 9, 1, 4] has two instances of the number 1, so we'd return True to indicate that the array has a case of duplicate numbers.

One of the first approaches that may come to mind is the use of nested loops, as follows:

```
def has_duplicate_value(array):
    for i in range(len(array)):
        for j in range(len(array)):
            if (i != j) and (array[i] == array[j]):
                return True

    return False
```

In this function, we iterate through each value of the array using the variable i. As we focus on each value in i, we then run a *second* loop that looks through all the values in the array—using j—and checks if the values at positions i and j are the same. If they are, it means we've encountered duplicate values and we return True. If we get through all of the looping and we haven't encountered any duplicates, we return False, since we know that there are no duplicates in the array.

While this certainly works, is it efficient? Now that we know a bit about Big O notation, let's take a step back and see what Big O would say about this function.

Remember that Big O expresses how many steps the algorithm takes relative to N data values. To apply this to our situation, we'd ask ourselves: for N values in the array provided to our has_duplicate_value function, how many steps would our algorithm take in a worst-case scenario?

To answer the preceding question, we need to analyze what steps our function takes as well as what the worst-case scenario would be.

The preceding function has one type of step, namely *comparisons*. It repeatedly compares array[i] and array[j] to see if they are equal and therefore represent a duplicate pair. In a worst-case scenario, the array contains no duplicates, which would force our code to complete all of the loops and exhaust every possible comparison before returning False.

Based on this, we can conclude that for N values in the array, our function would perform N^2 comparisons. This is because we perform an outer loop that must iterate N times to get through the entire array, and for *each iteration*, we must iterate *another N times* with our inner loop. That's N steps * N steps, which is N^2 steps, leaving us with an algorithm of $O(N^2)$.

We can actually prove that our function takes N^2 steps by adding some code to our function that tracks the algorithm's number of steps:

```python
def has_duplicate_value(array):
    steps = 0  # count of steps
    for i in range(len(array)):
        for j in range(len(array)):
            steps += 1  # increment number of steps
            if (i != j) and (array[i] == array[j]):
                return True

    print(steps)  # print number of steps if no duplicates
    return False
```

This added code will print the number of steps taken when there are no duplicates. If we run has_duplicate_value([1, 4, 5, 2, 9]), for example, we'll see an output of 25 in the Python console, indicating that there were twenty-five comparisons for the five elements in the array. If we test this for other values, we'll see that the output is always the size of the array squared. This is classic $O(N^2)$.

Very often (but not always), when an algorithm nests one loop inside another, the algorithm is $O(N^2)$. So whenever you see a nested loop, $O(N^2)$ alarm bells should go off in your head.

Now, the fact that our function is $O(N^2)$ should give us pause. This is because $O(N^2)$ is considered a relatively slow algorithm. Whenever you encounter a slow algorithm, it's worth spending some time to consider whether there are any faster alternatives. There may *not* be any better alternatives, but let's first make sure.

A Linear Solution

What follows is another implementation of the has_duplicate_value function that doesn't rely on nested loops. It's a bit clever, so let's first look at how it works and then we'll see if it's any more efficient than our first implementation.

```
def has_duplicate_value(array):
    existing_numbers = [0] * 11

    for i in range(len(array)):
        if existing_numbers[array[i]] == 1:
            return True
        else:
            existing_numbers[array[i]] = 1

    return False
```

Here's what this function does. It creates an array called existing_numbers, which starts out as an array containing eleven zeroes. We're ensuring that our array has at least eleven slots so we can keep track of the eleven possible ratings users can leave (0 to 10).

Then we use a loop to check each number in the array. As it encounters each number, it places an arbitrary value (we've chosen to use a 1) in the existing_numbers array at the *index* of the number we're encountering.

For example, let's say our input array is [3, 5, 8]. When we encounter the 3, we place a 1 at index 3 of existing_numbers. So the existing_numbers array will now be the rough equivalent of this:

```
[0, 0, 0, 1, 0, 0, 0, 0, 0, 0, 0]
```

There's now a 1 at index 3 of existing_numbers, to indicate and remember for the future that we've already encountered a 3 in our given array.

When our loop then encounters the 5 from the given array, it adds a 1 to index 5 of existing_numbers:

```
[0, 0, 0, 1, 0, 1, 0, 0, 0, 0, 0]
```

Finally, when we reach the 8, existing_numbers will now look like this:

```
[0, 0, 0, 1, 0, 1, 0, 0, 1, 0, 0]
```

Essentially, we're using the indexes of existing_numbers to remember which numbers from the array we've seen so far.

Now, here's the real trick. Before the code stores a 1 in the appropriate index, it *first checks to see whether that index already has a 1 as its value*. If it does, this means we've already encountered that number, meaning we found a duplicate. If this is the case, we simply return True and cut the function short. If we get to the end of the loop without having returned True, it means there are no duplicates and we return False.

To determine the efficiency of this new algorithm in terms of Big O, we once again need to determine the number of steps the algorithm takes in a worst-case scenario.

Here, the significant type of step is looking at each number and checking whether the value of its index in existing_numbers is a 1:

```
if existing_numbers[array[i]] == 1:
```

(In addition to the comparisons, we also make *insertions* into the existing_numbers array, but we're considering that kind of step trivial in this analysis. More on this in the next chapter.)

In terms of the worst-case scenario, such a scenario would occur when the array contains no duplicates, in which case our function must complete the entire loop.

This new algorithm appears to make N comparisons for N data elements. This is because there's only one loop, and it simply iterates for as many numbers as there are in the array. We can test out this theory by tracking the steps in the Python console:

```python
def has_duplicate_value(array):
    steps = 0
    existing_numbers = [0] * 11

    for i in range(len(array)):
        steps += 1
        if existing_numbers[array[i]] == 1:
            return True
        else:
            existing_numbers[array[i]] = 1

    print(steps)
    return False
```

If we run has_duplicate_value([1, 4, 5, 2, 9]) now, we'll see that the output in the Python console is 5, which is the same as the size of our array. We'd find this to be true across arrays of all sizes. This algorithm, then, is O(N).

We know that O(N) is much faster than $O(N^2)$, so by using this second approach, we've optimized our has_duplicate_value function significantly. This is a *huge* speed boost.

(One disadvantage with this new implementation is that this approach will consume more memory than the first approach. Don't worry about this for now; we'll discuss this at length in Chapter 19, Dealing with Space Constraints, on page 385.)

Wrapping Up

It's clear that having a solid understanding of Big O notation can enable you to identify slow code and select the faster of two competing algorithms.

However, in some situations Big O notation will have us believe that two algorithms have the same speed, while one is actually faster. In the next chapter, you're going to learn how to evaluate the efficiencies of various algorithms even when Big O isn't nuanced enough to do so.

Exercises

The following exercises provide you with the opportunity to practice with speeding up your code. The solutions to these exercises are found in the section Chapter 4, on page 438.

1. Replace the question marks in the following table to describe how many steps occur for a given number of data elements across various types of Big O:

N Elements	O(N)	O(log N)	O(N^2)
100	100	?	?
2000	?	?	?

2. If we have an O(N^2) algorithm that processes an array and find that it takes 256 steps, what is the size of the array?

3. Use Big O notation to describe the time complexity of the following function. It finds the greatest product of any pair of two numbers within a given array:

```python
def greatest_product(array):
    if len(array) < 2:
        return None

    greatest_product_so_far = array[0] * array[1]

    for index_i, value_i in enumerate(array):
        for index_j, value_j in enumerate(array):
            if (index_i != index_j and
                    value_i * value_j > greatest_product_so_far):
                greatest_product_so_far = value_i * value_j

    return greatest_product_so_far
```

4. The following function finds the greatest single number within an array, but it has an efficiency of $O(N^2)$. Rewrite the function so that it becomes a speedy $O(N)$:

```python
def greatest_number(array):
    if not array:
        return None

    for i in array:
        # Assume for now that i is the greatest:
        is_i_the_greatest = True

        for j in array:
            # If we find another value that is greater than i,
            # i is not the greatest:
            if j > i:
                is_i_the_greatest = False

        # If, by the time we checked all the other numbers, i
        # is still the greatest, it means that i is the greatest number:
        if is_i_the_greatest:
            return i
```

CHAPTER 5

Optimizing Code With and Without Big O

We've seen that Big O notation is a great tool for comparing algorithms and determining which algorithm should be used for a given situation. However, it's certainly not the *only* tool. In fact, there may be times when two competing algorithms are described in the same way using Big O, yet one algorithm is faster than the other.

In this chapter, you're going to learn how to discern between two algorithms that *seem* to have the same efficiency and how to select the faster of the two.

Selection Sort

In the previous chapter, we explored a sorting algorithm known as Bubble Sort, which had an efficiency of $O(N^2)$. We're now going to dig into another sorting algorithm called Selection Sort and see how it measures up to Bubble Sort.

The steps of Selection Sort are as follows:

1. We check each cell of the array from left to right to determine which value is least. As we move from cell to cell, we keep track of the lowest value we've encountered so far. (We'll do this by storing its index in a variable.) If we encounter a cell that contains a value that is even lower than the one in our variable, we replace it so that the variable now points to the new index. See the following diagram:

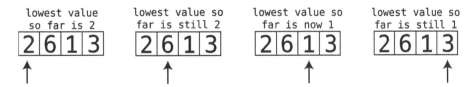

2. Once we've determined which index contains the lowest value, we swap its value with the value we began the pass-through with. This would be index 0 in the first pass-through, index 1 in the second pass-through, and so on. The diagram here illustrates making the swap of the first pass-through.

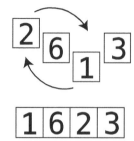

3. Each pass-through consists of Steps 1 and 2. We repeat the pass-throughs until we reach a pass-through that would start at the end of the array. By this point, the array will have been fully sorted.

Selection Sort in Action

Let's walk through the steps of Selection Sort using the example array [4, 2, 7, 1, 3].

We begin our first pass-through:

We set things up by inspecting the value at index 0. By definition, it's the lowest value in the array we've encountered so far (as it's the *only* value we've encountered so far), so we keep track of its index in a variable:

lowest value so far is 4, which is at index 0

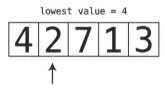

Step 1: We compare the 2 with the lowest value so far (which happens to be 4):

lowest value = 4

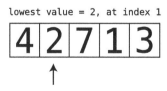

The 2 is even less than the 4, so it becomes the lowest value so far:

lowest value = 2, at index 1

Step 2: We compare the next value—the 7—with the lowest value so far. The 7 is greater than the 2, so 2 remains our lowest value:

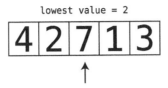

Step 3: We compare the 1 with the lowest value so far:

lowest value = 2

Because the 1 is even less than the 2, 1 becomes our new lowest value:

lowest value = 1, at index 3

Step 4: We compare the 3 to the lowest value so far, which is the 1. We've reached the end of the array, and we've determined that 1 is the lowest value out of the entire array:

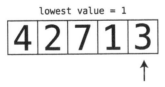

Step 5: Because 1 is the lowest value, we swap it with whatever value is at index 0—the index we began this pass-through with:

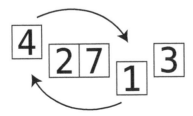

Since we've moved the lowest value to the beginning of the array, that means the lowest value is now in its correct spot:

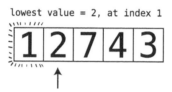

We're now ready to begin our second pass-through.

Setup: The first cell—index 0—is already sorted, so this pass-through begins at the next cell, which is index 1. The value at index 1 is the number 2, and it's the lowest value we've encountered in this pass-through so far:

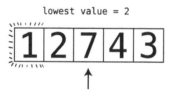

Step 6: We compare the 7 with the lowest value so far. The 2 is less than the 7, so 2 remains our lowest value:

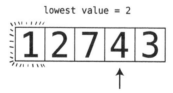

Step 7: We compare the 4 with the lowest value so far. The 2 is less than the 4, so 2 remains our lowest value:

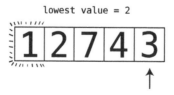

Step 8: We compare the 3 with the lowest value so far. The 2 is less than the 3, so 2 remains our lowest value:

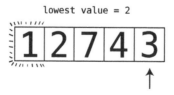

We've reached the end of the array. Since the lowest value from this pass-through was already in its correct spot, we don't need to perform a swap. This ends our second pass-through, leaving us with:

We now begin the third pass-through.

Setup: We begin at index 2, which contains the value 7. The 7 is the lowest value we've encountered so far in this pass-through:

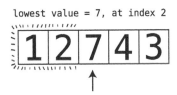

Step 9: We compare the 4 with the 7:

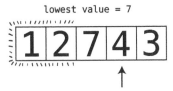

We note that 4 is our new lowest value:

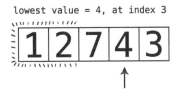

Step 10: We encounter the 3, which is even lower than the 4:

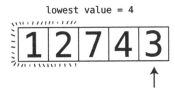

The 3 becomes our new lowest value:

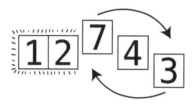

Step 11: We've reached the end of the array, so we swap the 3 with the value we started our pass-through with, which is the 7:

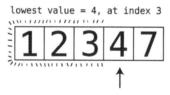

We now know that the 3 is in the correct place within the array:

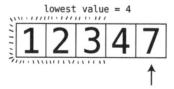

While you and I can both see that the entire array is correctly sorted at this point, the *computer* doesn't know this yet, so it must begin a fourth pass-through.

Setup: We begin the pass-through with index 3. The 4 is the lowest value so far:

lowest value = 4, at index 3

```
1 2 3 4 7
        ↑
```

Step 12: We compare the 7 with the 4:

lowest value = 4

```
1 2 3 4 7
          ↑
```

The 4 remains the lowest value we've encountered in this pass-through so far, so we don't need to swap it, since it's already in the correct place.

Because all the cells besides the last one are correctly sorted, that must mean the last cell is also in the correct order, and our entire array is properly sorted:

Code Implementation: Selection Sort

Here's an implementation of Selection Sort in Python:

```python
def selection_sort(array):
    for i in range(len(array) - 1):
        lowest_number_index = i

        for j in range(i + 1, len(array)):
            if array[j] < array[lowest_number_index]:
                lowest_number_index = j

        if lowest_number_index != i:
            array[i], array[lowest_number_index] = \
                array[lowest_number_index], array[i]

    return array
```

Let's break this down line by line.

We begin a loop that represents each pass-through. It uses the variable i to point to each index of the array and goes up through the second-to-last value:

```python
for i in range(len(array) - 1):
```

It doesn't need to run for the last value itself, since the array will be fully sorted by that point.

Next, begin keeping track of the *index* containing the lowest value we encounter so far:

```python
lowest_number_index = i
```

This lowest_number_index will be 0 at the beginning of the first pass-through, 1 at the beginning of the second, and so on.

The reason we specifically keep track of the index is because we'll need access to both the lowest value and its index in the rest of our code, and we can use the index to reference both. (We can check the lowest value by calling array[lowest_number_index]).

Within each pass-through, we check the remaining values of the array to see if there might be a lower value than the current lowest value:

```python
for j in range(i + 1, len(array)):
```

Indeed, if we find a lower value, we store this new value's index in lowest_number_index:

```
if array[j] < array[lowest_number_index]:
    lowest_number_index = j
```

By the end of the inner loop, we'll have found the index of the lowest number from this pass-through.

If the lowest value from this pass-through is already in its correct place (which would happen when the lowest value is the first value we encounter in the pass-through), we don't need to do anything. But if the lowest value is *not* in its correct place, we need to perform a swap. Specifically, we swap the lowest value with the value at i, which was the index we started the pass-through with:

```
if lowest_number_index != i:
    array[i], array[lowest_number_index] = array[lowest_number_index], array[i]
```

Finally, we return the sorted array:

```
return array
```

The Efficiency of Selection Sort

Selection Sort contains two types of steps: comparisons and swaps. We compare each value with the lowest number we've encountered in each pass-through, and we swap the lowest number into its correct position.

Looking back at our example array that contains five elements, we had to make a total of 10 comparisons. Let's break it down in the following table:

Pass-Through #	# of Comparisons
1	4 comparisons
2	3 comparisons
3	2 comparisons
4	1 comparison

That's a grand total of 4 + 3 + 2 + 1 = 10 comparisons.

To put it in a way that works for arrays of all sizes, we'd say that for N elements, we make

(N - 1) + (N - 2) + (N - 3) ... + 1 comparisons.

As for *swaps*, though, we only need to make a maximum of one swap per pass-through. This is because in each pass-through, we make either one or zero swaps, depending on whether the lowest number of that pass-through is already in the correct position. Contrast this with Bubble Sort, where in a worst-case scenario we have to make a swap for *each and every* comparison.

Here's a side-by-side comparison of Bubble Sort and Selection Sort:

N Elements	Max # of Steps in Bubble Sort	Max # of Steps in Selection Sort
5	20	14 (10 comparisons + 4 swaps)
10	90	54 (45 comparisons + 9 swaps)
20	380	209 (190 comparisons + 19 swaps)
40	1560	819 (780 comparisons + 39 swaps)
80	6320	3239 (3160 comparisons + 79 swaps)

From this comparison, it's clear Selection Sort takes about half the number of steps Bubble Sort does, indicating that Selection Sort is twice as fast.

Ignoring Constants

But here's the funny thing: in the world of Big O notation, Selection Sort and Bubble Sort are described in *exactly the same way.*

Again, Big O notation answers the key question: if there are N data elements, how many steps will the algorithm take? Because Selection Sort takes roughly half of N^2 steps, it would seem reasonable that we'd describe the efficiency of Selection Sort as being $O(N^2 / 2)$. That is, for N data elements, there are $N^2 / 2$ steps. The following table bears this out:

N Elements	$N^2 / 2$	Max # of Steps in Selection Sort
5	$5^2 / 2 = 12.5$	14
10	$10^2 / 2 = 50$	54
20	$20^2 / 2 = 200$	209
40	$40^2 / 2 = 800$	819
80	$80^2 / 2 = 3200$	3239

In reality, however, Selection Sort is described in Big O as $O(N^2)$, just like Bubble Sort. This is because of a major rule of Big O that I'm now introducing for the first time:

Big O notation ignores constants.

This is simply a mathematical way of saying that Big O notation never includes regular numbers that aren't an exponent. We simply drop these regular numbers from the expression.

In our case, then, even though the algorithm takes N^2 / 2 steps, we drop the "/ 2" because it's a regular number and express the efficiency as $O(N^2)$.

Here are a few more examples:

For an algorithm that takes N / 2 steps, we'd call it O(N).

An algorithm that takes N^2 + 10 steps would be expressed as $O(N^2)$ since we drop the 10, which is a regular number.

With an algorithm that takes 2N steps (meaning N * 2), we drop the regular number and call it O(N).

Even O(100N), which is *100 times slower than O(N)*, is also referred to as O(N).

Offhand, it would seem that this rule would render Big O notation entirely useless, as you can have two algorithms that are described in exactly the same way with Big O, and yet one can be *100 times faster* than the other. And that's exactly what we're seeing here with Selection Sort and Bubble Sort. Both are described in Big O as $O(N^2)$, but Selection Sort is twice as fast as Bubble Sort.

So, what gives?

Big O Categories

This leads us to the next concept within Big O: Big O notation only concerns itself with *general categories* of algorithm speeds.

As an analogy, let's talk about physical buildings. There are, of course, many different types of buildings. There are one-floor single-family homes, and two-floor single-family homes, and three-floor single-family homes. There are high-rise apartment buildings with varying numbers of floors. And there are skyscrapers with various heights and shapes.

If we were to compare two buildings, one of which is a single-family home and one of which is a skyscraper, it becomes almost moot to mention how many floors each one has. Because the two buildings are so incredibly different in their sizes and functions, we don't need to say, "This one is a two-story home, while the other is a one-hundred-floor skyscraper." We may as well just call one a house and the other a skyscraper. Calling them by their general categories is enough to signify their vast differences.

The same applies to algorithm efficiencies. If we compare, say, an O(N) algorithm with an $O(N^2)$ algorithm, the two efficiencies are so different that it doesn't really matter whether the O(N) algorithm is actually O(2N), or O(N / 2) or even O(100N).

Now, here's why O(N) and O(N^2) are considered two separate categories, while O(N) and O(100N) are part of the same category.

Remember The Soul of Big O, on page 37. Big O notation doesn't care merely about the number of steps an algorithm takes. It cares about the long-term trajectory of the algorithm's steps as the data increases. O(N) tells a story of straight growth—that the steps increase in a straight line according to some proportion of the data. This is true even when the steps are 100N. O(N^2) tells a different story—one of exponential growth.

Exponential growth is a completely different category compared to any form of O(N). This point is really driven home when we consider that O(N^2) will, at some point in data growth, become slower than O(N) multiplied by *any* factor.

In the following graph, you can see how O(N^2) becomes slower than various factors of N:

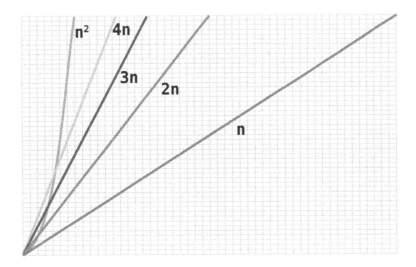

Therefore, when comparing two efficiencies that belong to two different categories of Big O, it's enough to identify them by their general category. Talking about O(2N) when compared to O(N^2) is like talking about a two-story house compared to a skyscraper. We may as well just say that O(2N) is part of the general category of O(N).

All the types of Big O we've encountered, whether it's O(1), O(log N), O(N), O(N^2), or the types we'll encounter later in this book, are general categories of Big O that are widely different from each other. Multiplying or dividing the number of steps by a regular number doesn't make them change to another category.

However, when two algorithms fall under the *same* classification of Big O, it doesn't necessarily mean that both algorithms have the same speed. After all, Bubble Sort is twice as slow as Selection Sort even though both are O(N^2). So while Big O is perfect for contrasting algorithms that fall under different classifications of Big O, when two algorithms fall under the *same* classification, further analysis is required to determine which algorithm is faster.

A Practical Example

Let's return to the first code example from Chapter 1, with minor changes:

```
def print_numbers_version_one(upper_limit):
    number = 2

    while number <= upper_limit:
        if number % 2 == 0:
            print(number)

        number += 1


def print_numbers_version_two(upper_limit):
    number = 2

    while number <= upper_limit:
        print(number)

        number += 2
```

Here we have two algorithms for accomplishing the same task, namely printing all even numbers starting from 2 to some upper_limit. (In Chapter 1, the upper limit was fixed at 100, while here, we let the user pass in a number as the upper_limit.)

I noted in Chapter 1 that the first version takes twice as many steps as the second version, but now let's see how this plays out in terms of Big O.

Again, Big O expresses the answer to the key question: if there are N data elements, how many steps will the algorithm take? In this case, though, N isn't the size of an array, but simply the number we pass into the function to serve as the upper_limit.

The first version takes about N steps. That is, if the upper_limit is 100, the function takes about 100 steps. (It really takes 99 steps, since it starts the count at 2.) So we can safely say that the first algorithm has a time complexity of O(N).

The second version takes N / 2 steps. When the upper_limit is 100, the function takes just 50 steps. While it would be tempting to call this O(N / 2), you've now learned that we drop the constants and reduce the expression to O(N).

Now, the second version is twice as fast as the first one and would naturally be the better choice. This is another great example of where two algorithms can be expressed the same way using Big O notation but further analysis is needed to figure out which algorithm is faster.

Significant Steps

Let's apply one more level of analysis to the previous example. If we look again at the first version, print_numbers_version_one, we said that it takes N steps. This is because the loop runs N times, with N being the upper_limit.

But does the function really take just N steps?

If we really break things down, we can see that *multiple* steps occur in each round of the loop.

First, we have the comparison step (if number % 2 == 0), which checks whether the number is divisible by 2. This comparison happens in each round of the loop.

Second, we have the print step (print(number)), which happens just for the even numbers. This, then, occurs in every *other* round of the loop.

And third, we have number += 1, which runs in each round of the loop.

In the previous chapters, I alluded to the fact that you'd learn how to determine which steps are significant enough to be counted when expressing the Big O of an algorithm. In our case, then, which of these steps are considered significant? Do we care about the comparisons, the printing, or the incrementing of number?

The answer is that *all* steps are significant. It's just that when we express the steps in Big O terms, we drop the constants and thereby simplify the expression.

Let's apply this here. If we count all the steps, we have N comparisons, N incrementings, and N / 2 printings. This adds up to 2.5N steps. However, because we eliminate the constant of 2.5, we express this as O(N). So which step was significant? They all were, but by dropping the constant, we effectively focus more on the number of times the loop runs, rather than the exact details of what happens within the loop.

Wrapping Up

We now have some powerful analysis tools at our disposal. We can use Big O to broadly determine the efficiency of an algorithm, and we can also compare two algorithms that fall within one classification of Big O.

However, another important factor must be taken into account when comparing the efficiencies of two algorithms. Until now, we've focused on how fast an algorithm is in a worst-case scenario. Now, worst-case scenarios, by definition, don't happen all the time. On average, most scenarios that occur are...well...average-case scenarios. In the next chapter, you'll learn how to take all scenarios into account.

Exercises

The following exercises provide you with the opportunity to practice analyzing algorithms. The solutions to these exercises are found in the section Chapter 5, on page 438.

1. Use Big O notation to describe the time complexity of an algorithm that takes 4N + 16 steps.

2. Use Big O notation to describe the time complexity of an algorithm that takes $2N^2$.

3. Use Big O notation to describe the time complexity of the following function, which returns the sum of all numbers of an array after the numbers have been doubled:

```
def double_then_sum(array):
    doubled_array = []

    for number in array:
        doubled_array.append(number * 2)

    sum = 0

    for number in doubled_array:
        sum += number

    return sum
```

4. Use Big O notation to describe the time complexity of the following function, which accepts an array of strings and prints each string in multiple cases:

```
def multiple_cases(array):
    for string in array:
        print(string.upper())
        print(string.lower())
        print(string.capitalize())
```

5. The next function iterates over an array of numbers. As it does so, it focuses on every *other* number while ignoring the numbers in between. For each "focus number," the function proceeds to print out *every* number from the array—one at a time—after being added to the focus number.

What is this function's efficiency in terms of Big O notation?

```python
def every_other(array):
    for index, number in enumerate(array):
        if index % 2 == 0:
            for other_number in array:
                print(number + other_number)
```

CHAPTER 6

Optimizing for Optimistic Scenarios

Until this point, we've focused primarily on how many steps an algorithm would take in a worst-case scenario. The rationale behind this is simple: if you're prepared for the worst, things will turn out okay.

However, you'll discover in this chapter that the worst-case scenario isn't the *only* situation worth considering. Being able to consider *all* scenarios is an important skill that can help you choose the appropriate algorithm for every situation.

Insertion Sort

We've previously encountered two different sorting algorithms: Bubble Sort and Selection Sort. Both have efficiencies of O(N^2), but Selection Sort is actually twice as fast. Now you'll learn about a third sorting algorithm called Insertion Sort that will reveal the power of analyzing scenarios beyond the worst case.

Insertion Sort consists of the following steps:

1. In the first pass-through, we temporarily remove the value at index 1 (the second cell) and store it in a temporary variable. This will leave a gap at that index, since it contains no value:

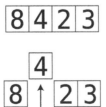

In subsequent pass-throughs, we remove the values at the subsequent indexes.

2. We then begin a shifting phase, where we take each value to the left of the gap and compare it to the value in the temporary variable:

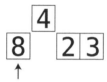

If the value to the left of the gap is greater than the temporary variable, we shift that value to the right:

As we shift values to the right, inherently the gap moves leftward. As soon as we encounter a value that is lower than the temporarily removed value, or we reach the left end of the array, this shifting phase is over.

3. We then insert the temporarily removed value into the current gap:

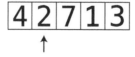

4. Steps 1 through 3 represent a single pass-through. We repeat these pass-throughs until the pass-through begins at the final index of the array. By then, the array will have been fully sorted.

Insertion Sort in Action

Let's apply Insertion Sort to the array [4, 2, 7, 1, 3].

We begin the first pass-through by inspecting the value at index 1. This happens to contain the value 2:

4 2 7 1 3

Step 1: We temporarily remove the 2 and keep it inside a variable called temp_value. We represent this value by shifting it above the rest of the array:

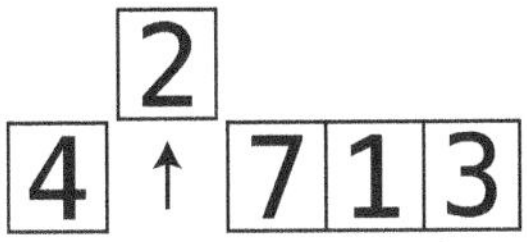

```
  2
4 ↑ 7 1 3
```

Step 2: We compare the 4 to the temp_value, which is 2:

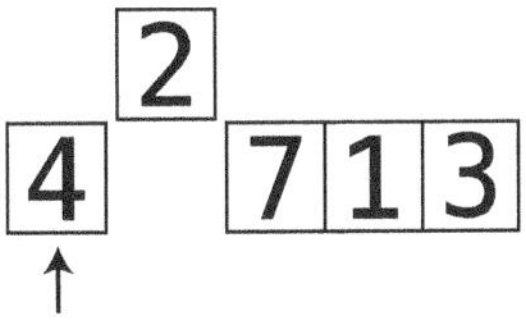

```
    2
4     7 1 3
↑
```

Step 3: Because 4 is greater than 2, we shift the 4 to the right:

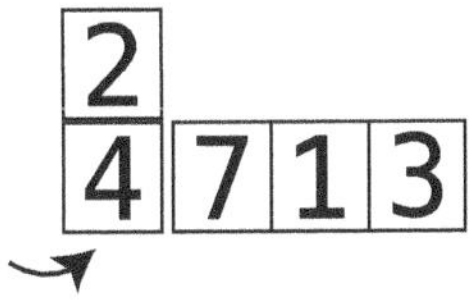

```
2
  4 7 1 3
 ↘
```

Nothing is left to shift, as the gap is now at the left end of the array.

Step 4: We insert the temp_value into the gap, completing our first pass-through:

```
 ↙
2 4 7 1 3
```

Next, we begin the second pass-through:

Step 5: In our second pass-through, we temporarily remove the value at index 2. We'll store this in temp_value. In this case, the temp_value is 7:

```
      7
2 4 ↑ 1 3
```

Step 6: We compare the 4 to the temp_value:

```
      7
2 4     1 3
  ↑
```

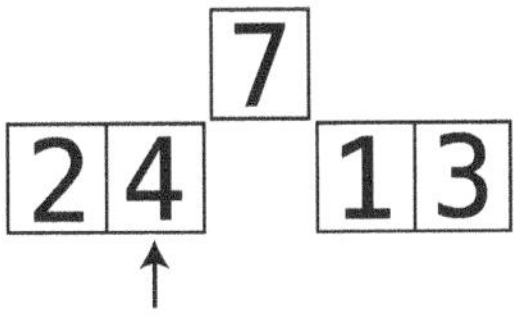

The 4 is lower, so we won't shift it. Since we reached a value that is less than the temp_value, this shifting phase is over.

Step 7: We insert the temp_value back into the gap, ending the second pass-through:

$$\boxed{2}\boxed{4}\boxed{7}\boxed{1}\boxed{3}$$

We now begin the third pass-through:

Step 8: We temporarily remove the 1 and store it in temp_value:

$$\boxed{2}\boxed{4}\boxed{7}\boxed{3}$$

Step 9: We compare the 7 to the temp_value:

$$\boxed{2}\boxed{4}\boxed{7}\boxed{3}$$

Step 10: The 7 is greater than 1, so we shift the 7 to the right:

$$\boxed{2}\boxed{4}\boxed{7}\boxed{3}$$

Step 11: We compare the 4 to the temp_value:

$$\boxed{2}\boxed{4}\boxed{7}\boxed{3}$$

Step 12: The 4 is greater than 1, so we shift it as well:

$$\boxed{2}\boxed{4}\boxed{7}\boxed{3}$$

Step 13: We compare the 2 to the temp_value:

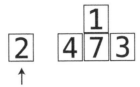

Step 14: The 2 is greater, so we shift it:

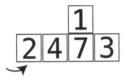

Step 15: The gap has reached the left end of the array, so we insert the temp_value into the gap, concluding this pass-through:

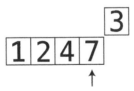

Now, we begin the fourth pass-through:

Step 16: We temporarily remove the value from index 4, making it our temp_value. This is the value 3:

Step 17: We compare the 7 to the temp_value:

Step 18: The 7 is greater, so we shift the 7 to the right:

Step 19: We compare the 4 to the temp_value:

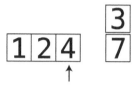

Step 20: The 4 is greater than the 3, so we shift the 4:

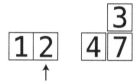

Step 21: We compare the 2 to the temp_value. The 2 is less than 3, so our shifting phase is complete:

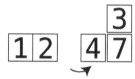

Step 22: We insert the temp_value back into the gap:

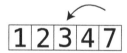

Our array is now fully sorted:

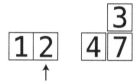

Code Implementation: Insertion Sort

Here's a Python implementation of Insertion Sort:

```python
def insertion_sort(array):
    for index in range(1, len(array)):
        temp_value = array[index]
        position = index - 1

        while position >= 0:
            if array[position] > temp_value:
                array[position + 1] = array[position]
                position = position - 1
```

```
        else:
            break

    array[position + 1] = temp_value

return array
```

Let's walk through this code step by step.

First, we start a loop beginning at index 1 that runs through the entire array. Each round of this loop represents a pass-through:

```
for index in range(1, len(array)):
```

Within each pass-through, we save the value we're "removing" in a variable called temp_value:

```
temp_value = array[index]
```

Next, we create a variable called position, which will start immediately to the left of the index of the temp_value. This position will represent each value we compare against the temp_value:

```
position = index - 1
```

As we move through the pass-through, this position will keep moving leftward as we compare each value to the temp_value.

We then begin an inner while loop, which runs as long as position is greater than or equal to 0:

```
while position >= 0:
```

We then perform our comparison; that is, we check whether the value at position is greater than the temp_value:

```
if array[position] > temp_value:
```

If it is, we shift that left value to the right:

```
array[position + 1] = array[position]
```

We then decrement position by 1 to compare the next left value against the temp_value in the next round of the while loop:

```
position = position - 1
```

If at any point we encounter a value at position that is less than or equal to the temp_value, we can get ready to end our pass-through, since it's time to move the temp_value into the gap:

```
else:
    break
```

The final step of each pass-through is moving the temp_value into the gap:

```
array[position + 1] = temp_value
```

After all pass-throughs have been completed, we return the sorted array:

```
return array
```

The Efficiency of Insertion Sort

Four types of steps occur in Insertion Sort: removals, comparisons, shifts, and insertions. To analyze the efficiency of Insertion Sort, we need to tally up each of these steps.

First, let's dig into comparisons. A comparison takes place each time we compare a value to the left of the gap with the temp_value. In a worst-case scenario, where the array is sorted in reverse order, we have to compare every number to the left of temp_value with temp_value in each pass-through. This is because each value to the left of temp_value will always be greater than temp_value, so the pass-through will only end when the gap reaches the left end of the array.

During the first pass-through, in which temp_value is the value at index 1, a maximum of one comparison is made, since there's only one value to the left of the temp_value. On the second pass-through, the maximum number of comparisons made is two, and so on. On the final pass-through, we need to compare the temp_value with every single value in the array besides temp_value itself. In other words, if there are N elements in the array, the maximum number of comparisons made in the final pass-through is N - 1.

We can, therefore, formulate the total number of comparisons as:

1 + 2 + 3 + ... + (N - 1) comparisons.

In our example array that contains five elements, that's a maximum of:

1 + 2 + 3 + 4 = 10 comparisons.

For an array containing 10 elements, there would be:

1 + 2 + 3 + 4 + 5 + 6 + 7 + 8 + 9 = 45 comparisons.

For an array containing 20 elements, there would be a total of 190 comparisons, and so on.

When examining this pattern, it emerges that for an array containing N elements, there are approximately $N^2 / 2$ comparisons. ($10^2 / 2$ is 50, and $20^2 / 2$ is 200. We'll look at this pattern more closely in the next chapter.)

Let's continue analyzing the other types of steps.

Shifts occur each time we move a value one cell to the right. When an array is sorted in reverse order, there will be as many shifts as there are comparisons since every comparison will force us to shift a value to the right.

Let's add up comparisons and shifts for a worst-case scenario:

N^2 / 2 comparisons

+ N^2 / 2 shifts

_____

N^2 steps

Removing and inserting the temp_value from the array happens once per pass-through. Since there are always N - 1 pass-throughs, we can conclude that there are N - 1 removals and N - 1 insertions.

So now we've got:

N^2 comparisons and shifts combined

N - 1 removals

+ N - 1 insertions

_____

N^2 + 2N - 2 steps

You've already learned one major rule of Big O: that Big O ignores constants. With this rule in mind, we'd—at first glance—simplify this to O(N^2 + N).

However, I'll now reveal another major rule of Big O:

Big O notation only takes into account the highest order of N when we have multiple orders added together.

In other words, if we have an algorithm that takes N^4 + N^3 + N^2 + N steps, we only consider N^4 to be significant—and just call it O(N^4). Why is this?

Look at the following table:

N	N^2	N^3	N^4
2	4	8	16
5	25	125	625
10	100	1,000	10,000
100	10,000	1,000,000	100,000,000

As N increases, N^4 becomes so much more significant than any other order of N that the smaller orders are considered trivial. For example, when looking at the bottom row of the table, when we add $N^4 + N^3 + N^2 + N$, we get a total of 101,010,100. But we may as well round that down to 100,000,000, which is accomplished by ignoring those lower orders of N.

We can apply this same concept to Insertion Sort. Even though we've already simplified Insertion Sort down to $N^2 + N$ steps, we simplify the expression further by throwing out the lower order, reducing it to $O(N^2)$.

It emerges that in a worst-case scenario, Insertion Sort has the same time complexity as Bubble Sort and Selection Sort. They're all $O(N^2)$.

I noted in the previous chapter that although Bubble Sort and Selection Sort are both $O(N^2)$, Selection Sort is faster because Selection Sort has $N^2 / 2$ steps compared with Bubble Sort's N^2 steps. At first glance, then, we'd say that Insertion Sort is as slow as Bubble Sort, since it too takes about N^2 steps.

If I stop the book here, you'd walk away thinking that Selection Sort is the best choice out of the three, since it's twice as fast as either Bubble Sort or Insertion Sort. But it's actually not that simple.

The Average Case

Indeed, in a worst-case scenario, Selection Sort *is* faster than Insertion Sort. However, it's critical we also take into account the *average-case scenario.*

Why?

By definition, the cases that occur most frequently are average scenarios. Take a look at this simple bell curve:

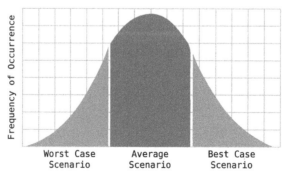

Best- and worst-case scenarios happen relatively infrequently. In the real world, average scenarios are what occur most of the time.

Take a randomly sorted array, for example. What are the odds that the values will occur in perfect ascending or descending order? It's much more likely that the values will be all over the place.

Let's examine Insertion Sort, then, in the context of all scenarios.

We've looked at how Insertion Sort performs in a worst-case scenario—where the array is sorted in descending order. In the worst case, we saw that in each pass-through, we compare and shift every value we encounter. (We calculated this to be a total of N^2 comparisons and shifts.)

In the best-case scenario, where the data is already sorted in ascending order, we end up making just one comparison per pass-through and not a single shift, since each value is already in its correct place.

Where data is randomly sorted, however, we'll have pass-throughs in which we compare and shift all of the data, some of the data, or possibly none of the data. If you look at the preceding walk-through example in Insertion Sort in Action, on page 80, you'll notice that in the first and third pass-throughs, we compare and shift all the data we encounter. In the fourth pass-through, we compare and shift just some of it, and in the second pass-through, we make just one comparison and shift no data at all.

(This variance occurs because some pass-throughs compare all the data to the left of the temp_value, while other pass-throughs end early, due to encountering a value that is less than the temp_value.)

So in the worst-case scenario, we compare and shift *all* the data, and in the best-case scenario, we shift *none* of the data (and just make one comparison per pass-through). For the average scenario, we can say that in the aggregate, we probably compare and shift about *half* the data. Thus, if Insertion Sort takes N^2 steps for the worst-case scenario, we'd say that it takes about $N^2 / 2$ steps for the average scenario. (In terms of Big O, however, both scenarios are $O(N^2)$.)

Let's dive into some specific examples.

The array [1, 2, 3, 4] is already presorted, which is the best case. The worst case for the same data would be [4, 3, 2, 1], and an example of an average case might be [1, 3, 4, 2].

In the worst case ([4, 3, 2, 1]), there are six comparisons and six shifts, for a total of twelve steps. In an average case of [1, 3, 4, 2], there are four comparisons and two shifts, for a total of six steps. In the best case ([1, 2, 3, 4]), there are three comparisons and zero shifts.

We can now see that the performance of Insertion Sort *varies greatly* based on the scenario. In the worst-case scenario, Insertion Sort takes N^2 steps. In an average scenario, it takes $N^2 / 2$ steps. And in the best-case scenario, it takes about N steps.

You can see these three types of performance in the following graph:

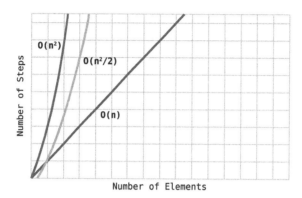

Contrast this with Selection Sort. Selection Sort takes $N^2 / 2$ steps in *all* cases, from worst to average to best-case scenarios. This is because Selection Sort doesn't have any mechanism for ending a pass-through early at any point. Each pass-through compares every value to the right of the chosen index no matter what.

Here's a table that compares Selection Sort and Insertion Sort:

	Best Case	Average Case	Worst Case
Selection Sort	$N^2 / 2$	$N^2 / 2$	$N^2 / 2$
Insertion Sort	N	$N^2 / 2$	N^2

So which is better: Selection Sort or Insertion Sort? The answer is, well, it depends. In an average case—where an array is randomly sorted—they perform similarly. If you have reason to assume you'll be dealing with data that is *mostly* sorted, Insertion Sort will be a better choice. If you have reason to assume you'll be dealing with data that is mostly sorted in reverse order, Selection Sort will be faster. If you have no idea what the data will be like, that's essentially an average case, and both will be equal.

A Practical Example

Suppose you're writing a Python application, and somewhere in your code you find that you need to get the intersection between two arrays. The intersection is a list of all the values that occur in *both* of the arrays. For example, if you have the arrays [3, 1, 4, 2] and [4, 5, 3, 6], the intersection would be a third array [3, 4] since both of those values are common to the two arrays.

Here's one possible implementation:

```
def intersection(first_array, second_array):
    result = []

    for i in first_array:
        for j in second_array:
            if i == j:
                result.append(i)

    return result
```

Here, we're running nested loops. In the outer loop, we iterate over each value in the first array. As we point to each value in the first array, we then run an inner loop that checks each value of the second array to see if it can find a match with the value being pointed to in the first array.

Two types of steps are taking place in this algorithm: comparisons and insertions. We compare every value of the two arrays against each other, and we insert matching values into the array result. Let's start by seeing how many comparisons there are.

If the two arrays are of equal size, and say that N is the size of either array, the number of comparisons performed are N^2. This is because we compare each element of the first array to each element of the second array. Thus, if we have two arrays that each contain five elements, we'd end up making twenty-five comparisons. So this intersection algorithm has an efficiency of $O(N^2)$.

The insertions, at most, would take N steps (if the two arrays happened to be identical). This is a lower order compared to N^2, so we'd still consider the algorithm to be $O(N^2)$. If the arrays are different sizes—say N and M—we'd say that the efficiency of this function is $O(N * M)$. (More on this can be found in Chapter 7, Big O in Everyday Code, on page 95.)

Is there any way we can improve this algorithm?

This is where it's important to consider scenarios beyond the worst case. In the current implementation of the intersection function, we make N^2 comparisons in *all* scenarios, no matter whether the arrays are identical or the arrays don't share a single common value.

However, where the two arrays share common values, we really shouldn't have to check *every* value of the second array against a value of the first array.

Let's see why:

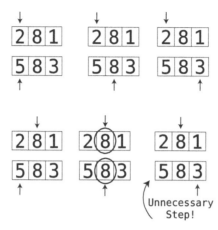

In this example, as soon as we find a common value (the 8), there's really no reason to complete the second loop. What are we checking for at this point? We've already determined that the second array contains the same 8 that the first array does and can add it to result. We're performing an unnecessary step.

To fix this, we can add a single word to our implementation:

```python
def intersection(first_array, second_array):
    result = []

    for i in first_array:
        for j in second_array:
            if i == j:
                result.append(i)
                break

    return result
```

With the addition of the break, we can cut the inner loop short and save steps (and therefore time).

It's still true that in a worst-case scenario, where the two arrays do not contain a single shared value, we have no choice but to perform N^2 comparisons. But now, in cases where the arrays share values, we can cut down the number of steps.

This is a significant optimization to our intersection function, since our first implementation would make N^2 comparisons in all scenarios.

Wrapping Up

Being able to discern between best-, average-, and worst-case scenarios is a key skill in choosing the best algorithm for your needs, as well as taking existing algorithms and optimizing them further to make them significantly faster. Remember, while it's good to be prepared for the worst case, average cases are what happen most of the time.

Now that we've covered the important concepts related to Big O notation, let's apply our knowledge to practical algorithms. In the next chapter, we're going to take a look at various everyday algorithms that may appear in real codebases and identify the time complexity of each one in terms of Big O.

Exercises

The following exercises provide you with the opportunity to practice with optimizing for best- and worst-case scenarios. The solutions to these exercises are found in the section Chapter 6, on page 439.

1. Use Big O notation to describe the efficiency of an algorithm that takes $3N^2 + 2N + 1$ steps.

2. Use Big O notation to describe the efficiency of an algorithm that takes $N + \log N$ steps.

3. The following function checks whether an array of numbers contains a pair of two numbers that add up to 10.

```python
def two_sum(array):
    for index_i, i in enumerate(array):
        for index_j, j in enumerate(array):
            if (index_i != index_j) and (i + j == 10):
                return True

    return False
```

What are the best-, average-, and worst-case scenarios? Then, express the worst-case scenario in terms of Big O notation.

4. The following function returns whether or not a capital "X" is present within a string.

```python
def contains_X(string):
    found_X = False

    for char in string:
        if char == "X":
            found_X = True

    return found_X
```

What is this function's time complexity in terms of Big O notation?

Then, modify the code to improve the algorithm's efficiency for best- and average-case scenarios.

CHAPTER 7

Big O in Everyday Code

In the previous chapters, you learned how to use Big O notation to express the time complexity of code. As you've seen, quite a few details go into Big O analysis. In this chapter, we'll use everything you've learned so far to analyze the efficiency of practical code samples that might be found in real-world codebases.

Determining the efficiency of our code is the first step in optimizing it. After all, if we don't know how fast our code is, how would we know if our modifications would make it faster?

Additionally, once we know how our code is categorized in terms of Big O notation, we can make a judgment call as to whether it may need optimization in the first place. For example, an algorithm that is $O(N^2)$ is generally considered to be a slow algorithm. So if we've determined that our algorithm falls into such a category, we should take pause and wonder if there are ways to optimize it.

Of course, $O(N^2)$ may be the best we can do for a given problem. However, knowing that our algorithm is considered slow can signal to us to dig deeper and analyze whether faster alternatives are available.

In the future chapters of this book, you're going to learn many techniques for optimizing our code for speed. But the first step of optimization is being able to determine how fast our code currently is.

So let's begin.

Mean Average of Even Numbers

The following method accepts an array of numbers and returns the mean average of all its *even* numbers. How would we express its efficiency in terms of Big O?

```
def average_of_even_numbers(array):
    sum = 0
    count_of_even_numbers = 0

    for number in array:
        if number % 2 == 0:
            sum += number
            count_of_even_numbers += 1

    if count_of_even_numbers == 0:
        return None

    return sum // count_of_even_numbers
```

Here's how to break the code down to determine its efficiency.

Remember that Big O is all about answering the key question: if there are N data elements, how many steps will the algorithm take? Therefore, the first thing we want to do is determine what the N data elements are.

In this case, the algorithm is processing the array of numbers passed into this method. These, then, would be the N data elements, with N being the size of the array.

Next, we have to determine how many steps the algorithm takes to process these N values.

We can see the guts of the algorithm is the loop that iterates over each number inside the array, so we'll want to analyze that first. Since the loop iterates over each of the N elements, we know the algorithm takes at least N steps.

Looking *inside* the loop, though, we can see that a varying number of steps occur within each round of the loop. For each and every number, we check whether the number is even. Then, if the number is even, we perform two more steps: we modify the sum variable, and we modify the count_of_even_numbers variable. So we execute two more steps for even numbers than we do for odd numbers.

As you've learned, Big O focuses primarily on worst-case scenarios. In our case, the worst case is when all the numbers are even, in which case we perform three steps during each round of the loop. Because of this, we can say that for N data elements, our algorithm takes 3N steps. That is, for each of the N numbers, our algorithm executes three steps.

Now, our method performs a few other steps outside of the loop as well. Before the loop, we initialize the two variables and set them to 0. Technically, these are two steps. After the loop, we perform another step: the division of sum / count_of_even_numbers. Technically, then, our algorithm takes three extra steps in addition to the 3N steps, so the total number of steps is 3N + 3.

However, you also learned that Big O notation ignores constant numbers, so instead of calling our algorithm O(3N + 3), we simply call it O(N).

Word Builder

The next example is an algorithm that collects every combination of two-character strings built from an array of single characters. For example, given the array ["a", "b", "c", "d"], we'd return a new array containing the following string combinations:

```
[
  'ab', 'ac', 'ad', 'ba', 'bc', 'bd',
  'ca', 'cb', 'cd', 'da', 'db', 'dc'
]
```

Following is an implementation of this algorithm. Let's see if we can figure out its Big O efficiency:

```
def word_builder(array):
    collection = []

    for index_i, i in enumerate(array):
        for index_j, j in enumerate(array):
            if index_i != index_j:
                collection.append(i + j)

    return collection
```

Here we're running one loop nested inside another. The outer loop iterates over each character in the array, keeping track of the index of i. For each index_i, we run an inner loop that iterates again over each character in the same array using the index index_j. Within this inner loop, we concatenate the characters at index_i and index_j, with the exception of when index_i and index_j are pointing to the same index.

To determine the efficiency of our algorithm, we once again need to determine what the N data elements are. In our case, as in the previous example, N is the number of items inside the array passed to the function.

The next step is to determine the number of steps our algorithm takes relative to the N data elements. In our case, the outer loop iterates over all N elements, and for each element, the inner loop iterates again over all N elements, which amounts to N steps multiplied by N steps. This is the classic case of O(N^2) and is often what nested-loop algorithms turn out to be.

Now, what would happen if we modified our algorithm to compute each combination of *three-character* strings? For our example array of ["a", "b", "c", "d"], our function would return the following array:

```
[
  'abc', 'abd', 'acb',
  'acd', 'adb', 'adc',
  'bac', 'bad', 'bca',
  'bcd', 'bda', 'bdc',
  'cab', 'cad', 'cba',
  'cbd', 'cda', 'cdb',
  'dab', 'dac', 'dba',
  'dbc', 'dca', 'dcb'
]
```

Here's an implementation that uses three nested loops. What is its time complexity?

```
def word_builder(array):
    collection = []

    for index_i, i in enumerate(array):
        for index_j, j in enumerate(array):
            for index_k, k in enumerate(array):
                if (index_i != index_j and
                        index_j != index_k and index_i != index_k):
                    collection.append(i + j + k)

    return collection
```

In this algorithm, for N data elements, we have N steps of the i loop multiplied by the N steps of the j loop multiplied by the N steps of the k loop. This is N * N * N, which is N^3 steps, which is described as $O(N^3)$.

If we had four or five nested loops, we'd have algorithms that are $O(N^4)$ and $O(N^5)$, respectively. Let's see how these all appear on a graph:

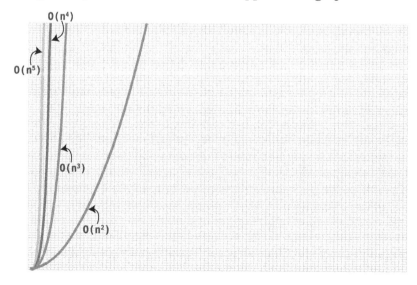

Optimizing any code from a speed of $O(N^3)$ to $O(N^2)$ would be a big win since the code becomes exponentially faster. However, the algorithm above remains stuck at $O(N^3)$.

Array Sample

In the next example, we create a function that takes a small sample of an array. We expect to have very large arrays, so our sample is just the first, middlemost, and last value from the array.

Here's an implementation of this function. See if you can identify its efficiency in Big O:

```python
def sample(array):
    if not array:
        return None

    first = array[0]
    middle = array[len(array) // 2]
    last = array[-1]

    return [first, middle, last]
```

In this case again, the array passed into this function is the primary data, so we can say that N is the number of elements in this array.

However, our function ends up taking the same number of steps no matter what N is. Reading from the beginning, midpoint, and last indexes of an array each takes one step no matter the size of the array. Similarly, finding the array's length and dividing it by 2 also takes one step.

Since the number of steps is constant—that is, it remains the same no matter what N is—this algorithm is considered $O(1)$.

Average Celsius Reading

Here's another example that involves mean averages. Let's say we're building weather-forecasting software. To determine the temperature of a city, we take temperature readings from many thermometers across the city, and we calculate the mean average of those temperatures.

We'd also like to display the temperatures in both Fahrenheit and Celsius, but our readings are initially only provided to us in Fahrenheit.

To get the average Celsius temperature, our algorithm does two things: first, it converts all the readings from Fahrenheit to Celsius. Then it calculates the mean average of all the Celsius numbers.

Below is some code that accomplishes this. What is its Big O?

```python
def average_celsius(fahrenheit_readings):
    if not fahrenheit_readings:
        return None

    celsius_numbers = []

    # Convert each reading to Celsius and append to array:
    for fahrenheit_reading in fahrenheit_readings:
        celsius_conversion = (fahrenheit_reading - 32) / 1.8
        celsius_numbers.append(celsius_conversion)

    # Calculate average:
    sum = 0

    for celsius_number in celsius_numbers:
        sum += celsius_number

    return sum // len(celsius_numbers)
```

First, we can say that N is the number of fahrenheit_readings passed into our method.

Inside the method, we run two loops. The first converts the readings to Celsius, and the second sums all the Celsius numbers. Since we have two loops that each iterate over all N elements, we have N + N, which is 2N (plus a few constant steps). Because Big O notation drops the constants, this gets reduced to O(N).

Don't get thrown off by the fact that in the earlier word builder example, two loops led to an efficiency of $O(N^2)$. There, the loops were *nested*, which led to N steps *multiplied* by N steps. In our case, however, we simply have two loops, one after the other. This is N steps *plus* N steps (2N), which is a mere O(N).

Clothing Labels

Suppose we're writing software for a clothing manufacturer. Our code accepts an array of newly produced clothing items (stored as strings) and creates text for every possible label we'll need.

Specifically, our labels should contain the item name plus its size, ranging from 1 to 5. For example, if we have the array, ["Purple Shirt", "Green Shirt"], we want to produce label text for those shirts like this:

```
[
"Purple Shirt Size: 1",
"Purple Shirt Size: 2",
"Purple Shirt Size: 3",
"Purple Shirt Size: 4",
"Purple Shirt Size: 5",
```

```
"Green Shirt Size: 1",
"Green Shirt Size: 2",
"Green Shirt Size: 3",
"Green Shirt Size: 4",
"Green Shirt Size: 5"
]
```

Here's code that will create this text for an entire array of clothing items:

```
def mark_inventory(clothing_items):
    clothing_options = []

    for item in clothing_items:
        for size in range(1, 6):
            clothing_options.append(item + " Size: " + str(size))

    return clothing_options
```

Let's determine this algorithm's efficiency. The clothing_items are the primary data being processed, so N is the size of the array, clothing_items.

This code contains nested loops, so it's tempting to declare this algorithm to be $O(N^2)$. However, we need to analyze this case a little more carefully. While code containing nested loops often is $O(N^2)$, in this case, it's not.

Nested loops that result in $O(N^2)$ occur when each loop revolves around N. In our case, however, while our outer loop runs N times, our inner loop runs a constant five times; that is, this inner loop will always run five times no matter what N is.

So while our outer loop runs N times, the inner loop runs five times for each of the N strings. This means our algorithm runs 5N times, but this is reduced to O(N), since Big O notation ignores constants.

Count the Ones

Here's another algorithm where the Big O is different from what it seems at first glance. This function accepts an *array of arrays*, where the inner arrays contain 1s and 0s. The function then returns how many 1s there are.

So take a look at this example input:

```
[
  [0, 1, 1, 1, 0],
  [0, 1, 0, 1, 0, 1],
  [1, 0]
]
```

Our function will return 7 since there are seven 1s.

Here's the function:

```python
def count_ones(outer_array):
    count = 0

    for inner_array in outer_array:
        for number in inner_array:
            if number == 1:
                count += 1

    return count
```

What's the Big O of this algorithm?

Again, it's easy to notice the nested loops and jump to the conclusion that it's $O(N^2)$. However, the two loops are iterating over two completely different things.

The outer loop is iterating over the inner arrays, and the inner loop is iterating over the actual numbers. At the end of the day, our inner loop only runs for as many numbers as there are *in total*.

Because of this, we can say that N represents how many numbers there are. And since our algorithm simply processes each number, the function's time complexity is O(N).

Palindrome Checker

A *palindrome* is a word or phrase that reads the same both forward and backward. Some examples include *racecar*, *kayak*, and *deified*.

Here's a function that determines whether a string is a palindrome:

```python
def is_palindrome(string):
    left_index = 0
    right_index = len(string) - 1

    # Iterate until left_index reaches the middle of the array:
    while left_index < len(string) // 2:

        # If the character on the left doesn't equal the character
        # on the right, the string is not a palindrome:
        if (string[left_index] != string[right_index]):
            return False

        left_index += 1
        right_index -= 1

    # If we got through the entire loop without finding any
    # mismatches, the string must be a palindrome:
    return True
```

Let's determine the Big O of this algorithm.

In this case, N is the size of the string passed to this function.

The guts of the algorithm takes place within the while loop. Now, this loop is somewhat interesting because it only runs until it reaches the midpoint of the string. That would mean that the loop runs N / 2 steps.

However, Big O ignores constants. Because of this, we drop the division by 2, and our algorithm is O(N).

Get All the Products

Our next example is an algorithm that accepts an array of numbers and returns the product of every combination of two numbers.

For example, if we passed in the array [1, 2, 3, 4, 5], the function returns:

```
[2, 3, 4, 5, 6, 8, 10, 12, 15, 20]
```

This is because we first multiply the 1 by the 2, 3, 4, and 5. Then we multiply the 2 by the 3, 4, and 5. Next, we multiply the 3 by the 4 and the 5. And finally, we multiply the 4 by the 5.

Note something interesting: when we multiply, say, the 2 by the other numbers, we only have to multiply it by the numbers that are to the right of it. We don't have to go back and multiply 2 by the 1, because that was already covered back when we multiplied the 1 by the 2. So each number only needs to be multiplied by the remaining numbers to the right of it.

Here's an implementation of this algorithm:

```python
def two_number_products(array):
    products = []

    for i in range(len(array)):
        for j in range(i + 1, len(array)):
            products.append(array[i] * array[j])

    return products
```

Let's break this down. N is the number of items in the array passed to this function.

We run the outer loop N times. (We actually run it N - 1 times, but we'll drop that constant.) The inner loop, though, is different. Since j always begins one index to the right of i, the inner loop's number of steps decreases each time that it's launched by the outer loop.

Let's see how many times the inner loop runs for our example array, which contains five elements:

When i is 0, the inner loop runs while j is 1, 2, 3, and 4. When i is 1, the inner loop runs while j is 2, 3, and 4. When i is 2, the inner loop runs while j is 3, and 4. When i is 3, the inner loop runs while j is 4. When all is said and done, the inner loop runs:

4 + 3 + 2 + 1 times.

To put this in terms of N, we can say that the inner loop runs approximately:

N + (N - 1) + (N - 2) + (N - 3) ... + 1 times.

This formula always turns out to compute to about $N^2 / 2$. We can visualize this in the following diagram. For the purposes of the diagram, we'll say that N is 8, so there are 8^2, or 64, squares.

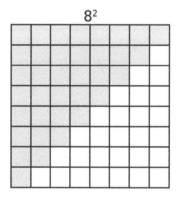

If you work your way from the top row to the bottom, you'll see that the top row has all N squares shaded gray. The next row has N - 1 squares shaded gray, and the one after that has N - 2 gray squares. This pattern continues until the bottom row, which has just one shaded square.

You can also see at a glance that approximately half of the squares are shaded. This demonstrates that the pattern of N + (N - 1) + (N - 2) + (N - 3)... + 1 is equivalent to $N^2 / 2$.

We've figured out, then, that the inner loop runs for $N^2 / 2$ steps. But because Big O ignores constants, we express this as $O(N^2)$.

Dealing with Multiple Datasets

Now, what happens if instead of computing the product of every two numbers from a single array, we instead compute the product of every number from one array by every number of a *second* array?

For example, if we had the array [1, 2, 3] and the array [10, 100, 1000], we'd compute the products as follows:

```
[10, 100, 1000, 20, 200, 2000, 30, 300, 3000]
```

Our code would be similar to the previous snippet, with some slight modifications:

```python
def two_number_products(array1, array2):
    products = []

    for i in array1:
        for j in array2:
            products.append(i * j)

    return products
```

Let's analyze the time complexity of this function.

First, what is N? This is the first hurdle, as we now have *two* datasets, namely, the two arrays.

It's tempting to lump everything together and say N is the total number of items of both arrays combined. But this is problematic for the following reason:

Here's a tale of two scenarios. In Scenario 1, there are two arrays of size 5. In Scenario 2, there's one array of size 9 and another of size 1.

In both scenarios, we'd end up saying that N is 10, since 5 + 5 = 10 and 9 + 1 = 10. However, the efficiency of each scenario is *very* different.

In Scenario 1, our code takes twenty-five (5 * 5) steps. Because N is 10, this is equivalent to $(N / 2)^2$ steps.

In Scenario 2, though, our code takes nine (9 * 1) steps, which is close to about N steps. This is dramatically faster than Scenario 1!

So, we don't want to consider N to be the total number of integers from both arrays, since we'd never be able to pin down the efficiency in terms of Big O notation, as it varies based on the different scenarios.

We're in a bit of a bind here. We have no choice but to express the time complexity as O(N * M), where N is the size of one array and M is the size of the other.

This is a new concept: whenever we have two distinct datasets that have to interact with each other through multiplication, we have to identify both sources separately when we describe the efficiency in terms of Big O.

While this is the correct way of expressing this algorithm in terms of Big O notation, it's a little less useful than other expressions of Big O. Comparing an O(N * M) algorithm to algorithms that only have an N (and not an M) is a little like comparing apples to oranges.

However, we do know that there's a specific range in which O(N * M) lies. That is, if N and M are the same, it's equivalent to $O(N^2)$. And if they're not the same, and we arbitrarily assign the smaller number to be M, even if M is as low as 1, we end up with O(N). In a sense then, O(N * M) can be construed as a range between O(N) and $O(N^2)$.

Is this great? No, but it's the best we can do.

Password Cracker

You're a hacker (an ethical one, of course) who's trying to figure out someone's password. You decide on a brute-force approach and write some code that produces every possible string of a given length. Here's the code you whipped up:

```python
from string import ascii_lowercase
import itertools

def every_password(length):
    for s in itertools.product(ascii_lowercase, repeat=length):
        print("".join(s))
```

In our code, we've imported the entire alphabet using ascii_lowercase from Python's string module so we don't have to actually type out the entire alphabet. We've also used Python's itertools module to allow us to run an arbitrary number of nested loops with minimum code.

In truth, we're not going to focus on how this code works, but rather what this code *does*.

When we call the every_password function, we pass in an integer, which becomes the variable length.

If length is 3, the code will return all possible strings within the range of "aaa" and "zzz". Running this code will print the following:

```
aaa
aab
aac
aad
aae

...

zzx
zzy
zzz
```

If length is 4, your code will print all possible strings of length 4:

```
aaaa
aaab
aaac
aaad
aaae

. . .

zzzx
zzzy
zzzz
```

If you try running this code even for a mere length of 5, you may be waiting some time for it to finish. This is a slow algorithm! But how do we express it in terms of Big O?

Let's break it down.

If we simply print each letter from the alphabet once, it would take 26 steps.

When we print every two-character combination, we end up with 26 characters multiplied by 26 characters.

When printing every three-character combination, we end up with 26 * 26 * 26 combinations.

Do you see the pattern?

Length	Combinations
1	26
2	26^2
3	26^3
4	26^4

If we look at this in terms of N, it emerges that if N is the length of each string, *the number of combinations is 26^N.*

Therefore, in Big O notation, we express this as $O(26^N)$. This is an utterly glacial algorithm! The truth is that even an algorithm that is a "mere" $O(2^N)$ is incredibly slow. Let's see how it looks on a graph, shown on page 108, compared to some of the other algorithms we've seen so far.

As you can see, $O(2^N)$ gets even slower than $O(N^3)$ at a point.

In a certain sense, $O(2^N)$ is the opposite of $O(\log N)$. With an algorithm of $O(\log N)$ (like binary search), each time the data is doubled, the algorithm takes

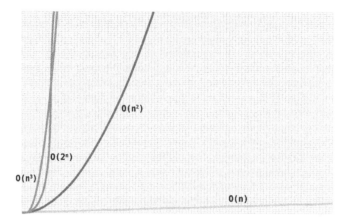

one additional step. With an algorithm of $O(2^N)$, each time we add *one* element of data, the algorithm *doubles* in steps!

In our password cracker, each time we increase N by one, the number of steps get multiplied by *26*. This takes an incredible amount of time, which is why brute force is such an inefficient way to crack a password.

Wrapping Up

Congratulations! You're now a Big O pro. You can analyze all sorts of algorithms and categorize their time complexities. Armed with this knowledge, you'll be able to methodically optimize your code for speed.

Speaking of which, in the next chapter, we'll discover a new data structure that is one of the most useful and common tools for speeding up algorithms. And I'm talking about some serious speed.

Exercises

The following exercises provide you with the opportunity to practice with algorithms in practical situations. The solutions to these exercises are found in the section Chapter 7, on page 440.

1. Use Big O notation to describe the time complexity of the following function. The function returns True if the array is a 100-sum array, and False if it is not.

   A 100-sum array meets the following criteria:

   - Its first and last numbers add up to 100.
   - Its second and second-to-last numbers add up to 100.
   - Its third and third-to-last numbers add up to 100, and so on.

Here's the function:

```python
def one_hundred_sum(array):
    if (len(array) % 2 != 0) or not array:
        return False

    left_index = 0
    right_index = len(array) - 1

    while left_index < (len(array) // 2):
        if array[left_index] + array[right_index] != 100:
            return False

        left_index += 1
        right_index -= 1

    return True
```

2. Use Big O notation to describe the time complexity of the following function. It merges two sorted arrays to create a new sorted array containing all the values from both arrays:

```python
def merge(array_1, array_2):
    new_array = []
    array_1_pointer = 0
    array_2_pointer = 0

    # Run the loop until we've reached end of both arrays:
    while array_1_pointer < len(array_1) or array_2_pointer < len(array_2):

        # If we already reached the end of the first array,
        # add item from second array:
        if array_1_pointer >= len(array_1):
            new_array.append(array_2[array_2_pointer])
            array_2_pointer += 1
        # If we already reached the end of the second array,
        # add item from first array:
        elif array_2_pointer >= len(array_2):
            new_array.append(array_1[array_1_pointer])
            array_1_pointer += 1
        # If the current number in first array is less than current
        # number in second array, add from first array:
        elif array_1[array_1_pointer] < array_2[array_2_pointer]:
            new_array.append(array_1[array_1_pointer])
            array_1_pointer += 1
        # If the current number in second array is less than or equal
        # to current number in first array, add from second array:
        else:
            new_array.append(array_2[array_2_pointer])
            array_2_pointer += 1

    return new_array
```

3. Use Big O notation to describe the time complexity of the following func-
    tion. This function solves a famous problem known as "finding a needle
    in the haystack."

    Both the needle and haystack are strings. For example, if the needle is
    "def" and the haystack is "abcdefghi", the needle is contained somewhere in
    the haystack, as "def" is a substring of "abcdefghi". However, if the needle
    is "dd", it cannot be found in the haystack of "abcdefghi".

    This function returns True or False depending on whether the needle can
    be found in the haystack:

```python
def find_needle(needle, haystack):
    needle_start_index = 0

    while needle_start_index <= len(haystack) - len(needle):
        if needle[0] == haystack[needle_start_index]:
            needle_offset = 0

            while needle_offset < len(needle):
                if (needle[needle_offset]
                        != haystack[needle_start_index + needle_offset]):
                    break
                else:
                    if needle_offset == len(needle) - 1:
                        return True

                needle_offset += 1

        needle_start_index += 1

    return False
```

4. Use Big O notation to describe the time complexity of the following func-
    tion. This function finds the greatest product of three numbers from a
    given array:

```python
def largest_product(array):
    if len(array) < 3:
        return None

    largest_product_so_far = array[0] * array[1] * array[2]
    i = 0

    while i < len(array):
        j = i + 1

        while j < len(array):
            k = j + 1

            while k < len(array):
                if array[i] * array[j] * array[k] > largest_product_so_far:
                    largest_product_so_far = array[i] * array[j] * array[k]
                k += 1
```

```
        j += 1
    i += 1
return largest_product_so_far
```

5. I once saw a joke aimed at HR people: "Want to immediately eliminate the unluckiest people from your hiring process? Just take half of the resumes on your desk and throw them in the trash."

If we were to write software that kept reducing a pile of resumes until we had one left, it might take the approach of alternating between throwing out the top half and the bottom half; that is, it will first eliminate the top half of the pile, and then proceed to eliminate the bottom half of what remains. It keeps alternating between eliminating the top and bottom until one lucky resume remains, and that's who we'll hire!

Describe the efficiency of this function in terms of Big O:

```
def pick_resume(resumes):
    if not resumes:
        return None

    eliminate = "top"

    while len(resumes) > 1:
        midpoint = len(resumes) // 2

        if eliminate == "top":
            resumes = resumes[:midpoint]
            eliminate = "bottom"
        elif eliminate == "bottom":
            resumes = resumes[-midpoint:]
            eliminate = "top"

    return resumes[0]
```

CHAPTER 8

Blazing Fast Lookup with Hash Tables

Imagine you're writing a program that allows customers to order fast food from a restaurant, and you're implementing a menu of foods with their respective prices. You could, technically, use an array:

```
menu = [
    ["french fries", 0.75],
    ["hamburger", 2.5],
    ["hot dog", 1.5],
    ["soda", 0.6]
]
```

This array contains several subarrays, and each subarray contains two elements. The first element is a string representing the food on the menu, and the second element represents the price of that food.

As you learned in Chapter 2, Why Algorithms Matter, on page 21, if this array were unordered, searching for the price of a given food would take O(N) steps since the computer would have to perform a linear search. If it's an *ordered* array, the computer could do a binary search, which would take O(log N).

While O(log N) isn't bad, we can do better. In fact, we can do *much* better. By the end of this chapter, you'll learn how to use a special data structure called a *hash table*, which can be used to look up data in just O(1) time. By knowing how hash tables work under the hood and the right places to use them, you can leverage their tremendous lookup speeds in many situations.

Hash Tables

Most programming languages include a data structure called a *hash table*, and it has an amazing superpower: fast reading. Note that hash tables are called by different names in various programming languages. In Python they're called *dictionaries*, and other languages call them hashes, maps, hash maps, dictionaries, or associative arrays. We'll refer to them as hash tables, since that's a common universal way to refer to this data structure.

Here's an example of the menu as implemented with a hash table:

```
menu = { "french fries": 0.75, "hamburger": 2.5,
"hot dog": 1.5, "soda": 0.6 }
```

A hash table is a list of paired values. The first item in each pair is called the *key*, and the second item is called the *value*. In a hash table, the key and value have some significant association with one another. In this example, the string, "french fries" is the key, and 0.75 is the value. They are paired together to indicate that french fries cost 75 cents.

In Python, you can look up a key's value using this syntax:

```
menu.get("french fries")
```

This would return the value 0.75.

Alternatively, you can look up a key's value this way:

```
menu["french fries"]
```

However, this latter approach triggers an error if the key doesn't exist in the hash table. Therefore, we'll use the former approach, which simply returns None if the key isn't found.

Looking up a value in a hash table has an efficiency of O(1) on average, as it usually takes *just one step*. Let's see why.

Hashing with Hash Functions

Do you remember those secret codes you used as a kid to create and decipher messages? For example, here's a simple way to map letters to numbers:

A = 1
B = 2
C = 3
D = 4
E = 5

and so on. According to this code,

ACE converts to 135,
CAB converts to 312,
DAB converts to 412,

and

BAD converts to 214.

This process of taking characters and converting them to numbers is known as *hashing*. And the code that is used to convert those letters into particular numbers is called a *hash function*.

Many other hash functions exist besides this one. Another example of a hash function may be to take each letter's corresponding number and return the *sum* of all the numbers. If we did that, BAD would become the number 7 following a two-step process:

Step 1: First, BAD converts to 214.

Step 2: We then take each of these digits and get their sum:

2 + 1 + 4 = 7

Another example of a hash function may be to return the *product* of all the letters' corresponding numbers. This would convert the word BAD into the number 8:

Step 1: First, BAD converts to 214.

Step 2: We then take the product of these digits:

2 * 1 * 4 = 8

In our examples for the remainder of this chapter, we're going to stick with this last version of the hash function. Real-world hash functions are more complex than this, but this multiplication hash function will keep our examples clear and simple.

The truth is that a hash function needs to meet only one criterion to be valid: a hash function must convert the same string to the *same number* every single time it's applied. If the hash function can return inconsistent results for a given string, it's not valid.

Examples of invalid hash functions include functions that use random numbers or the current time as part of their calculation. With these functions, BAD might convert to 12 one time and 106 another time.

With our multiplication hash function, however, BAD will *always* convert to 8. That's because B is always 2, A is always 1, and D is always 4. And 2 * 1 * 4 is *always* 8. There's no way around this.

Note that with this hash function, DAB will *also* convert into 8 just as BAD will. This will cause some issues that I'll address later.

Armed with the concept of hash functions, we can now understand how a hash table works.

Building a Thesaurus for Fun and Profit, but Mainly Profit

On nights and weekends, you're single-handedly working on a stealth startup that will take over the world. It's...a thesaurus app. But this isn't any *old* thesaurus app—this is Quickasaurus. And you know that it will totally disrupt the billion-dollar thesaurus market. When a user looks up a word in Quickasaurus, it returns just *one* synonym, instead of *every* possible synonym, as old-fashioned thesaurus apps do.

Since every word has an associated synonym, this is a great use case for a hash table. After all, a hash table is a list of paired items. Let's get started.

We can represent our thesaurus using a hash table:

```
thesaurus = {}
```

Under the hood, a hash table stores its data in a bunch of cells in a row, similar to an array. Each cell has a corresponding number. For example:

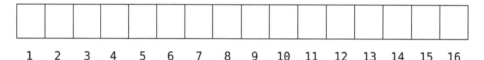

(We left off index 0 since nothing would be stored there given our multiplication hash function.)

Let's add our first entry into the hash table:

```
thesaurus["bad"] = "evil"
```

In code, our hash table now looks like this:

```
{"bad": "evil"}
```

Let's explore how the hash table stores this data.

First, the computer applies the hash function to the key. Again, we'll be using the multiplication hash function described previously. So this would compute as:

BAD = 2 * 1 * 4 = 8

Since our key ("bad") hashes into 8, the computer places the value ("evil") into cell 8:

Now, let's add another key-value pair:

```
thesaurus["cab"] = "taxi"
```

Again, the computer hashes the key:

CAB = 3 * 1 * 2 = 6

Since the resulting value is 6, the computer stores the value ("taxi") inside cell 6.

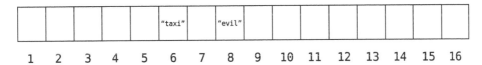

Let's add one more key-value pair:

```
thesaurus["ace"] = "star"
```

To sum up what's happening here: for every key-value pair, each *value* is stored at the *index* of the *key*, after the key has been hashed.

ACE hashes into 15, since ACE = 1 * 3 * 5 = 15, so "star" gets placed into cell 15:

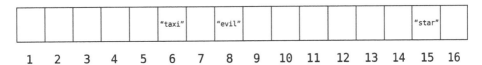

In code, our hash table currently looks like this:

```
{"bad": "evil", "cab": "taxi", "ace": "star"}
```

Hash Table Lookups

When we look up items from a hash table, we use a key to find its associated value. Let's see how this works with our Quickasaurus example hash table.

Suppose we want to look up the value associated with the key "bad". In our code, we'd say:

```
thesaurus.get("bad")
```

To find the value associated with "bad", the computer executes two simple steps:

1. The computer hashes the key we're looking up: BAD = 2 * 1 * 4 = 8.
2. Since the result is 8, the computer looks inside cell 8 and returns the value stored there. In this case, that is the string "evil".

Let's take a step back and look at the big picture here. In a hash table, the placement of each value is determined by its key; that is, by hashing the key itself, we compute the index number where the key's associated value should be placed.

Because the key determines the placement of the value, we use this principle to make lookups a cinch. When we have any key and want to find its value, the key itself tells us where the value will be found. Just as we hashed the key to insert the value in the appropriate cell, we can hash the key again to find where we previously put that value.

It now becomes clear why looking up a value in a hash table is typically O(1): it's a process that takes a constant amount of time. The computer hashes the key, turns it into a number, and jumps to the index with that number to retrieve the value stored there.

We can now understand why a hash table would yield faster lookups for our restaurant menu than an array. With an array, when we look up the price of a menu item, we would have to search through each cell until we find it. For an unordered array, this would take up to O(N), and for an ordered array, this would take up to O(log N). Using a hash table, however, we can now use the actual menu items as keys, allowing us to do a hash table lookup of O(1). And *that's* the beauty of a hash table.

One-Directional Lookups

It's important to point out that the ability to find any value within the hash table in a single step only works if we know the value's key. If we tried to find a particular value without knowing its key, we'd still have to resort to searching each and every key-value pair within the hash table, which is O(N).

Similarly, we can only do O(1) lookups when using a *key* to find the *value*. If, on the other hand, we want to use a *value* to find its associated *key*, we can't take advantage of the hash table's fast lookup ability.

This is because the whole premise of the hash table is that the key determines the value's location. But this premise only works in one direction: we use the key to find the value. The value does not determine the key's location, so we have no way to easily find any key without combing through all of them.

Come to think of it, where are the keys stored? In the previous diagrams, we only saw how the values are stored in the hash table.

While this detail may vary from language to language, some languages store the keys next to the values themselves. This is useful in case of collisions, which I'll discuss in the next section.

In any case, another aspect of the hash table's one-directional nature is worth noting. Each key can exist only once in the hash table, but there can be multiple instances of a value.

If we think about the menu example from the beginning of this chapter, we can't have the hamburger listed twice (nor would we want to, as it only has one price). However, we *could* have multiple foods that cost $2.50.

In many languages, if we try to store a key-value pair where the key already exists, it simply overwrites the old value while keeping the same key.

Dealing with Collisions

Hash tables are awesome but are not without complications.

Continuing our thesaurus example: what happens if we want to add the following entry into our thesaurus?

```
thesaurus["dab"] = "pat"
```

First, the computer would hash the key:

DAB = 4 * 1 * 2 = 8

Then, it would try to add "pat" to our hash table's cell 8:

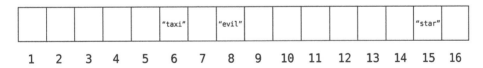

Uh-oh. Cell 8 is already filled with "evil"—literally!

Trying to add data to a cell that is already filled is known as a *collision*. Fortunately, there are ways around it.

One classic approach for handling collisions is known as *separate chaining*. When a collision occurs, instead of placing a *single* value in the cell, it places in it a reference to an array.

Let's look more carefully at a subsection of our hash table's underlying data storage:

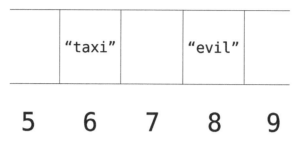

In our example, the computer wants to add "pat" to cell 8, but it already contains "evil". So it replaces the contents of cell 8 with an array, as shown here:

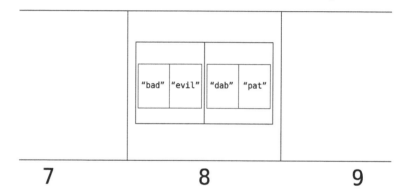

This array contains subarrays, where the first value is the word and the second value is its synonym.

Let's walk through how a hash table lookup works in this case. Say we look up the following word:

`thesaurus.get("dab")`

The computer takes the following steps:

1. It hashes the key: DAB = 4 * 1 * 2 = 8.

2. It looks up cell 8. The computer takes note that cell 8 contains an array of arrays rather than a single value.

3. It searches through the array linearly, looking at index 0 of each subarray until it finds our key ("dab"). It then returns the value at index 1 of the correct subarray.

Let's walk through these steps visually.

We hash DAB into 8, so the computer inspects that cell:

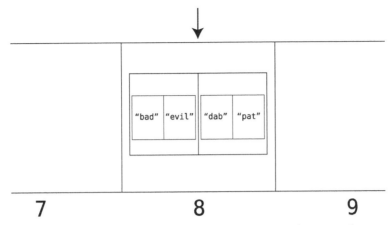

Because cell 8 contains an array of subarrays, we begin a linear search through each subarray, starting at the first one. We inspect index 0 of the first subarray:

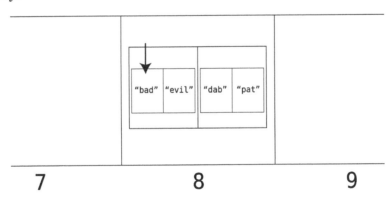

It doesn't contain the key we're looking for ("dab"), so we move on to index 0 of the next subarray:

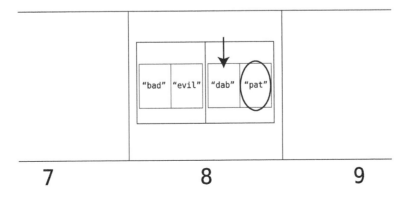

We found "dab", which would indicate that the value at index 1 of that subarray ("pat") is the value we're looking for.

In a scenario where the computer hits upon a cell that references an array, its search can take some extra steps, as it needs to conduct a linear search within an array of multiple values. If somehow all of our data ended up within a single cell of our hash table, our hash table would be no better than an array. So, it actually turns out that the worst-case performance for a hash table lookup is O(N).

Because of this, it's critical that a hash table is designed in such a way that it will have few collisions and, therefore, typically perform lookups in O(1) time rather than O(N) time.

Luckily, most programming languages implement hash tables and handle these details for us. However, by understanding how it all works under the hood, we can appreciate how hash tables eke out O(1) performance.

Let's see how hash tables can be set up to avoid frequent collisions.

Making an Efficient Hash Table

Ultimately, a hash table's efficiency depends on three factors:

- How much data we're storing in the hash table
- How many cells are available in the hash table
- Which hash function we're using

It makes sense why the first two factors are important. If you have a lot of data and only a few cells, there will be many collisions and the hash table will lose its efficiency. Let's explore, however, why the hash function itself is important for efficiency.

Let's say we're using a hash function that always produces a value that falls in the range from 1 to 9. An example of this is a hash function that converts letters into their corresponding numbers and keeps adding the resulting digits together until it ends up with a single digit.

For example:

PUT = 16 + 21 + 20 = 57

Because 57 contains more than one digit, the hash function breaks up the 57 into 5 + 7:

5 + 7 = 12

12 also contains more than one digit, so it breaks up the 12 into 1 + 2:

1 + 2 = 3

In the end, PUT hashes into 3.

This hash function by its very nature will *always* return a number 1 through 9.

Let's return to our example hash table:

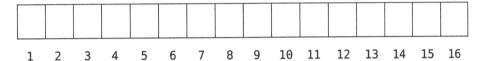

With this hash function, the computer would never even use cells 10 through 16 even though they exist. All data would be stuffed into cells 1 through 9.

A good hash function, therefore, is one that distributes its data across *all* available cells. The more we can spread out our data, the fewer collisions we'll have.

The Great Balancing Act

You learned that a hash table's efficiency goes up as its number of collisions goes down. In theory, then, the best way to avoid collisions would be to have a hash table with a large number of cells. Imagine we want to store just five items in our hash table. A hash table with 1,000 cells would seem to be wonderful for our case, since odds are there would be no collisions.

However, while avoiding collisions is important, we have to balance that with avoiding memory hogging as well.

Although a hash table with 1,000 cells for our five pieces of data is great for avoiding collisions, we'd be using up 1,000 cells to store just five pieces of data, and that's a poor use of memory.

This is the balancing act that a hash table must perform. A good hash table *strikes a balance of avoiding collisions while not consuming lots of memory.*

To accomplish this, computer scientists have developed the following rule of thumb: for every seven data elements stored in a hash table, it should have ten cells.

So if you're planning on storing fourteen elements, you'd want to have twenty available cells, and so on.

This ratio of data to cells is called the *load factor*. Using this terminology, we'd say that the ideal load factor is 0.7 (7 elements / 10 cells).

If you initially stored seven pieces of data in a hash table, the computer might allocate a hash table with ten cells. When you begin to add more data, though, the computer will expand the hash table by adding more cells and changing the hash function so that the new data will be distributed evenly across the new cells.

Again, most of the internals of a hash table are managed by the computer language you're using. It decides how big the hash table needs to be, what hash function to use, and when it's time to expand the hash table. You have the right to assume that your programming language has implemented its hash table to allow for peak performance.

Now that we've seen how hashes work, it's clear that they have a superior lookup efficiency of O(1). We're going to use this knowledge shortly to optimize our code for speed.

But let's first take a quick tour of the many different use cases for hash tables when it comes to simple data organization.

Hash Tables for Organization

Because hash tables keep data in pairs, they're useful in many scenarios for organizing data.

Some data exists naturally in paired form. The fast-food menu and thesaurus scenarios from this chapter are classic examples. The menu contains each food item paired with its price. The thesaurus contains each word paired with its synonym. In fact, this is why Python refers to hash tables as dictionaries. A dictionary is a common form of paired data; it's a list of words with their respective definitions.

Other examples of naturally paired data can include tallies, such as political candidates and the number of votes each received:

```
{"Candidate A": 1402021, "Candidate B": 2321443, "Candidate C": 432}
```

An inventory tracking system, which keeps track of how much of each item is in supply, is another tally example:

```
{"Yellow Shirt": 1203, "Blue Jeans": 598, "Green Felt Hat": 65}
```

Hash tables are such a natural fit for paired data that we can even use them to simplify conditional logic in certain instances.

Say we encounter a function that returns the meaning of common HTTP status code numbers:

```python
def status_code_meaning(number):
    if number == 200:
        return "OK"
    elif number == 301:
        return "Moved Permanently"
    elif number == 401:
        return "Unauthorized"
    elif number == 404:
        return "Not Found"
    elif number == 500:
        return "Internal Server Error"
```

If we think about this code, we'll realize that the conditional logic revolves around paired data, namely, the status code numbers and their respective meanings.

By using a hash table, we can completely eliminate the conditional logic:

```python
status_codes = {200: "OK", 301: "Moved Permanently",
                401: "Unauthorized", 404: "Not Found",
                500: "Internal Server Error"}

def status_code_meaning(number):
    return status_codes.get(number)
```

Another common use for hash tables is to represent objects that have various attributes. For example, here's a representation of a dog:

```python
{"name": "Fido", "breed": "Pug", "age": 3, "gender": "Male"}
```

As you can see, attributes are a kind of paired data, since the attribute name becomes the key, and the actual attribute becomes the value.

We can create an entire list of dogs if we place multiple hash tables inside an array:

```python
[
  {"name": "Fido", "breed": "Pug", "age": 3, "gender": "Male"},
  {"name": "Lady", "breed": "Poodle", "age": 6, "gender": "Female"},
  {"name": "Spot", "breed": "Dalmatian", "age": 2, "gender": "Male"}
]
```

Hash Tables for Speed

While hash tables are a perfect fit for paired data, they can also be used to make your code faster—even if your data doesn't exist as pairs. And this is where things get exciting.

Here's a simple array:

```
array = [61, 30, 91, 11, 54, 38, 72]
```

If you want to search for a number in this array, how many steps would it take?

Because the array is unordered, you'd have to perform a linear search, which would take N steps—you learned this back at the beginning of the book.

However, what would happen if we ran some code that would convert these numbers into a hash table that looked like this?

```
hash_table = {61: True, 30: True, 91: True,
11: True, 54: True, 38: True, 72: True}
```

Here, we've stored each number as a key and assigned the Boolean True as the associated value for each number.

Now, if I asked you to search this hash table for a certain number as a key, how many steps would it take?

Well, I could use this simple code:

```
hash_table.get(72)
```

And I could look up the number 72 in a single step.

In other words, by doing a hash table lookup using 72 as the key, I can determine in one step whether the 72 is present in the hash table. The reasoning is straightforward: if 72 is a key in the hash table, I'd get back True, since the 72 has True as its value. On the other hand, if the 72 is *not* a key in the hash table, I'd get back None.

Since doing a hash table lookup takes just one step, I can therefore find any number in the hash table (as a key) in one step.

Can you see the magic?

By converting an array into a hash table in this way, we can go from O(N) searches to O(1) searches.

Here's what's interesting about using a hash table in this way. Even though hash tables are often used for naturally paired data, our data here is *not* paired. We just care about a list of single numbers.

While we did assign a value to each key, it doesn't really matter what the value is. We used True as the value for each key, but any arbitrary value (that is "truthy") would achieve the same results.

The trick here is that by placing each number in the hash table as a key, we can later look up each of those keys in one step. If our lookup returns any value, it means the key itself must be in the hash table. If we get back None, then the key must not be in the hash table.

I refer to using a hash table in this way as "using it as an index." (It's my own term.) An index at the back of a book tells you whether the topic can be found in the book instead of you having to flip through all the pages to find it. Here as well, we created the hash table to serve as a kind of index; in our case, it's an index that tells us whether a specific item is contained within the original array.

Let's use this technique to boost the speed of a very practical algorithm.

Array Subset

Let's say we need to determine whether one array is a subset of another array. Take these two arrays, for example:

```
["a", "b", "c", "d", "e", "f"]
["b", "d", "f"]
```

The second array, ["b", "d", "f"], is a subset of the first array, ["a", "b", "c", "d", "e", "f"], because every value of the second array is contained within the first array.

However, say our arrays were these:

```
["a", "b", "c", "d", "e", "f"]
["b", "d", "f", "h"]
```

The second array is *not* a subset of the first array, because the second array contains the value "h", which does not exist within the first array.

How would we write a function that compares two arrays and lets us know if one is a subset of the other?

One way we can do this is by using nested loops. Essentially, we'd iterate through every element of the smaller array, and for each element in the smaller array, we'd then begin a second loop that iterates through each element of the larger array. If we ever find an element in the smaller array that isn't contained within the larger array, our function will return False. If the code gets past the loops, it means it never encountered a value in the smaller array that wasn't contained within the larger array, so it returns True.

Here's a Python implementation of this approach:

```python
def is_subset(array1, array2):
    # Determine which array is smaller:
    if len(array1) > len(array2):
        larger_array = array1
        smaller_array = array2
    else:
        larger_array = array2
        smaller_array = array1

    # Iterate through smaller array:
    for i in smaller_array:

        # Assume temporarily that the current value from
        # smaller array is not found in larger array:
        found_match = False

        # For each value in smaller array, iterate through
        # larger array:
        for j in larger_array:

            # If the two values are equal, it means the current
            # value in smaller array is present in the larger array:
            if i == j:
                found_match = True
                break

        # If the current value in smaller array doesn't exist
        # in larger array, return false:
        if not found_match:
            return False

    # If we get to the end of the loops, it means that all
    # values from smaller array are present in larger array:
    return True
```

When we analyze the efficiency of this algorithm, we find that it's O(N * M) since it runs for the number of items in the first array multiplied by the number of items in the second array.

Now, let's harness the power of a hash table to dramatically improve the efficiency of our algorithm. Let's ditch our original approach and start again from scratch.

In our new approach, after we've determined which array is larger and which is smaller, we're going to run a single loop through the larger array and store each value inside of a hash table:

```python
hash_table = {}

for value in larger_array:
    hash_table[value] = True
```

In this code snippet, we create an empty hash table inside the hash_table variable. Then we iterate through each value in the larger_array and add the item from the array to the hash table. We add the item itself as a key, and True as the value.

For the earlier example, ["a", "b", "c", "d", "e", "f"], once we've run it through this loop, we end up with a hash table that looks like this:

```
{"a": True, "b": True, "c": True, "d": True, "e": True, "f": True}
```

This becomes our "index" that will allow us to conduct O(1) lookups of these items later on.

Now, here's the brilliant part. Once the first loop is complete and we have this hash table to work with, we can then begin a second (non-nested) loop that iterates through the *smaller* array:

```
for value in smaller_array:
    if not hash_table.get(value):
        return False
```

This loop looks at each item in the smaller_array and checks to see whether it exists as a key inside the hash_table. Remember, the hash_table stores all the items from larger_array as its keys. So if we find an item in hash_table, it means the item is also in larger_array. And if we don't find an item in hash_table, it means it's also not inside the larger_array.

So for each item in smaller_array, we check whether it's a key in hash_table. If it's not, that means the item isn't contained within the larger_array, and the smaller_array is therefore not a subset of the larger array, and we return False. (However, if we get past this loop, it means the smaller array *is* a subset of the larger one.)

Let's put this altogether in one complete function:

```
def is_subset(array1, array2):
    hash_table = {}

    # Determine which array is smaller:
    if len(array1) > len(array2):
        larger_array = array1
        smaller_array = array2
    else:
        larger_array = array2
        smaller_array = array1

    for value in larger_array:
        hash_table[value] = True
```

```
    for value in smaller_array:
        if not hash_table.get(value):
            return False

    return True
```

Now, how many steps did this algorithm take? We iterated through each item of the *larger* array once to build the hash table.

And we iterated through each item of the *smaller* array, taking just one step per item to look up the item in the hash table. Remember, a hash table lookup takes just one step.

If we say that N is the total number of items of both arrays combined, our algorithm is O(N), since we touched each item just once. We spent one step on each item from the larger array, followed by one step on each item from the smaller array.

That's a *huge* win over our first algorithm, which was O(N * M).

This technique of using a hash table as an "index" comes up frequently in algorithms that require multiple searches within an array; that is, if your algorithm will need to keep searching for values inside an array, each search would itself take up to N steps. By creating a hash table "index" of the array, we reduce each search to only one step.

As I pointed out, what makes this technique particularly interesting is that when using a hash table as an "index," we aren't even dealing with naturally paired data. Instead, we just want to know whether the key itself is in the hash table. When we use the key to perform a lookup in the hash table and receive any value (no matter how arbitrary it is), it means the key must be present in the hash table.

Wrapping Up

Hash tables are indispensable when it comes to building efficient software. With their O(1) reads and insertions, it's a difficult data structure to beat.

Until now, our analysis of various data structures revolved around their efficiency and speed. But did you know that some data structures provide advantages other than speed? In the next lesson, we're going to explore two data structures that can help improve code elegance and maintainability.

Exercises

The following exercises provide you with the opportunity to practice with hash tables. The solutions to these exercises are found in the section Chapter 8, on page 440.

1. Write a function that returns the intersection of two arrays. The intersection is a third array that contains all values contained within the first two arrays. For example, the intersection of [1, 2, 3, 4, 5] and [0, 2, 4, 6, 8] is [2, 4]. Your function should have a complexity of O(N). (If your programming language has a built-in way of doing this, don't use it. The idea is to build the algorithm yourself.)

2. Write a function that accepts an array of strings and returns the first duplicate value it finds. For example, if the array is ["a", "b", "c", "d", "c", "e", "f"], the function should return "c", since it's duplicated within the array. (You can assume that there's one pair of duplicates within the array.) Make sure the function has an efficiency of O(N).

3. Write a function that accepts a string that contains all the letters of the alphabet except one and returns the missing letter. For example, the string, "the quick brown box jumps over a lazy dog" contains all the letters of the alphabet except the letter "f". The function should have a time complexity of O(N).

4. Write a function that returns the first *non*-duplicated character in a string. For example, the string, "minimum" has two characters that only exist once—the "n" and the "u", so your function should return the "n", since it occurs first. The function should have an efficiency of O(N).

CHAPTER 9

Crafting Elegant Code
with Stacks and Queues

Until now, our discussion around data structures has focused primarily on how they affect the *performance* of various operations. However, having a variety of data structures in your programming arsenal also allows you to create code that is simpler and easier to read.

In this chapter, you're going to discover two new data structures: stacks and queues. The truth is that these two structures are not entirely new. They're simply arrays with restrictions. Yet these restrictions are exactly what make them so elegant.

More specifically, stacks and queues are elegant tools for handling temporary data. From operating system architecture to printing jobs to traversing data, stacks and queues serve as temporary containers that can be used to form beautiful algorithms.

Think of temporary data like the food orders in a diner. What each customer orders is important until the meal is made and delivered; then you throw the order slip away. You don't need to keep that information around. Temporary data is information that doesn't have any meaning after it's processed, so you can throw it away once you're done with it.

Stacks and queues handle this kind of temporary data but have a special focus on the *order* in which the data is handled, as you'll now learn.

Stacks

A *stack* stores data in the same way arrays do—it's simply a list of elements. The one catch is that stacks have the following three constraints:

- Data can be inserted only at the end of a stack.
- Data can be deleted only from the end of a stack.
- Only the last element of a stack can be read.

You can think of a stack as an actual stack of dishes; you can't look at the face of any dish other than the one at the top. Similarly, you can't add any dish except to the top of the stack, nor can you remove any dish besides the one at the top. (At least, you shouldn't.) In fact, most computer science literature refers to the end of the stack as its *top* and the beginning of the stack as its *bottom*.

Our diagrams will reflect this terminology by viewing stacks as vertical arrays, like so:

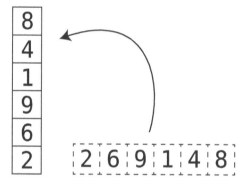

As you can see, the first item in the array becomes the bottom of the stack, while the last item becomes the stack's top.

While the restrictions of a stack seem—well—restrictive, we'll see shortly how they're to our benefit.

To see a stack in action, let's start with an empty stack.

Inserting a new value into a stack is also called *pushing onto the stack*. Think of it as adding a dish onto the top of the dish stack.

Let's push a 5 onto the stack:

Again, there's nothing fancy going on here. All we're really doing is just inserting a data element into the end of an array.

Now let's push a 3 onto the stack:

Next, let's push a 0 onto the stack:

Note that we're always adding data to the top (that is, the end) of the stack. If we wanted to insert the 0 into the bottom or middle of the stack, we couldn't, because that's the nature of a stack: data can only be added to the top.

Removing elements from the top of the stack is called *popping from the stack.* Because of a stack's restrictions, we can only pop data from the top.

Let's pop some elements from our example stack.

First, we pop the 0:

Our stack now contains only two elements: the 5 and the 3.

Next, we pop the 3:

Our stack now only contains the 5:

5

A handy acronym used to describe stack operations is LIFO, which stands for *last in, first out*. All this means is the *last* item *pushed* onto a stack is always the *first* item *popped* from it. It's sort of like students who slack off—they're always the last to arrive to class but the first to leave.

Abstract Data Types

Most programming languages don't come with the stack as a built-in data type or class. Instead, it's up to you to implement it yourself. This is a stark contrast with arrays, which are available in most languages.

To create a stack, then, you generally have to use one of the built-in data structures to hold the data. Here's one way to implement a stack using Python, which uses an array under the hood:

```python
class Stack:
    def __init__(self):
        self.data = []

    def push(self, element):
        self.data.append(element)

    def pop(self):
        if len(self.data) > 0:
            return self.data.pop()
        else:
            return None

    def read(self):
        if len(self.data) > 0:
            return self.data[-1]
        else:
            return None
```

As you can see, our stack implementation stores the data in an array called self.data.

Whenever a stack is initiated, we automatically build an empty array with self.data = []. Our stack also contains methods that push a new element onto the end of self.data, pop an element from the beginning of self.data, and read the first element from the self.data array. (The read and pop methods return None if the stack is empty.)

However, by building the Stack class around the array, we've built an interface that forces the user to interact with the array in limited ways. While one can normally read from any index of an array, when using the array through the stack interface, one can only read the last item. The same goes for inserting and deleting data.

The stack data structure, then, isn't the same kind of data structure that an array is. The array is built into most programming languages and interacts directly with the computer's memory. The stack, on the other hand, is a set of rules and processes around how we should interact with an array so that we can achieve a particular result.

In fact, a stack doesn't even care about *what* data structure is under the hood. All it cares about is that there's a list of data elements that act in a LIFO way. Whether we accomplish this with an array or some other type of built-in data structure doesn't matter. Because of this, the stack is an example of what is known as an *abstract data type*—it's a kind of data structure that is a set of theoretical rules that revolve around some other built-in data structure.

The set we encountered in Chapter 1, Why Data Structures Matter, on page 1, is another example of an abstract data type. Some implementations of sets use arrays under the hood, while other implementations use hash tables. The set itself, though, is simply a theoretical concept: it's a list of non-duplicated data elements.

Many of the data structures we'll encounter in the remainder of this book are abstract data types—they're pieces of code that are written on top of other built-in data structures.

It should be noted that even a built-in data structure can be an abstract data type. Even if a programming language does implement its own Stack class, it doesn't change the fact that the stack data structure is still a concept that allows for various data structures to be used under the hood.

Stacks in Action

Although a stack isn't typically used to store data on a long-term basis, it can be a great tool to handle temporary data as part of various algorithms. Let's look at an example.

Let's create the beginnings of a JavaScript linter—that is, a program that inspects a programmer's JavaScript code and ensures that each line is syntactically correct. JavaScript is notorious for having an abundance of parentheses in its code, so that's the aspect of syntax we'll be focusing on. This includes parentheses, square brackets, and curly braces—all common causes of frustrating syntax errors.

To solve this problem, let's first analyze what type of syntax is incorrect when it comes to braces. If we break it down, we'll find three situations of erroneous syntax.

The first is when there's an opening brace that doesn't have a corresponding closing brace, such as this:

```
(var x = 2;
```

We'll call this Syntax Error Type #1.

The second is when there is a closing brace that was never preceded by a corresponding opening brace:

```
var x = 2;)
```

We'll call that Syntax Error Type #2.

The third, which we'll refer to as Syntax Error Type #3, is when a closing brace is not the same *type* of brace as the immediately preceding opening brace, such as:

```
(var x = [1, 2, 3)];
```

In the preceding example, there's a matching set of parentheses and a matching pair of square brackets, but the closing parenthesis is in the wrong place, as it doesn't match the immediately preceding opening brace, which is a square bracket.

How can we implement an algorithm that inspects a line of JavaScript code and ensures that there are no brace-related syntax errors? This is where a stack allows us to implement a beautiful linting algorithm, which works as follows:

We prepare an empty stack, and then we read each character from left to right following these rules:

1. If we find any character that isn't a type of brace (parenthesis, square bracket, or curly brace), we ignore it and move on.

2. If we find an *opening* brace, we push it onto the stack. Having it on the stack means we're waiting to close that particular brace.

3. If we find a *closing* brace, we pop the top element in the stack and inspect it. We then analyze:

   • If the item we popped (which is always an opening brace) does not match the current closing brace, it means we've encountered Syntax Error Type #3.

   • If we couldn't pop an element because the stack was empty, that means the current closing brace doesn't have a corresponding opening brace beforehand. This is Syntax Error Type #2.

- If the item we popped *is* a corresponding match for the current closing brace, it means we've successfully closed that opening brace, and we can continue parsing the line of JavaScript code.

4. If we make it to the end of the line and there's still something left on the stack, that means there's an opening brace without a corresponding closing brace, which is Syntax Error Type #1.

Let's see this in action using the following example:

$$(var\ x\ =\ \{y:\ [1,\ 2,\ 3]\})$$

After we prepare an empty stack, we begin reading each character from left to right.

Step 1: We begin with the first character, which happens to be an opening parenthesis:

$$\downarrow$$
$$(var\ x\ =\ \{y:\ [1,\ 2,\ 3]\})$$

Step 2: Since it's a type of opening brace, we push it onto the stack:

We then ignore all the characters, var x = , since they aren't brace characters.

Step 3: We encounter our next opening brace:

$$\downarrow$$
$$(var\ x\ =\ \{y:\ [1,\ 2,\ 3]\})$$

Step 4: We push it onto the stack:

We then ignore the y:.

Step 5: We encounter the opening square bracket:

$$\downarrow$$
$$(var\ x\ =\ \{y:\ [1,\ 2,\ 3]\})$$

Step 6: We add that to the stack as well:

We then ignore the 1, 2, 3.

Step 7: We encounter our first closing brace—a closing square bracket:

$$\downarrow$$
$$(var\ x\ =\ \{y:\ [1,\ 2,\ 3]\})$$

Step 8: We pop the element at the top of the stack, which happens to be an *opening* square bracket:

Since our closing square bracket is a corresponding match to this top element of the stack, it means we can continue with our algorithm without throwing any errors.

Step 9: We move on, encountering a closing curly brace:

$$\downarrow$$
$$(var\ x\ =\ \{y:\ [1,\ 2,\ 3]\})$$

Step 10: We pop the top item from stack:

It's an opening curly brace, so we've found a match with the current closing brace.

Step 11: We encounter a closing parenthesis:

$$\downarrow$$
$$(var\ x\ =\ \{y:\ [1,\ 2,\ 3]\})$$

Step 12: We pop the last element in the stack. It's a corresponding match, so there are no errors so far.

Because we've made it through the entire line of code and our stack is empty, our linter can conclude that there are no syntactical errors on this line (relating to opening and closing braces).

Code Implementation: Stack-Based Code Linter

Here's an implementation of the preceding algorithm. Note that we're using our earlier implementation of the Stack class:

```
import stack

class Linter:
    def __init__(self):
        self.stack = stack.Stack()
```

```
def lint(self, text):
    while self.stack.read():
        self.stack.pop()

    matching_braces = {"(": ")", "[": "]", "{": "}"}

    for char in text:

        if char in matching_braces.keys():
            self.stack.push(char)

        elif char in matching_braces.values():
            if not self.stack.read():
                return char + " does not have opening brace"
            else:
                popped_opening_brace = self.stack.pop()

                if char != matching_braces.get(popped_opening_brace):
                    return char + " has mismatched opening brace"
    # If we get to the end of line, and the stack isn't empty:
    if self.stack.read():
        return self.stack.read() + " does not have closing brace"

    # Return True if line has no errors:
    return True
```

The import stack allows our code to use our own stack implementation from above, as we saved it in a file called stack.py.

As soon as we create an instance of the Linter class, we create a stack that our algorithm can use. This is accomplished with the following code:

```
def __init__(self):
    self.stack = stack.Stack()
```

The main linting algorithm takes place within the lint method, which accepts a string of JavaScript code and assigns it to a variable called text.

The very first thing we do is ensure that the stack is empty, as it still may have data in it from a previous linting. We accomplish this by popping data from the stack until there's no data left:

```
while self.stack.read():
    self.stack.pop()
```

We then define what we consider to be sets of matching brackets:

```
matching_braces = {"(": ")", "[": "]", "{": "}"}
```

We're now up to the main part of the algorithm, which runs using a loop that analyzes each character of text, one at a time:

```
for char in text:
```

If the character we're up to is an opening brace, we push it onto the stack:

```
if char in matching_braces.keys():
    self.stack.push(char)
```

If the current character is *not* an opening brace, we then check to see if it's perhaps a closing brace:

```
elif char in matching_braces.values():
```

If it is, we then consider a couple of possibilities. We first check to see if there's anything on the stack. If there isn't, we trigger Syntax Error #2:

```
if not self.stack.read():
    return char + " does not have opening brace"
```

If there *is* something on the stack, we pop it off and check to see if it's a matching opening brace. If it isn't, we trigger Syntax Error #3:

```
else:
    popped_opening_brace = self.stack.pop()

    if char != matching_braces.get(popped_opening_brace):
        return char + " has mismatched opening brace"
```

The loop continues this way until it processes the entire text.

However, we're not quite done. We still have to check whether the stack contains anything, because if it does, it means we have a stray opening brace that was never closed. This, again, is Syntax Error #1:

```
if self.stack.read():
    return self.stack.read() + " does not have closing brace"
```

At the end of our method we return True if we process the entire text and don't encounter any errors.

Here's some sample code to run our linter:

```
linter = Linter()
linter.lint("(var x = 2;")
```

This example will trigger Syntax Error #1 since the opening parenthesis has no closing parenthesis.

In this example, we used a stack to implement our linter with a neat algorithm. But if a stack actually uses an array under the hood, why bother with a stack? Couldn't we have accomplished the same task using an array?

The Importance of Constrained Data Structures

By definition, if a stack is just a constrained version of an array, that means an array can do anything a stack can do. If so, what advantage does a stack provide?

Constrained data structures like the stack (and the queue, which we'll encounter shortly) are important for several reasons.

First, when we work with a constrained data structure, we can prevent potential bugs. The linting algorithm, for example, only works if we exclusively remove items from the top of the stack. If a programmer inadvertently writes code that removes items from the middle of the array, the algorithm will break down. By using a stack, we're forced into only removing items from the top, as it's impossible to get the stack to remove any other item.

Second, data structures like stacks give us a new mental model for tackling problems. The stack, for example, gives us the whole idea of a last-in, first-out process. We can then apply this LIFO mindset to solve all sorts of problems, such as the linter just described.

And once we're familiar with the stack and its LIFO nature, the code we write using the stack becomes familiar and elegant to other developers who read our code. As soon as someone sees a stack being used within an algorithm, they immediately know that the algorithm is working with a LIFO-based process.

Stack Wrap-Up

Stacks are ideal for processing any data that should be handled last in, first out. The undo function in a word processor, for example, is a great use case for a stack. As the user types, we keep track of each keystroke by pushing the keystroke onto the stack. Then, when the user hits the undo key, we pop the most recent keystroke from the stack and eliminate it from the document. At this point, their next-to-most recent keystroke is now sitting at the top of the stack, ready to be undone if need be.

Queues

A *queue* is another data structure designed to process temporary data. It's like a stack in many ways, except that it processes data in a different order. Like a stack, a queue is also an abstract data type.

You can think of a queue as a line of people at the movie theater. The first one in the line is the first one to leave the line and enter the theater. With queues, the first item added to the queue is the first item to be removed. That's why computer scientists apply the acronym FIFO to queues: *first in, first out.*

As with a line of people, a queue is usually depicted horizontally. It's also common to refer to the beginning of the queue as its *front* and the end of the queue as its *back.*

Like stacks, queues are arrays with three restrictions (it's just a different set of restrictions):

- Data can be inserted only at the *end* of a queue. (This is identical behavior to the stack.)

- Data can be deleted only from the *front* of a queue. (This is the opposite behavior of the stack.)

- Only the element at the *front* of a queue can be read. (This, too, is the opposite of behavior of the stack.)

Let's see a queue in action, beginning with an empty queue.

First, we insert a 5 (a common term for inserting into a queue is *enqueue*, but we'll use the terms insert and enqueue interchangeably):

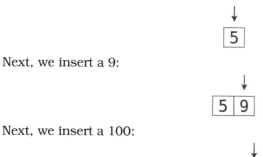

Next, we insert a 9:

Next, we insert a 100:

As of now, the queue has functioned just like a stack. However, removing data happens in the reverse, as we remove data from the *front* of the queue. (Removing an element from a queue is also known as *dequeuing.*)

If we want to remove data, we must start with the 5, since it's at the front of the queue:

Next, we remove the 9:

Our queue now only contains one element, the 100.

Queue Implementation

I mentioned that the queue is an abstract data type. Like many other abstract data types, it doesn't come implemented in many programming languages. Here's an implementation of a queue:

```
class Queue:
    def __init__(self):
        self.data = []

    def enqueue(self, element):
        self.data.append(element)

    def dequeue(self):
        if len(self.data) > 0:
            return self.data.pop(0)
        else:
            return None

    def read(self):
        if len(self.data) > 0:
            return self.data[0]
        else:
            return None
```

Again, our Queue class wraps the array with an interface that restricts our interaction with the data, only allowing us to process the data in specific ways. The enqueue method allows us to insert data at the end of the array, while the dequeue removes the first item from the array. And the read method allows us to peek at just the very first element of the array.

Queues in Action

Queues are common in many applications, ranging from printing jobs to background workers in web applications.

Let's say we're programming a simple Python interface for a printer that can accept printing jobs from various computers across a network. We want to make sure we print each document in the order in which it was received.

This code uses our implementation of the `Queue` class from earlier:

```python
import queue

class PrintManager:

    def __init__(self):
        self.queue = queue.Queue()

    def queue_print_job(self, document):
        self.queue.enqueue(document)

    def run(self):
        while self.queue.read():
            self.print_document(self.queue.dequeue())

    def print_document(self, document):
        # Code to run the actual printer goes here.
        # For demo purposes, we'll print to the terminal:
        print(document)
```

We can then utilize this class as follows:

```python
print_manager = PrintManager()
print_manager.queue_print_job("First Document")
print_manager.queue_print_job("Second Document")
print_manager.queue_print_job("Third Document")
print_manager.run()
```

Each time we call `queue_print_job`, we add the "document" (represented by a string, in this example) to the queue:

```python
def queue_print_job(self, document):
    self.queue.enqueue(document)
```

When we call `run`, we print each document by processing it in the order in which it was received. That is, we dequeue each document from the queue and print it:

```python
def run(self):
    while self.queue.read():
        self.print_document(self.queue.dequeue())
```

When we run the previous code, the program will output the three documents in the same order in which they were received:

```
First Document
Second Document
Third Document
```

While this example is simplified and abstracts away some of the nitty-gritty details that a real live printing system may have to deal with, the fundamental use of a queue for such an application is very real and serves as the foundation for building such a system.

Queues are also the perfect tool for handling asynchronous requests—they ensure that the requests are processed in the order in which they were received. They're also commonly used to model real-world scenarios where events need to occur in a certain order, such as airplanes waiting for takeoff and patients waiting for their doctor.

Wrapping Up

As you've seen, stacks and queues are programmers' tools for elegantly handling all sorts of practical algorithms.

Now that you've learned about stacks and queues, you've unlocked a new achievement: you can learn about recursion, which depends upon a stack. Recursion also serves as the foundation for many of the more advanced and super-efficient algorithms that I'll cover in the rest of this book.

Exercises

The following exercises provide you with the opportunity to practice with stacks and queues. The solutions to these exercises are found in the section Chapter 9, on page 442.

1. If you were writing software for a call center that places callers on hold and then assigns them to "the next available representative," would you use a stack or a queue?

2. If you pushed numbers onto a stack in the following order: 1, 2, 3, 4, 5, 6, and then popped two items, which number would you be able to read from the stack?

3. If you inserted numbers into a queue in the following order: 1, 2, 3, 4, 5, 6, and then dequeued two items, which number would you be able to read from the queue?

4. Write a function that uses a stack to reverse a string. (For example, "abcde" would become "edcba".) You can work with our earlier implementation of the Stack class.

CHAPTER 10

Recursively Recurse with Recursion

Recursion is a key concept in computer science that will unlock the more advanced algorithms we're going to encounter in this book. When used correctly, recursion can be used to solve certain types of tricky problems in surprisingly simple ways. Sometimes, it even seems like magic.

But before we dive in, a pop quiz!

What happens when the blah() function defined here is called?

```
def blah():
    blah()
```

As you probably guessed, it will call itself infinitely, since blah() calls itself, which in turn calls itself, and so on.

Recursion is the term for a function calling itself. Indeed, infinite recursion, as in the above example, is utterly useless. When harnessed correctly, though, recursion can be a powerful tool.

Recurse Instead of Loop

Let's say you work at NASA and need to program a countdown function for launching spacecraft. The particular function that you're asked to write should accept a number—such as 10—and display the numbers from 10 down to 0.

Take a moment and implement this function yourself. When you're done, read on.

Odds are that you wrote a simple loop, along the lines of this implementation:

```
def countdown(number):
    while number >= 0:
        print(number)
        number -= 1
```

Nothing is wrong with this implementation, but it may have never occurred to you that you don't *have* to use a loop.

How?

Let's try recursion instead. Here's a first attempt at using recursion to implement our countdown function:

```python
def countdown(number):
    print(number)

    countdown(number - 1)
```

Let's walk through this code step by step.

Step 1: We call countdown(10), so the argument variable number starts out as 10.

Step 2: We print number (which contains the value 10) to the console.

Step 3: Before the countdown function is complete, it calls countdown(9), since number - 1 is 9.

Step 4: countdown(9) begins running. In it, we print number (which is currently 9) to the console.

Step 5: Before countdown(9) is complete, it calls countdown(8).

Step 6: countdown(8) begins running. We print 8 to the console.

Before we continue stepping through the code, note how we're using recursion to achieve our goal. We're not using any loop constructs, but by simply having the countdown function call itself, we're able to count down from 10 and print each number to the console.

In almost any case in which you can use a loop, you can also use recursion. Now, just because you *can* use recursion doesn't mean that you *should* use recursion. Recursion is a tool that allows for writing elegant code. In the preceding example, the recursive approach isn't necessarily any more beautiful or efficient than using a classic loop. However, we'll soon encounter examples in which recursion shines. In the meantime, let's continue exploring how recursion works.

The Base Case

Let's continue our walk-through of the countdown function. We'll skip a few steps for brevity...

Step 21: We call countdown(0).

Step 22: We print number (that is, 0) to the console.

Step 23: We call countdown(-1).

Step 24: We print number (that is, -1) to the console.

Uh-oh. As you can see, our solution isn't perfect, as we'll end up infinitely printing negative numbers.

To perfect our solution, we need a way to end our countdown at 0 and prevent the recursion from continuing on forever.

We can solve this problem by adding a conditional statement that ensures that if number is currently 0, we don't call countdown() again:

```python
def countdown(number):
    print(number)
    if number == 0:
        return
    else:
        countdown(number - 1)
```

Now when number is 0, our code will not call the countdown() function again but instead just return, thereby preventing another call of countdown().

In recursion terminology, the case in which our function will *not* recurse is known as the *base case*. So 0 is the base case for our countdown() function. Again, every recursive function needs at least one base case to prevent it from calling itself indefinitely.

Reading Recursive Code

It takes time and practice to get used to recursion, and you'll ultimately learn *two* sets of skills: *reading* recursive code and *writing* recursive code. Reading recursive code is somewhat easier, so let's get some practice with that first.

We'll do this by looking at another example: calculating factorials.

A *factorial* is best illustrated with some examples.

The factorial of 3 is:

3 * 2 * 1 = 6

The factorial of 5 is:

5 * 4 * 3 * 2 * 1 = 120

And so on and so forth.

Here's a recursive implementation that returns a number's factorial:

```
def factorial(number):
    if number <= 1:
        return 1
    else:
        return number * factorial(number - 1)
```

This code can look somewhat confusing at first glance. To walk through the code to see what it does, here's the process I recommend:

1. Identify the base case.

2. Walk through the function for the base case.

3. Identify the next-to-last case. This is the case just before the base case, as I'll demonstrate momentarily.

4. Walk through the function for the next-to-last case.

5. Repeat this process by identifying the case before the one you just analyzed and walking though the function for that case.

Let's apply this process to the preceding code. If we analyze the code, we'll quickly notice that there are two paths. One path is where number is less than or equal to 1, and the other path is where number is greater than 1:

```
if number <= 1:  # Path 1
    ...
  else:  # Path 2: number is greater than 1
    ...
```

We can see that the recursion happens inside the else path, since factorial calls itself:

```
else:
    return number * factorial(number - 1)
```

So it must be that the base case is the first path, since it's the path where no recursion is taking place:

```
if number <= 1:
    return 1
```

We can conclude, then, that the base case is when number is less than or equal to 1.

Next, let's walk through the factorial method assuming it's dealing with a base case, such as factorial(1). Again, the relevant code from our method is the following:

```
if number <= 1:
    return 1
```

Well, that's pretty simple—it's the base case, so no recursion actually happens. If we call factorial(1), the method simply returns 1. Okay, so grab a napkin and write this fact down:

factorial (1) returns 1

Next, let's move up to the next case, which would be factorial(2). The relevant line of code from our method is:

```
else:
    return number * factorial(number - 1)
```

So calling factorial(2) will return 2 * factorial(1). To calculate 2 * factorial(1), we need to know what factorial(1) returns. If you check your napkin, you'll see that it returns 1. So 2 * factorial(1) will return 2 * 1, which just happens to be 2.

Add this fact to your napkin:

factorial (2) returns 2

factorial (1) returns 1

Now, what happens if we call factorial(3)? Again, the relevant line of code is:

```
else:
    return number * factorial(number - 1)
```

So that would translate into return 3 * factorial(2). What does factorial(2) return? You don't have to figure that out all over again, since it's on your napkin! It returns 2. So, factorial(3) will return 6 (because 3 * 2 = 6). Go ahead and add this wonderful factoid to your napkin:

factorial (3) returns 6

factorial (2) returns 2

factorial (1) returns 1

Take a moment and figure out for yourself what factorial(4) will return.

As you can see, starting the analysis from the base case and building up is a great way to reason about recursive code.

Recursion in the Eyes of the Computer

To complete your understanding of recursion, we need to see how the computer itself processes a recursive function. It's one thing for humans to reason about recursion using the earlier "napkin" method. However, the computer has to do the tricky work of calling a function from within the function itself.

So let's break down the process of how the computer executes a recursive function.

Say that we call factorial(3). Since 3 isn't the base case, the computer reaches this line:

```
return number * factorial(number - 1)
```

This then launches the function factorial(2).

But there's a catch. When the computer begins to run factorial(2), did the computer yet complete running factorial(3)?

This is what makes recursion tricky for the computer. Until the computer reaches the end keyword of factorial(3), it's not done with factorial(3). So we enter into a weird situation. The computer didn't yet complete executing factorial(3), yet it's starting to run factorial(2) while *still in the middle* of factorial(3).

And factorial(2) isn't the end of the story, because factorial(2) triggers factorial(1). So it's a crazy thing: while still in the middle of running factorial(3), the computer calls factorial(2). And while running factorial(2), the computer runs factorial(1). It turns out, then, that factorial(1) runs in the middle of *both* factorial(2) and factorial(3).

How does the computer keep track of all of this? It needs some way to remember that after it finishes factorial(1), it needs to go back and finish running factorial(2). And then it needs to remember to complete factorial(3) once it completes factorial(2).

The Call Stack

Luckily, you recently learned about stacks in Chapter 9, Crafting Elegant Code, on page 133. The computer uses a stack to keep track of which functions it's in the middle of calling. This stack is known, appropriately enough, as the *call stack.*

Here's how the call stack works in the context of our factorial example.

The computer begins by calling factorial(3). Before the method completes executing, however, factorial(2) gets called. To track that the computer is still in the middle of factorial(3), the computer pushes that information onto a call stack:

This indicates that the computer is in the middle of factorial(3). (Really, the computer also needs to save which line it's in the middle of, and some other things like variable values, but I'm keeping the diagrams simple.)

The computer then proceeds to execute factorial(2). Now, factorial(2), in turn, calls factorial(1). Before the computer dives into factorial(1), though, the computer needs to remember that it's still in the middle of factorial(2), so it pushes that onto the call stack as well:

The computer then executes factorial(1). Since 1 is the base case, factorial(1) completes without calling the factorial method again.

After the computer completes factorial(1), it checks the call stack to see whether it's in the middle of any other functions. If there's something in the call stack, it means that the computer still has work to do—namely, wrap up some other functions it was in the middle of.

If you recall, stacks are restricted in that we can only pop its top element. This is ideal for recursion, since the top element will be *the most recently called function*, which is what the computer needs to wrap up next. It's a LIFO situation: the function that was called last (that is, most recently) is the function we need to complete first.

The next thing the computer does is pop the top element of the call stack, which currently is factorial(2):

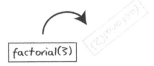

The computer then completes its execution of factorial(2).

Now, the computer pops the next item from the stack. By this time, only factorial(3) is left on the stack, so the computer pops it and therefore completes running factorial(3).

At this point, the stack is empty, so the computer knows it's done executing all of the methods, and the recursion is complete.

Looking back at this example from a bird's-eye view, you'll see that the order in which the computer calculates the factorial of 3 is as follows:

1. factorial(3) is called first. Before it's done...
2. factorial(2) is called second. Before it's done...
3. factorial(1) is called third.

4. factorial(1) is *completed* first.
5. factorial(2) is completed based on the result of factorial(1).
6. Finally, factorial(3) is completed based on the result of factorial(2).

The factorial function is a calculation made based on recursion. The calculation is ultimately made by factorial(1) passing its result (which is 1) to factorial(2). Then factorial(2) multiplies this 1 by 2, yielding 2, and passes this result to factorial(3). Finally, factorial(3) takes this result and multiplies it by 3, computing the result of 6.

Some refer to this idea as *passing a value up through the call stack*; that is, each recursive function returns its computed value to its "parent" function. Eventually, the function that was initially called first computes the final value.

Stack Overflow

Let's take a look back at the infinite recursion example from the beginning of the chapter. Recall that blah() called itself ad infinitum. What do you think will happen to the call stack?

In the case of infinite recursion, the computer keeps pushing the same function again and again onto the call stack. The call stack grows and grows until, eventually, the computer reaches a point where there's simply no more room in its short-term memory to hold all this data. This causes an error known as *stack overflow*—the computer just shuts down the recursion and says, "I refuse to call the function again, because I'm running out of memory!"

Filesystem Traversal

Now that you've seen how recursion works, we can use it to solve certain problems that would otherwise be uncrackable.

One type of problem in which recursion is a natural fit is when we need to delve into multiple layers of a problem without knowing how many layers there are.

Take the example of traversing through a filesystem. Let's say you have a script that does something with all the contents inside a directory, such as printing all the subdirectory names. However, you don't want the script to only handle the immediate subdirectories—you want it to act on all the subdirectories *within* the subdirectories of the directory and all of *their* subdirectories, and so on.

Let's create a simple script that prints the names of all subdirectories within a given directory:

```
import os

def print_subdirectories(directory_name):
    for filename in os.listdir(directory_name):
        if os.path.isdir(filename):
            path = os.path.join(directory_name, filename)
            print(path)
```

We can call this function by passing in a directory name. If we want to call it on the current directory, we could write the following:

```
print_subdirectories(".")
```

In this script, we look through each file within the given directory. If the file is itself a subdirectory, we print the subdirectory name.

While this works well, it only prints the names of the subdirectories *immediately* within the current directory. It doesn't print the names of the subdirectories *within* those subdirectories.

Let's update our script so that it can search one level deeper:

```
import os

def print_subdirectories(directory_name):
    for filename in os.listdir(directory_name):
        if os.path.isdir(filename):
            path = os.path.join(directory_name, filename)
            print(path)

            for filename2 in os.listdir(path):
                path2 = os.path.join(path, filename2)
                if os.path.isdir(path2):
                    print(path2)
```

Now, every time our script discovers a directory, it then conducts an identical loop through the subdirectories of *that* directory and prints the names of the subdirectories. But this script also has its limitations because it's only searching two levels deep. What if we want to search three, four, or five levels deep? We would need five levels of nested loops.

And what if we want to search as deep as our subdirectories go? That would seem to be impossible, as we don't even know how many levels there are.

And *this* is where recursion really shines. With recursion, we can write a script that goes arbitrarily deep—and with a lot less code!

```
import os

def print_subdirectories(directory_name):
    for filename in os.listdir(directory_name):
        path = os.path.join(directory_name, filename)
        if os.path.isdir(path):
            print(path)
            print_subdirectories(path)
```

As this script encounters files that are themselves subdirectories, it calls the print_subdirectories method upon that very subdirectory. The script can therefore dig as deep as it needs to, leaving no subdirectory unturned.

To visualize how this algorithm acts on an example filesystem, examine this diagram, which specifies the order in which the script traverses the subdirectories.

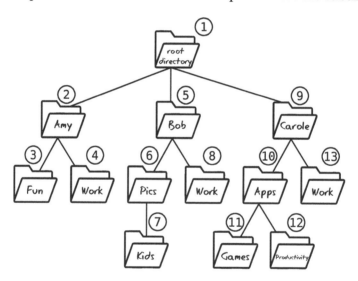

We'll encounter this process again with a detailed visual walk-through in Depth-First Search, on page 336.

Wrapping Up

As you've seen with the filesystem example, recursion is often a great choice for an algorithm in which the algorithm needs to dig an arbitrary number of levels deep into something.

You've now seen how recursion works and how incredibly useful it can be. You've also learned how to walk through and read recursive code. However, most people have a difficult time writing their own recursive functions when they're first starting out. In the next chapter, we'll explore techniques to help you learn to write recursively. Along the way, you'll also discover other important use cases where recursion can be an incredible tool.

Exercises

The following exercises provide you with the opportunity to practice with recursion. The solutions to these exercises are found in the section Chapter 10, on page 443.

1. The following function prints every other number from a low number to a high number. For example, if low is 0 and high is 10, it would print:

    ```
    0
    2
    4
    6
    8
    10
    ```

    Identify the base case in the function:

    ```python
    def print_every_other(low, high):
        if low > high:
            return

        print(low)
        print_every_other(low + 2, high)
    ```

2. My kid was playing with my computer and changed my factorial function so that it computes factorial based on (n - 2) instead of (n - 1). He also changed number <= 1 to number == 1. Predict what will happen when we run factorial(10) using this function:

    ```python
    def factorial(number):
        if number == 1:
            return 1
        else:
            return number * factorial(number - 2)
    ```

3. Following is a function in which we pass in two numbers called low and high. The function returns the sum of all the numbers from low to high. For example, if low is 1 and high is 10, the function will return the sum of all numbers from 1 to 10, which is 55. However, our code is missing the base case and will run indefinitely! Fix the code by adding the correct base case:

    ```python
    def sum(low, high):
        return high + sum(low, high - 1)
    ```

4. Here's an array containing both numbers and arrays, which in turn contain numbers and arrays:

```
array = [  1,
           2,
           3,
           [4, 5, 6],
           7,
           [8,
             [9, 10, 11,
               [12, 13, 14]
             ]
           ],
           [15, 16, 17, 18, 19,
             [20, 21, 22,
               [23, 24, 25,
                 [26, 27, 29]
               ], 30, 31
             ], 32
           ], 33
         ]
```

Write a recursive function that prints all the numbers (and *just* numbers).

CHAPTER 11

Learning to Write in Recursive

In the previous chapter, you learned what recursion is and how it works. I found on my own learning journey that even once I understood how recursion works, I still struggled to write my own recursive functions.

Through deliberate practice and taking note of various recursive patterns, I discovered some techniques that helped me to learn to "write in recursive" more easily, and I'd like to share them with you. Along the way, you'll discover additional areas where recursion shines.

Note that we won't be discussing the efficiency of recursion in this chapter. Recursion can actually have a terribly negative impact on the time complexity of an algorithm, but this is the subject of the next chapter. For now, we're just going to focus on developing the recursive mindset.

Recursive Category: Repeatedly Execute

Over the course of tackling various recursive problems, I began to find that there are various categories of problems. Once I learned an effective technique for a certain category, when I found another problem that belonged to the same category, I was able to apply the same technique to solve it.

The category that I found to be the easiest was one in which the goal of the algorithm was to repeatedly execute a task.

The NASA spacecraft countdown algorithm from the previous chapter is a great example. The code prints a number such as 10, and then 9, then 8, all the way down to 0. While the number the function prints is different each time, we boil down the code's essence to the fact that it is repeatedly executing a task—namely, the printing of a number.

This was our implementation of that algorithm:

```python
def countdown(number):
    print(number)

    if number == 0:
        return
    else:
        countdown(number - 1)
```

I found that for problems of this category, the last line of code in the function was a simple, single call to the function again. In the previous snippet, this takes the form of countdown(number - 1). This line does one thing: it makes the next recursive call.

The directory-printing algorithm from the previous chapter is another example of this. This function repeatedly executes the task of printing directory names.

Our code looked like this:

```python
import os

def print_subdirectories(directory_name):
    for filename in os.listdir(directory_name):
        path = os.path.join(directory_name, filename)
        if os.path.isdir(path):
            print(path)
            print_subdirectories(path)
```

Here as well, the last line of code is print_subdirectories(path), which is a simple call to the recursive function, triggering it again.

Recursive Trick: Passing Extra Parameters

Let's try our hand at another problem of the "repeatedly execute" category. We're going to write an algorithm that takes an array of numbers and doubles each of the numbers within the array. Note that we're not going to produce a new array; instead, we're going to modify the array in place.

This algorithm, too, is one in which we repeatedly execute a task. Specifically, we repeatedly double a number. We start with the first number and double it. We move onto the second number and double it—and so on.

Let's take a stab at writing this algorithm in Python, which we'll call double_array(). We know that our final line will be the recursive call, so let's include that line:

```python
def double_array(array):
    double_array(array)
```

In-Place Modifications

Let's take a look at the concept of *in-place* modifications, just in case it's not clear.

Generally speaking, there are two basic approaches to manipulating data. Let's take the example of doubling the values in an array. If I had the array [1, 2, 3, 4, 5] and wanted to "double" it to produce the array [2, 4, 6, 8, 10], I could do one of two things.

The first option is to create a new array that contains the doubled data but leave the original array alone. Take the following code:

```
a = [1, 2, 3, 4, 5]
b = double_array(a)
```

Since the double_array function is creating and returning a brand-new array, if we were to check the values of a and b, we'd get the following:

```
a # [1, 2, 3, 4, 5]
b # [2, 4, 6, 8, 10]
```

The original array a was unmodified, and b holds a brand-new array.

The second option is called *in-place* modification, meaning the function actually changes the *original array* passed into function.

With in-place modification, if we now check a and b, we'd find this:

```
a # [2, 4, 6, 8, 10]
b # [2, 4, 6, 8, 10]
```

The in-place function modifies a, and b is just pointing to the very same array that a is.

Whether we choose to create a new array or modify the original one in place is up to us and depends on the context of our project. We're going to talk more about in-place algorithms in *Dealing with Space Constraints*.

Next, we need to add the code that will actually double the number. But which number will we double? Let's try to double the first number:

```
def double_array(array):
    array[0] *= 2
    double_array(array)
```

Okay, so we've doubled the number at index 0, but how do we proceed to double the number at index 1?

Now, if we were to use a loop instead of recursion, we would have used a variable to keep track of the index and continuously increased it by 1, something along these lines:

```
def double_array(array):
    index = 0

    while index < len(array):
        array[index] *= 2
        index += 1
```

In our recursive version, though, the only argument to our function is the array. We need some way to keep track of and increment an index. How do we pull this off?

And now for our next trick…

Let's pass in extra parameters!

Let's modify the beginning of our function so that it accepts *two* arguments—the array itself and an index to keep track of. Here's the code:

```
def double_array(array, index):
```

As things stand right now, when we call this function, we need to pass in the array and the starting index, which will be 0:

```
double_array([1, 2, 3, 4, 5], 0)
```

Once we have the index as a function argument, we have a way of incrementing and tracking the index as we make each successive recursive call. Here's the code for this:

```
def double_array(array, index):
    array[index] *= 2
    double_array(array, index + 1)
```

In each successive call, we pass in the array again as the first argument, but we also pass along an incremented index. This allows us to keep track of an index just as we would in a classical loop.

Our code isn't perfect just yet, though. Our function will throw an error once the index goes past the end of the array and tries to multiply a nonexistent number. To solve this, we need our base case:

```
def double_array(array, index):
    # Base case: when the index goes past the end of the array
    if index >= len(array):
        return

    array[index] *= 2
    double_array(array, index + 1)
```

We can test this function out with the following code:

```
array = [1, 2, 3, 4]
double_array(array, 0)
print(array)
```

Our recursive function is now complete. However, if our programming language supports default arguments as Python does, we can make things even prettier.

Right now, we need to call the function like this:

```
double_array([1, 2, 3, 4, 5], 0)
```

Admittedly, passing in that 0 as a second parameter isn't beautiful—it's just so we can achieve our trick of maintaining an index. After all, we *always* want to start our index off at 0.

However, we can use default parameters to allow us to simply call the function the original way:

```
double_array([1, 2, 3, 4, 5])
```

Here's our updated code to make this work:

```
def double_array(array, index=0):
    # Base case: when the index goes past the end of the array
    if index >= len(array):
        return

    array[index] *= 2
    double_array(array, index + 1)
```

All we updated here was setting a default argument of index=0. This way, the first time we call the function, we don't have to pass in the index parameter. However, we still get to use the index parameter for all successive calls.

The "trick" of using extra function parameters is a common technique in writing recursive functions, and a handy one.

Recursive Category: Calculations

In the previous section, we discussed the first category of recursive functions—those whose job it is to repeatedly execute a task. For the remainder of this chapter, I'll elaborate on a second general category: performing a calculation based on a subproblem.

The goal of many functions is to perform a calculation. A function that returns the sum of two numbers, or a function that finds the greatest value within an array, are examples. These functions receive some sort of input and return the result of calculations involving that input.

In Chapter 10, Recursively Recurse with Recursion, on page 149, we found that one area in which recursion shines is where we need to act on a problem that has an arbitrary number of levels of depth. A second area in which recursion shines is where *it is able to make a calculation based on a subproblem of the problem at hand.*

Before I define what a subproblem is, let's refer back to the factorial problem of the previous chapter. As you learned, the factorial of 6 is as follows:

6 * 5 * 4 * 3 * 2 * 1

To write a function that calculates the factorial of a number, we could use a classic loop that starts with the 1 and builds up from there. That is, we'd multiply the 2 by the 1, and then multiply 3 by the result, and then 4, and so on until we reach 6.

Such a function may look like this:

```
def factorial(n):
    product = 1

    for num in range(1, n + 1):
        product *= num

    return product
```

However, we could approach the problem differently: we could calculate the factorial based on its subproblem.

A *subproblem* is a version of the very same problem applied to a smaller input. Let's apply this to our case.

If you think about it, factorial(6) will be 6 multiplied by whatever the result of factorial(5) is.

Since factorial(6) is:

6 * 5 * 4 * 3 * 2 * 1

and factorial(5) is:

5 * 4 * 3 * 2 * 1

we can conclude that factorial(6) is equivalent to:

6 * factorial(5).

That is, once we have the result of factorial(5), we can simply multiply that result by 6 to get the answer to factorial(6).

Since factorial(5) is the smaller problem that can be used to compute the result for the bigger problem, we call factorial(5) a *subproblem* of factorial(6).

Here's the implementation of this from the last chapter:

```
def factorial(number):
    if number <= 1:
        return 1
    else:
        return number * factorial(number - 1)
```

Again, the key line here is return number * factorial(number - 1), in which we compute the result as number multiplied by our subproblem, which is factorial(number - 1).

Two Approaches to Calculations

We've seen that when writing a function that makes a calculation, there are two potential approaches: we can try to build the solution from the "bottom-up," or we can attack the problem going "top-down" by making the calculation based on the problem's subproblem. Indeed, computer science literature refers to the terms *bottom-up* and *top-down* in regard to recursion strategies.

The truth is that both approaches can be achieved through recursion. We previously saw the bottom-up approach using a classic loop; we can also use recursion to implement the bottom-up strategy.

To do this, we need to use our trick of passing extra parameters, as follows:

```
def factorial(n, i=1, product=1):
    if i > n:
        return product
    return factorial(n, i + 1, product * i)
```

In this implementation, we have three parameters. n, as before, is the number whose factorial we're computing. i is a simple variable that starts at 1 and increments by one in each successive call until it reaches n. Finally, product is the variable in which we store the calculation as we keep multiplying each successive number. We keep passing the product to the successive call so we can keep track of it as we go.

While we can use recursion in this way to achieve the bottom-up approach, it's not particularly elegant and doesn't add much value over using a classic loop.

When going bottom-up, we're employing the same strategy for making the calculation whether we're using a loop or recursion. The computational approach is the same.

But to go top-down, we *need* recursion. And because recursion is the only way to achieve a top-down strategy, it's one of the key factors that makes recursion a powerful tool.

Top-Down Recursion: A New Way of Thinking

This brings us to the central point of this chapter: recursion shines when implementing a top-down approach because going top-down *offers a new mental strategy for tackling a problem.* That is, a recursive top-down approach allows one to think about a problem in a completely different way.

Specifically, when we go top-down, we get to mentally "kick the problem down the road." We can free our mind from some of the nitty-gritty details we normally have to think about when going bottom-up.

To see what I mean, let's take another look at the key line from our top-down factorial implementation:

```
return number * factorial(number - 1)
```

This line of code makes its calculation based on factorial(number - 1). When we write this line of code, do we have to understand how the factorial function it's calling works? Technically, we don't. Whenever we write code that calls another function, we assume that the function will return the correct value without necessarily understanding how its internals work.

Here as well, when we calculate our answer based on calling the factorial function, we don't need to understand how the factorial function works; we can just expect it to return the correct result. Of course, the weird part is that *we're the ones writing the factorial function!* This line of code exists *within the factorial function itself.* But that's what is so great about top-down thinking: in a way, we can solve the problem without even knowing how to solve the problem.

When we write "in recursive" to implement a top-down strategy, we get to relax our brains a little. We can even choose to ignore the details of how the calculation actually works. We get to say, "Let's just rely on the subproblem to deal with the details."

The Top-Down Thought Process

If you haven't done a lot of top-down recursion before, it takes time and practice to learn to think in this way. I found that when tackling a top-down problem, it helps to think the following three thoughts:

1. Imagine the function you're writing has already been implemented by someone else.

2. Identify the subproblem of the problem.

3. See what happens when you call the function on the subproblem and go from there.

While these steps sound vague at the moment, they'll become more clear through the following examples.

Array Sum

Say we have to write a function called sum that sums up all the numbers in a given array. For example, if we pass the array [1, 2, 3, 4, 5] into the function, it'll return 15, which is the sum of those numbers.

The first thing we'll do is imagine that the sum function has already been implemented. Admittedly, this takes a certain suspension of disbelief, since we know that we're in the middle of writing this function as we speak! But let's try to let go and pretend that the sum function already works.

Next, let's identify the subproblem. This can be more of an art than a science, but practice will help you get better at it. In our case, we can say that the subproblem is the array [2, 3, 4, 5]—that is, all the numbers from the array save the first one.

Finally, let's see what happens when we apply the sum function to our subproblem. If the sum function "already works," and the subproblem is [2, 3, 4, 5], what happens when we call sum([2, 3, 4, 5])? Well, we get the sum of 2 + 3 + 4 + 5, which is 14.

To solve our problem of finding the sum of [1, 2, 3, 4, 5] then, we can just add the first number, 1, to the result of sum([2, 3, 4, 5]).

In pseudocode, we'd write something like this:

```
return array[0] + sum(the remainder of the array)
```

In Python, we can write this like so:

```
return array[0] + sum(array[1:])
```

(In Python, the syntax array[1:] returns a new array that has the contents of the original array starting from index 1 until the end.)

Now, believe it or not, we're done! Save for the base case, which we'll get to in a moment, our sum function can be written like this:

```
def sum(array):
    return array[0] + sum(array[1:])
```

Note that we didn't think about how we're going to add all the numbers together. All we did was imagine that someone else wrote the sum function for us, which we applied to the subproblem. We kicked the problem down the road, but in doing so, we solved the entire problem.

The last thing we need to do is handle the base case. That is, if each subproblem recursively calls its own subproblem, we will eventually reach the subproblem of sum([5]). This function will eventually try to add the 5 to the remainder of the array, but there *are* no other elements in the array.

To deal with this, we can add the base case:

```
def sum(array):
    # Base case: only one element in the array:
    if len(array) == 1:
        return array[0]

    return array[0] + sum(array[1:])
```

And now we're done.

Technically, there's another case we haven't handled, and that's if the input array is completely empty. Currently, our code will throw an error for such an input.

In this book, our code doesn't necessarily attempt to handle every edge case. (For example, what if the input array contains strings instead of numbers?) However, we'll sometimes put in a guard against an empty array by throwing an extra clause, as follows:

```
def sum(array):
    # If array is empty:
    if not array:
        return 0

    # Primary base case:
    if len(array) == 1:
        return array[0]

    return array[0] + sum(array[1:])
```

We now technically have *two* base cases. The possibility of the array being empty is *kind* of a base case unto itself but will only be triggered if the original input is empty. On the other hand, an array of length 1 is the *primary* base case since that case will always be triggered by the recursion itself.

However, a neat little trick can allow us to reduce our code to having just one base case again—all while still dealing with the possibility of an empty array.

It relies upon the fact that in Python, when we call array[1:] on an array with only one value in it, we get back an empty array. With this in mind, we only need the base case of an empty array, since the recursion will eventually trigger such a case. We can eliminate the base case of an array of length 1 altogether, since recursively calling the sum method on such an array will yield a case of an empty array. So the following code works perfectly:

```python
def sum(array):
    # Base case: an empty array
    if not array:
        return 0

    return array[0] + sum(array[1:])
```

And now we're *really* done.

String Reversal

Let's try another example. We're going to write a reverse function that reverses a string. So if the function accepts the argument "abcde", it'll return "edcba".

First, let's identify the subproblem. Again, this takes practice, but very often the first thing to try is the next-to-smallest version of the problem at hand. So for the string "abcde", let's assume the subproblem is "bcde". This subproblem is the same as the original string minus its first character.

Next, let's imagine that someone did us the great favor of implementing the reverse function for us. How nice of them!

Now, if the reverse function is available for our use and our subproblem is "bcde", that means we can already call reverse("bcde"), which would return "edcb".

Once we can do that, dealing with the "a" is a piece of cake. We just need to throw it onto the end of the string.

So, we can write:

```python
def reverse(string)
    return reverse(string[1:]) + string[0]
```

Our computation is simply the result of calling reverse on the subproblem and then adding the first character to the end.

Once again, save for the base case, we're done. I know, it's crazy magical.

The base case occurs when the string has one character, so we can add the following line of code to handle it:

```
if len(string) == 1:
    return string[0]
```

However, as in the previous example, we can make the base case an empty string and thereby handle such an input as well. Again, this works since calling string[1:] on a one-character string yields an empty string:

```
def reverse(string):
    if not string:
        return ""

    return reverse(string[1:]) + string[0]
```

And we're done.

Counting X

We're on a roll, so let's try another example. Let's write a function called count_x that returns the number of "x"s in a given string. If our function is passed the string "axbxcxd", it'll return 3, since there are three instances of the character "x".

Let's first identify the subproblem. As in the previous example, we'll say the subproblem is the original string minus its first character. So for "axbxcxd", the subproblem is "xbxcxd".

Next, let's imagine count_x has already been implemented. If we call count_x on our subproblem, by calling count_x("xbxcxd"), we get 3. To that, we just need to add 1 if our first character is also an "x". (If our first character is *not* an "x", we don't need to add anything to the result of our subproblem.)

So, we can write:

```
def count_x(string):
    if string[0] == "x":
        return 1 + count_x(string[1:])
    else:
        return count_x(string[1:])
```

This conditional statement is straightforward. If the first character is an "x", we add 1 to the result of the subproblem. Otherwise, we return the result of our subproblem as is.

Here too, we're basically done. All we need to do is deal with the base case.

We can say that the base case here is when a string has only one character. But this leads to some awkward code, since we really have two base cases, as the single character may be an "x" but may also *not* be an "x":

```python
def count_x(string):
    # Two base cases:
    if len(string) == 1:
        if string[0] == "x":
            return 1
        else:
            return 0

    if string[0] == "x":
        return 1 + count_x(string[1:])
    else:
        return count_x(string[1:])
```

But again, we can simplify our code and just have one single base case if we make our base case an empty string:

```python
def count_x(string):
    # Base case: an empty string
    if not string:
        return 0

    if string[0] == "x":
        return 1 + count_x(string[1:])
    else:
        return count_x(string[1:])
```

By definition, an empty string will always contain zero "x"s, so we truly have only one base case.

The Staircase Problem

You've now learned to use a new mental strategy for solving certain computational problems using top-down recursion. However, you may still be skeptical and ask, "Why do we need this new mental strategy anyway? I've been able to solve these problems with loops just fine until now."

Indeed, you may not need a new mental strategy for simpler computations. But when it comes to more complex functions, you may find that the recursive mindset makes the writing of code much easier. It certainly does for me!

Here's one of my favorite examples. A famous question—known as the *staircase problem*—goes like this:

Let's say we have a staircase of N steps, and a person has the ability to climb one, two, or three steps at a time. How many different possible "paths" can someone take to reach the top? Write a function that will calculate this for N steps. The following image displays three possible paths of jumping up a five-step staircase.

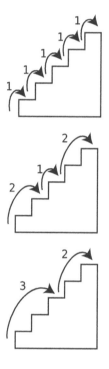

These are just three of many possible paths.

Let's first explore this problem with a bottom-up approach. That is, we'll work our way up from the simplest cases to the more complex ones.

Obviously, if there's only one step, there's only one possible path.

With two steps, there are two paths. The person can climb one step twice, or the person can jump up two steps at once. I'll write this like so:

```
1, 1
2
```

With a staircase of three steps, someone could take one of four possible paths:

```
1, 1, 1
1, 2
2, 1
3
```

With four steps, there are seven options:

```
1, 1, 1, 1
1, 1, 2
1, 2, 1
1, 3
2, 1, 1
2, 2
3, 1
```

Go ahead and try to draw up all the combinations for a five-step staircase. It's not that easy! And this is just five steps. Imagine how many combinations there are for, say, eleven steps.

Now, let's get to the question at hand: how would we *write the code* to count all the paths?

Without the recursive mindset, it can be difficult to wrap one's mind around the algorithm for making this calculation. However, with the top-down way of thinking, the problem can become surprisingly easy.

For an eleven-step staircase, the first subproblem that comes to mind is a ten-step staircase. Let's go with that for now. If we knew how many possible paths there are to climb a ten-step staircase, can we use that as a base for calculating the paths for an eleven-step staircase?

For starters, we do know that climbing an eleven-step staircase will take *at least* as many steps as climbing a ten-step staircase. That is, we have all the paths to get to stair number 10, and from there, one can climb one more step to get to the top.

However, this can't be the complete solution, since we know that someone can also jump to the top from stair numbers 9 and 8 as well.

If we think about it further, we'll realize that if you're taking any path that includes going from stair 10 to stair 11, you're not taking any of the paths that include jumping from stair 9 to stair 11. Conversely, if you jump from stair 9 to stair 11, you're not taking any of the paths that include stepping on stair 10.

So we know that the number of paths to the top will include at least the number of paths to stair 10 plus the number of paths to stair 9.

And since it's possible to also jump from stair 8 to stair 11, as one can jump three steps at a time, we need to include the count of those paths as well.

We've determined, then, that the number of steps to the top is at least the sum of all the paths to stairs 10, 9, and 8.

However, in thinking about it even further, it's evident there aren't any other possible paths to the top beyond these. After all, one can't jump from stair 7 to stair 11. So we can conclude that for N steps, the number of paths is the following:

```
number_of_paths(n - 1) + number_of_paths(n - 2) + number_of_paths(n - 3)
```

Other than the base case, this will be the code for our function!

```
def number_of_paths(n):
    return (number_of_paths(n - 1)
            + number_of_paths(n - 2)
            + number_of_paths(n - 3))
```

It seems too good to be true that this is almost all the code we need. But it *is* true. All that's left to deal with is the base case.

Staircase Problem Base Case

Determining the base case for this problem is slightly tricky. That's because when this function gets to an n of 3, 2, or 1, the function will call itself on n of 0 or below. For example, number_of_paths(2) calls itself for number_of_paths(1), number_of_paths(0), and number_of_paths(-1).

One way we can deal with this is by hardcoding all the bottom cases:

```
def number_of_paths(n):
    if n <= 0:
        return 0
    if n == 1:
        return 1
    if n == 2:
        return 2
    if n == 3:
        return 4

    return (number_of_paths(n - 1)
            + number_of_paths(n - 2)
            + number_of_paths(n - 3))
```

Another way to devise the base cases here is to cleverly rig the system by using strange but effective base cases that just happen to compute the right numbers. Let me show you what I mean.

We know that we definitely want the result of number_of_paths(1) to be 1, so we'll start with the following base case:

```
if n == 1:
    return 1
```

Now, we know that we want number_of_paths(2) to return 2, but we don't *have* to create that base case explicitly. Instead, we can take advantage of the fact that number_of_paths(2) will compute as number_of_paths(1) + number_of_paths(0) + number_of_paths(-1). Since number_of_paths(1) returns 1, if we made number_of_paths(0) also return 1, and number_of_paths(-1) return 0, we'd end up with a sum of 2, which is what we want.

So we can add the following base cases:

```
if n < 0:
    return 0
if n == 0 or n == 1:
    return 1
```

Let's move on to number_of_paths(3), which will return the sum of number_of_paths(2) + number_of_paths(1) + number_of_paths(0). We know that we want the result to be 4, so let's see if the math works out. We already rigged number_of_paths(2) to return 2. number_of_paths(1) will return 1, and number_of_paths(0) will also return 1, so we end up getting the sum of 4, which is just what we need.

Our complete function can also be written as:

```
def number_of_paths(n):
    if n < 0:
        return 0
    if n == 0 or n == 1:
        return 1

    return (number_of_paths(n - 1)
            + number_of_paths(n - 2)
            + number_of_paths(n - 3))
```

While this is less intuitive than our previous version, we cover all the base cases with just two lines of code.

As you can see, the top-down recursive approach made solving this problem much easier than it might have been otherwise.

Anagram Generation

To top off our conversation, let's tackle our most complex recursive problem yet. We're going to use everything we've got in our recursion toolbox to make this work.

We're going to write a function that returns an array of all anagrams of a given string. An anagram is a reordering of all the characters within a string. For example, the anagrams of "abc" are:

```
["abc",
"acb",
"bac",
"bca",
"cab",
"cba"]
```

Now, let's say we were to collect all the anagrams of the string "abcd". Let's apply our top-down mindset to this problem.

Presumably, we could say that the subproblem of "abcd" is "abc". The question then is this: if we had a working anagrams function that returned all the anagrams of "abc", how can we use them to produce all the anagrams of "abcd"? Think about this for a bit and see if you can come up with any approaches.

Here's the approach that occurred to me. (There are others, though.)

If we had all six anagrams of "abc", we can come up with every permutation of "abcd" if we stick the "d" in every possible spot within each anagram of "abc":

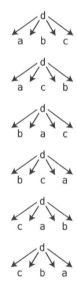

Here is a Python implementation of this algorithm. You'll note that it's certainly more involved than the previous examples in this chapter:

```python
def anagrams_of(string):
    if len(string) == 1:
        return [string[0]]

    collection = []

    substring_anagrams = anagrams_of(string[1:])

    for substring_anagram in substring_anagrams:
```

```
        for index in range(len(substring_anagram) + 1):
            new_string = (substring_anagram[:index]
                            + string[0]
                            + substring_anagram[index:])
            collection.append(new_string)

    return collection
```

This code is not trivial, so let's break it down. For now, we'll skip over the base case.

We start by creating an empty array in which we'll collect the entire collection of anagrams:

```
collection = []
```

This is the same array we'll return at the end of our function.

Next, we grab the array of all anagrams from the substring of our string. This substring is the subproblem string—namely, from the second character until the end. For example, if the string is "hello", the substring is "ello":

```
substring_anagrams = anagrams_of(string[1:])
```

Note how we use the top-down mentality to assume that the anagrams_of function already works on the substring.

We then iterate over each of the substring_anagrams:

```
for substring_anagram in substring_anagrams:
```

Before moving on, it's worth noting at this point that we are using a combination of loops and recursion together. Using recursion doesn't mean that you *have* to eliminate loops from your code altogether! We're using each tool in the way that most naturally helps us solve the problem at hand.

For each substring anagram, we iterate over each of its indexes—plus an extra index at the end. For each index, we create a brand new string (called new_string), and fill it with the substring anagram plus the first character of our current string inserted at the current index:

```
for index in range(len(substring_anagram) + 1):
    new_string = (substring_anagram[:index]
                    + string[0]
                    + substring_anagram[index:])
```

For example, if the string is "abcd" and the substring anagram is "bcd", we iterate over each index (plus an extra index at the end), which comes out to 0 through 3, and create the following new strings:

```
"abcd"   # inserted 'a' at index 0
"bacd"   # inserted 'a' at index 1
"bcad"   # inserted 'a' at index 2
"bcda"   # inserted 'a' at index 3
```

Really, the substring anagram "bcd" doesn't *have* an index 3, but we iterate through index 3 so we can insert the "a" at the very end of the substring anagram.

Each new_string represents a new anagram, so we add it to our collection:

```
collection.append(new_string)
```

When we're done, we return the collection of anagrams.

The base case is where the substring contains only one character, in which case there's only one anagram—the character itself!

The Efficiency of Anagram Generation

As an aside, let's stop for a moment to analyze the efficiency of our anagram-generating algorithm, since we'll discover something interesting. In fact, the time complexity of generating anagrams is a new category of Big O that we haven't encountered before.

If we think about how many anagrams we generate, we'll notice an interesting pattern.

For a string containing three characters, we create permutations that start with each of the three characters. Each permutation then picks its middle character from one of the two remaining characters, and its last character from the last character that's left. This is 3 * 2 * 1, which is six permutations.

Looking at this for other string lengths, we get:

```
4 characters: 4 * 3 * 2 * 1         anagrams
5 characters: 5 * 4 * 3 * 2 * 1     anagrams
6 characters: 6 * 5 * 4 * 3 * 2 * 1 anagrams
```

Do you recognize this pattern? It's a factorial!

So if the string has six characters, the number of anagrams is whatever the factorial of 6 is. This is 6 * 5 * 4 * 3 * 2 * 1, which computes to 720.

The mathematical symbol for factorial is the exclamation point. So, factorial 6 is expressed as 6!, and the factorial of 10 is expressed as 10!.

Remember that Big O expresses the answer to the key question: if there are N data elements, how many steps will the algorithm take? In our case, N would be the length of the string.

For a string of length N, we produce N! anagrams. In Big O notation then, this is expressed as O(N!). This is also known as *factorial time.*

O(N!) is the slowest category of Big O we'll encounter in this book. Let's see how it looks compared to other "slow" Big O categories:

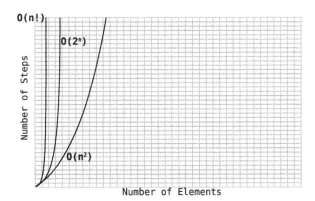

Although O(N!) is extremely slow, we don't have a better option here, since our task is to generate *all* the anagrams, and there simply are N! anagrams for an N-character word.

In any case, recursion played a pivotal role in this algorithm, which is an important example of how recursion can be used to solve a complex problem.

Wrapping Up

Learning to write functions that use recursion certainly takes practice. But you're now armed with tricks and techniques that will make the learning process easier for you.

We're not done with our journey through recursion just yet, though. While recursion is a great tool for solving a variety of problems, it can actually slow your code down *a lot* if you're not careful. In the next chapter, you'll learn how to wield recursion while still keeping your code nice and speedy.

Exercises

The following exercises provide you with the opportunity to practice with recursion. The solutions to these exercises are found in the section Chapter 11, on page 444.

1. Use recursion to write a function that accepts an array of strings and returns the total number of characters across all the strings. For example,

if the input array is ["ab", "c", "def", "ghij"], the output should be 10 since there are ten characters in total.

2. Use recursion to write a function that accepts an array of numbers and returns a new array containing just the even numbers.

3. A particular numerical sequence is known as *triangular numbers*. The pattern begins as 1, 3, 6, 10, 15, 21, and continues onward. To calculate the next number in the sequence, we add the previous number from the sequence plus N, where N corresponds to the place in the sequence where the number lies. For example, the seventh number in the sequence is 28, since it's the seventh number in the pattern, so we add the number 7 plus 21 (the previous number in the sequence). Write a function that accepts a number for N and returns the correct number from the series; that is, if the function was passed the number 7, the function would return 28.

4. Use recursion to write a function that accepts a string and returns the first index that contains the character "x". For example, the string, "abcdefghijklmnopqrstuvwxyz" has an "x" at index 23. To keep things simple, assume the string *definitely* has at least one "x".

5. This problem is known as the *unique paths problem:* Let's say you have a grid of rows and columns. Write a function that accepts a number of rows and a number of columns and calculates the number of possible "shortest" paths from the upper-leftmost square to the lower-rightmost square.

    For example, here's what the grid looks like with three rows and seven columns. You want to get from the S (Start) to the F (Finish).

    By "shortest" path, I mean that at every step, either you're moving one step to the right:

Or you're moving one step downward:

Again, your function should calculate the *number* of shortest paths.

CHAPTER 12

Dynamic Programming

In the previous chapter, you learned how to write recursively and how to use recursion to solve some rather complex problems.

While recursion can certainly solve *some* problems, it can also create *new* ones if not used properly. In fact, recursion is often the culprit behind some of the slowest categories of Big O, such as $O(2^N)$.

The good news, though, is that many of these problems can be avoided. In this chapter, you'll learn how to identify some of the most common speed traps found in recursive code and how to express such algorithms in terms of Big O. More important, you'll learn the techniques to fix these problems.

Here's some more good news: the techniques found in this chapter are pretty simple. Let's take a look at how to use these easy but effective methods for turning our recursive nightmares into recursive bliss.

Unnecessary Recursive Calls

Here's a recursive function that finds the greatest number from an array:

```
def max(array):
    if not array:
        return None

    if len(array) == 1:
        return array[0]

    if array[0] > max(array[1:]):
        return array[0]
    else:
        return max(array[1:])
```

The essence of each recursive call is the comparison of a single number (array[0]) to the maximum number from the remainder of the array. (To calculate the maximum number from the remainder of the array, we call the very max function we're in, which is what makes the function recursive.)

We achieve the comparison with a conditional statement. The first half of the conditional statement is as follows:

```
if array[0] > max(array[1:]):
    return array[0]
```

This snippet says that if the single number (array[0]) is greater than what has already been determined to be the maximum number of the rest of the array (max(array[1:])), then by definition, array[0] must be the greatest number, so we return it.

Here is the second half of the conditional statement:

```
else:
    return max(array[1:])
```

This second snippet says that if array[0] is *not* greater than the greatest number from the rest of the array, then the greatest number from the rest of the array must be the greatest number overall, and we return it.

While this code works, it contains a hidden inefficiency. If you look carefully, you'll note that our code contains the phrase, max(array[1:]) twice, once in each half of the conditional statement.

The problem with this is that each time we mention max(array[1:]), we trigger an entire avalanche of recursive calls.

Let's break this down for an example array of [1, 2, 3, 4].

We know that we're going to start by comparing the 1 with the maximum number of the remaining array, [2, 3, 4]. That, in turn, will compare the 2 against the max of the remaining [3, 4], which in turn will compare the 3 against the [4]. This, too, triggers one more recursive call on the [4] itself, which is the base case.

However, to really see how our code plays out, we're going to start by analyzing the bottom call and working our way up the call chain.

Let's begin.

Max Recursive Walk-Through

When we call max([4]), the function simply returns the number 4. Again, this is because our base case is when the array only contains one element, as dictated by the following line of code:

```
if len(array) == 1:
    return array[0]
```

This is pretty straightforward—it's a single function call:

$$max([4])$$

Moving up the call chain, let's see what happens when we call max([3, 4]). In the first half of the conditional statement (if array[0] > max(array[1:]):), we compare the 3 to max([4]). But calling max([4]) is itself a recursive call. The following diagram depicts max([3, 4]) calling max([4]):

```
max([3,4])
   1st |
       ↓
   max([4])
```

Note that next to the arrow, we put the label "1st" to indicate that this recursive call was triggered by the *first* half of the conditional statement within max([3, 4]).

After this step has been completed, our code can now compare the 3 with the result of max([4]). Since the 3 is not greater than that result (4), we trigger the second half of the conditional. (This is the code, return max(array[1:]).) In this case, we return max([4]).

But when our code returns max([4]), it triggers the actual function call of max([4]). This is now the second time we've triggered the max([4]) call:

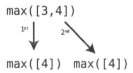

As you can see, the function, max([3, 4]) ends up calling max([4]) twice. Of course, we'd rather try to avoid doing this if we don't have to. If we've already computed the result of max([4]) once, why should we call the same function again just to get the same result?

This problem gets a lot worse when we move just one level up the call chain.

Here's what happens when we call max([2, 3, 4]).

During the first half of the conditional, we compare the 2 against max([3, 4]), which we've already determined looks like this:

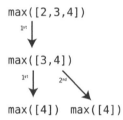

So max([2, 3, 4]) calling max([3, 4]) then, would look like this:

```
max([2,3,4])
  1st │
      ▼
max([3,4])
  1st │    2nd ↘
      ▼
max([4])  max([4])
```

But here's the kicker. This is just for the *first* half of the conditional of max([2, 3, 4]). For the second half of the conditional, we end up calling max([3, 4]) *again*:

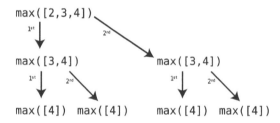

Yikes!

Let's dare to move to the top of the call chain, calling max([1, 2, 3, 4]). When all is said and done, after we call max for both halves of the conditional, we get what is shown in the diagram on page 189.

So when we call max([1, 2, 3, 4]), we actually end up triggering the max function fifteen times.

We can see this visually by adding the statement, print("RECURSION") to the beginning of our function:

```
def max(array)
  print("RECURSION")

  # remaining code omitted for brevity
```

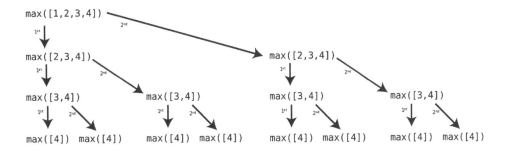

When we then run our code, we'll see the word RECURSION printed to our terminal fifteen times.

Now, we do need *some* of those calls, but not all of them. We do need to calculate max([4]), for example, but one such function call is enough to get the computed result. But here, we call that function *eight* times.

The Little Fix for Big O

Thankfully, there's an easy way to eliminate all these extra recursive calls. We'll call max only once within our code, and *save* the result to a variable:

```python
def max(array):
    if not array:
        return None

    if len(array) == 1:
        return array[0]

    # Calculate the max of the remainder of the array
    # and store it inside a variable:
    max_of_remainder = max(array[1:])

    # Comparison of first number against this variable:
    if array[0] > max_of_remainder:
        return array[0]
    else:
        return max_of_remainder
```

By implementing this simple modification, we end up calling max a mere four times. Try it out yourself by adding the print("RECURSION") line and running the code.

The trick here is that we're making each necessary function call once and saving the result in a variable so that we don't have to ever call that function again.

The difference in efficiency between our initial function and our ever-so-slightly modified function is stark.

The Efficiency of Recursion

In our second, improved version of the max function, the function recursively calls itself as many times as there are values in the array. We'd call this O(N).

Up until this point, the cases of O(N) we've seen involved loops, with a loop running N times. However, we can apply the same principles of Big O to recursion as well.

As you'll recall, Big O answers the key question: if there are N data elements, how many steps will the algorithm take?

Since the improved max function runs N times for N values in the array, it has a time complexity of O(N). Even if the function itself contains multiple steps, such as five, its time complexity would be O(5N), which is reduced to O(N).

In the first version, though, the function called itself *twice* during each run (save for the base case). Let's see how this plays out for different array sizes.

The following table shows how many times max gets called on arrays of various sizes:

N Elements	Number of Calls
1	1
2	3
3	7
4	15
5	31

Can you see the pattern? When we increase the data by one, we roughly *double* the number of steps the algorithm takes. As you learned by our discussion of the Password Cracker, on page 106, this is the pattern of $O(2^N)$. We already know that this is an extremely slow algorithm.

The improved version of the max function, however, only calls max for as many elements as there are inside the array. This means that our second max function has an efficiency of O(N).

This is a powerful lesson: avoiding extra recursive calls is key to keeping recursion fast. What at first glance was a very small change to our code—the mere storing of a computation in a variable—ended up changing the speed of our function from $O(2^N)$ to $O(N)$.

Overlapping Subproblems

The Fibonacci sequence is a mathematical sequence of numbers that goes like this until infinity:

0, 1, 1, 2, 3, 5, 8, 13, 21, 34, 55...

This sequence begins with the numbers 0 and 1, and each subsequent number is the sum of the previous two numbers of the sequence. For example, the number 55 was computed because it is the sum of the previous two numbers, which are 21 and 34.

The following Python function returns the Nth number in the Fibonacci sequence. For example, if we pass the number 10 to the function, it will return 55, as 55 is the tenth number in the series. (The 0 is considered the 0th number in the series.)

```python
def fib(n):
    if n == 0 or n == 1:
        return n
    return fib(n - 2) + fib(n - 1)
```

The key line in this function is the following:

```python
return fib(n - 2) + fib(n - 1)
```

This line sums the previous two numbers in the Fibonacci series. It's a beautiful recursive function.

However, alarm bells should be going off in your head right now because our function calls itself *twice*.

Let's take the computation of the sixth Fibonacci number, for example. The function fib(6) makes a call to both fib(4) and fib(5), as shown in the following diagram:

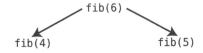

As we've seen, a function calling itself twice can easily lead us down the road to $O(2^N)$. Indeed, here are all the recursive calls made by fib(6) shown in the diagram on page 192.

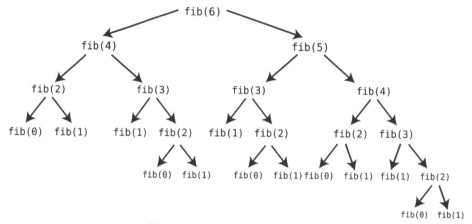

You've got to admit, $O(2^N)$ can look pretty scary.

While one simple change worked to optimize the first example in this chapter, optimizing our Fibonacci sequence isn't as simple.

And that's because there isn't just one single piece of data we can save in a variable. We *need* to calculate both fib(n - 2) and fib(n - 1) (as each Fibonacci number is the sum of those two numbers), and storing the result of one won't alone give us the result for the other.

This is a case of what computer scientists call *overlapping subproblems*. Let's unpack that term.

When a problem is solved by solving smaller versions of the same problem, the smaller problem is called a *subproblem*. This concept isn't new—we've been dealing with it frequently throughout our discussion of recursion. In the case of the Fibonacci sequence, we compute each number by first computing the smaller numbers in the sequence. The computations of these smaller numbers are the subproblems.

What makes these subproblems *overlapping*, though, is the fact that fib(n - 2) and fib(n - 1) end up calling many of the same functions as each other. Specifically, fib(n - 1) ends up making some of the very same calculations already made by fib(n - 2). For example, you can see in the previous diagram that fib(5) calls fib(3) even though fib(4) has itself already done so. Many other calls are duplicated too.

Well, it seems that we're at a dead end. Our Fibonacci example requires us to make many overlapping function calls, and our algorithm oozes along at a pace of $O(2^N)$. There's just nothing we can do.

Or is there?

Dynamic Programming Through Memoization

Luckily, we *do* have options, and that is through something called dynamic programming. *Dynamic programming* is the process of optimizing recursive problems that have overlapping subproblems.

(Don't pay too much attention to the word *dynamic*. There's some debate about how the term came about, and there's nothing obviously dynamic about the techniques I'm about to demonstrate.)

Optimizing an algorithm with dynamic programming is typically accomplished with one of two techniques.

The first technique is something called *memoization*. And no, that's not a typo. Pronounced meh-moe-ih-ZAY-shun, memoization is a simple, but brilliant, technique for reducing recursive calls in cases of overlapping subproblems.

Essentially, memoization reduces recursive calls by *remembering* previously computed functions. (In this respect, memoization really is like its similar-sounding word memorization.)

In our Fibonacci example, the first time fib(3) is called, the function does its computation and returns the number 2. However, before moving on, the function stores this result inside a hash table. The hash table will look something like this:

{3: 2}

This indicates that the result of fib(3) is the number 2.

Similarly, our code will memoize the results of all new computations it encounters. After encountering fib(4), fib(5), and fib(6), for example, our hash table will look like this:

```
{
  3: 2,
  4: 3,
  5: 5,
  6: 8
}
```

Now that we have this hash table, we can use it to prevent future recursive calls. Here's the way this works:

Without memoization, fib(4) would normally call fib(3) and fib(2), which in turn make their own recursive calls. Now that we have this hash table, we can approach things differently. Instead of fib(4) just blithely calling fib(3), for example, it first checks the hash table to see if the result of fib(3) has already been computed. Only if the 3 key is *not* in the hash table does the function proceed to call fib(3).

Memoization goes for the jugular of overlapping subproblems. The whole issue with overlapping subproblems is that we end up computing the same recursive calls over and over again. With memoization, though, each time we make a new calculation, we store it in the hash table for future use. This way, we only make a calculation if it hasn't ever been made before.

Okay, this all sounds good, but there's one glaring problem. How does each recursive function get access to this hash table?

The answer is this: we pass the hash table as a second parameter to the function.

Because the hash table is a specific object in memory, we're able to pass it from one recursive call to the next, even though we're modifying it as we go. This is true even as we unwind the call stack. Even though the hash table may have been empty when the original call was made, that same hash table can be full of data by the time the original call has finished executing.

Implementing Memoization

To pass the hash table along, we modify our function to accept *two* arguments, with the hash table as the second. We call this hash table, memo, as in memoization:

```
def fib(n, memo):
```

When calling the function the first time, we pass in both the number and an empty hash table:

```
fib(6, {})
```

Each time fib calls itself, it also passes along the hash table, which gets filled up along the way.

Here's the rest of the function:

```
def fib(n, memo):
    if n == 0 or n == 1:
        return n
    if n not in memo:
        memo[n] = fib(n - 2, memo) + fib(n - 1, memo)
    return memo[n]
```

Let's analyze this line by line.

Again, our function now accepts two parameters, namely n and the memo hash table:

```
def fib(n, memo):
```

First off, the base cases of 0 and 1 both automatically return n and are unaffected by memoization.

Before making any recursive calls, our code first checks to see whether fib(n) has already been calculated for the given n:

```
if n not in memo:
```

(If the calculation for n is already in the hash table, we simply return the result with return memo[n].)

Only if the calculation for n has not yet been made do we proceed with the calculation:

```
memo[n] = fib(n - 2, memo) + fib(n - 1, memo)
```

Here, we store the result of the calculation in the memo hash table so we never have to calculate it again.

Also note how we pass memo along as an argument to the fib function each time we call it. This is the key to sharing the memo hash table across all the calls to the fib function.

As you can see, the guts of the algorithm remain the same. We're still using recursion to solve our problem, as the computation of fib is still essentially fib(n - 2) + fib(n - 1). However, if the number we're computing is new, we store the result in a hash table, and if the number we're computing was already computed once before, we simply grab the result from the hash table instead of computing it again.

When we map out the recursive calls in our memoized version, we get this:

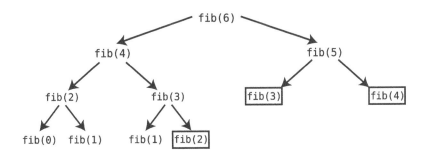

In this diagram, each call that is surrounded by a box is one in which the result was retrieved from the hash table.

So what is the Big O of our function now? Let's look at how many recursive calls we make for different types of N:

N Elements	Number of Calls
1	1
2	3
3	5
4	7
5	9
6	11

We can see that for N, we make (2N) - 1 calls. Since in Big O we drop the constants, this is an O(N) algorithm.

This is an incredible improvement over $O(2^N)$. Go memoization!

Dynamic Programming Through Going Bottom-Up

I mentioned earlier that dynamic programming can be achieved through one of two techniques. We looked at one technique, memoization, which is quite nifty.

The second technique, known as *going bottom-up*, is a lot less fancy and may not even seem like a technique at all. All going bottom-up means is to ditch recursion and use some other approach (like a loop) to solve the same problem.

The reason that going bottom-up is considered part of dynamic programming is because dynamic programming means taking a problem *that could be solved recursively* and ensuring that it doesn't make duplicate calls for overlapping subproblems. Using iteration (that is, loops) instead of recursion is, technically, a way to achieve this.

Going bottom-up becomes more of a "technique" when the problem is more naturally solved with recursion. Generating Fibonacci numbers is one example where recursion is a neat, elegant solution. Having to solve the same problem with iteration may take more brainpower, as an iterative approach may be less intuitive. (Imagine solving the staircase problem from the previous chapter with a loop. Ugh.)

Let's see how we might implement a bottom-up approach for our Fibonacci function.

Bottom-Up Fibonacci

In the following bottom-up approach, we start with the first two Fibonacci numbers: 0 and 1. We then use good ol' iteration to build up the sequence:

```python
def fib(n):
    if n == 0:
        return 0

    a = 0
    b = 1

    for _ in range(1, n):
        a, b = b, a + b

    return b
```

The very first thing we do is return 0 if the input n is 0. Officially, fib(0) should return 0, so we easily dispense with that with a simple conditional statement.

Now, we get to the meat of the code. We initialize variables a and b as 0 and 1 respectively, as those are the first two numbers of the Fibonacci sequence.

We then start a loop so we can calculate each number of the sequence until we reach n:

```python
for _ in range(1, n):
```

In Python, this is equivalent to for i in range(1, n), except that we're not going to need an i variable.

To calculate the next number in the sequence, we need to add the two previous numbers together, namely a + b. We'll update b to be this new number, since b always is supposed to point to the last number in the sequence. We also update a to what b was, so that a continues to point to the second-to-last number:

```python
a, b = b, a + b
```

Because our code is a simple loop from 1 to N, our code takes N steps. Like the memoization approach, it's O(N).

Memoization vs. Bottom-Up

You've now seen the two primary techniques of dynamic programming: memoization and going bottom-up. Is one technique better than the other?

Usually, it depends on the problem and why you're using recursion in the first place. If recursion presents an elegant and intuitive solution to a given problem, you may want to stick with it and use memoization to deal with any overlapping subproblems. However, if the iterative approach is equally intuitive, you may want to go with that.

It's important to point out that even with memoization, recursion does carry some extra overhead versus iteration. Specifically, with any recursion, the computer needs to keep track of all the calls in a call stack, which consumes memory. The memoization itself also requires the use of a hash table, which will take up additional space on your computer as well. (More on this in Chapter 19, Dealing with Space Constraints, on page 385.)

Generally speaking, going bottom-up is often the better choice, unless the recursive solution is more intuitive. Where recursion is more intuitive, you can keep the recursion and keep it fast by using memoization.

Wrapping Up

Now that you're able to write efficient recursive code, you've also unlocked a superpower. You're about to encounter some really efficient—yet advanced—algorithms, and many of them rely on the principles of recursion.

Exercises

The following exercises provide you with the opportunity to practice with dynamic programming. The solutions to these exercises are found in the section Chapter 12, on page 446.

1. The following function accepts an array of numbers and returns the sum, as long as a particular number doesn't bring the sum above 100. If adding a particular number will make the sum higher than 100, that number is ignored. However, this function makes unnecessary recursive calls. Fix the code to eliminate the unnecessary recursion:

```
def add_until_100(array):
    if not array:
        return 0

    if array[0] + add_until_100(array[1:]) > 100:
        return add_until_100(array[1:])
    else:
        return array[0] + add_until_100(array[1:])
```

2. The following function uses recursion to calculate the Nth number from a mathematical sequence known as the Golomb sequence. It's terribly

inefficient, though! Use memoization to optimize it. (You don't have to understand how the Golomb sequence works to do this exercise.)

```
def golomb(n):
    if n == 1:
        return 1

    return 1 + golomb(n - golomb(golomb(n - 1)))
```

3. Here is a solution to the unique paths problem from an exercise in the previous chapter. (Sorry, it's a bit of a spoiler if you haven't tried doing that exercise yet.) Use memoization to improve its efficiency:

```
def unique_paths(rows, columns):
    if rows == 1 or columns == 1:
        return 1

    return unique_paths(rows - 1, columns) + unique_paths(rows, columns - 1)
```

CHAPTER 13

Recursive Algorithms for Speed

We've seen that understanding recursion unlocks all sorts of new algorithms, such as traversing a filesystem or producing anagrams. In this chapter, you're going to learn that recursion is also the key to algorithms that can make our code run much, much faster.

In previous chapters, we've encountered a number of sorting algorithms, including Bubble Sort, Selection Sort, and Insertion Sort. In real life, however, none of these methods are actually used to sort arrays. Most computer languages have built-in sorting functions for arrays that save us the time and effort of implementing our own. And in many of these languages, the sorting algorithm that is employed under the hood is Quicksort.

The reason we're going to dig into Quicksort (even though it's already built into many computer languages) is because by studying how it works, you can learn how to use recursion to greatly speed up an algorithm, and you can do the same for other practical algorithms of the real world.

Quicksort is an extremely fast sorting algorithm that is particularly efficient for average scenarios. While in worst-case scenarios (that is, inversely sorted arrays) it performs similarly to Insertion Sort and Selection Sort, it's much faster for average scenarios—which are what occur most of the time.

Quicksort relies on a concept called *partitioning*, so we'll jump into that first.

Partitioning

To *partition* an array is to take a random value from the array—which is then called the *pivot*—and make sure that every number that is less than the pivot ends up to the left of the pivot and that every number greater than the pivot ends up to the right of the pivot. We accomplish partitioning through a simple algorithm that will be described in the following example.

Let's say we have the following array:

0 5 2 1 6 3

For consistency's sake, we'll always select the rightmost value to be our pivot (although we can technically choose other values). In this case, the number 3 is our pivot. We indicate this by circling it:

0 5 2 1 6 ③

We then assign *pointers*—one to the leftmost value of the array, and one to the rightmost value of the array, excluding the pivot itself:

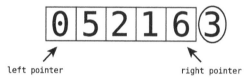

left pointer   right pointer

We're now ready to begin the actual partition, which follows these steps. Don't worry—the steps will become clearer shortly, when we walk through our example.

1. The left pointer continuously moves one cell to the right until it reaches a value that is greater than or equal to the pivot and then stops.

2. Then the right pointer continuously moves one cell to the left until it reaches a value that is less than or equal to the pivot and then stops. The right pointer will also stop if it reaches the beginning of the array.

3. Once the right pointer has stopped, we reach a crossroads. If the left pointer has reached (or gone beyond) the right pointer, we move on to Step 4. Otherwise, we swap the values that the left and right pointers are pointing to, and then we go back to repeat Steps 1, 2, and 3 again.

4. Finally, we swap the pivot with the value that the left pointer is currently pointing to.

When we're done with a partition, we are now assured that all values to the left of the pivot are less than the pivot, and all values to the right of the pivot are greater than it. And that means the pivot itself is now in its correct place within the array, although the other values are not yet necessarily completely sorted.

Let's apply this to our example:

Step 1: Compare the left pointer (now pointing to 0) to our pivot (the value 3):

0 5 2 1 6 ③

left pointer   right pointer

Since 0 is less than the pivot, the left pointer moves on in the next step.

Step 2: The left pointer moves on:

0 5 2 1 6 ③

We compare the left pointer (the 5) to our pivot. Is the 5 lower than the pivot? It's not, so the left pointer stops, and we activate the right pointer in our next step.

Step 3: Compare the right pointer (6) to our pivot. Is the value greater than the pivot? It is, so our pointer will move on in the next step.

Step 4: The right pointer moves on:

0 5 2 1 6 ③

We compare the right pointer (1) to our pivot. Is the value greater than the pivot? It's not, so our right pointer stops.

Step 5: Since both pointers have stopped, we swap the values of the two pointers:

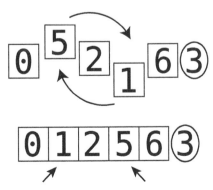

0 1 2 5 6 ③

We then activate our left pointer again in the next step.

Step 6: The left pointer moves on:

$$0 \quad 1 \quad 2 \quad 5 \quad 6 \quad ③$$

We compare the left pointer (2) to our pivot. Is the value less than the pivot? It is, so the left pointer moves on.

Step 7: The left pointer moves on to the next cell. Note that at this point, both the left and right pointers are pointing to the same value:

$$0 \quad 1 \quad 2 \quad 5 \quad 6 \quad ③$$

We compare the left pointer to our pivot. Because our left pointer is pointing to a value that is greater than our pivot, it stops. At this point, since our left pointer has reached our right pointer, we're done with moving pointers.

Step 8: For our final step of the partition, we swap the value that the left pointer is pointing to with the pivot:

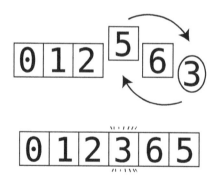

Although our array isn't completely sorted, we've successfully completed a partition; that is, since our pivot was the number 3, all numbers that are less than 3 are to its left, while all numbers greater than 3 are to its right. This also means, by definition, that the 3 is *now in its correct place within the array.*

Code Implementation: Partitioning

Following is an implementation of a SortableArray class in Python that includes a partition method that partitions the array as we've described:

```
class SortableArray:

    def __init__(self, array):
        self.array = array

    def partition(self, left_pointer, right_pointer):
        pivot_index = right_pointer
        pivot = self.array[pivot_index]

        right_pointer -= 1

        while True:

            while self.array[left_pointer] < pivot:
                left_pointer += 1

            while self.array[right_pointer] > pivot:
                right_pointer -= 1

            if left_pointer >= right_pointer:
                break
            else:
                self.array[left_pointer], self.array[right_pointer] = \
                    self.array[right_pointer], self.array[left_pointer]
                left_pointer += 1

        self.array[left_pointer], self.array[pivot_index] = \
            self.array[pivot_index], self.array[left_pointer]

        return left_pointer
```

Let's break this code down a bit.

The partition method accepts the starting points of the left and right pointers as parameters:

```
def partition(self, left_pointer, right_pointer):
```

When this method is first called on an array, these pointers will point to the left and right ends of the array, respectively. However, we'll see that Quicksort will call this method on subsections of the array as well. Because of this, we can't always assume the left and right pointers are always the two extremities of the array, so they need to become method arguments. This point will be clearer when I explain the complete Quicksort algorithm.

Next, we select our pivot, which is always the rightmost element in the range we're dealing with:

```
pivot_index = right_pointer
pivot = self.array[pivot_index]
```

Once our pivot has been identified, we move the right_pointer to the item immediately left of the pivot:

```
right_pointer -= 1
```

We then begin a loop (while True) that will seem to run indefinitely. However, later within the loop is a break statement that will terminate the loop as soon as the left_pointer and right_pointer cross paths. Within this loop, we use another loop to keep moving the left_pointer to the right until it reaches an item that is greater than or equal to the pivot:

```
while self.array[left_pointer] < pivot:
    left_pointer += 1
```

Similarly, we move the right_pointer to the left until it hits an item that is less than or equal to the pivot:

```
while self.array[right_pointer] > pivot:
    right_pointer -= 1
```

Once the left_pointer and right_pointer have stopped moving, we check whether the two pointers have met:

```
if left_pointer >= right_pointer:
    break
```

If they have, we exit the loop and get ready to swap out the pivot, which we'll get to momentarily. However, if the two pointers have stopped but not yet met each other, we swap the values at the two pointers:

```
self.array[left_pointer], self.array[right_pointer] = \
    self.array[right_pointer], self.array[left_pointer]
```

We then move the left_pointer to get ready for the next round of left- and right-pointer movements:

```
left_pointer += 1
```

Finally, once the two pointers have met, we swap the pivot with the value at the left_pointer:

```
self.array[left_pointer], self.array[pivot_index] = \
    self.array[pivot_index], self.array[left_pointer]
```

The method concludes by returning the left_pointer, as this will be needed by the Quicksort algorithm (which I'll explain shortly).

Quicksort

The Quicksort algorithm is a combination of partitions and recursion. It works as follows:

1. Partition the array. The pivot is now in its proper place.

2. Treat the subarrays to the left and right of the pivot as their own arrays, and recursively repeat Steps 1 and 2. That means we'll partition each subarray and end up with even smaller sub-subarrays to the left and right of each subarray's pivot. We then partition those sub-subarrays, and so on and so forth.

3. When we have a subarray that has zero or one elements, that's our base case and we do nothing.

Let's return to our example. We began with the array of [0, 5, 2, 1, 6, 3] and ran a single partition on the entire array. Since Quicksort begins with such a partition, that means we're already partly through the Quicksort process. We left off with:

As you can see, the value 3 was the original pivot. Now that the pivot is in the correct place, we need to sort whatever is to the left and right of the pivot. Note that in our example, it just so happens that the numbers to the left of the pivot are already sorted, but the computer doesn't know that yet.

The next step after the partition is to treat everything to the left of the pivot as its own array and partition it.

We'll obscure the rest of the array for now, as we're not focusing on it at the moment:

Now, of this [0, 1, 2] subarray, we'll make the rightmost element the pivot. So that would be the number 2:

We'll establish our left and right pointers:

And now we're ready to partition this subarray. Let's continue from after Step 8, where we left off previously.

Step 9: We compare the left pointer (0) to the pivot (2). Since the 0 is less than the pivot, we continue moving the left pointer.

Step 10: We move the left pointer one cell to the right, and it now happens to be pointing to the same value the right pointer is pointing to:

We compare the left pointer to the pivot. Since the value 1 is less than the pivot, we move on.

Step 11: We move the left pointer one cell to the right, which just happens to be the pivot:

At this point, the left pointer is pointing to a value that is equal to the pivot (since it *is* the pivot!), and so the left pointer stops.

Note how the left pointer managed to sneak past the right pointer. That's okay, though. The algorithm is designed to work even with such an occurrence.

Step 12: Now we activate the right pointer. However, because the right pointer's value (1) is less than the pivot, it stays still.

Since our left pointer has passed our right pointer, we're done moving pointers altogether in this partition.

Step 13: Next, we swap the pivot with the left pointer's value. Now, it just so happens that the left pointer is pointing to the pivot itself, so we swap the pivot with itself, which results in no change at all. At this point, the partition is complete and the pivot (2) is now in its correct spot:

We now have a subarray of [0, 1] to the left of the pivot (the 2) and no subarray to its right. The next step is to recursively partition the subarray to the pivot's left, which again, is [0, 1]. We don't have to deal with any subarray to the right of the pivot since no such subarray exists.

Because all we'll focus on in the next step is the subarray [0, 1], we'll block out the rest of the array so it looks like this:

To partition the subarray [0, 1], we'll make the rightmost element (the 1) the pivot. Where will we put the left and right pointers? Well, the left pointer will point to the 0, but the right pointer will also point to the 0 since we always start the right pointer at one cell to the left of the pivot. That gives us this:

We're now ready to begin the partition.

Step 14: We compare the left pointer (0) with the pivot (1):

It's less than the pivot, so we move on.

Step 15: We shift the left pointer one cell to the right. It now points to the pivot:

Since the left pointer's value (1) is not lower than the pivot (since it *is* the pivot), the left pointer stops moving.

Step 16: We compare the right pointer with the pivot. Since it's pointing to a value that is less than the pivot, we don't move it anymore. And since the left pointer has passed the right pointer, we're done moving pointers for this partition.

Step 17: We now swap the left pointer with the pivot. Again, in this case, the left pointer is actually pointing to the pivot itself, so the swap doesn't actually change anything. The pivot is now in its proper place, and we're done with this partition.

That leaves us with this:

Next up, we need to partition the subarray to the left of the most recent pivot. In this case, that subarray is [0]—an array of just one element. An array of zero or one elements is our base case, so we don't do anything. The element is just considered to be in its proper place automatically. So now we've got this:

We started out by treating 3 as our pivot, and recursively partitioned the subarray to its left ([0, 1, 2]). As promised, we now need to come back to recursively partitioning the subarray to the right of the 3, which is [6, 5].

We'll obscure the [0, 1, 2, 3], since we've already sorted those, and now we're only focusing on the [6, 5]:

In the next partition, we'll treat the rightmost element (the 5) as the pivot. That gives us this:

When setting up our next partition, our left and right pointers both end up pointing to the 6:

Step 18: We compare the left pointer (6) with the pivot (5). Since 6 is greater than the pivot, the left pointer doesn't move further.

Step 19: The right pointer is pointing to the 6 as well, so we would theoretically move on to the next cell to the left. However, there are no more cells to the left of the 6, so the right pointer stops moving. Since the left pointer has reached the right pointer, we're done moving pointers altogether for this partition. That means we're ready for the final step.

Step 20: We swap the pivot with the value of the left pointer:

Our pivot (5) is now in its correct spot, leaving us with this:

Next up, we technically need to recursively partition the subarray to the left and right of the [5, 6] subarray. Since there's no subarray to its left, that means we only need to partition the subarray to the right. Since the subarray to the right of the 5 is a single element of [6], that's our base case and we do nothing—the 6 is automatically considered to be in its proper place:

And we're done!

Code Implementation: Quicksort

Following is a quicksort method we can add to the previous SortableArray class that would successfully complete the Quicksort:

```
def quicksort(self, left_index, right_index):
    if right_index - left_index <= 0:
        return

    pivot_index = self.partition(left_index, right_index)

    self.quicksort(left_index, pivot_index - 1)

    self.quicksort(pivot_index + 1, right_index)
```

The code here is surprisingly concise, but let's look at each line. For now, we'll skip over the first line of code, which represents the base case. Let's jump straight to the meaty recursion.

We begin by partitioning the range of elements between the left_index and right_index:

```
pivot_index = self.partition(left_index, right_index)
```

The first time we run quicksort, we partition the entire array. In subsequent calls, though, this line of code partitions whatever range of elements that lies between the left_index and right_index, which may be a subsection of the original array.

Note that we assign the return value of partition to a variable called pivot_index. If you'll recall, this value was the left_pointer which pointed to the pivot by the time the partition method was complete.

We then recursively call quicksort on the subarrays to the left and right of the pivot:

```
self.quicksort(left_index, pivot_index - 1)
self.quicksort(pivot_index + 1, right_index)
```

The recursion ends when we reach the base case, which is when the subarray at hand contains no more than one element:

```
if right_index - left_index <= 0:
    return
```

We can take our Quicksort implementation for a test drive using the following code:

```
array = [0, 5, 2, 1, 6, 3]
sortable_array = SortableArray(array)
sortable_array.quicksort(0, len(array) - 1)
print(sortable_array.array)
```

The Efficiency of Quicksort

To figure out the efficiency of Quicksort, let's first determine the efficiency of a *single* partition.

When we break down the steps of a partition, we'll note that a partition involves two primary types of steps:

- *Comparisons*: We compare each of the values at hand to the pivot.
- *Swaps*: When appropriate, we swap the values being pointed to by the left and right pointers.

Each partition has at least N comparisons—that is, we compare each element of the array with the pivot. This is true because a partition always has the left and right pointers move through each cell until the left and right pointers reach each other.

The number of swaps, however, will depend upon how the data is sorted. A single partition can have, at most, N / 2 swaps, as even if we'd swap values at every opportunity, each swap takes care of two values. As you can see in the following diagram, we partition six elements in just three swaps:

Now, in most cases, we're not making a swap every step of the way. For *randomly* sorted data, we generally swap about half of the values. On average, then, we're making about N / 4 swaps.

So on average, we make about N comparisons and N / 4 swaps. We can say, then, that there are about 1.25N steps for N data elements. In Big O notation, we ignore constants, so we'd say that a partition runs in O(N) time.

Now, that's the efficiency of a *single* partition. But Quicksort involves *many* partitions, so we need to conduct further analysis to determine the efficiency of Quicksort.

Quicksort from a Bird's-Eye View

To visualize this more easily, see the diagram on page 214, depicting a typical Quicksort on an array of eight elements from a bird's-eye view. In particular, the diagram shows how many elements each partition acts upon. We've left out the actual numbers from the array since the exact values don't matter. Note that in the diagram, the active subarray is the group of cells that's not grayed out.

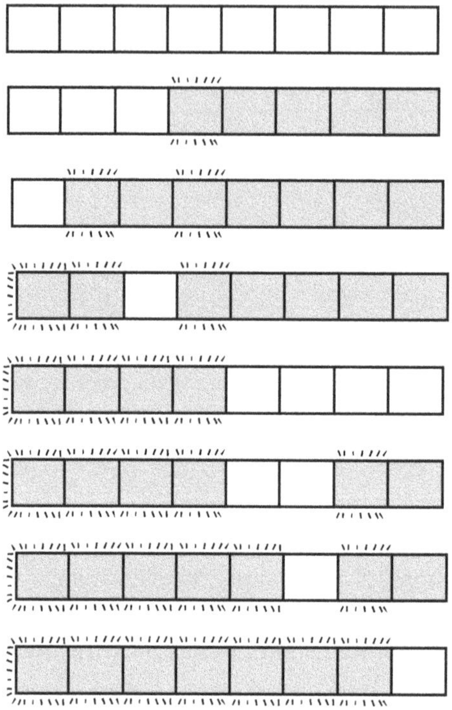

We can see that we have eight partitions, but each partition takes place on subarrays of various sizes. We perform a partition on the original array of eight elements but also perform partitions on subarrays of sizes 4, 3, and 2, and another four partitions on arrays of size 1.

Since Quicksort is essentially comprised of this series of partitions, and each partition takes about N steps for N elements of each subarray, if we add the sizes of all the subarrays together, we'll get the total number of steps Quicksort takes:

```
  8 elements

  3 elements

  1 element

  1 element

  4 elements

  2 elements

  1 element

+ 1 element
  _____

Total = About 21 steps
```

We see that where the original array has 8 elements, Quicksort takes about 21 steps. This assumes a best- or average-case scenario, where the pivot ends up roughly in the middle of the subarray after each partition.

For an array of 16 elements, Quicksort takes about 64 steps, and for an array of 32 elements, Quicksort takes about 160 steps. Take a look at this table:

N	Quicksort Steps (approx.)
4	8
8	24
16	64
32	160

(While in our example earlier, the number of Quicksort steps for an array of size 8 was 21, I put 24 in this table. The exact number can vary from case to case, and 24 is also a reasonable approximation. I specifically made it 24 to make the following explanation a little clearer.)

The Big O of Quicksort

How do we categorize Quicksort in terms of Big O notation?

If we look at the pattern shown earlier, we'll note that the number of Quicksort steps for N elements in the array is about *N multiplied by log N*, as shown in the following table:

N	log N	N * log N	Quicksort Steps (approx.)
4	2	8	8
8	3	24	24
16	4	64	64
32	5	160	160

In fact, this is exactly how to express the efficiency of Quicksort. It's an algorithm of *O(N log N)*. We've discovered a new category of Big O!

The graph on page 216 shows how O(N log N) looks beside other categories of Big O.

Now, it's not a coincidence that the number of steps in Quicksort just happens to align with N * log N. If we think about Quicksort more broadly, we can see *why* it's this way.

Each time we partition the array, we end up breaking it down into two subarrays. Assuming the pivot ends up somewhere in the middle of the array—which

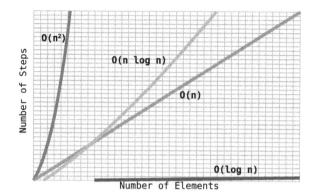

is what happens in the average case—these two subarrays are of roughly equal sizes.

How many times can we break an array into halves until we've broken it completely down to the point where each subarray is of size 1? For an array of size N, this will take us log N times. Take a look at the following diagram:

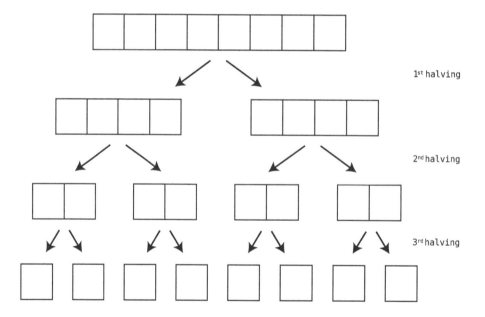

As you can see, for an array of size 8, it takes us three halvings until we've reduced the array into eight individual elements. This is log N, and fits with our definition of log N as being the number of times it takes to halve something until we reach 1.

So this is why Quicksort takes N * log N steps. We have log N halvings, and for each halving, we perform a partition on all the subarrays whose elements add up to N. (They add up to N because all the subarrays are simply pieces of the original array of N elements.)

This is illustrated in the previous diagram. At the top of the diagram, for example, we partition the original array of eight elements, creating two sub-arrays of size 4. We then partition both subarrays of size 4, which means that we're again partitioning eight elements.

Bear in mind that O(N * log N) is just an approximation. In reality, we first perform an extra O(N) partition on the original array as well. Additionally, an array doesn't cleanly break into two even halves, since the pivot is not part of the halving.

Here's what a more realistic example looks like, where we ignore the pivot after each partition:

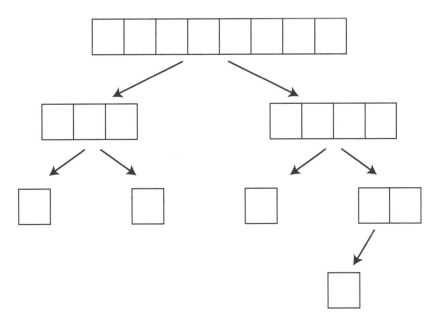

Quicksort in the Worst-Case Scenario

For many other algorithms we've encountered, the best case was one where the array was already sorted. When it comes to Quicksort, however, the best-case scenario is one in which the pivot always ends up smack in the middle of the subarray after the partition. Interestingly, this generally occurs when the values in the array are mixed up pretty well.

The worst-case scenario for Quicksort is one in which the pivot always ends up on one side of the subarray instead of in the middle. This can happen where the array is in perfect ascending or descending order. The visualization for this process is shown here:

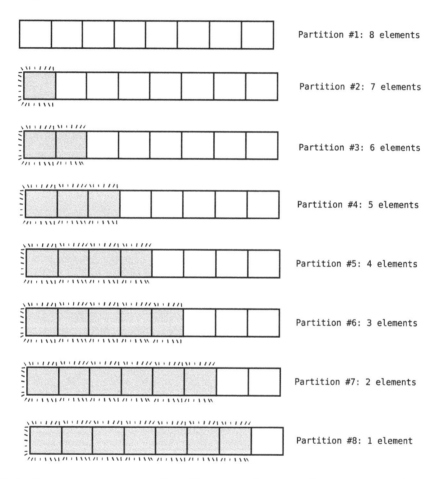

In this diagram you can see that the pivot always ends up on the left end of each subarray.

While in this case each partition still involves only one swap, we lose out because of the increased number of comparisons. In the first example, when the pivot always ended up toward the middle, each partition after the first one was conducted on relatively small subarrays (the largest subarray had a size of 4). In this example, however, the first five partitions take place on subarrays of size 4 or greater. And each of these partitions has as many comparisons as there are elements in the subarray.

So in this worst-case scenario, we have partitions of 8 + 7 + 6 + 5 + 4 + 3 + 2 + 1 elements, which yields a total of 36 comparisons.

To put this a little more formulaically, we'd say that for N elements, there are N + (N - 1) + (N - 2) + (N - 3) ... + 1 steps. We saw in our discussion of Get All the Products, on page 103, that this computes to $N^2 / 2$ steps, which for the purposes of Big O is $O(N^2)$.

So in a worst-case scenario, Quicksort has an efficiency of $O(N^2)$.

Quicksort vs. Insertion Sort

Now that we've got Quicksort down, let's compare it with one of the simpler sorting algorithms, such as Insertion Sort:

	Best Case	Average Case	Worst Case
Insertion Sort	$O(N)$	$O(N^2)$	$O(N^2)$
Quicksort	$O(N \log N)$	$O(N \log N)$	$O(N^2)$

We can see they have identical worst-case scenarios and that Insertion Sort is faster than Quicksort in a best-case scenario. However, the reason Quicksort is superior to Insertion Sort is because of the average scenario—which, again, is what happens most of the time. For average cases, Insertion Sort takes a whopping $O(N^2)$, while Quicksort is much faster at $O(N \log N)$.

Because of Quicksort's superiority in average circumstances, many programming languages use Quicksort under the hood of their built-in sorting functions. So it's unlikely you'll be implementing Quicksort yourself. However, a very similar algorithm can come in handy for practical cases—and it's called Quickselect.

Quickselect

Let's say you have an array in random order, and you don't need to sort it, but you do want to know the tenth-lowest value in the array, or the fifth-highest. This can be useful if we have a lot of test grades and want to know what the 25th percentile is, or if we want to find the median grade.

One way to solve this would be to sort the entire array and then jump to the appropriate index.

However, even were we to use a fast sorting algorithm like Quicksort, this algorithm would take at least $O(N \log N)$ for average cases. And while that isn't bad, we can do even better with a brilliant little algorithm known as

Quickselect. Like Quicksort, Quickselect relies on partitioning and can be thought of as a hybrid of Quicksort and binary search.

As you've seen earlier in this chapter, after a partition, the pivot value ends up in the appropriate spot in the array. Quickselect takes advantage of this in the following way:

Let's say we have an array of eight values, and we want to find the second-to-lowest value within the array.

First, we partition the entire array:

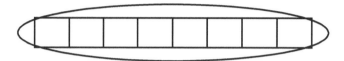

After the partition, the pivot will hopefully end up somewhere toward the middle of the array:

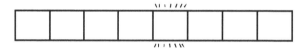

This pivot is now in its correct spot, and since it's in the fifth cell, we now know which value is the fifth-lowest value within the array.

Now, we're looking for the second-lowest value, not the fifth-lowest. But we *do* know that the second-lowest value is *somewhere to the left* of the pivot. We can now ignore everything to the right of the pivot and focus on the left subarray. It's in this respect that Quickselect is similar to binary search: we keep dividing the array in half and focus on the half in which we know the value we're seeking will be found.

Next, we partition the subarray to the left of the pivot:

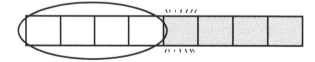

Let's say the new pivot of this subarray ends up the third cell:

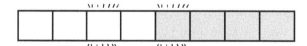

We now know that the value in the third cell is in its correct spot, meaning it's the third-to-lowest value in the array. By definition, then, the second-to-lowest value will be somewhere to its left. We can now partition the subarray to the left of the third cell:

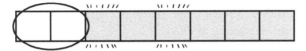

After this next partition, the lowest and second-lowest values will end up in their correct spots within the array:

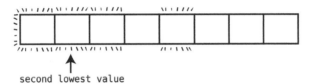

second lowest value

We can then grab the value from the second cell and know with confidence that it's the second-lowest value in the entire array. One of the beautiful things about Quickselect is that we can find the correct value *without having to sort the entire array.*

With Quicksort, each time we halved the array, we needed to re-partition every single element again (in their subarray form), giving us O(N log N). With Quickselect, on the other hand, each time we cut the array in half, we only had to partition the one half we cared about—the half in which we know our value is to be found.

The Efficiency of Quickselect

When analyzing the efficiency of Quickselect, we'll see that it's O(N) for average scenarios. Why is this?

In our earlier example of an array of eight elements, we executed three partitions: one on an array of eight elements, one on a subarray of four elements, and one on a subarray of two elements.

Recall that each partition takes about N steps for the subarray it's run upon. The total steps, then, for the three partitions is 8 + 4 + 2 = 14 steps. So an array of eight elements yields roughly 14 steps.

For an array of 64 elements, we run about 64 + 32 + 16 + 8 + 4 + 2 = 126 steps. For 128 elements, we would need about 254 steps. And for 256 elements, we would end up with 510 steps.

We can see that we need about 2N steps for N elements in the array.

(Another way to formulate this is to say that for N elements, we would need N + (N/2) + (N/4) + (N/8) + ... 2 steps. This always turns out to be roughly 2N steps.)

Since Big O ignores constants, we drop the 2 from the 2N and say that Quickselect has an efficiency of O(N).

Code Implementation: Quickselect

Following is an implementation of a quickselect method that can be dropped into the SortableArray class described earlier. You'll note that it's very similar to the quicksort method:

```python
def quickselect(self, kth_lowest_value, left_index, right_index):
    if right_index - left_index <= 0:
        return self.array[left_index]

    pivot_index = self.partition(left_index, right_index)

    if kth_lowest_value < pivot_index:
        return self.quickselect(kth_lowest_value, left_index, pivot_index - 1)
    elif kth_lowest_value > pivot_index:
        return self.quickselect(kth_lowest_value, pivot_index + 1, right_index)
    else:
        return self.array[pivot_index]
```

The variable kth_lowest_value allows us to choose which value we're searching for. We can search for the second-to-lowest value, the fifth-to-lowest value, or any other value we'd like.

If you want to find the second-to-lowest value of an unsorted array, you'd run the following code:

```python
array = [0, 50, 20, 10, 60, 30]
sortable_array = SortableArray(array)
print(sortable_array.quickselect(1, 0, len(array) - 1))
```

The first argument of the quickselect method accepts the position you're looking for, starting at index 0. We've put in a 1 to represent the second-to-lowest value. The second and third values are the left and right indexes of the array, respectively.

Sorting as a Key to Other Algorithms

As of this writing, the fastest sorting algorithms we know of have speeds of O(N log N). While Quicksort is one of the most popular among them, there are many others as well. Mergesort is another well-known O(N log N) sorting algorithm and will be covered in Volume 2 of this book.

The fact that the fastest sorting algorithms are O(N log N) is important, as this has implications for other algorithms as well. This is because there are algorithms that use sorting as a component of a larger process.

For example, if you'll recall from Chapter 4, Speeding Up Your Code with Big O, on page 47, we dealt with the problem of checking whether there are duplicate values within an array.

The first solution we looked at involved nested loops and had an efficiency of O(N²). While we found a solution that took O(N), I parenthetically hinted at a disadvantage with that approach having to do with extra memory consumption. (I'll eventually discuss this at length in Chapter 19, Dealing with Space Constraints, on page 385.) So let's assume that the O(N) approach is out. Are there any other ways we can improve upon the quadratic O(N²) solution? Hint: the solution has something to do with sorting!

We can build a beautiful algorithm if we presort the array.

Let's say the original array was [5, 9, 3, 2, 4, 5, 6]. This array has two instances of 5, so we do have a case of duplicates.

Now, if we first sorted this array, it would become [2, 3, 4, 5, 5, 6, 9].

Next, we can use a single loop to iterate over each number. As we inspect each number, we'd check whether it's identical to the *next* number. If it is, we've found a duplicate. If we get to the end of the loop without finding a duplicate, then we know that we have no duplicates.

The trick here is that by presorting the numbers, we end up bunching duplicate numbers together.

In our example, we'd start by looking at the first number, which is the 2. We'd check whether it's identical to the next number. The next number is 3, so they're not duplicates.

We'd then check the 3 against the following number, which happens to be a 4, allowing us to move on. We'd check the 4 against the 5, and we'd move on again.

At this point, we'd inspect the first 5 and check it against the following number, which is the second 5. Aha! We found a pair of duplicate numbers, and we can return true.

Here's a Python implementation of this:

```python
def has_duplicate_value(array):
    array.sort()

    for index in range(len(array) - 1):
```

```
    if array[index] == array[index + 1]:
        return True

return False
```

Now, this is an algorithm that used sorting as one of its components. What's the Big O of this algorithm?

We start out by sorting the array. We can assume that Python's sort() function uses something like Quicksort under the hood and has an efficiency of O(N log N). Next, we spend up to N steps iterating through the array. Our algorithm, then, takes (N log N) + N steps.

You learned that when we have multiple orders added together, Big O notation keeps only the highest order of N because the lower orders are trivial beside the higher orders. Here as well, N is trivial beside N log N, so we reduce the expression to O(N log N).

So, that's it! We've used sorting to develop an algorithm that is O(N log N), which is a significant improvement over the original $O(N^2)$ algorithm.

Plenty of algorithms employ sorting as part of a larger process. We now know that any time we do so, we have an algorithm that is at *least* O(N log N). Of course, the algorithm may be slower than this if it has other things going on, but we know that O(N log N) will always be the baseline.

Wrapping Up

The Quicksort and Quickselect algorithms are recursive algorithms that present beautiful and efficient solutions to thorny problems. They're great examples of how a non-obvious but well-thought-out algorithm can boost performance.

Now that we've seen some more advanced algorithms, we're now going to head in a new direction and explore a trove of additional data structures. Some of these data structures have operations that involve recursion, so we'll be fully prepared to tackle those now. Besides their being really interesting, we'll see that each data structure has a special power that can bring significant advantages to a variety of applications.

Exercises

The following exercises provide you with the opportunity to practice with fast sorting. The solutions to these exercises are found in the section Chapter 13, on page 447.

1. Given an array of positive numbers, write a function that returns the greatest product of any three numbers. The approach of using three nested loops would clock in at $O(N^3)$, which is very slow. Use sorting to implement the function in a way that it computes at $O(N \log N)$ speed. (Some other implementations are even faster, but we're focusing on using sorting as a technique to make code faster.)

2. The following function finds the missing number from an array of integers; that is, the array is expected to have all integers from 0 up to the array's length, but one is missing. As examples, the array [5, 2, 4, 1, 0] is missing the number 3, and the array [9, 3, 2, 5, 6, 7, 1, 0, 4] is missing the number 8.

   Here's an implementation that is $O(N^2)$ (the clause if number not in array is itself already $O(N)$, since the computer needs to search the entire array to find number):

```
def find_missing_number(array):
    for number in range(len(array) + 1):
        if number not in array:
            return number

    return None
```

   Use sorting to write a new implementation of this function that only takes $O(N \log N)$. (Some other implementations are even faster, but we're focusing on using sorting as a technique to make code faster.)

3. Write three different implementations of a function that finds the greatest number within an array. Write one function that is $O(N^2)$, one that is $O(N \log N)$, and one that is $O(N)$.

CHAPTER 14

Node-Based Data Structures

For the next several chapters, we're going to explore a variety of data structures that all build upon a single concept—the *node*. As you'll see shortly, nodes are pieces of data that may be dispersed throughout the computer's memory. Node-based data structures offer new ways to organize and access data that provide a number of major performance advantages.

In this chapter, we'll explore the linked list, which is the simplest node-based data structure and the foundation for future chapters. You'll discover that linked lists seem almost identical to arrays but come with their own set of trade-offs in efficiency that can give us a performance boost for certain situations.

Linked Lists

Like an array, a *linked list* is a data structure that represents a list of items. While on the surface arrays and linked lists look and act quite similarly, under the hood there are big differences.

As mentioned in Chapter 1, Why Data Structures Matter, on page 1, memory inside a computer can be visualized as a giant set of cells in which bits of data are stored. You learned that when creating an array, your code finds a contiguous group of empty cells in memory and designates them to store data for your application, as shown on page 228.

You also saw that the computer has the ability to access any memory address in one step and can use that power to also immediately access any index within the array. If you wrote code that said, "Look up the value at index 4," your computer could locate that cell in a single step. Again, this is because your program knows which memory address the array starts at—say, memory address 1000—and therefore knows that if it wants to look up index 4, it should simply jump to memory address 1004.

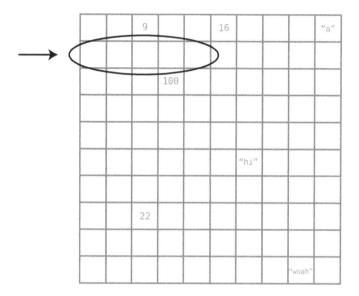

Linked lists, on the other hand, work differently. Instead of being a contiguous block of memory, the data from linked lists can be scattered across different cells throughout the computer's memory.

Connected data that are dispersed throughout memory are known as *nodes*. In a linked list, each node represents one item in the list. The big question, then, is this: if the nodes are not next to each other in memory, how does the computer know which nodes are part of the same linked list?

This is the key to the linked list: each node also comes with a little extra information—namely, the memory address of the *next* node in the list.

This extra piece of data—this pointer to the next node's memory address—is known as a *link*. Here's a visual depiction of a linked list:

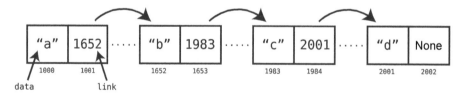

In this example, we have a linked list that contains four pieces of data: "a", "b", "c", and "d". However, it uses *eight* cells of memory to store this data, because each node consists of two memory cells. The first cell holds the actual data, while the second cell serves as a link that indicates where in memory the next node begins. The final node's link contains None since the linked list ends there.

A linked list's first node is also referred to as its *head*, and its last node its *tail*. We may use the terms *head* and *first node* interchangeably.

If the computer knows at which memory address the linked list begins, it has all it needs to begin working with the list! Since each node contains a link to the next node, all the computer needs to do is follow each link to string together the entire list.

The fact that a linked list's data can be spread throughout the computer's memory is a potential advantage it has over the array. An array, by contrast, needs to find an entire block of contiguous cells to store its data, which can get increasingly difficult as the array size grows. These details are managed by your programming language under the hood, so you may not have to worry about them. However, you'll see shortly that there are more tangible differences between linked lists and arrays that we can sink our teeth into.

Implementing a Linked List

Some programming languages, such as Java, come with linked lists built into the language. Many languages don't, but it's fairly simple to implement them on our own.

Let's create our own linked list using Python. We'll use two classes to implement this: Node and LinkedList. Let's create the Node class first:

```python
class Node:

    def __init__(self, data):
        self.data = data
        self.next_node = None
```

The Node class has two attributes: data contains the node's primary value (for example, the string "a"), while next_node contains the link to the next node in the list. We can use this class as follows:

```python
node_1 = Node("once")
node_2 = Node("upon")
node_3 = Node("a")
node_4 = Node("time")

node_1.next_node = node_2
node_2.next_node = node_3
node_3.next_node = node_4
```

With this code, we've created a list of four nodes that serve as a list containing the strings "once", "upon", "a", and "time".

Note that in our implementation, the next_node refers to another Node *instance* rather than an actual memory address number. The effect, however, is the same—the nodes are likely dispersed throughout the computer's memory, and yet we can use the nodes' links to string the list together.

Going forward, then, we're simply going to discuss each link as pointing to another node rather than to a specific memory address. Accordingly, we're going to use simplified diagrams to depict linked lists, such as this one:

Each node in this diagram consists of two cells. The first cell contains the node's data, and the second cell points to the next node.

This reflects our implementation of the Node class. In it, the data method returns the node's data, while the next_node method returns the next node in the list. *In this context, the next_node method serves as the node's link.*

While we've been able to create this linked list with the Node class alone, we still need an easy way to tell our program where the linked list begins. To do this, we'll create a LinkedList class in addition to our previous Node class. Here's the LinkedList class in its basic form:

```
import node

class LinkedList:
    def __init__(self, first_node=None):
        self.first_node = first_node
```

Note that we import node at the beginning of our code, since we placed the Node class in a separate file from this LinkedList class.

At this point, all a LinkedList instance does is keep track of the first node of the list.

Previously we created a chain of nodes containing node_1, node_2, node_3, and node_4. We can now use our LinkedList class to reference this list by writing the following code:

```
list = LinkedList(node_1)
```

This list variable now acts as a handle on the linked list, as it's an instance of LinkedList that has access to the list's first node.

An important point emerges: *when dealing with a linked list, we have immediate access only to its head.* This is going to have serious ramifications, as we'll see shortly.

At first glance, though, linked lists and arrays are similar—they're both just lists of stuff. When we dig into the analysis, though, we'll see some dramatic differences in these two data structures' performances! Let's jump into the four classic operations: reading, searching, insertion, and deletion.

Reading

As you know, a computer can read from an array in O(1) time. But now let's figure out the efficiency of reading from a linked list.

If you want to read, say, the value of the third item of a linked list, the computer cannot look it up in one step, because it wouldn't immediately know where to find it in the computer's memory. After all, each node of a linked list could be *anywhere* in memory! All our program knows immediately is the memory address of the *first* node of the linked list; it doesn't know offhand where any of the other nodes are.

To read from the third node, then, the computer must go through a process. First, it accesses the first node. It then follows the first node's link to the second node and then the second node's link to the third node.

To get to any node, then, we always need to start with the first node (the only node we initially have access to), and follow the chain of nodes until we reach the node we want.

It turns out, then, that if we were to read from the last node in the list, it would take N steps for N nodes in the list. Linked lists having a worst-case read of O(N) is a major disadvantage when compared with arrays that can read any element in just O(1). But don't fret, as linked lists will have their moment to shine, as we'll see soon.

Code Implementation: Linked List Reading

Let's go ahead and add a read method to our LinkedList class:

```
def read(self, index):
    current_node = self.first_node
    current_index = 0
```

```
    while current_index < index:
        current_node = current_node.next_node
        current_index += 1

        if not current_node:
            return None

    return current_node.data
```

If we want to read the fourth node from a list, for example, we'd call our method by passing in the node's index as follows:

```
list.read(3)
```

Let's walk through how this method works.

First, we create a variable called current_node that refers to the node we're currently accessing. Since we're going to start by accessing the head, we say this:

```
current_node = self.first_node
```

Recall that first_node is an instance variable of the LinkedList class.

We also track the index of current_node so that we can know when we reach the desired index. We start at 0 since the first node's index is 0:

```
current_index = 0
```

We then launch a loop that runs while current_index is less than the index we're attempting to read:

```
while current_index < index:
```

In each pass-through of the loop, we access the next node in the list and make it the new current_node:

```
current_node = current_node.next_node
```

We also bump up the current_index by 1:

```
current_index += 1
```

At the end of each pass-through, we check whether we've reached the end of the list, and we return None if the index we're trying to read isn't in our list:

```
if not current_node:
    return None
```

This works because the final node of the list will actually have a next_node that is None since the last node was never assigned a next_node of its own. This being the case, when current_node refers to the final node and we then execute current_node = current_node.next_node, the current_node becomes None.

Finally, if we do break out of the loop, it's because we reached the desired index. We can then return the node's value with the following:

```
return current_node.data
```

Searching

As you know, searching means looking for a value within the list and returning its index. We've seen that linear search on an array has a speed of O(N), since the computer needs to inspect each value one at a time.

Linked lists also have a search speed of O(N). To search for a value, we need to go through a similar process to the one we did with reading; that is, we begin with the head and follow the links of each node to the next one. Along the way, we inspect each value until we find what we're looking for.

Code Implementation: Linked List Search

Here's how we can implement the search operation in Python. We'll call this method search and pass in the value we're searching for:

```
def search(self, value):
    current_node = self.first_node
    current_index = 0

    while True:
        if current_node.data == value:
            return current_index

        current_node = current_node.next_node

        if not current_node:
            break

        current_index += 1

    return None
```

We can then search for any value within the list, like so:

```
list.search("time")
```

Using this, we would get back the index of where "time" is located within the list. In our example above, this would be 3.

As you can see, the mechanics of searching are similar to reading. The main difference is that the loop doesn't stop at a particular index but runs until we either find the value or reach the end of the list.

Insertion

Admittedly, linked lists have yet to impress us from a performance standpoint. They're no better than arrays at search, and much worse at reading. But not to worry—linked lists will have their moment. In fact, that moment is now.

Insertion is one operation in which linked lists have a distinct advantage over arrays *in certain situations*.

Recall that the worst-case scenario for insertion into an array is when the program inserts data into index 0, because it first has to shift the rest of the data one cell to the right, which ends up yielding an efficiency of O(N). With linked lists, however, insertion at the beginning of the list takes just one step—which is O(1). Let's see why.

Say we have the following linked list:

If we want to add "yellow" to the beginning of the list, all we have to do is create a new node and have its link point to the node containing "blue":

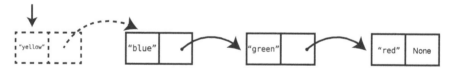

(In our code, we'd also need to update the LinkedList instance so that its first_node attribute now points to this "yellow" node.)

In contrast with an array, the linked list provides the flexibility of inserting data to the front of the list without requiring the shifting of any data. How sweet is that?

The truth is that, theoretically, inserting data *anywhere* within a linked list takes just one step, but there's one gotcha. Let's continue with our example. Here's our linked list now:

Say we now want to insert "purple" at index 2 (which would be between "blue" and "green"). The actual insertion takes just one step; that is, we can create the new purple node and simply change the blue node's link to point to the purple node, as shown here:

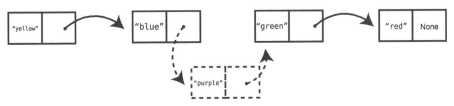

However, for the computer to do this, it first needs to *get to* the node at index 1 ("blue") so that it can modify its link to point to the newly created node. As we've seen, though, reading—which is accessing an item at a given index—from a linked list already takes O(N). Let's see this in action.

We know that we want to add a new node after index 1. So the computer needs to get to index 1 of the list. To do this, we must start at the beginning of the list:

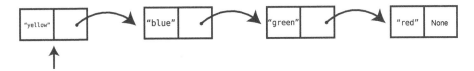

We then access the next node by following the first link:

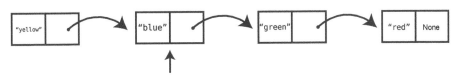

Now that we've found index 1, we can finally add the new node:

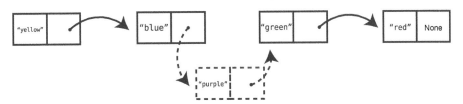

In this case, adding "purple" took three steps. If we were to add it to the *end* of our list, it would take five steps: four steps to access index 3 and one step to insert the new node.

Practically speaking, then, inserting into a linked list is O(N), as the worst-case scenario of inserting at the end of the list will take N + 1 steps.

However, we've seen that the best-case scenario of inserting at the *beginning* of the list is only O(1).

Interestingly, our analysis shows that the best- and worst-case scenarios for arrays and linked lists are the opposite of one another. The following table breaks this all down:

Scenario	Array	Linked List
Insert at beginning	Worst case	Best case
Insert at middle	Average case	Average case
Insert at end	Best case	Worst case

As you can see, arrays favor insertions at the end, while linked lists favor insertions at the beginning.

We've now found one thing that linked lists are great at—inserting things at the beginning of the list. Later in this chapter, we'll see a great practical example of where we can take advantage of this.

Code Implementation: Linked List Insertion

Let's add an insertion method to our LinkedList class. We'll call it insert:

```
def insert(self, index, value):
    new_node = node.Node(value)

    if index == 0:
        new_node.next_node = self.first_node
        self.first_node = new_node
        return

    current_node = self.first_node
    current_index = 0

    while current_index < (index - 1):
        current_node = current_node.next_node
        current_index += 1

    new_node.next_node = current_node.next_node

    current_node.next_node = new_node
```

To use the method, we pass in both the new value as well as the index of where we want to insert it.

For example, to insert "purple" at index 2, we'd say this:

```
list.insert(2, "purple")
```

Let's break this insert method down.

First, we create a new Node instance with the value provided to our method:

```
new_node = node.Node(value)
```

(Here, the node from node.Node refers to the node module we imported at the beginning of the file, as we placed the Node class in a separate file from the LinkedList class.)

Next, we deal with the case where we're inserting into index 0—that is, at the beginning of our list. The algorithm for this case is different than if we insert elsewhere into the list, so we deal with this case separately.

To insert at the beginning of the list, we simply have our new_node link to the first node of the list and declare our new_node to be the first node going forward:

```
if index == 0:
    new_node.next_node = self.first_node
    self.first_node = new_node
    return
```

The return keyword ends the method early, as there's nothing left to do.

The rest of the code deals with a case in which we're inserting anywhere other than at the beginning.

As with reading and searching, we start off by accessing the head of the list:

```
current_node = self.first_node
current_index = 0
```

We then use a while loop to access the node *just before* the spot where we want to insert our new_node:

```
while current_index < (index - 1):
    current_node = current_node.next_node
    current_index += 1
```

At this point, the current_node is the node that'll immediately precede our new_node.

Next, we set the link of our new_node to point to the node after the current_node:

```
new_node.next_node = current_node.next_node
```

Finally, we change the link of the current_node (which, again, is to be the node that precedes our new_node) to point to our new_node:

```
current_node.next_node = new_node
```

And we're done!

Deletion

Linked lists also shine when it comes to deletion, especially when deleting from the beginning of the list.

To delete a node from the beginning of a linked list, all we need to do is perform one step: we change the first_node of the linked list to now point to the second node.

Let's return to our example of the linked list containing the values "once", "upon", "a", and "time". If we want to delete the value "once", we could simply change the linked list to begin at "upon":

```
list.first_node = node_2
```

Contrast this with an array, in which deleting the first element means shifting all remaining data one cell to the left, which takes O(N) time.

When it comes to deleting the *final* node of a linked list, the actual deletion takes one step—we just take the second-to-last node and make its link None. However, it takes N steps to even access the second-to-last node in the first place, since we need to start at the beginning of the list and follow the links until we reach it.

The following table contrasts the various scenarios of deletion for both arrays and linked lists. Note how it's identical to insertion:

Situation	Array	Linked List
Delete at beginning	Worst case	Best case
Delete at middle	Average case	Average case
Delete at end	Best case	Worst case

While deleting from the beginning or end of a linked list is straightforward, deleting from anywhere in the middle is slightly more involved.

Say we want to delete the value at index 2 ("purple") from our example linked list of colors, as shown in the following diagram:

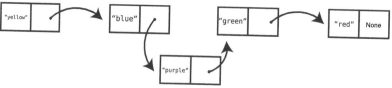

To accomplish this, we need to first access the node immediately *preceding* the one we're deleting ("blue"). Then we change its link to point to the node that is immediately *after* the node we're deleting ("green").

The following visualization demonstrates us changing the link of the "blue" node from "purple" to "green":

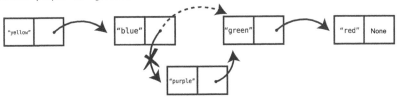

It's interesting to note that whenever we delete a node from our linked list, the node still exists in memory somewhere. We're just removing the node from our list by ensuring that no other node from the list links to it. This has the *effect* of deleting the node from our list, even if the node still exists in memory.

(Different programming languages handle these deleted nodes in various ways. Some will automatically detect that they're not being used and will "garbage collect" them, freeing up memory.)

Code Implementation: Linked List Deletion

Here's what the delete operation might look like in our LinkedList class. It's called delete, and we pass in the index we're going to delete:

```python
def delete(self, index):
    if index == 0:
        self.first_node = self.first_node.next_node
        return

    current_node = self.first_node
    current_index = 0

    while current_index < (index - 1):
        current_node = current_node.next_node
        current_index += 1

    node_after_deleted_node = current_node.next_node.next_node

    current_node.next_node = node_after_deleted_node
```

This method is pretty similar to the insert method we saw earlier. Let's highlight some of the novel points.

The method first deals with a case in which index is 0, meaning we intend to delete the first node of the list. The code for this is ridiculously simple:

```python
if index == 0:
    self.first_node = self.first_node.next_node
    return
```

All we do is change our list's first_node to point to what is currently the second node, and we're done!

The rest of the method handles deletions anywhere else from the list. To do this, we use a while loop to access the node immediately preceding the one we want to delete. This becomes our current_node.

We then grab the node that comes immediately *after* the node we're going to delete and store it in a variable called node_after_deleted_node:

```
node_after_deleted_node = current_node.next_node.next_node
```

Notice our little trick in accessing that node. It's simply the node that comes two nodes after the current_node!

Then we modify the link of the current_node to point to the node_after_deleted_node:

```
current_node.next_node = node_after_deleted_node
```

Efficiency of Linked List Operations

After our analysis, it emerges that the comparison of linked lists and arrays breaks down as follows:

Operation	Array	Linked list
Reading	O(1)	O(N)
Search	O(N)	O(N)
Insertion	O(N) (O(1) at end)	O(N) (O(1) at beginning)
Deletion	O(N) (O(1) at end)	O(N) (O(1) at beginning)

In the grand scheme of things, linked lists seem to be lackluster when it comes to time complexity. They perform similarly to arrays for search, insertion, and deletion, and are much slower when it comes to reading. If so, why would one ever want to use a linked list?

The key to unlocking the linked list's power is in the fact that the *actual insertion and deletion steps* are just O(1).

But isn't that only relevant when inserting or deleting at the beginning of the list? We saw that to insert or delete elsewhere, it takes up to N steps just to access the node we want to delete or insert after!

Well, it just so happens that there are scenarios in which we may already have accessed the right node for some other purpose. The next example is a case in point.

Linked Lists in Action

One case where linked lists shine is when we examine a single list and delete many elements from it. Let's say, for example, we're building an application that combs through existing lists of email addresses and removes any email address that has an invalid format.

No matter whether the list is an array or a linked list, we need to comb through the entire list one element at a time to inspect each email address. This, naturally, takes N steps. However, let's examine what happens when we actually delete each email address.

With an array, each time we delete an email address, we need another O(N) steps to shift the remaining data to the left to close the gap. All this shifting will happen before we can even inspect the next email address.

Let's assume that 1 in 10 email addresses are invalid. If we had a list of 1,000 email addresses, we'd have about 100 invalid ones. Our algorithm, then, would take 1,000 steps to read all 1,000 email addresses. On top of that, though, it might take up to an additional 100,000 steps for deletion, as for each of the 100 deleted addresses, we might shift up to 1,000 other elements.

With a linked list, however, as we comb through the list, each deletion takes just one step, as we can simply change a node's link to point to the appropriate node and move on. For our 1,000 emails, then, our algorithm would take just 1,100 steps, as there are 1,000 reading steps, and 100 deletion steps.

It turns out, then, that linked lists are an amazing data structure for moving through an entire list while making insertions or deletions, as we never have to worry about shifting other data as we make an insertion or deletion.

Doubly Linked Lists

Linked lists come in a number of different flavors. The linked list we've discussed until this point is the *classic* linked list, but with some slight modifications we can grant linked lists additional superpowers.

One variant form of the linked list is the *doubly linked list*.

A doubly linked list is like a linked list except that each node has *two* links—one that points to the next node and another that points to the *previous* node. In addition, the doubly linked list always keeps track of both the head *and* tail nodes, instead of just the head.

Here's what a doubly linked list looks like:

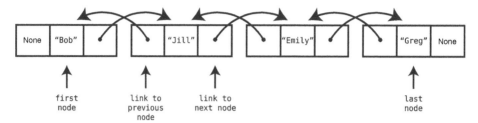

first
node

link to
previous
node

link to
next node

last
node

We can implement the core of a doubly linked list in Python like this. First, we must create a new kind of "double-ended" node:

```
class Node:

    def __init__(self, data):
        self.data = data
        self.next_node = None
        self.previous_node = None
```

You'll notice how each node now contains not just a next_node attribute but a previous_node attribute as well.

Once we have that in place, we can now implement our doubly linked list:

```
import double_ended_node

class DoublyLinkedList:

    def __init__(self, first_node=None, last_node=None):
        self.first_node = first_node
        self.last_node = last_node
```

Since a doubly linked list always knows where both its head and tail are, we can access each of them in a single step, or O(1). So just as we can read, insert, or delete from the beginning of the list in O(1), we can do the same from the end of the list in O(1) as well.

Here's a depiction of inserting at the end of a doubly linked list:

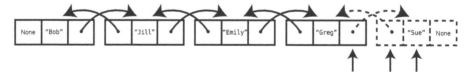

As you can see, we create a new node ("Sue") and have its previous_node point to what used to be the last_node ("Greg") of the linked list. Then we change the next_node of the last_node ("Greg") to point to this new node ("Sue"). Finally, we declare the new node ("Sue") to be the last_node of the linked list.

Code Implementation: Doubly Linked List Insertion

We'll look next at the implementation of a new append method that we can add to our DoublyLinkedList class. Instead of inserting a value anywhere in the list, the append method simply adds a new value at the end of the list. We're focusing on appending, rather than classical inserting, simply to highlight how easy and fast it is to append to a doubly linked list. Here's the append method:

```python
def append(self, value):
    new_node = double_ended_node.Node(value)

    if not self.first_node:
        self.first_node = new_node
        self.last_node = new_node
    else:
        new_node.previous_node = self.last_node
        self.last_node.next_node = new_node
        self.last_node = new_node
```

Let's highlight the most important parts of this method.

First, we create the new node:

```python
new_node = double_ended_node.Node(value)
```

At first, our code handles the case where the list doesn't contain any nodes yet. But let's jump to the case where we append to an existing list.

We set the previous_node link of the new_node to point to what until this point was the last node:

```python
new_node.previous_node = self.last_node
```

Then we change the last node's link (which was None until this point) and have it point to our new_node:

```python
self.last_node.next_node = new_node
```

Last, we tell our instance of the DoublyLinkedList that its last node is our new_node:

```python
self.last_node = new_node
```

Moving Forward and Backward

With a classic linked list, we can only move *forward* through the list; that is, we can access the first node and follow the links to find all the other nodes of the list. But we're not able to move backward, as no node is aware of what the previous node is.

A doubly linked list allows for a lot more flexibility, as we can move both forward *and* backward through the list. In fact, we can even start with the tail and work our way backward to the head.

Queues as Doubly Linked Lists

Because doubly linked lists have immediate access to both the front and end of the list, they can insert data on either side at O(1) as well as delete data on either side at O(1).

Because doubly linked lists can insert data at the end in O(1) time and delete data from the front in O(1) time, *they make the perfect underlying data structure for a queue.*

We looked at Queues, on page 143, and you'll recall that they are lists of items in which data can only be inserted at the end and removed from the beginning. You learned there that queues are an example of an abstract data type and that we were able to use an array to implement them under the hood.

Now, since queues insert at the end and delete from the beginning, arrays are only so good as the underlying data structure. While arrays are O(1) for insertions at the end, they're O(N) for deleting from the beginning.

A doubly linked list, on the other hand, is O(1) for both inserting at the end *and* for deleting from the beginning. That's what makes it a perfect fit for serving as the queue's underlying data structure.

Code Implementation: Queue Built upon a Doubly Linked List

Before implementing the queue itself, we'll first add one more method to our DoublyLinkedList class. This pop_head method removes the head from the list and returns it:

```
def pop_head(self):
    popped_node = self.first_node
    self.first_node = self.first_node.next_node
    self.first_node.previous_node = None
    return popped_node
```

As you can see, we effectively delete the first node by changing the list's self.first_node to be what is currently the second node. We also make sure that the new head doesn't link to any previous node. Finally, we return the node we just deleted.

With this in place, we can now create a queue implementation that is built upon a doubly linked list:

```
import doubly_linked_list

class Queue:
    def __init__(self):
        self.data = doubly_linked_list.DoublyLinkedList()

    def enqueue(self, element):
        self.data.append(element)

    def dequeue(self):
        dequeued_node = self.data.pop_head()
        return dequeued_node.data

    def read(self):
        if not self.data.first_node:
            return None
        return self.data.first_node.data
```

The Queue class implements its methods on top of our DoublyLinkedList. The enqueue method relies on the append method of our DoublyLinkedList:

```
def enqueue(self, element):
    self.data.append(element)
```

Similarly, the dequeue method takes advantage of the linked list's ability to delete from the front of the list:

```
def dequeue(self):
    dequeued_node = self.data.pop_head()
    return dequeued_node.data
```

By implementing our queue with a doubly linked list, we can now both insert and delete from the queue at a speedy O(1). And that's doubly awesome.

Wrapping Up

As we've seen, the subtle differences between arrays and linked lists unlock new ways to make our code faster than ever.

By looking at linked lists, you've also learned the concept of nodes. However, the linked list is only the simplest of node-based data structures. In the coming chapters, you'll learn about node-based structures that are both more complex and more interesting—and that will reveal new worlds about how nodes can yield tremendous power and efficiency.

Exercises

The following exercises provide you with the opportunity to practice with linked lists. The solutions to these exercises are found in the section Chapter 14, on page 449.

1. Add a method to the classic LinkedList class that prints all the values of the list.

2. Add a method to the DoublyLinkedList class that prints all the values of the list in *reverse* order.

3. Add a method to the classic LinkedList class that returns the last value from the list. Assume you don't know how many elements are in the list.

4. Here's a tricky one. Add a method to the classic LinkedList class that reverses the list; that is, if the original list is A -> B -> C, all of the list's links should change so that C -> B -> A.

5. Here's a brilliant little linked list puzzle for you. Let's say you have access to a node from somewhere in the middle of a classic linked list but not to the linked list itself; that is, you have a variable that points to an instance of Node, but you don't have access to the LinkedList instance. In this situation, if you follow this node's link, you can find all the values from this middle node until the end, but you have no way to find the nodes that precede this node in the list.

    Write code that will effectively delete this node from the list. The entire remaining list should remain complete, with only this node removed.

CHAPTER 15

Speeding Up All the Things with Binary Search Trees

Sometimes, we may want to arrange our data in a specific order. For example, we may want an alphabetized list of names or a list of products in order of lowest price to highest.

While we can use a sorting algorithm such as Quicksort to arrange our data into perfect ascending order, it comes at a cost. As we've seen, even the fastest algorithms take O(N log N) time. So if we're going to want our data sorted *often*, it would be sensible to always keep our data in sorted order in the first place so that we never need to resort it.

An ordered array is a simple but effective tool for keeping data in order. It's also fast for certain operations, as it has O(1) reads and O(log N) search (when using binary search).

However, ordered arrays have a drawback.

When it comes to insertions and deletions, ordered arrays are relatively slow. Whenever a value is inserted into an ordered array, we first shift all greater values one cell to the right. And when a value is deleted from an ordered array, we shift all greater values one cell to the left. This takes N steps in a worst-case scenario (inserting into or deleting from the first cell of the array), and N / 2 steps on average. Either way, it's O(N), and O(N) is relatively slow for a simple insertion or deletion.

Now, if we were looking for a data structure that delivers all-around amazing speed, a hash table is a great choice. Hash tables are O(1) for search, insertion, and deletion. However, they don't maintain order, and order is what we need for our alphabetized-list application.

So what do we do if we want a data structure that maintains order yet *also* has fast search, insertion, and deletion? Neither an ordered array nor a hash table is ideal.

Enter the binary search tree.

Trees

You were introduced to node-based data structures in the previous chapter with linked lists. In a classic linked list, each node contains a link that connects the node to a single other node. A *tree* is also a node-based data structure, but within a tree each node can have links to *multiple* nodes.

Here is a visualization of a simple tree:

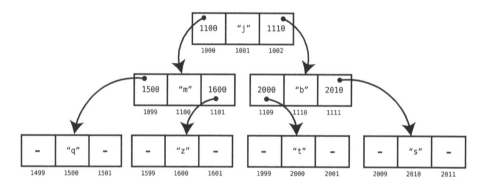

In this example, each node has links that lead to two other nodes. For the sake of simplicity, we can represent this tree visually without showing all the memory addresses:

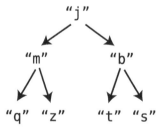

Trees come with their own unique nomenclature:

- The uppermost node (in our example, "j") is called the *root*. Yes, in our picture the root is at the *top* of the tree; it's how trees are typically depicted.

- In our example, we'd say that "j" is a *parent* to "m" and "b". Conversely, "m" and "b" are *children* of "j". Similarly, the "m" is a parent of "q" and "z", and "q" and "z" are children of "m".

- As in a family tree, a node can have *descendants* and *ancestors*. A node's descendants are *all* the nodes that stem from a node, while a node's ancestors are *all* the nodes that it stems from. In our example, "j" is the ancestor of all the other nodes in the tree, and all the other nodes are, therefore, descendants of "j".

- Trees are said to have *levels*. Each level is a row within the tree. Our example tree has three levels:

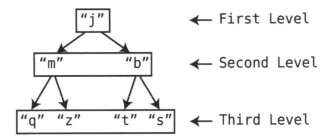

- One property of a tree is how *balanced* it is. A tree is balanced when its nodes' subtrees have the same number of nodes in it.

For instance, the preceding tree is said to be perfectly balanced. If you look at each node, its two subtrees have the same number of nodes. The root node ("j") has two subtrees, which each contain three nodes. You'll see that the same is also true for every node in the tree. For example, the "m" node also has two subtrees where the two subtrees each contain one node.

The following tree, on the other hand, is *imbalanced*:

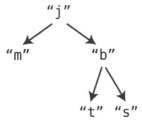

As you can see, the root's right subtree contains more nodes than its left subtree, causing an imbalance.

Binary Search Trees

Many different kinds of tree-based data structures exist, but in this chapter, we'll focus on a particular tree known as a *binary search tree*.

Note that there are two adjectives here: *binary* and *search*.

A *binary* tree is a tree in which each node has zero, one, or two children.

A binary *search* tree is a binary tree that also abides by the following rules:

- Each node can have at most one *left* child and one *right* child.
- A node's *left* descendants can only contain values that are less than the node itself. Likewise, a node's *right* descendants can only contain values that are greater than the node itself.

Here's an example of a binary search tree, in which the values are numbers:

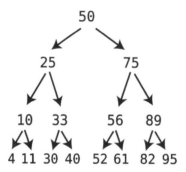

Note that each node has one child with a lesser value than itself, which is depicted using a left arrow, and one child with a greater value than itself, which is depicted using a right arrow.

Additionally, notice that all of the 50's left descendants are less than it. At the same time, all of the 50's right descendants are greater than it. The same pattern goes for each and every node.

While the following example is a binary tree, it's not a binary *search* tree:

It's a binary tree because each node has zero, one, or two children. But it's not a binary *search* tree, because the root node has two left children; that is, it has two children than are less than it. For a binary search tree to be valid, it can have at most one left (lesser) child and one right (greater) child.

The implementation of a tree node in Python might look something like this:

```python
class TreeNode:
    def __init__(self, value, left=None, right=None):
        self.value = value
        self.left_child = left
        self.right_child = right
```

We can then build a simple tree like this:

```python
node1 = TreeNode(25)
node2 = TreeNode(75)
root = TreeNode(50, node1, node2)
```

Because of the unique structure of a binary search tree, we can search for any value within it very quickly, as we'll now see.

Searching

Here, again, is a binary search tree:

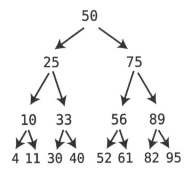

The algorithm for searching within a binary search tree is as follows:

1. Designate a node to be the *current node*. (At the beginning of the algorithm, the root node is the first current node.)

2. Inspect the value at the current node.

3. If we've found the value we're looking for, great!

4. If the value we're looking for is less than the current node, search for it in its left subtree.

5. If the value we're looking for is greater than the current node, search for it in its right subtree.

6. Repeat Steps 1 through 5 until we find the value we're searching for, or until we hit the bottom of the tree, in which case our value must not be in the tree.

Say we want to search for the 61. Let's see how many steps it would take, by walking through this visually.

When searching through a tree, we must always begin at the root:

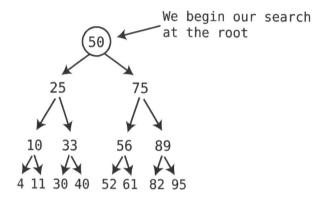

Next, the computer asks itself: is the number we're searching for (61) greater or less than the value of this node? If the number we're looking for is less than the current node, look for it in the left child. If it's greater than the current node, look for it in the right child.

In this example, because 61 is greater than 50, we know it must be somewhere to the right, so we search the right child. In the following picture, we've shaded out all the nodes we've eliminated from our search, since we know that the 61 cannot possibly be there:

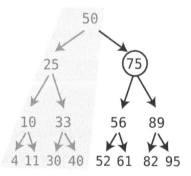

"Are you my mother?" asks the algorithm. Since the 75 is not the 61 we're looking for, we need to move down to the next level. And because 61 is less than 75, we'll check the left child, since the 61 could only be in that subtree, as shown in the diagram on page 253.

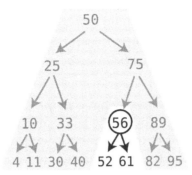

The 56 is not the 61 we're looking for, so we continue our search. Since 61 is greater than 56, we search for the 61 in the right child of the 56:

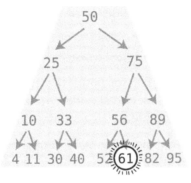

We found it! In this example, it took us four steps to find our desired value.

The Efficiency of Searching a Binary Search Tree

If you take another look at the steps we just walked through, you'll notice that each step eliminates half of the remaining nodes from our search. For example, when we begin our search, we start at the root node, and our desired value may be found among any of the root's descendants. However, when we then decide to continue the search with, say, the root's right child, we eliminate the left child and *all of its descendants* from the search.

We'd say, then, that searching in a binary search tree is O(log N), which is the apt description for any algorithm that eliminates half of the remaining values with each step. (We'll see soon, though, that this is only for a perfectly balanced binary search tree, which is a best-case scenario.)

Log(N) Levels

Here's yet another way of describing why search in a binary search tree is O(log N), which will reveal another property about binary trees in general: *if there are N nodes in a balanced binary tree, there will be about log N levels (that is, rows).*

To understand this, let's assume each row in the tree is completely filled with nodes, and that there aren't any empty positions. If you think about it, each time we add a new full level to the tree, we end up roughly doubling the number of nodes that the tree has. (Really, we're doubling the nodes and adding one.)

For example, a binary tree with four complete levels has fifteen nodes. (Go ahead, count them.) If we add a fifth complete level, that means we add two children to each of the eight nodes in the fourth level. This means we add sixteen new nodes, roughly doubling the size of the tree.

It emerges that each new level doubles the size of the tree. Accordingly, *a tree containing N nodes will require log(N) levels* to hold all the nodes.

In the context of binary search, we noted that the pattern of log(N) is that with each step of the search, we can eliminate half of the remaining data. The number of levels needed in a binary tree follows this pattern as well.

Let's take a binary tree that needs to hold thirty-one nodes. With our fifth level, we can hold sixteen of those nodes. This took care of roughly half of the data, leaving us with just fifteen nodes that we still need to find room for. With the fourth level, we take care of eight of those nodes, leaving us with seven unaccounted for. With the third level, we take care of four of those nodes, and so on.

Indeed, log 31 is (approximately) 5. So we've now concluded that a balanced tree with N nodes will have log(N) levels.

Since this is the case, it makes a lot of sense as to why searching a binary search tree takes up to log(N) steps: because each step of the search causes us to move down a level, we take up to as many steps as there are levels in the tree.

However you prefer to think about it, searching a binary search tree takes O(log N).

Now, while search in a binary search tree is O(log N), so is binary search within an ordered array, in which each number we select also eliminates half of the remaining possible values. In this regard, then, searching a binary search tree has the same efficiency as binary search within an ordered array.

Where binary search trees really shine over ordered arrays, though, is with insertion. We'll get to that soon.

Code Implementation: Searching a Binary Search Tree

To implement the search operation, as well as the other binary search tree operations, we're going to make heavy use of recursion. You learned back in Chapter 10, Recursively Recurse with Recursion, on page 149, that recursion is key when dealing with data structures that have an arbitrary number of levels of depth. A tree is such a data structure, as it can have an infinite number of levels.

Here's how we can use recursion to implement search with Python. While we could have alternatively used a loop instead, the recursive code for search is more concise and elegant:

```python
def search(search_value, node):
    if not node or node.value == search_value:
        return node

    elif search_value < node.value:
        return search(search_value, node.left_child)

    else:
        return search(search_value, node.right_child)
```

This search function accepts the search_value we're searching for and a node that we'll use as the base for our search. The first time we call search, the node will be the root node. However, in the subsequent recursive calls, the node may be another node within the tree.

Our function deals with four possible cases, two of which are the base cases:

```python
if not node or node.value == search_value:
    return node
```

One base case is when the node contains the search_value we're looking for, in which case we can return the node and not make any recursive calls.

The other base case is when there is no node. This will make more sense after we've examined the other cases, so let's come back to this shortly.

The next case is when the search_value is less than the value of the current node:

```python
elif search_value < node.value:
    return search(search_value, node.left_child)
```

In this case, we know that if it exists in the tree, the search_value will have to be found somewhere among this node's left descendants. So we recursively call the search function on this node's left child.

The next case is the inverse; it's when the search_value is greater than the current node:

```
else:
    return search(search_value, node.right_child)
```

In this case, we recursively call search on the current node's right child.

Now, when we make these recursive calls on the current node's children, note that we didn't check whether the current node even has any children. That's where the first base case comes in:

```
if not node
```

That is to say, if it turns out that we called search on a child node that doesn't actually exist, we end up returning None (since the node variable will actually contain None). This case will happen if the search_value doesn't exist within our tree, as we'll try to access the node where the search_value *should* be found, but our search hits a dead end. In this case, it's appropriate that we return None, indicating that the search_value is not within the tree.

Insertion

As I mentioned earlier, binary search trees are at their best when it comes to insertion. Now we'll see why.

Say we want to insert the number 45 into our example tree. The first thing we'd have to do is find the correct node to attach the 45 to. To begin our search, we start at the root:

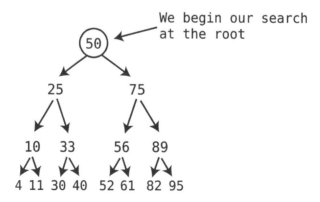

Since 45 is less than 50, we drill down to the left child:

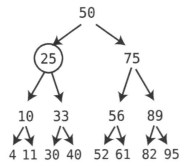

Since 45 is greater than 25, we must inspect the right child:

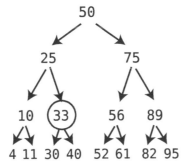

Since 45 is greater than 33, we check the 33's right child:

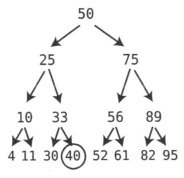

At this point, we've reached a node that has no children, so we have nowhere to go. This means we're ready to perform our insertion.

Since 45 is greater than 40, we insert it as a right child of the 40:

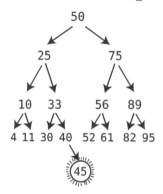

In this example, insertion took five steps, consisting of four search steps plus one insertion step. Insertion always takes just one extra step beyond a search, which means insertion takes (log N) + 1 steps. In Big O notation, which ignores constants, this is O(log N).

In an ordered array, by contrast, insertion takes O(N), because in addition to search, we must shift a lot of data to the right to make room for the value we're inserting.

This is what makes binary search trees so efficient. While ordered arrays have O(log N) search and O(N) insertion, binary search trees have O(log N) search *and* O(log N) insertion. This becomes critical in an application in which you anticipate a lot of changes to your data.

Code Implementation: Binary Search Tree Insertion

Here's a Python implementation of inserting a new value into a binary search tree. Like the search function, it's recursive:

```python
import tree_node

def insert(value, node):
    if value < node.value:

        if not node.left_child:
            node.left_child = tree_node.TreeNode(value)
        else:
            insert(value, node.left_child)

    elif value > node.value:

        if not node.right_child:
            node.right_child = tree_node.TreeNode(value)
        else:
            insert(value, node.right_child)
```

The insert function accepts a value that we're going to insert and a node that serves as the ancestor node for which our value will become a descendant.

First, we check whether the value is less than the value of the current node:

```
if value < node.value:
```

If the value is less than the node, we know that we need to insert the value somewhere among the left descendants of the node.

We then check to see whether the current node has a left child. If the node doesn't have a left child, we make the value into the left child, since that's exactly where the value belongs:

```
if not node.left_child:
    node.left_child = tree_node.TreeNode(value)
```

This is the base case, since we don't need to make any recursive calls.

However, if the node already has a left child, we can't place the value there. Instead, we recursively call insert on the left child so that we continue to search for the spot in which we'll place the value:

```
else:
    insert(value, node.left_child)
```

Eventually, we'll hit a descendant node that doesn't have its own child, and that's where the value is going to go.

The rest of the function is the exact inverse; it handles cases where the value is greater than the current node.

The Order of Insertion

It's important to note that only when creating a tree out of randomly sorted data do trees usually wind up being well-balanced. However, if we insert *sorted* data into a tree, it can become imbalanced and less efficient. For example, if we were to insert the following data in this order—1, 2, 3, 4, 5—we'd end up with a tree that looks like this:

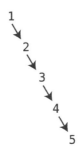

This tree is completely linear, so searching for the 5 within this tree would take O(N).

However, if we inserted the same data in the following order—3, 2, 4, 1, 5—the tree would be evenly balanced:

Only with a balanced tree does search take O(log N).

Because of this, if you ever want to convert an ordered array into a binary search tree, you'd want to first randomize the order of the data.

It emerges that in a worst-case scenario, when a tree is completely *imbalanced*, search is O(N). In a best-case scenario, when it is perfectly balanced, search is O(log N). In the typical scenario, in which data is inserted in random order, a tree will be pretty well balanced and search will take about O(log N).

Deletion

Deletion is the least straightforward operation within a binary search tree and requires some careful maneuvering.

Let's say we want to delete the 4 from this binary search tree:

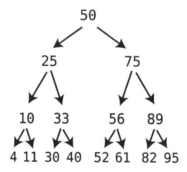

First, we perform a search to find the 4. We won't visualize this search again, since you've already got that down.

Once we find the 4, we can delete it in one step:

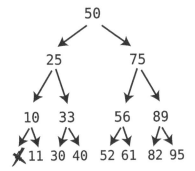

Well, that was simple. But let's see what happens when we try to delete the 10:

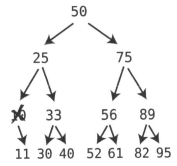

We end up with an 11 that isn't connected to the tree anymore. And we can't have that, because we'd lose the 11 forever.

However, to solve this problem, we can plug the 11 into where the 10 used to be:

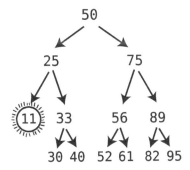

So far, our deletion algorithm follows these rules:

- If the node being deleted has no children, simply delete it.
- If the node being deleted has one child, delete the node and plug the child into the spot where the deleted node was.

Deleting a Node with Two Children

Deleting a node that has two children is the most complex scenario. Let's say we want to delete the 56 in this tree:

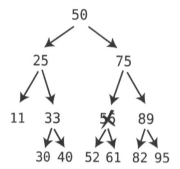

What are we going to do with its former children, 52 and 61? We can't move *both* of them to where the 56 was. This is where the next rule of the deletion algorithm comes into play:

- When deleting a node with two children, replace the deleted node with the *successor* node. The successor node is the child node whose value is the *least of all values that are greater than the deleted node.*

That was a tricky sentence. To put it in other words: if we were to put the deleted node and all of its descendants in ascending order, the successor node would be the next number after the one we just deleted.

In this case, it's easy to figure out which node is the successor since the deleted node had only two descendants. If we put the numbers 52-56-61 in ascending order, the next number after 56 is 61.

Once we find the successor node, we plug it into where the deleted node was. So we replace the 56 with the 61:

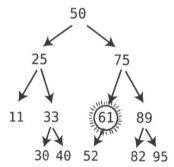

Finding the Successor Node

How does the computer find the successor node? This can be tricky when we delete a node high up in the tree.

Here's the algorithm for finding the successor node:

- Visit the right child of the deleted value, and then keep on visiting the left child of each subsequent child until there are no more left children. The bottom value is the successor node.

Let's see this again in action in a more complex example. Let's delete the root node:

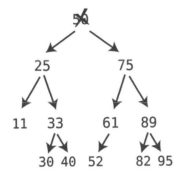

We now need to plug the successor node into where the 50 was and turn it into the root node. So let's find the successor node.

To do this, we first visit the *right* child of the deleted node, and then keep descending *leftward* until we reach a node that doesn't have a left child:

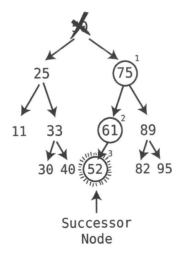

Successor
Node

It turns out that the 52 is the successor node.

Now that we've found the successor node, we plug it into the node we deleted:

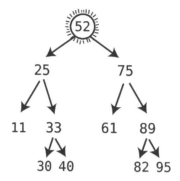

And we're done!

Successor Node with a Right Child

We haven't accounted for one case yet, though, and that's where the successor node has a right child of its own. Let's re-create the preceding tree but add a right child to the 52:

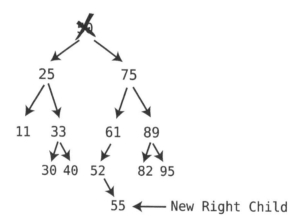

In this case, we can't simply plug the successor node—the 52—into the root, since we'd leave its child of 55 hanging. This leads us to one more rule for our deletion algorithm:

- If the successor node has a right child, after plugging the successor node into the spot of the deleted node, take the former right child of the successor node and place it where the successor node used to be.

That was another tricky sentence, so let's walk through the steps.

First, we plug the successor node (52) into the root. This leaves the 55 dangling without a parent:

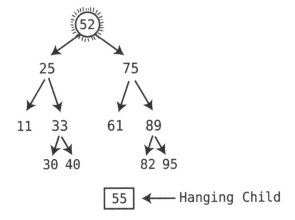

Next, we place the 55 in the spot where the successor node used to be, which is the left child of the 61:

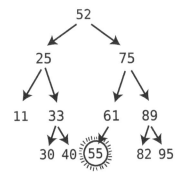

Successor Node is a Right Child

It can sometimes happen that the successor node is *itself* a right child. And sometimes this successor node can have a right child of its own. For example, in the following tree, if we delete the 3, the 4 becomes the successor node, since the 4 has no left children:

Here, when we plug the successor node into the spot where the deleted 3 was, we don't make the 5 dangling and reattach it elsewhere. Instead, we simply keep the 5 as the 4's right child.

And now we're *really* done.

The Complete Deletion Algorithm

Putting all the steps together, here is the algorithm for deletion from a binary search tree:

- If the node being deleted has no children, simply delete it.

- If the node being deleted has one child, delete the node and plug the child into the spot where the deleted node was.

- When deleting a node with two children, replace the deleted node with the *successor* node. The successor node is the child node whose value is the *least of all values that are greater than the deleted node.*

- To find the successor node: visit the right child of the deleted node, and then keep on visiting the left child of each subsequent child until there are no more left children. The bottom node is the successor node. If the deleted node's right child has no left children, the deleted node's right child itself becomes the successor node.

- If the successor node has a right child (and the successor node was itself a left child of its parent), after plugging the successor node into the spot of the deleted node, take the former right child of the successor node and turn it into the *left child of the former parent of the successor node.*

Code Implementation: Binary Search Tree Deletion

Here's a Python implementation of deletion from a binary search tree. The primary method here is delete, which in turn relies on a helper method called replace_with_successor_node:

```python
def replace_with_successor_node(node):
    successor_node = node.right_child

    if not successor_node.left_child:
        node.value = successor_node.value
        node.right_child = successor_node.right_child
        return

    while successor_node.left_child:
        parent_of_successor_node = successor_node
        successor_node = successor_node.left_child
```

```
    if successor_node.right_child:
        parent_of_successor_node.left_child = successor_node.right_child
    else:
        parent_of_successor_node.left_child = None

    node.value = successor_node.value
    return successor_node

def delete(value_to_delete, node):
    current_node = node
    parent_of_current_node = None
    node_to_delete = None

    while current_node:
        if current_node.value == value_to_delete:
            node_to_delete = current_node
            break

        parent_of_current_node = current_node
        if value_to_delete < current_node.value:
            current_node = current_node.left_child
        elif value_to_delete > current_node.value:
            current_node = current_node.right_child

    if not node_to_delete:
        return None

    if node_to_delete.left_child and node_to_delete.right_child:
        replace_with_successor_node(node_to_delete)
    else:  # deleted node has 0 or 1 children

        child_of_deleted_node = (node_to_delete.left_child or
                                 node_to_delete.right_child)

        if not parent_of_current_node:
            node_to_delete.value = child_of_deleted_node.value
            node_to_delete.left_child = child_of_deleted_node.left_child
            node_to_delete.right_child = child_of_deleted_node.right_child
        elif node_to_delete == parent_of_current_node.left_child:
            parent_of_current_node.left_child = child_of_deleted_node
        elif node_to_delete == parent_of_current_node.right_child:
            parent_of_current_node.right_child = child_of_deleted_node

    return node_to_delete
```

That's a decent amount of code, but we'll walk through it step by step.

In contrast with search and insertion, we wrote the deletion code *without* recursion. While we could have written the deletion method recursively, I find that the recursive code for deletion is considerably more difficult to grasp. Instead, we use a loop to move about the tree.

Let's begin by walking through the delete method.

When we call this method, we pass in the value we'd like to delete (value_to_delete) as well as the root node of the tree (node).

At first, we set three variables:

```
current_node = node
parent_of_current_node = None
node_to_delete = None
```

The current_node initially points to the root but will be updated as we move down the tree looking for the value we are to delete. The parent_of_current_node is, as the name implies, the parent of the current_node. The reason we need to track this will become apparent later on. Finally, the node_to_delete will *eventually* point to the node we'll be deleting, but until we find that node, this variable is set to None.

We then begin a loop that searches for the value_to_delete within the tree. This is essentially a search operation, but again, this time we use iteration instead of recursion:

```
while current_node:
    if current_node.value == value_to_delete:
        node_to_delete = current_node
        break

    parent_of_current_node = current_node
    if value_to_delete < current_node.value:
        current_node = current_node.left_child
    elif value_to_delete > current_node.value:
        current_node = current_node.right_child
```

This snippet moves down through the tree, updating current_node as we go, searching for the value_to_delete. If we don't find it, which will be the case if the value is not present in the tree, the loop will terminate on its own because current_node will be None.

If, however, we *do* find the value_to_delete, we declare the current_node to be the node_to_delete and break out of the loop. Note that we also keep track of the parent_of_current_node, which is now the parent of the node we'll be deleting.

Next, we have this snippet:

```
if not node_to_delete:
    return None
```

This returns None if the value we'd like to delete isn't even in our tree to begin with.

The remainder of this method performs the actual deletion. We first handle the most complex case, where the node we're deleting has two children:

```
if node_to_delete.left_child and node_to_delete.right_child:
    replace_with_successor_node(node_to_delete)
```

Here, we outsource the heavy lifting to the replace_with_successor_node helper method, which we'll analyze soon. In the meantime, though, let's move on.

Next, we handle the case in which the deleted node has 0 or 1 children:

```
else:  # deleted node has 0 or 1 children
    child_of_deleted_node = (node_to_delete.left_child or
                            node_to_delete.right_child)

    if not parent_of_current_node:
        node_to_delete.value = child_of_deleted_node.value
        node_to_delete.left_child = child_of_deleted_node.left_child
        node_to_delete.right_child = child_of_deleted_node.right_child
    elif node_to_delete == parent_of_current_node.left_child:
        parent_of_current_node.left_child = child_of_deleted_node
    elif node_to_delete == parent_of_current_node.right_child:
        parent_of_current_node.right_child = child_of_deleted_node
```

Here, we first set a new variable called child_of_deleted_node, which will represent the deleted node's child. In a case where the deleted node had no children, this variable will be set to None. This variable is crucial, for when we delete our node_to_delete, we need to place its child in the spot where the deleted node used to be.

And that's exactly what the code above does in the two elif clauses. It determines whether the deleted node was a left or right child of its parent, and attaches the child_of_deleted_node to the deleted node's parent accordingly.

The first clause in the if statement handles the case where we're deleting the root node. To ensure that we mark the deleted root's child as the new root, we overwrite the root with its child.

This brings us to the final line of our method, which simply returns the deleted node in case we may want to use it for some other purpose:

```
return node_to_delete
```

Let's now return to the case where the deleted node had two children. Our previous code called the helper method replace_with_successor_node, so let's walk through that now.

When calling this method, we pass in the node that we'll be deleting, which will be called node.

Next, we identify the successor node using the following code:

```
successor_node = node.right_child

if not successor_node.left_child:
    node.value = successor_node.value
    node.right_child = successor_node.right_child
    return

while successor_node.left_child:
    parent_of_successor_node = successor_node
    successor_node = successor_node.left_child
```

Here, we begin at the deleted node's right child, and then move down the tree following left children until we can't go any further. That bottom node is our successor node. We also keep track of the successor node's parent.

However, in the case that the successor node happens to be the deleted node's right child (which occurs when the deleted node's right child has no left children), we simply plug the successor node into the spot where the deleted node was. If this is the case, this is all we need to do. But if the successor node is a left child of its parent, we move on.

Next, we remove the successor node from its spot:

```
if successor_node.right_child:
    parent_of_successor_node.left_child = successor_node.right_child
else:
    parent_of_successor_node.left_child = None
```

Our code deals with two possible cases. The second case (in the else clause) is the simpler case, which is when the successor node had no children. In that case, we wipe away the successor node by replacing it with None.

In the more complex case, where the successor node has a right child, we place that right child in the spot where the successor node used to be.

We've successfully removed the successor node from the tree, but there's one more critical step. Remember we didn't initially set out to delete the successor node. Our entire goal was to delete the node from higher up in the tree.

To do that, we plug the successor node into the spot of the node we're deleting:

```
node.value = successor_node.value
```

Note that we don't plug in the actual successor node; instead, we simply use its value to overwrite the value of node, effectively deleting node.

And that's it! It was a journey, but we did it.

The Efficiency of Binary Search Tree Deletion

Like search and insertion, deleting from trees is also typically O(log N). This is because deletion requires a search plus a few extra steps to deal with any hanging children. Contrast this with deleting a value from an ordered array, which is O(N) due to shifting elements to the left to close the gap of the deleted value.

Binary Search Trees in Action

We've seen that binary search trees boast efficiencies of O(log N) for search, insertion, and deletion, making it an efficient choice for scenarios in which we need to store and manipulate ordered data. This is particularly true if we'll be modifying the data often, because while ordered arrays are just as fast as binary search trees when searching data, binary search trees are significantly faster when it comes to inserting and deleting data.

For example, let's say we're creating an application that maintains a list of book titles. We'd want our application to have the following functionality:

- Our program should be able to print the list of book titles in alphabetical order.

- Our program should allow for constant changes to the list.

- Our program should allow the user to search for a title within the list.

If we didn't anticipate that our book list would be changing that often, an ordered array would be a suitable data structure to contain our data. However, we're building an app that should be able to handle many changes in real time. If our list had millions of titles, a binary search tree may be a better choice.

Such a tree might look something like this:

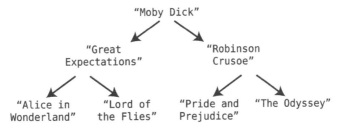

Here, the titles are positioned based on their alphabetical order. A title that comes earlier in the alphabet is considered a "lower" value, while titles that come later are "greater" values.

Binary Search Tree Traversal

Now, we've already seen how to search, insert, and delete data from a binary search tree. I mentioned, though, that we also want to be able to print the entire list of book titles in alphabetical order. How can we do that?

First, we need the ability to *visit* every single node in the tree. *Visiting* nodes is another term for accessing them. The process of visiting every node in a data structure is known as *traversing* the data structure.

Second, we need to make sure we traverse the tree in alphabetically ascending order so that we can print the list in that order. You can traverse a tree in multiple ways, but for this application, we'll perform what is known as *inorder traversal*, so that we can print each title in alphabetical order.

Recursion is a great tool for performing traversal. We'll create a recursive function called traverse that can be called on a particular node. The function then performs the following steps:

1. Call itself (traverse) recursively on the node's left child. The function will keep getting called until we hit a node that does not have a left child.

2. Visit the node. (For our book title app, we print the value of the node at this step.)

3. Call itself (traverse) recursively on the node's right child. The function will keep getting called until we hit a node that does not have a right child.

For this recursive algorithm, the base case is when we call traverse on a child that does not exist, in which case we return without doing anything further.

Here's a Python traverse_and_print function that works for our list of book titles. Note how concise it is:

```python
def traverse_and_print(node):
    if not node:
        return
    traverse_and_print(node.left_child)
    print(node.value)
    traverse_and_print(node.right_child)
```

Let's walk through the inorder traversal step by step.

We first call traverse_and_print on "Moby Dick". This, in turn, calls traverse_and_print on the left child of "Moby Dick", which is "Great Expectations":

```python
traverse_and_print(node.left_child)
```

Before we move on to that, though, we're going to add to the call stack the fact that we're in the middle of the function in "Moby Dick" and the fact that we're in the middle of traversing its left child:

"Moby Dick": left child

We then proceed with traverse_and_print("Great Expectations"), which calls traverse_and_print on the left child of "Great Expectations", which is "Alice in Wonderland".

Let's add traverse_and_print("Great Expectations") to the call stack before moving on:

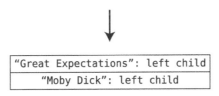

"Great Expectations": left child
"Moby Dick": left child

The traverse_and_print("Alice in Wonderland") calls traverse_and_print on the left child of "Alice in Wonderland". However, there *isn't* any left child (the base case), so nothing happens. The next line of traverse_and_print is the following:

print(node.value)

This line prints "Alice in Wonderland".

Next, the function attempts to traverse_and_print the *right* child of "Alice in Wonderland":

traverse_and_print(node.right_child)

However, there's no right child (the base case), so the function returns without doing anything further.

Since we've completed the function traverse_and_print("Alice in Wonderland"), we check the call stack to see where we're up to in this recursive soup:

"Great Expectations": left child
"Moby Dick": left child

Ah, that's right. We were in the middle of traverse_and_print("Great Expectations"), and we had just completed calling traverse_and_print on its left child. Let's pop this from the call stack:

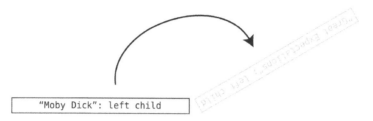

And let's continue. The function next prints "Great Expectations" and then calls traverse_and_print on the right child, which is "Lord of the Flies". Before moving on to that, though, let's hold our place within this function in the call stack:

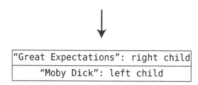

We now execute traverse_and_print("Lord of the Flies"). First, we call traverse_and_print on its left child, but it doesn't have one. Next, we print "Lord of the Flies". Finally, we call traverse_and_print on its right child, but that doesn't exist either, so the function is now done.

We look at our call stack and see that we were in the process of executing traverse_and_print on the right child of "Great Expectations". We can pop that from the stack and continue as shown in the following diagram:

Now, it just so happens that we've also now completed everything we have to do in traverse_and_print("Great Expectations"), so we can go back to the call stack to see what to do next:

We can see that we were in the middle of traverse_and_print of the left child of "Moby Dick". We can pop that from the call stack (which leaves the stack empty for now) and continue with the next step within traverse_and_print("Moby Dick"), which is to print "Moby Dick".

Then, we call traverse_and_print on the right child of "Moby Dick". We'll add this to the call stack:

For the sake of brevity (although it's probably too late for that), I'll let you walk through the rest of the traverse_and_print function from here.

By the time our function has finished executing, we'll have printed the nodes in this order:

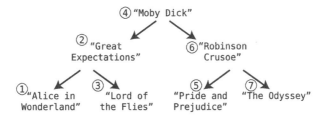

And that's how we achieve our goal of printing the book titles in alphabetical order. Note that tree traversal is O(N), since by definition, traversal visits all N nodes of the tree.

Wrapping Up

The binary search tree is a powerful node-based data structure that provides order maintenance, while also offering fast search, insertion, and deletion. It's more complex than its linked list cousin, but it offers tremendous value.

However, the binary search tree is just one type of tree. Trees are of many different kinds, and each type brings unique advantages to specialized situations. In the next chapter, we're going to discover another tree that will bring unique speed advantages to a specific, but common, scenario.

Exercises

The following exercises provide you with the opportunity to practice with binary search trees. The solutions to these exercises are found in the section Chapter 15, on page 452.

1. Imagine you were to take an empty binary search tree and insert the following sequence of numbers in this order: [1, 5, 9, 2, 4, 10, 6, 3, 8].

   Draw a diagram showing what the binary search tree would look like. Remember, the numbers are being inserted in the order presented here.

2. If a well-balanced binary search tree contains 1,000 values, what is the maximum number of steps it would take to search for a value within it?

3. Write an algorithm that finds the greatest value within a binary search tree.

4. In the text, I demonstrated how to use *inorder* traversal to print a list of all the book titles. Another way to traverse a tree is known as *preorder* traversal. Here's the code for it as applied to our book app:

```
def traverse_and_print(node):
    if not node:
        return
    print(node.value)
    traverse_and_print(node.left_child)
    traverse_and_print(node.right_child)
```

   For the example tree in the text (the one with "Moby Dick" and the other book titles), write out the order in which the book titles are printed with preorder traversal. As a reminder, here's the example tree:

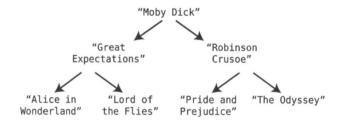

5. Yet another form of traversal is called *postorder* traversal. Here's the code as applied to our book app:

```
def traverse_and_print(node):
    if not node:
        return
    traverse_and_print(node.left_child)
    traverse_and_print(node.right_child)
    print(node.value)
```

   For the example tree in the text (which also appears in the previous exercise), write out the order in which the book titles are printed with postorder traversal.

CHAPTER 16

Keeping Your Priorities Straight with Heaps

Now that we've discovered the tree, we've unlocked many new data structures. In the previous chapter, we focused specifically on the binary search tree, but there are many other types of trees as well. Like all data structures, each type of tree comes with its own benefits and drawbacks, and the trick is knowing which one to harness in a specific situation.

In this chapter, we'll explore the heap, a type of tree data structure that has special powers that can be leveraged for specific scenarios, in particular when we want to constantly keep tabs on the greatest or least data element in a dataset.

To appreciate what a heap can do, let's take a look at a completely different data structure: the priority queue.

Priority Queues

You learned about Queues, on page 143, and discovered that the queue is a list in which items are processed first in, first out (FIFO). Essentially, this means that data is inserted only at the *end* of the queue, and data is accessed and removed only from the *front* of the queue. In accessing the queue's data, we give precedence to the order in which the data was inserted.

A *priority queue* is a list whose deletions and access are just like a classic queue but whose insertions are like an ordered array. So we only delete and access data from the *front* of the priority queue, but when we insert data, we always make sure the data remains sorted in a specific order.

One classic example of where a priority queue is helpful is an application that manages the triage system for a hospital emergency room. In the ER, we don't treat people strictly in the order in which they arrived. Instead, we treat people in the order of the severity of their symptoms. If someone suddenly arrives with a life-threatening injury, that patient will be placed at the front of the queue, even if the person with the flu had arrived hours earlier.

Let's say our triage system ranked the severity of a patient's condition on a scale of 1 to 10, with 10 being the most critical. Our priority queue may look like this:

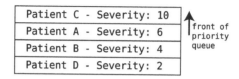

In determining the next patient to treat, we'll always select the patient at the front of the priority queue, since that person's need is the most urgent. In this case, the next patient we'd treat is Patient C.

If a new patient now arrives with a condition severity of 3, we'll initially place this patient at the appropriate spot within the priority queue. We'll call this person Patient E:

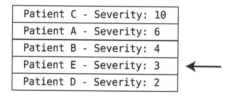

The priority queue is an example of an abstract data type—one that can be implemented using other, more fundamental, data structures. One straightforward way we can implement a priority queue is by using an ordered array; that is, we use an array and apply the following constraints:

- When we insert data, we ensure we always maintain proper order.
- Data can only be removed from the end of the array. (This will represent the front of the priority queue.)

This approach is straightforward, but now let's analyze its efficiency.

The priority queue has two primary operations: deletions and insertions.

We saw in Chapter 1, Why Data Structures Matter, on page 1, that deleting from the front of an array is O(N), since we have to shift all the data over to fill the gap created at index 0. However, we've cleverly tweaked our implementation so that we consider the *end* of the array to be the *front* of the priority queue. This way, we're always deleting from the end of the array, which is O(1).

With O(1) deletions, our priority queue is in good shape so far. But what about insertions?

You learned that inserting into an ordered array is O(N), since we have to inspect up to all N elements of the array to determine where our new data should go. (And even if we find the correct spot early, we need to then shift all the remaining data over to the right.)

Our array-based priority queue, then, has deletions that are O(1) and insertions that are O(N). If we expect there to be many items in our priority queue, the O(N) insertions may cause some real unwanted drag in our application.

Because of this, computer scientists discovered another data structure that serves as a more efficient foundation for the priority queue. This data structure is the heap.

Heaps

Heaps are of several different types, but we're going to focus on the *binary heap*.

The binary heap is a specific kind of binary tree. As a reminder, a binary tree is a tree where each node has a maximum of two child nodes. (The binary *search* tree from the last chapter was one specific type of binary tree.)

Now, even binary heaps come in two flavors: the max-heap and the min-heap. We're going to work with the max-heap for now, but as you'll see later, the difference between the two is trivial.

Going forward, I'm going to refer to this data structure simply as a heap, even though we're specifically working with a binary max-heap.

The *heap* is a binary tree that maintains the following conditions:

- The value of each node must be greater than each of its descendant nodes. This rule is known as the *heap condition*.

- The tree must be *complete*. (I'll explain the meaning of this shortly.)

Let's break down both of these conditions, starting with the heap condition.

The Heap Condition

The *heap condition* says that each node's value must be greater than each and every one of its descendants.

For example, the following tree meets the heap condition since each node is greater than any of its descendants, as shown in the diagram on page 280.

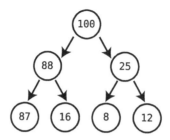

In this example, the root node of 100 has no descendant that is greater than it. Similarly, the 88 is greater than both of its children, and so is the 25.

The following tree isn't a valid heap, because it doesn't meet the heap condition:

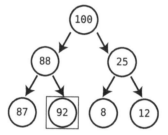

As you can see, the 92 is greater than its parent of 88. This violates the heap condition.

Note how the heap is structured very differently than the binary search tree. In a binary search tree, each node's right child is greater than it. In a heap, however, a node *never* has any descendant that is greater than it. As they say, "A binary search tree doth not a heap make." (Or something like that.)

We can also construct a heap that has the opposite heap condition, which is each node must contain a *smaller* value than any of its descendants. Such a heap is known as the min-heap, which I mentioned earlier. We're going to continue to focus on the max-heap, where each node must be *greater* than all of its descendants. Ultimately, whether a heap is a max-heap or a min-heap is trivial, as everything else about both heaps is identical; they only have reversed heap conditions. Otherwise, the fundamental idea is the same.

Complete Trees

Now, let's get to the second rule of heaps—that the tree needs to be complete.

A *complete tree* is a tree that is completely filled with nodes; no nodes are missing. So if you read each level of the tree from left to right, all of the nodes are there. However, the bottom row *can* have empty positions, as long as there aren't any nodes to the right of these empty positions. This is best demonstrated with examples.

The following tree is complete, since each level (meaning, each row) of the tree is completely filled in with nodes:

The following tree is *not* complete, since there's an empty position on the third level (and other nodes exist on the third level to the right of that empty position):

Now, the next tree is actually considered complete, since its empty positions are limited to the bottom row, and there aren't any nodes found to the right of the empty positions:

A heap, then, is a tree that meets the heap condition *and* is also complete. Here's one more example of a heap:

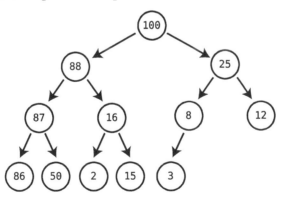

This is a valid heap since each node is greater than any of its descendants, and the tree is also complete. While it does have some gaps in the bottom row, these gaps are limited to the very right of the tree.

Heap Properties

Now that you know what a heap is, let's examine some of its interesting properties.

While the heap condition dictates that the heap be ordered a certain way, this ordering is still useless when it comes to searching for a value within the heap.

For example, let's say that in the above heap, we want to search for the value 3. If we start at the root node of 100, should we search among its left or right descendants? In a binary search tree, we'd know that the 3 must be among the 100's left descendants. In a heap, however, all we know is that the 3 has to be a descendant of the 100, and can't be its ancestor. But we'd have no idea as to which child node to search next. Indeed, the 3 happens to be among the 100's *right* descendants, but it could have also easily been among its left descendants.

Because of this, heaps are said to be *weakly ordered* as compared to binary search trees. While heaps have *some* order, as descendants cannot be greater than their ancestors, this isn't enough order to make heaps worth searching through.

Another property of heaps, that may be obvious by now but is worth calling attention to, is in a heap, the root node will always have the *greatest* value. (In a min-heap, the root will contain the smallest value.) This will be the key as to why the heap is a great tool for implementing priority queues. In the priority queue, we always want to access the value with the greatest priority. With a heap, we always know that we can find this in the root node. Thus, the root node will represent the item with the highest priority.

The heap has two primary operations: inserting and deleting. As we noted, searching within a heap would require us to inspect each node, so search isn't an operation usually implemented in the context of heaps. (A heap can also have an optional read operation, which would simply look at the value of the root node.)

Before we move on to how the heap's primary operations work, let me define one more term, since it'll be used heavily in the upcoming algorithms.

The heap has something called a *last node*. A heap's *last node* is the rightmost node in its bottom level.

Take a look at the heap on page 283.

In this heap, the 3 is the last node, since it's the rightmost node in the bottom row.

Next, let's get into the heap's primary operations.

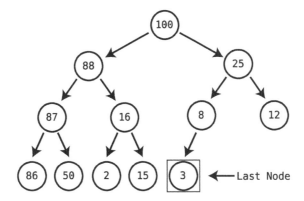

Heap Insertion

To insert a new value into the heap, we perform the following algorithm:

1. We create a node containing the new value and insert it at the next available rightmost spot in the bottom level. Thus, this value becomes the heap's last node.

2. Next, we compare this new node with its parent node.

3. If the new node is greater than its parent node, we swap the new node with the parent node.

4. We repeat Step 3, effectively moving the new node up through the heap, until the new node has a parent whose value is greater than it.

Let's see this algorithm in action. Here's what would happen if we were to insert a 40 into the heap.

Step 1: We add the 40 as the heap's last node:

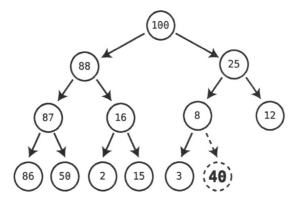

Note that doing the following would have been incorrect:

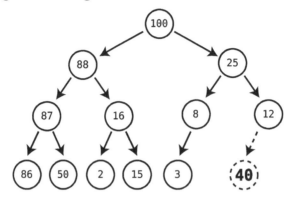

Placing the 40 as a child of the 12 node makes the tree *incomplete* since we'd now have a node to the right of an empty position. For a heap to remain a heap, it must always be complete.

Step 2: We compare the 40 with its parent node, which happens to be the 8. Since the 40 is greater than the 8, we swap the two nodes:

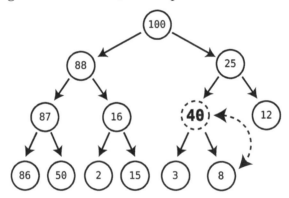

Step 3: We compare the 40 with its new parent, the 25. Since the 40 is greater than the 25, we swap them:

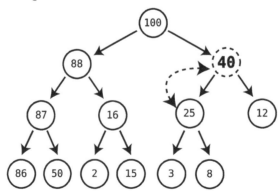

Step 4: We compare the 40 to its parent, which is the 100. Since the 40 is smaller than the 100, we're done!

This process of moving the new node up the heap, is called *trickling* the node up through the heap. Sometimes it moves up to the right, and sometimes it moves up to the left, but it always moves up until it settles into the correct position.

The efficiency of inserting into a heap is O(log N). As you saw in the previous chapter, for N nodes in any binary tree, the tree is organized into about log(N) rows. Since at most we'd have to trickle the new value up to the top row, this will take log(N) steps at most.

Looking for the Last Node

While the insertion algorithm seems straightforward, there's one little snag. The first step has us place the new value as the heap's last node. But this begs the question: how do we find the spot that will be the last node?

Let's take a look again at the heap before we inserted the 40:

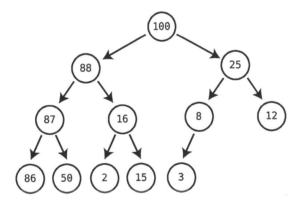

We know by looking at the diagram that to make the 40 into the last node, we'd make it the right child of the 8, as that's the next available spot in the bottom row.

But a computer doesn't have eyeballs and doesn't see the heap as a bunch of rows. All it sees is the root node, and it can follow links to child nodes. So how do we create an algorithm for the computer to find the spot for the new value?

Take our example heap. When we start at the root node of 100, do we tell the computer to look among the 100's right descendants to find the next available spot for the new last node?

While it's true that in our example heap the next available spot is among the 100's right descendants, take a look at the following alternative heap:

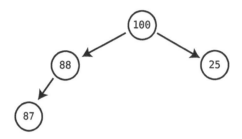

In this heap, the next available spot for the new last node would be the 88's right child, which is among the 100's *left* descendants.

Essentially, then, just as it's impossible to search through a heap, it's impossible to efficiently find the heap's last node (or next available spot to hold a new last node) without having to inspect each and every node.

So how *do* we find the next available node? I'll explain this later on, but for now, let's call this issue the *problem of the last node*. I promise we'll come back to it.

In the meantime, let's explore the heap's other primary operation, which is deletion.

Heap Deletion

The first thing to know about deleting a value from a heap is that *we only ever delete the root node.* This is right in line with the way a priority queue works, in that we only access and remove the highest-priority item.

The algorithm for deleting the root node of a heap is as follows:

1. Move the *last node* into where the root node was, effectively removing the original root node.

2. Trickle the root node down into its proper place. I'll explain how trickling down works shortly.

Let's say we're going to remove the root node from the heap on page 287.

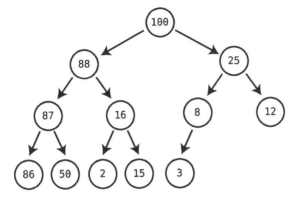

In this example, the root node is the 100. To delete it, we overwrite the root by placing the last node there instead. In this case, the last node is the 3. So we move the 3 and place it where the 100 was:

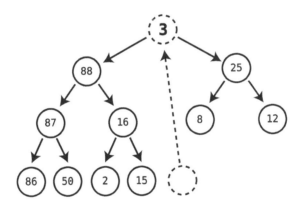

Now, we can't leave the heap as is, because the heap condition has been violated since the 3 is currently less than some (actually, most) of its descendants. To make things right again, we need to trickle the 3 down until its heap condition has been restored.

Trickling down is a tad more complex than trickling up, since each time we trickle a node down, we have two possible directions as to where we'll trickle it down; that is, we can either swap it with its left child or its right child. (When trickling up, on the other hand, each node has only one parent to swap with.)

Here's the algorithm for trickling *down*. For the sake of clarity, we're going to call the node we're trickling the "trickle node." (Sounds gross, I know.)

1. We check both children of the trickle node and see which one is larger.

2. If the trickle node is smaller than the larger of the two child nodes, we swap the trickle node with that larger child.

3. We repeat Steps 1 and 2 until the trickle node has no children who are greater than it.

Let's see this in action.

Step 1: The 3, which is the trickle node, currently has two children, the 88 and the 25. The 88 is larger of the two, and since the 3 is smaller than the 88, we swap the trickle node with the 88:

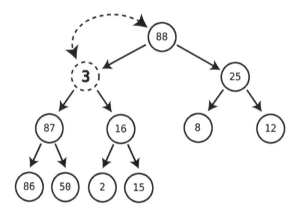

Step 2: The trickle node now has two new children, the 87 and the 16. The 87 is the larger one, and it's greater than the trickle node. So we swap the trickle node with the 87:

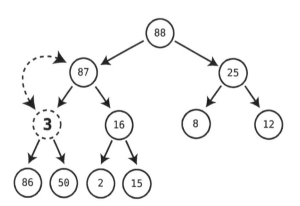

Step 3: The trickle node's children are currently the 86 and the 50. The 86 is the larger of the two, and it's also greater than the trickle node, so we swap the 86 with the trickle node:

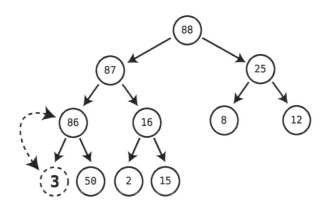

At this point, the trickle node has no children that are greater than it. (In fact, it has no children at all.) So we're done, as the heap condition has been restored.

The reason why we always swap the trickle node with the *greater* of its two children is because if we swap it the with the smaller one, we'd end up violating the heap condition immediately. Watch what happens when we try to swap the trickle node with a smaller child.

Let's start again with the trickle node of 3 as our root:

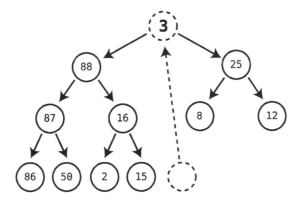

Let's swap the 3 with the 25, which is the smaller of the children:

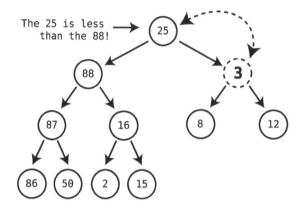

We've now placed the 25 in a situation where it is a parent of the 88. Since the 88 is greater than its parent, the heap condition has been broken.

Like insertion, the time complexity of deletion from a heap is O(log N), as we have to trickle a node from the root down through all log(N) levels of the heap.

Heaps vs. Ordered Arrays

Now that you know the efficiency of heaps, let's see why it's a great choice for implementing priority queues.

Here's a side-by-side comparison of ordered arrays versus heaps:

	Ordered Array	Heap
Insertion	O(N)	O(log N)
Deletion	O(1)	O(log N)

At first glance, it seems that it's a wash. Ordered arrays are slower than heaps when it comes to insertion but faster than heaps for deletion.

However, heaps are considered to be the better choice, and here's why.

While O(1) is extremely fast, O(log N) is still *very* fast. And O(N), by comparison, is slow. With this in mind, we can rewrite the earlier table this way:

	Ordered Array	Heap
Insertion	Slow	Very fast
Deletion	Extremely fast	Very fast

In this light, it becomes clearer as to why the heap is considered the better choice. We'd rather use a data structure that is consistently very fast than a data structure that is sometimes extremely fast and sometimes slow.

It's worth pointing out that priority queues generally perform insertions and deletions in about equal proportion. Think about the emergency room example, where we expect to treat everyone who comes in. So we want both our insertions and deletions to be fast. If either operation is slow, our priority queue will be inefficient.

With a heap, then, we ensure that both of the priority queue's primary operations—insertion and deletion—perform at a very fast clip.

The Problem of the Last Node…Again

While the heap deletion algorithm seems straightforward, it once again raises the problem of the last node.

I explained that the first step of deletion requires us to move the last node and turn it into the root node. But how do we find the last node in the first place?

Before we solve the problem of the last node, let's first explore why insertion and deletion are so dependent on the last node anyway. Why couldn't we insert new values elsewhere in the heap? And why, when deleting, can't we replace the root node with some other node other than the last node?

Now, if you think about it, you'll realize that if we were to use other nodes, the heap would become incomplete. But this begs the next question: why is completeness *important* for the heap?

The reason why completeness is important is because we want to ensure our heap remains *well balanced*.

To see this clearly, let's take another look at insertion. Let's say we have the following heap:

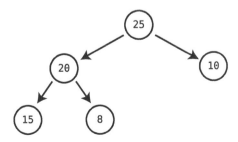

If we want to insert a 5 into this heap, the only way to keep the heap well balanced is by making the 5 the last node—in this case, making it a child of the 10:

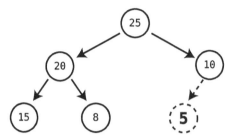

Any alternative to this algorithm would cause imbalance. Say, in an alternative universe, the algorithm was to insert the new node into the bottom leftmost node, which we could easily find by traversing the left children until we hit the bottom. This would make the 5 a child of the 15:

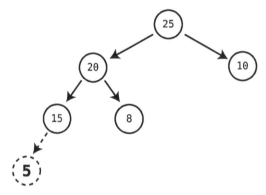

Our heap is now somewhat imbalanced, and it's easy to see how much more imbalanced it would become if we kept inserting new nodes at the bottom leftmost spot.

Similarly, when deleting from a heap, we always turn the last node into the root because, otherwise, the heap can become imbalanced. Take again our example heap:

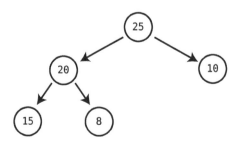

If, in our alternative universe, we always moved the bottom rightmost node into the root position, the 10 would become the root node, and we'd end up with an imbalanced heap with a bunch of left descendants and zero right descendants.

Now, the reason why this balance is so important is because it's what allows us to achieve O(log N) operations. In a severely imbalanced tree like the following one, traversing it could take O(N) steps instead:

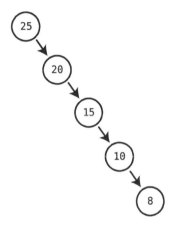

But this brings us back to the problem of the last node. What algorithm would allow us to consistently find the last node of any heap? (Again, without having to traverse all N nodes.)

And this is where our plot takes a sudden twist.

Arrays as Heaps

Because finding the last node is so critical to the heap's operations, and because we want to make sure that finding the last node is efficient, heaps are *usually implemented using arrays.*

While until now we always assumed that every tree consists of independent nodes connected to each other with links (just like a linked list), you'll now see that we can also use an array to implement a heap. The heap itself can be an abstract data type that really uses an array under the hood.

The diagram on page 294 shows how an array is used to store the values of a heap.

The way this works is that we assign each node to an index within the array. In the previous diagram, the index of each node is found in a square below

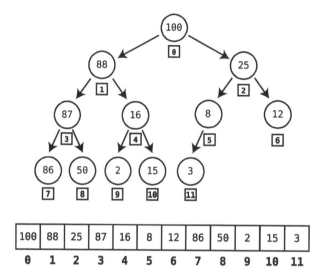

the node. If you look carefully, you'll see that we assign the index of each node according to a specific pattern.

The root node is always stored at index 0. We then move down a level and go from left to right, assigning each node to the next available index in the array. So on the second level, the left node (88) becomes index 1, and the right node (25) becomes index 2. When we reach the end of a level, we move down to the next level and repeat this pattern.

Now, the reason why we're using an array to implement the heap is because it solves the problem of the last node. How?

When we implement the heap in this fashion, *the last node will always be the final element of the array*. Since we move top-down and left to right when assigning each value to the array, the last node will always be the final value in the array. In the previous example, you can see that the 3, which is the last node, is the last value in the array.

Because the last node will always be found at the end of the array, it becomes trivial to find the last node: we just need to access the final element. Additionally, when we insert a new node into the heap, we do so at the end of the array to make it the last node.

Before we get into the other details of how an array-based heap works, we can already begin to code its basic structure. Here's the beginning of our heap implementation in Python:

```
class Heap:
    def __init__(self):
        self.data = []

    def root_node(self):
        return self.data[0]

    def last_node(self):
        return self.data[-1]
```

As you can see, we initialize the heap as an empty array. We have a root_node method, which returns the first item of this array, and we also have a last_node method that returns the last value of this array.

Traversing an Array-Based Heap

As you've seen, the heap's insertion and deletion algorithms require us to be able to trickle our way through the heap. Trickling, in turn, requires us to be able to traverse the heap by accessing a node's parent or children. But how do we move from node to node when all the values are merely stored in an array? Traversing a heap would have been straightforward if we could have simply followed each node's links. But now that the heap is an array under the hood, how do we know which nodes are connected to each other?

This has an interesting solution. It turns out that when we assign the indexes of the heap's nodes according to the pattern described earlier, the following traits of a heap are always true:

- To find the left child of any node, we can use the formula (index * 2) + 1.
- To find the right child of any node, we can use the formula (index * 2) + 2.

Take another look at the previous diagram and focus on the 16, which is at index 4. To find its left child, we multiply its index (4) by 2 and add 1, which yields 9. This means that index 9 is the left child of the node at index 4.

Similarly, to find the right child of index 4, we multiply the 4 by 2 and add 2, which yields 10. This means that index 10 is the right child of index 4.

Because these formulas always work, we're able to treat our array as a tree.

Let's add these two methods to our Heap class:

```
def left_child_index(self, index):
    return (index * 2) + 1

def right_child_index(self, index):
    return (index * 2) + 2
```

Each of these methods accepts an index within the array and returns the left or right child index, respectively.

Here's another important trait of array-based heaps:

- To find a node's parent, we can use the formula (index - 1) // 2.

Note that this formula uses *floor* division, meaning we throw away any numbers beyond the decimal point. For example, 3 // 2 returns 1, rather than the more accurate 1.5.

Again, in our example heap, focus on index 4. If we take that index, subtract 1, and then divide by 2, we get 1. And as you can see in the diagram, the parent of the node at index 4 is found at index 1.

So now we can add another method to our Heap class:

```
def parent_index(self, index):
    return (index - 1) // 2
```

This method accepts an index and calculates the index of its parent node.

Code Implementation: Heap Insertion

Now that we have the essential elements of our Heap in place, let's implement the insertion algorithm:

```
def insert(self, value):
    self.data.append(value)
    new_node_index = len(self.data) - 1

    while (new_node_index > 0 and
            (self.data[new_node_index]
              > self.data[self.parent_index(new_node_index)])):

        parent_index = self.parent_index(new_node_index)
        self.data[parent_index], self.data[new_node_index] = \
            self.data[new_node_index], self.data[parent_index]

        new_node_index = parent_index
```

As usual, let's break this thing down.

Our insert method accepts the value we're inserting into our heap. The first thing we do is make this new value the last node by adding it to the very end of the array:

```
self.data.append(value)
```

Next, we keep track of the index of the new node, as we'll need it later. Right now, the index is the last index in the array:

```
new_node_index = len(self.data) - 1
```

Next, we trickle up the new node to its proper place using a while loop:

```
while (new_node_index > 0 and
    (self.data[new_node_index]
      > self.data[self.parent_index(new_node_index)])):
```

This loop runs as long as two conditions are met. The main condition is that the new node is greater than its parent node. We also make a condition that the new node must have an index greater than 0, as funny things can happen if we try to compare the root node with its nonexistent parent.

Each time this loop runs, we swap the new node with its parent node, since the new node is currently greater than the parent:

```
parent_index = self.parent_index(new_node_index)
self.data[parent_index], self.data[new_node_index] = \
    self.data[new_node_index], self.data[parent_index]
```

We also then update the index of the new node appropriately:

```
new_node_index = parent_index
```

Since this loop only runs while the new node is greater than its parent, the loop ends once the new node is in its proper place.

Code Implementation: Heap Deletion

We'll next look at an implementation of deleting an item from a heap. We named the method pop, since the term *pop* implies a focus on *returning the deleted value* to be used by other code, such as in a priority queue (as we'll see soon). We're not merely trying to eliminate the root value; we also want to pass that value along to other code to be processed.

The main method is the pop method, but to make the code simpler, we've created two helper methods, has_greater_child and find_larger_child_index.

Here goes:

```
def pop(self):
    value_to_delete = self.root_node()
    self.data[0] = self.data.pop()
    trickle_node_index = 0

    while self.has_greater_child(trickle_node_index):
        larger_child_index = self.find_larger_child_index(trickle_node_index)

        self.data[trickle_node_index], self.data[larger_child_index] = \
            self.data[larger_child_index], self.data[trickle_node_index]

        trickle_node_index = larger_child_index

    return value_to_delete
```

```
def has_greater_child(self, index):
    return ((self.left_child_index(index) <= len(self.data) and
            self.data[self.left_child_index(index)] > self.data[index])
            or
            (self.right_child_index(index) <= len(self.data) and
            self.data[self.right_child_index(index)] > self.data[index]))

def find_larger_child_index(self, index):
    if not self.data[self.right_child_index(index)]:
        return self.left_child_index(index)

    if (self.data[self.right_child_index(index)]
            > self.data[self.left_child_index(index)]):
        return self.right_child_index(index)
    else:
        return self.left_child_index(index)
```

Let's first dive into the pop method.

The pop method doesn't accept any arguments, since the only node we ever delete is the root node. Here's how the method works.

First, we save the value we're going to delete so we can return it at the end of the function:

```
value_to_delete = self.root_node()
```

Next, we remove the last value from the array and make it the first value:

```
self.data[0] = self.data.pop()
```

This simple line effectively deletes the original root node, as we're overwriting the root node's value with the last node's value.

Next, we need to trickle the new root node down to its proper place. We called this the trickle node earlier, and our code reflects this.

Before we start the actual trickling, we keep track of the trickle node's index, as we'll need it later. Currently, the trickle node is at index 0:

```
trickle_node_index = 0
```

We then use a while loop to execute the trickle-down algorithm. The loop runs as long as the trickle node has any children that are greater than it:

```
while self.has_greater_child(trickle_node_index):
```

This line uses the has_greater_child method, which returns whether a given node has any children who are greater than that node.

Within this loop, we first find the index of the greater of the trickle node's children:

```
larger_child_index = self.find_larger_child_index(trickle_node_index)
```

This line uses the method find_larger_child_index, which returns the index of the trickle node's greater child. We store this index in a variable called larger_child_index.

Next, we swap the trickle node with its greater child:

```
self.data[trickle_node_index], self.data[larger_child_index] = \
    self.data[larger_child_index], self.data[trickle_node_index]
```

We update the index of the trickle node, which will be the index it was just swapped with:

```
trickle_node_index = larger_child_index
```

Finally, we return the value of the node we deleted from the heap:

```
return value_to_delete
```

Alternate Heap Implementations

Our heap implementation is now complete. It's worth noting that while we did use an array to implement the heap under the hood, it *is possible* to implement a heap using linked nodes as well. (This alternative implementation uses a different trick to solve the problem of the last node, one that involves binary numbers.)

However, the array implementation is the more common approach, so that's what I presented here. It's also interesting to see how an array can be used to implement a tree.

Indeed, it's possible to use an array to implement *any* sort of binary tree, such as the binary search tree from the previous chapter. However, the heap is the first case of a binary tree where an array implementation provides an advantage, as it helps us find the last node easily.

Heaps as Priority Queues

Now that you understand how heaps work, we can circle back to our old friend, the priority queue.

Again, the primary function of a priority queue is to allow us immediate access to the highest-priority item in the queue. In our emergency room example, we want to first address the person with the most serious problem.

It's for this reason that a heap is a natural fit for priority queue implementations. The heap gives us immediate access to the highest-priority item, which can always be found at the root node. Each time we take care of the highest-priority item (and then remove it from the heap), the next-highest item floats to the top of the heap and is on deck to be addressed next. And the heap accomplishes this while maintaining very fast insertions and deletions, both of which are O(log N).

Contrast this to the ordered array, which requires much slower insertions of O(N) to ensure that each new value is in its proper place.

It turns out that the heap's weak ordering *is its very advantage*. The fact that it doesn't have to be perfectly ordered allows us to insert new values in O(log N) time. At the same time, the heap is ordered *just enough* so that we can always access the one item we need at any given time, namely, the heap's greatest value.

Wrapping Up

So far, we've seen how different types of trees can optimize different types of problems. Binary search trees kept search fast while minimizing the cost of insertions, and heaps were the perfect tool for building priority queues.

In the next chapter, we'll explore another tree that's used to power some of the most common text-based operations you use on a day-to-day basis.

Exercises

The following exercises provide you with the opportunity to practice with heaps. The solutions to these exercises are found in the section Chapter 16, on page 453.

1. Draw what the following heap would look like after we insert the value 11 into it:

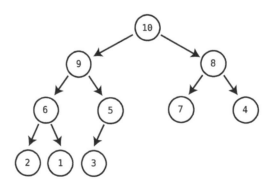

2. Draw what the previous heap would look like after we delete the root node.

3. Imagine you've built a brand-new heap by inserting the following numbers into the heap in this particular order: 55, 22, 34, 10, 2, 99, 68. If you then pop them from the heap one at a time and insert the numbers into a new array, in what order would the numbers now appear?

CHAPTER 17

It Doesn't Hurt to Trie

Did you ever wonder how your smartphone's autocomplete feature works? Autocomplete is the feature you see when you start typing "catn" and your phone suggests that the word you're about to type is either "catnip" or "catnap". (Yes, I text my friends about catnip all the time.)

For this to work, your phone has access to an entire dictionary of words. But what data structure are these words stored in?

Let's imagine, for a moment, that all the words in the English language are stored within an array. If the array were unsorted, we'd have to search *every word* in the dictionary to find all words that start with "catn". This is O(N), and a very slow operation considering that N is a pretty large number in this case, as it's the number of all the words in the dictionary.

A hash table wouldn't help us either, as it hashes the *entire word* to determine where in memory the value should be stored. As the hash table wouldn't have a "catn" key, we'd have no easy way to locate "catnip" or "catnap" within the hash table.

Things improve greatly if we store the words inside an ordered array. If the array contained all the words in alphabetical order, we could use binary search to find a word beginning with "catn" in O(log N) time. And while O(log N) isn't bad, we can do even better. In fact, if we use a special tree-based data structure, we can approach O(1) speeds in finding our desired words.

The examples in this chapter show how tries can be used for applications dealing with text, as tries allow for important features such as autocomplete and autocorrect. However, tries have other uses as well, including applications involving IP addresses or phone numbers.

Tries

The *trie* is a kind of tree that's ideal for text-based features such as autocomplete. Before we get into how the trie works, though, let's first address its pronunciation.

In my (unasked for) opinion, the trie is one of the most unfortunately named data structures out there. The word *trie* is derived from the word *retrieval*. So technically, it should be pronounced "tree." But since that would be confused with the word *tree*, which is the general term for all tree-based data structures, most people pronounce trie as "try." Some resources refer to this same data structure as the prefix tree or the digital tree, but trie, amazingly, remains the most popular name. So there you have it.

Here's one last comment before we dive into the details. The trie is not as well documented as the other data structures in this book, and many different resources implement the trie in slightly different ways. I've chosen a particular implementation that I find to be the most straightforward and understandable, but you'll find other implementations out there. In any case, the general ideas behind most of the implementations remain the same.

The Trie Node

Like most other trees, the trie is a collection of nodes that point to other nodes. However, the trie is *not* a binary tree. Whereas a binary tree doesn't allow any node to have more than two child nodes, a trie node can have *any number* of child nodes.

In our implementation, each trie node contains a hash table, where the keys are English characters and the values are other nodes of the trie. Take a look at the following diagram:

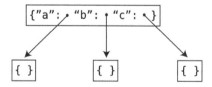

Here, the root node contains a hash table with the keys "a", "b", and "c". The values are other trie nodes, which are the children of this node. These children also contain hash tables, which will in turn point to *their* children. (For now, we left the children's hash tables empty, but they'll contain data in future diagrams.)

The implementation of the actual trie node itself is very simple. Here is our Python version of the TrieNode class:

```
class TrieNode:

    def __init__(self):
        self.children = {}
```

As you can see, the TrieNode just contains a hash table.

If we print (to the console) the data from our root node in the previous example, we'll get something like this:

```
{'a': <__main__.TrieNode instance at 0x108635638>,
 'b': <__main__.TrieNode instance at 0x108635878>,
 'c': <__main__.TrieNode instance at 0x108635ab8>}
```

Again, in this hash table, the keys are individual character strings, and the values are instances of other TrieNodes.

The Trie Class

To fully create our trie, we'll also need a separate Trie class, which will keep track of the root node:

```
import trie_node

class Trie:

    def __init__(self):
        self.root = trie_node.TrieNode()
```

This class keeps track of a self.root variable that points to the root node. In this implementation, when we create a new Trie, it begins with an empty TrieNode as its root.

As we progress through this chapter, we're going to add our trie operation methods to this Trie class as well.

Storing Words

Now, the point of our trie is to store words. Let's see how the following trie stores the words, "ace", "bad", and "cat", as shown in the diagram on page 306.

This trie stores the three words by turning each character of each word into its own trie node. If you start with the root node and follow its "a" key, for example, it points to a child node containing a key of "c". The "c" key, in turn, points to a node that contains a key of "e". When we string these three characters together, we get the word "ace".

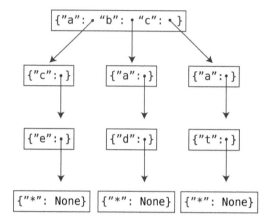

With this pattern, you can see how the trie also stores the words "bad" and "cat".

You'll note that the final characters in these words have children nodes of their own. If you look at the "e" node from the word "ace", for example, you can see that the "e" points to a child node that contains a hash table with a key of "*", an asterisk. (The value doesn't actually matter, so it can simply be None.) This indicates we've reached the end of a word, and that "ace", therefore, is a complete word. The need for this "*" key will become more apparent shortly.

Now, here's where tries become even more interesting. Let's say we want to also store the word "act". To do this, we keep the existing "a" and "c" keys, but we add one new node containing the key of "t". Look at the following diagram:

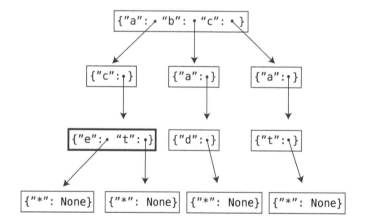

As you can see, the bolded node's hash table now contains *two* children nodes, an "e" and a "t". By doing this, we indicate that both "ace" and "act" are valid dictionary words.

To make things easier to visualize going forward, we're going to represent our tries using a simpler diagram. Here's the same trie using this new format:

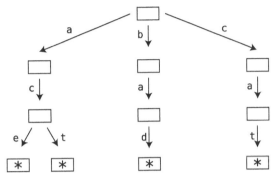

In this diagram style, we place each hash table key next to an arrow pointing to its child node.

The Need for the Asterisk

Let's say we want to store the words "bat" and "batter" in a trie. This is an interesting case, since the word "batter" actually contains the word "bat". Here's how we handle this:

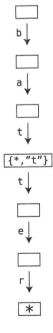

The first "t" points to a node that has *two* keys. One key is an "*" key (with a null value), while the other is a "t" whose value points to another node. This indicates that "bat" is itself a word even though it's also a prefix of the longer word "batter".

Note that in this diagram, we're not using classic hash table syntax anymore but instead using a condensed syntax to save space. We've used curly braces to indicate that the node contains a hash table. However, the {*, "t"} is not a key-value pair but simply two keys. The "*" key has a null value, and the "t" key has the next node as its value.

This is why those "*"s are critical. We need them to indicate when parts of a word are also words themselves.

Let's bring this all together with a more complex example. Here's a trie that contains the words "ace", "act", "bad", "bake", "bat", "batter", "cab", "cat", "catnap", and "catnip":

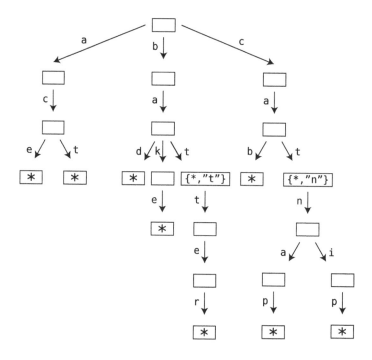

Tries used in real applications may contain thousands of words. If they don't contain the entire English language, they at least contain the most common words.

To build our autocomplete feature, let's first analyze the basic trie operations.

Trie Search

The most classic trie operation is search—namely, determining whether a string is found in the trie. Search has two flavors: we can search to see whether the string is a *complete* word, or we can search to see whether the string is at least a word *prefix* (that is, the beginning of a word). These two versions are similar, but we'll implement the latter one, where our search will look for prefixes. This search will end up finding complete words as well, since a complete word is at least as good as a prefix.

The algorithm for prefix search performs the following steps (they'll become clearer when we walk though an example that follows):

1. We establish a variable called current_node. At the beginning of our algorithm, this points to the root node.

2. We iterate over each character of our search string.

3. As we point to each character of our search string, we look to see if the current_node has a child with that character as a key.

4. If it does not, we return None, as it means our search string does not exist in the trie.

5. If the current_node *does* have a child with the current character as the key, we update the current_node to become that child. We then go back to Step 2, continuing to iterate over each character in our search string.

6. If we get to the end of our search string, it means we've found our search string.

Let's see this in action by searching for the string "cat" in our trie from earlier.

Setup: We set the current_node to be the root node. (The current_node is indicated in bold in the diagrams on the following pages.) We also point to the first character of our string, which is the "c", as shown in the top diagram on page 310.

Step 1: Since the root node has "c" as a child key, we update the current_node to become that key's value. We also continue iterating through the characters in our search string, so we point to the next character, which is the "a", as shown in the bottom diagram on page 310.

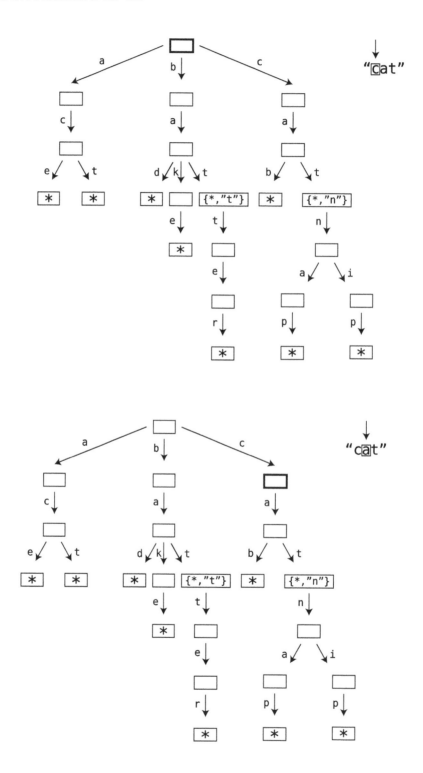

Step 2: We inspect the current_node for a child with the key of "a". It has one, so we make that child the new current_node. We then proceed to search for the next character in our string, which is the "t":

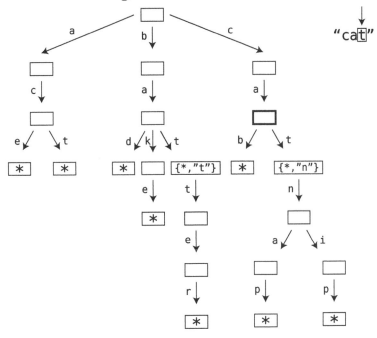

Step 3: We're now pointing to the "t" of our search string. Since the current_node has a "t" child, we follow it, as shown in the diagram on page 312.

Since we've reached the end of our search string, it means we've found "cat" in our trie.

Code Implementation: Trie Search

Let's implement trie search by adding a search method to our Trie class:

```python
def search(self, word):
    current_node = self.root

    for char in word:
        if current_node.children.get(char):
            current_node = current_node.children[char]
        else:
            return None

    return current_node
```

Our search method accepts a string that represents the word (or prefix) we're searching for.

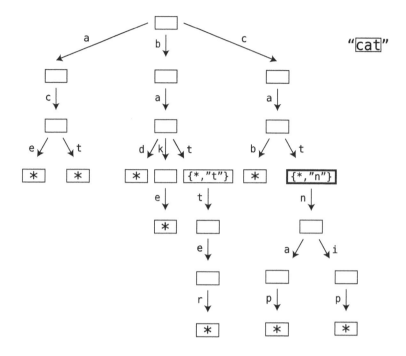

First, we establish the root node as our current_node:

```
current_node = self.root
```

Then we iterate over each character of our search word:

```
for char in word:
```

Within each round of the loop, we check whether the current node has any children with the current character as the key. If there is such a child, we update the current node to be the child node:

```
if current_node.children.get(char):
    current_node = current_node.children[char]
```

If there is no such child, we return None, as it means we've hit a dead end and our search word isn't contained in the trie.

If we get past the end of the loop, it means we've found the entire word in our trie. In this case, we return the current_node. The reason we return the current node, as opposed to just returning True, is to help us with the autocomplete feature, as I'll explain when we get there.

The Efficiency of Trie Search

The great thing about trie search is that it's incredibly efficient.

Let's analyze the number of steps it takes.

In our algorithm, we focus on each character of our search string one at a time. As we do so, we use each node's hash table to find the appropriate child node in one step. As you know, a hash table lookup takes just O(1) time. It turns out, then, that our algorithm takes as many steps *as there are characters in our search string*.

This can be much faster than using binary search on an ordered array. Binary search is O(log N), with N being the number of words in our dictionary. Trie search, on the other hand, takes only as many steps as the number of characters in our search term. For a word like "cat", that's just three steps.

Expressing trie search in terms of Big O is slightly tricky. We can't quite call it O(1), since the number of steps isn't constant, as it all depends on the search string's length. And O(N) can be misleading, since N normally refers to the amount of data in the data structure. This would be the number of nodes in our trie, which is a much greater number than the number of characters in our search string.

Most references have decided to call this O(K), where K is the number of characters in our search string. Any letter other than N would have worked here, but K it is.

Even though O(K) isn't constant, as the size of the search string can vary, O(K) is similar to constant time in one important sense. Most *non*-constant algorithms are tied to the amount of data at hand; that is, as N data increases, the algorithm slows down. With an O(K) algorithm, though, our trie can grow tremendously, but that will have no effect on the speed of our search. An O(K) algorithm on a string of three characters will always take three steps, no matter how large the trie is. The only factor that affects our algorithm's speed is the size of our input rather than all the available data. This makes our O(K) algorithm extremely efficient.

While search is the most common type of operation performed on tries, it's difficult to test drive it without populating our trie with data, so let's tackle insertion next.

Trie Insertion

Inserting a new word into a trie is similar to searching for an existing word. We first search to see if the word already exists in the trie. If it doesn't, we insert the new word.

Here's how the algorithm goes:

1. We establish a variable called current_node. At the beginning of our algorithm, this points to the root node.

2. We iterate over each character of our search string. Here, our search string represents the new word we're inserting. We call it a search string since we're also searching whether the string already exists in the trie.

3. As we point to each character of our search string, we look to see if the current_node has a child with that character as a key.

4. If it does, we update the current_node to become that child node, and we go back to Step 2, moving on to the next character of our search string.

5. If the current_node does *not* have a child node that matches the current character, we create such a child node and update the current_node to be this new node. We then go back to Step 2, moving on to the next character of our search string.

6. After we insert the final character of our new word, we add a "*" child to the last node to indicate the word is complete.

Let's see this in action by inserting the word "can" into our earlier example trie.

Setup: We set the current_node to be the root node. We also point to the first character of our string, which is the "c", as shown in the top diagram on page 315.

Step 1: The root node has a "c" child key, so we turn that key's value into the current_node. We also point to the next character of our new word, the "a", as shown in the bottom diagram on page 315.

Step 2: We inspect the current_node for a child with the key of "a". There is one, so we make that the current_node and point to the next character of our string, which is the "n", as shown in the top diagram on page 316.

Step 3: The current_node does *not* have an "n", so we need to create that child, as shown in the bottom diagram on page 316.

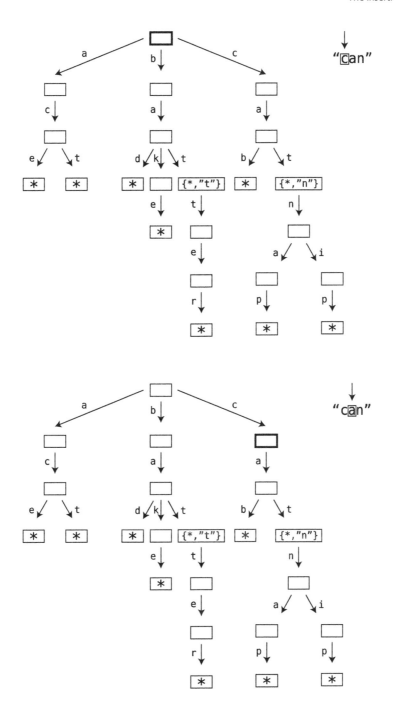

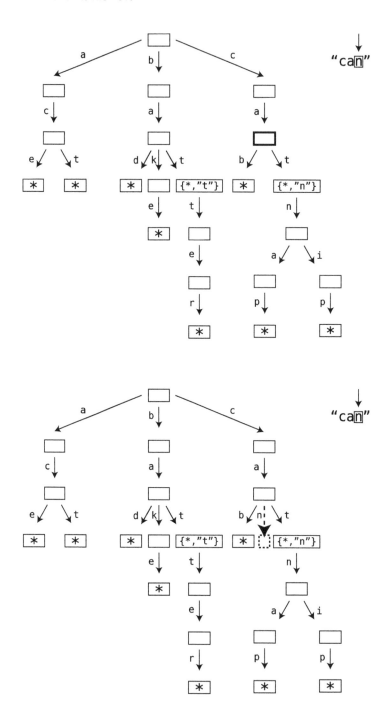

Step 4: We're done inserting "can" into our trie, so we cap it off with a child of "*":

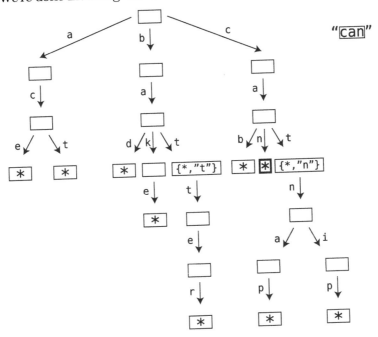

"can"

And we're done!

Code Implementation: Trie Insertion

Here's the insert method for our Trie class. You'll note that most of it looks the same as the earlier search method:

```
def insert(self, word):
    current_node = self.root

    for char in word:
        if current_node.children.get(char):
            current_node = current_node.children[char]
        else:
            new_node = trie_node.TrieNode()
            current_node.children[char] = new_node
            current_node = new_node

    current_node.children["*"] = None
```

The first part of this method is the same as search. It diverges when the current-Node doesn't have the child that matches the current character. When this is the case, we add a new key-value pair to the current_node's hash table, with the key being the current character and the value being a new TrieNode:

```
new_node = trie_node.TrieNode()
current_node.children[char] = new_node
```

We then update the current_node to be this new node:

```
current_node = new_node
```

We then repeat the loop until we're done inserting our new word. Once we're done, we add a "*" key to the final node's hash table, with the value as None:

```
current_node.children["*"] = None
```

Like search, trie insertion takes about O(K) steps. If we count the adding of the "*" at the end, it's technically K + 1 steps, but because we drop the constants, we express the speed as O(K).

Building Autocomplete

We're just about ready to build a real autocomplete feature. To make this a tad easier, let's first build a slightly simpler function that we'll use to help us with this feature.

Collecting All the Words

The next method we're going to add to our Trie class is a method that returns an array of *all* the words in the trie. Now, it's rare that we'd actually want to list the *entire* dictionary. However, we're going to allow this method to accept any node of the trie as an argument so that it can list all the words that start from that node.

The following method, called collect_all_words, collects a list of all the trie's words starting from a particular node:

```
def collect_all_words(self, words, node=None, word=""):
    current_node = node or self.root
    for key, child_node in current_node.children.items():
        if key == "*":
            words.append(word)
        else:
            self.collect_all_words(words, child_node, word + key)
    return words
```

This method relies heavily on recursion, so let's break it down carefully.

The method accepts three primary arguments: words, node, and word.

When we first call this method, we must pass in words as an empty array. As the method proceeds, it will fill this array with words from the trie. The method eventually returns this array once we've filled it with all the desired words.

The node argument allows us to specify which node in the trie to start collecting the words from. If we don't pass in this argument, our method will start from the root node, collecting every word in the entire trie.

The word argument defaults to an empty string. As we move through the trie, we add characters to this word. When we reach a "*", the word is considered complete and we add it to the words array.

Let's now break down each line of code.

The first thing we do is set the current_node:

```
current_node = node or self.root
```

By default, the current_node will be the root node, unless we passed in some other node as the method's first parameter. Let's assume for now that the current_node is indeed the root node.

Next, we begin a loop that iterates over all the key-value pairs in the current_node's children hash table:

```
for key, child_node in current_node.children.items():
```

In each iteration of the loop, the key is always a single-character string, and the value, child_node, is another instance of TrieNode.

Let's skip to the else clause, as this is where the magic happens:

```
self.collect_all_words(words, child_node, word + key)
```

This line recursively calls the collect_all_words function.

The first argument is the words array. By passing this array along in each recursive call, we're able to fill it with complete words, effectively building this list as we traverse the trie.

The second argument is the child_node. This allows us to recursively call the collect_all_words method on the child node, continuing to collect all the words from the child node and on.

The third argument is word + key, making it so that as we move through each node of the trie, we add the key to the current word, building up the word as we go.

The base case is when we reach a "*" key, indicating we've completed a word. At this point, we can add the word to the words array:

```
if key == "*":
    words.append(word)
```

At the end of the function, we return the words array. If we called this function without passing in a specific node, this will return the complete list of words in the trie.

Recursion Walk-Through

Let's run through a quick visual example of this using a simple trie. This trie holds two words, "can" and "cat":

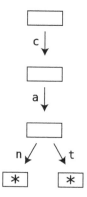

Call 1: In the very first call of collect_all_words, the current_node starts out at the root, word is an empty string, and the words array is empty:

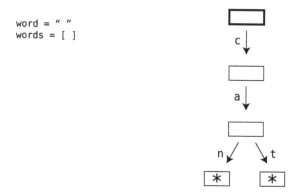

We iterate over the root node's children. The root node happens to only have one child key, the "c", which points to a child node. Before we recursively call collect_all_words on this child node, we need to add the current call to the call stack.

We then recursively call collect_all_words on the "c" child node. We also pass in word + key as the word argument. word + key is the string "c", since word was empty and the key is "c". And we also pass in the words array, which is still empty. The next image shows where we are once we make this recursive call:

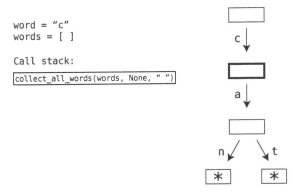

```
word = "c"
words = [ ]

Call stack:
collect_all_words(words, None, " ")
```

Call 2: We iterate over the current node's children. It has just one child key, the "a". Before recursively calling collect_all_words on the respective child node, we'll add the current call to the call stack. In the diagram that follows, we call this current node the "a" node, meaning it's the node that has "a" as a child.

We then recursively call collect_all_words. We pass in the child node, "ca" (which is word + key), and the still-empty words array:

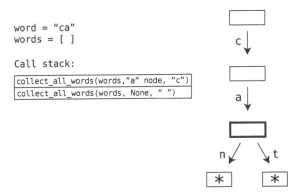

```
word = "ca"
words = [ ]

Call stack:
collect_all_words(words,"a" node, "c")
collect_all_words(words, None, " ")
```

Call 3: We iterate over the current node's children, which are "n" and "t". We'll start with the "n". Before making any recursive calls, though, we need to first add the current call to our call stack. In the diagram that follows, we call this current node the "n/t" node, meaning it's the node that has both "n" and "t" as children.

When we then call collect_all_words on the "n" child, we also pass in "can" as the word argument as well as the empty words array:

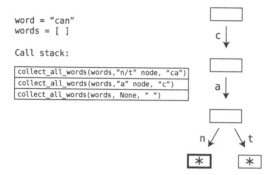

Call 4: We iterate over the current node's children. In this case, it has only one child, which is the "*". This is our base case. We add the current word, which is "can", to the words array:

$$words = [\text{"can"}]$$

Call 5: We now pop the top call from our call stack, which was the call of collect_all_words on the node with the children keys of "n" and "t", and where word was "ca". This means we now return to that call (as we return to whatever call we pop from the call stack):

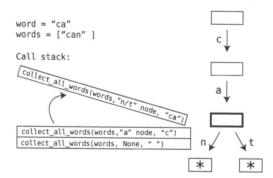

Here we can make a subtle but important point. In the current call, word is back to "ca", since that was the word argument when we first initiated this call. However, the words array now contains the word "can" even though the array was empty when we originally made this call.

Here's the reason why this works. In many programming languages, an array can be passed up and down a call stack because the array remains the same object in memory even when we add new values to it. (The same concept applies to hash tables as well, which was how we were able to pass it along as part of the memoization technique we looked at in *Dynamic Programming*.)

When a string is modified, on the other hand, the computer creates a new string instead of truly modifying the original string object. Therefore, when we updated word by changing it from "ca" to "can", the previous call still only has access to the original string, "ca". (In some languages, this may work slightly differently. For our purposes, though, this is the general idea.)

In any case, we're in the middle of a call where words contains the word "can", and word is "ca".

Call 6: At this point, we've already iterated over the "n" key, so the loop is now up to the "t" key. Before recursively calling collect_all_words on the "t" child node, we need to add the current call to the call stack again. (This will be the second time we add this call to the call stack. We previously popped it off, but now we're going to add it again.)

When we call collect_all_words on the "t" child, we pass in "cat" as the word argument (since that is word + key) and the words array:

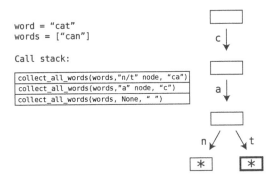

Call 7: We iterate over the current node's children. The only child here is "*", so we add the current word of "cat" to our words array:

words = ["can", "cat"]

At this point, we can unwind the call stack, popping off each call and completing its execution, each of which ends by returning the words array. The final call we complete—which was the first call to kick this all off—returns words as well. Because this contains the strings "can" and "cat", we've successfully returned the trie's entire word list.

Completing Autocomplete

We're finally ready to implement our autocomplete feature. In fact, we've pretty much done all the legwork already. All we need to do is put the pieces together.

Here's a basic autocomplete method that we can drop into our Trie class:

```
def autocomplete(self, prefix):
    current_node = self.search(prefix)

    if not current_node:
        return None

    return self.collect_all_words([], current_node)
```

Yes, that's it. By using our search method and collect_all_words method together, we can autocomplete any prefix. Here's how this works.

The autocomplete method accepts the prefix parameter, which is the string of characters the user begins typing in.

First, we search the trie for the existence of the prefix. If the search method doesn't find the prefix in the trie, the search method returns None, and so our method does as well.

However, if the prefix is found in the trie, the search method returns *the node in the trie that represents the final character in the prefix.* We noted earlier that we could have simply had the search method return True once it finds the word. The reason why we had it return the final node was so that we could use the search method to help us with the autocomplete feature.

Our autocomplete method continues by calling the collect_all_words method on the node returned by the search method. This finds and collects all words that stem from that final node, which represents all the complete words that can be appended to the original prefix to form a word.

Our method finally returns an array of all possible endings to the user's prefix, which we could then display to the user as possible autocomplete options.

Tries with Values: A Better Autocomplete

If we think about it, a good autocomplete feature isn't necessarily going to display *every* possible word the user might be intending to type. Showing, say, sixteen options would be overwhelming to the user, so we'd rather show just the most popular words from the available list.

For example, if the user starts typing "bal", the user might be intending to type "ball", "bald", or "balance". Now, it's also possible that the user is typing the obscure word "balter" (which means to dance clumsily, if you wanted to know). However, odds are that "balter" is *not* the intended word, since it's not a common word.

To display the most popular word options, we somehow need to store the word popularity data in our trie as well. And we're in luck, since we only need to make a slight modification to our trie to accomplish this.

In our current trie implementation, every time we've set a "*" key, we've made its value None. This is because we've only ever paid attention to the "*" key; the value carried no significance.

However, we can take advantage of these values to store additional data about the words themselves, such as how popular they are. To keep things simple, let's work with a simple range of 1 to 10, with 1 being the rarest kind of word, and 10 being an extremely popular word.

Let's say "ball" is a very popular word and has a popularity score of 10. The word "balance" may be slightly less popular, and have a score of 9. The word "bald" is used even less often, and has a score of 7. And since "balter" is a hardly known word, we'll give it a score of 1. We can store these scores in the trie this way:

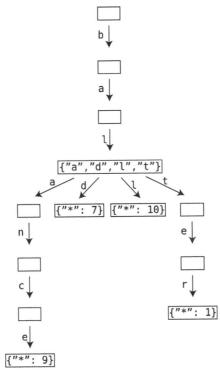

By using a number as the value of each "*" key, we can effectively store each word's popularity score. When we now collect all the words of the trie, we can collect their scores along with them and then sort the words in order of their popularity. We can then choose to only display the most popular word options.

Wrapping Up

We've now covered three types of trees: binary search trees, heaps, and tries. There are *many* other types of trees as well, such as AVL trees, red black trees (covered in Volume 2 of this book), 2-3-4 trees, and plenty of others. Each tree has unique traits and behaviors that can be leveraged for specific situations. I encourage you to learn more about these various trees, but for now, you have a taste for how different trees can solve different problems.

It's now time for the final data structure of the book. Everything you've learned about trees will help you understand graphs. Graphs are helpful in so many different situations, and that's why they're so popular. So let's dive in.

Exercises

The following exercises provide you with the opportunity to practice with tries. The solutions to these exercises are found in the section Chapter 17, on page 454.

1. List all the words stored in the following trie:

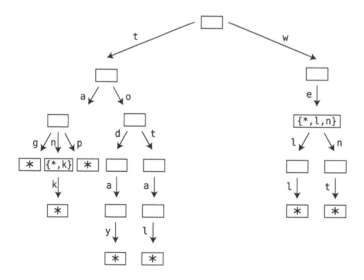

2. Draw a trie that stores the following words: "get", "go", "got", "gotten", "hall", "ham", "hammer", "hill", and "zebra".

3. Write a function that traverses each node of a trie and prints each key, including all "*" keys.

4. Write an *autocorrect* function that attempts to replace a user's typo with a correct word. The function should accept a string that represents text a user typed in. If the user's string is *not* in the trie, the function should return an alternative word that shares the longest possible prefix with the user's string.

   For example, let's say our trie contained the words "cat", "catnap", and "catnip". If the user accidentally types in "catnar", our function should return "catnap", since that's the word from the trie that shares the longest prefix with "catnar". This is because both "catnar" and "catnap" share a prefix of "catna", which is five characters long. The word "catnip" isn't as good, since it only shares the shorter, four-character prefix of "catn" with "catnar".

   One more example: if the user types in "caxasfdij", the words "cat", "catnap", and "catnip" are all valid replacements since they share the same prefix of "ca" with the user's typo. Our function just needs to return one valid option—it doesn't matter which.

   If the user's string is found in the trie, the function should just return the word itself. This should be true even if the user's text isn't a complete word, as we're only trying to correct typos, not suggest endings to the user's prefix.

CHAPTER 18

Connecting Everything with Graphs

Let's say we're building a social network that allows people to be friends with one another. These friendships are mutual, so if Alice is friends with Bob, then Bob is also friends with Alice.

How can we best organize this data?

One basic approach might be to use a two-dimensional array that stores the list of friendships:

```
friendships = [
  ["Alice", "Bob"],
  ["Bob", "Cynthia"],
  ["Alice", "Diana"],
  ["Bob", "Diana"],
  ["Elise", "Fred"],
  ["Diana", "Fred"],
  ["Fred", "Alice"]
]
```

Here, each subarray containing a pair of names represents a friendship between two people.

Unfortunately, with this approach, there's no quick way to see who Alice's friends are. If we look carefully, we can see that that Alice is friends with Bob, Diana, and Fred. But for the computer to determine this, it would have to comb through all the relationships in the list, since Alice can be present in any of them. This is O(N), which is very slow.

Thankfully, we can do much, *much* better than this. With a data structure known as a *graph*, we can find Alice's friends in *just O(1) time.*

Graphs

A *graph* is a data structure that specializes in relationships, as it easily conveys how data is connected.

Here's a visualization of our social network, displayed as a graph:

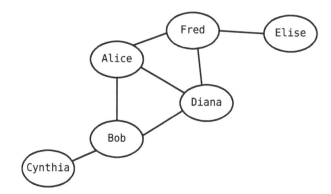

Each person is represented by a node, and each line indicates a friendship with another person. If you look at Alice, for example, you can see that she is friends with Bob, Diana, and Fred, since her node has lines that connect to their nodes.

Graphs vs. Trees

You might have noticed that graphs look similar to trees, which we've dealt with in the past few chapters. Indeed, *trees are a type of graph*. Both data structures consist of nodes connected to each other.

So what's the difference between a graph and a tree?

Here's the deal: while all trees are graphs, not all graphs are trees.

Specifically, for a graph to be considered a tree, it cannot have *cycles*, and all nodes must be *connected*. Let's see what that means.

A graph may have nodes that form what is known as a *cycle*—that is, nodes that reference each other circularly. In the previous example, Alice is friends with Diana, and Diana is connected to Bob, and Bob is connected…to Alice. These three nodes form a cycle.

Trees, on the other hand, are not "allowed" to have cycles. If a graph has a cycle, then it's not a tree.

Another characteristic specific to trees is that every node is somehow connected to every other node, even if the connections are indirect. However, it's
possible for a graph to not be fully connected.

See the following graph:

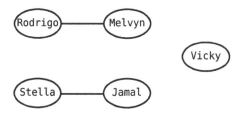

In this social network, we have two pairs of friends. However, no one from
either pair is friends with anyone from the other pair. Additionally, we can
see that Vicky has no friends yet, as perhaps she signed up for this social
network just minutes ago. With trees, however, there's never a node that's
disconnected from the rest of the tree.

Graph Jargon

Graphs have a bit of their own technical jargon. We're used to calling each
piece of data a *node*, but in "graph-speak," each node is called a *vertex*. The
lines between nodes, um—vertices, have their own name as well and are called
edges. And vertices that are connected by an edge are said to be *adjacent* to
each other. Some computer scientists also refer to adjacent vertices as
neighbors.

In our first graph, then, the vertices of Alice and Bob are adjacent to each
other, since they share an edge.

I mentioned earlier that it's possible for a graph to have a vertex that isn't
connected at all to other vertices. However, a graph where *all* the vertices are
connected in some way is said to be a *connected graph*.

The Bare-Bones Graph Implementation

For the sake of code organization, we're going to use object-oriented classes
to represent our graphs, but it's worth noting that we can also use a basic
hash table (see Chapter 8, Blazing Fast Lookup with Hash Tables, on page
113) to represent a rudimentary graph. Here's a bare-bones implementation
of our social network using a hash table:

```
friends = {
  "Alice": ["Bob", "Diana", "Fred"],
  "Bob": ["Alice", "Cynthia", "Diana"],
  "Cynthia": ["Bob"],
  "Diana": ["Alice", "Bob", "Fred"],
  "Elise": ["Fred"],
  "Fred": ["Alice", "Diana", "Elise"]
}
```

With a graph, we can look up Alice's friends in O(1), because we can look up the value of any key in the hash table with one step:

```
friends.get("Alice")
```

This immediately returns the array containing all of Alice's friends.

Directed Graphs

In some social networks, relationships are *not* mutual. For example, a social network may allow Alice to follow Bob, but Bob doesn't have to follow Alice back. Let's construct a new graph that demonstrates who follows whom:

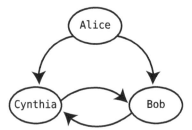

This is known as a *directed graph*. In this example, the arrows indicate the *direction* of the relationship. Alice follows both Bob and Cynthia, but no one follows Alice. We can also see that Bob and Cynthia follow each other.

We can still use our simple hash-table implementation to store this data:

```
followees = {
  "Alice": ["Bob", "Cynthia"],
  "Bob": ["Cynthia"],
  "Cynthia": ["Bob"]
}
```

The only difference here is that we're using the arrays to represent the people each person *follows*.

Object-Oriented Graph Implementation

I demonstrated how a hash table can be used to implement a graph, but going forward, we'll work with an object-oriented approach.

Here's the beginning of an object-oriented graph implementation, using Python:

```python
class Vertex:
    def __init__(self, value):
        self.value = value
        self.adjacent_vertices = []

    def add_adjacent_vertex(self, vertex):
        self.adjacent_vertices.append(vertex)
```

The Vertex class has two primary attributes, the value and an array of adjacent_vertices. In our social network example, each vertex represents a person, and the value might be a string containing the person's name. With a more complex application, we'd probably want to store multiple pieces of data inside a vertex, such as the person's additional profile information.

The adjacent_vertices array contains all the vertices this vertex connects to. We can add a new adjacent vertex to a given vertex using the add_adjacent_vertex method.

Here's how we can use this class to build a directed graph representing who follows whom in this image:

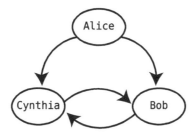

```python
alice = Vertex("alice")
bob = Vertex("bob")
cynthia = Vertex("cynthia")

alice.add_adjacent_vertex(bob)
alice.add_adjacent_vertex(cynthia)
bob.add_adjacent_vertex(cynthia)
cynthia.add_adjacent_vertex(bob)
```

Now, if we were building an *undirected* graph for the social network (where all friendships are mutual), it would make sense if we add Bob to Alice's list of friends, we should automatically add Alice to Bob's list of friends as well.

To do this, we can modify our add_adjacent_vertex method as follows:

```python
def add_adjacent_vertex(self, vertex):
    self.adjacent_vertices.append(vertex)
    vertex.adjacent_vertices.append(self)
```

Let's say we're calling this method on Alice and adding Bob to her list of friends. As with the previous version, we use self.adjacent_vertices.append(vertex) to add Bob to Alice's list of adjacent_vertices. However, we also call this very method on Bob's vertex, with vertex.adjacent_vertices.append(self). This adds Alice to Bob's list of friends as well.

To keep things simple going forward, we're going to work with graphs that are connected (again, meaning all vertices are connected to each other in some way). With such graphs, we can use this one Vertex class to achieve all the algorithms going forward. The general idea is if we have access to just one vertex, we can find all other vertices from there, since all the vertices are connected.

However, it's important to point out that if we're dealing with a disconnected graph, it may be impossible to discover all the vertices just from one vertex. In this case, we may need to store all the graph vertices in some additional data structure, such as an array, so that we have access to all of them. (It's common to see graph implementations use a separate Graph class to contain this array.)

Adjacency List vs. Adjacency Matrix

Our implementation of the graph uses a simple list (in the form of an array) to store a vertex's adjacent vertices. This approach is known as the *adjacency list* implementation.

However, it's good to know that there's another implementation that uses two-dimensional arrays instead of lists. This alternative approach is known as the *adjacency matrix*, and it can provide advantages in specific situations.

Both approaches are popular, and I've decided to stick with the adjacency list because I find it to be more intuitive. But I recommend you research the adjacency matrix as well, as it can be useful and is particularly interesting.

Graph Search

One of the most common graph operations is searching for a particular vertex.

When dealing with graphs, the term *search* can have several connotations. In the simplest sense, to search a graph means to find a particular vertex somewhere within the graph. This would be similar to searching for a value within an array or a key-value pair inside a hash table.

However, when applied to graphs, the term *search* usually has a more specific connotation, and that is: *if we have access to one vertex in the graph, we must find another particular vertex that is somehow connected to this vertex.*

For example, take a look at this example social network:

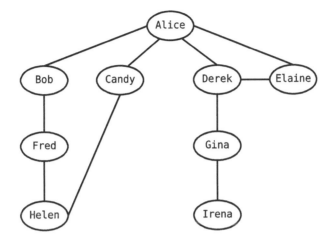

Let's say we currently have access to Alice's vertex. If we said that we'll search for Irena, it would mean that we're trying to find our way from Alice to Irena.

Interestingly, you can see that there are two different *paths* we can take to get from Alice to Irena.

The shorter path is obvious:

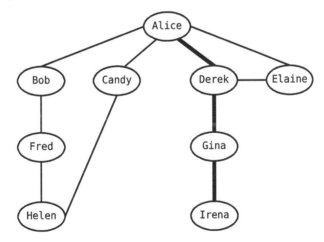

We can get from Alice to Irena in this sequence:

Alice -> Derek -> Gina -> Irena

However, we can take a slightly longer path to get to Irena as well:

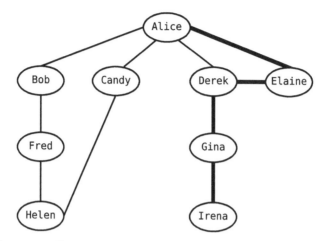

This is the longer path:

Alice -> Elaine -> Derek -> Gina -> Irena

The term *path* is an official graph term, and it means the specific sequence of edges to get from one vertex to another.

Now, searching a graph (which you now know means getting from one vertex to another) can be useful for a variety of use cases.

Perhaps the most obvious application for graph search is searching for a particular vertex within a connected graph. When this is the case, search can be used to find *any* vertex within the entire graph even if we have access to just one random vertex.

Another use for graph search is to discover whether two vertices are connected. For example, we may want to know whether Alice and Irena are somehow connected to each other in this network. A search would give us the answer.

Search can also be used even if we aren't looking for one particular vertex; that is, we can use graph search to merely traverse a graph, which can be useful if we want to perform an operation on every vertex in the graph. You'll see shortly how this works.

Depth-First Search

The two well-known approaches for graph search are *depth-first search* and *breadth-first search*. Both approaches can get the job done, but each provides unique advantages in particular situations. We're going to start with depth-first search, also referred to as DFS, because it's actually quite similar to the algorithm for binary tree traversal that we discussed back in Binary Search Tree Traversal, on page 272. In fact, it's *also* the same essential algorithm that we saw in Filesystem Traversal, on page 156.

As mentioned earlier, graph search can be used to either find a particular vertex, or it can be used to simply traverse the graph. We're going to begin by using depth-first search to traverse the graph since that algorithm is slightly simpler.

The key to any graph search algorithm is keeping track of which vertices we've visited so far. If we don't do this, we can end up in an infinite cycle. Take the following graph, for example:

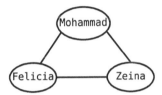

Here, Mohammad is friends with Felicia. And Felicia also happens to be friends with Zeina. But Zeina is friends with Mohammad. So our code would end up going in circles unless we keep track of which vertices we've already traversed.

This problem didn't occur when we dealt with trees (or filesystem traversal), since trees can't have cycles. But since a graph *can* have a cycle, we need to address this issue now.

One way to keep track of our visited vertices is by using a hash table. As we visit each vertex, we add the vertex (or its value) as a key in the hash table and assign it an arbitrary value, such as the Boolean True. If a vertex is present in the hash table, it means we've already visited it.

With this in mind, the depth-first search algorithm works as follows.

1. Start at any random vertex within the graph.

2. Add the current vertex to the hash table to mark it as having been visited.

3. Iterate through the current vertex's adjacent vertices.

4. For each adjacent vertex, if the adjacent vertex has already been visited, ignore it.

5. If the adjacent vertex has *not* yet been visited, recursively perform depth-first search on that vertex.

Depth-First Search Walk-Through

Let's see this in action.

In this walk-through, we're going to start with Alice. In the following diagrams, the vertex with lines around it is the current vertex. A check mark means we've officially marked the vertex as having been visited (and added to the hash table).

Step 1: We start with Alice and give her a check mark to indicate that we've officially visited her vertex:

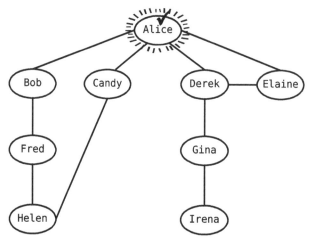

Next up, we'll iterate over Alice's neighbors using a loop. These will be Bob, Candy, Derek, and Elaine.

The order of which neighbor to visit first doesn't matter, so let's just start with Bob. He seems nice.

Step 2: We now perform depth-first search on Bob. Note that this is making a recursive call, as we're already in the middle of a depth-first search of Alice.

As with all recursion, the computer needs to remember which function calls it's still in the middle of, so it first adds Alice to the call stack:

We can now begin the depth-first search on Bob, which makes Bob the current vertex. We mark him as visited, as shown in the graph on page 339.

We then iterate over Bob's adjacent vertices. These are Alice and Fred.

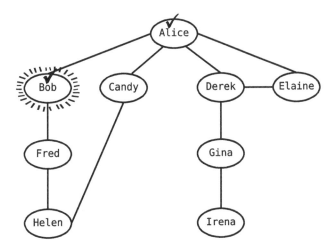

Step 3: Alice has already been visited, so we can ignore her.

Step 4: The only other neighbor, then, is Fred. We call the depth-first search function on Fred's vertex. The computer first adds Bob to the call stack to remember that it's still in the middle of searching Bob:

We now perform depth-first search on Fred. He's now the current vertex, so we mark him as visited:

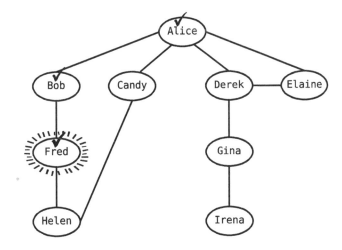

Next, we iterate over Fred's adjacent vertices, which are Bob and Helen.

Step 5: Bob has already been visited, so we ignore him.

Step 6: The only remaining adjacent vertex is Helen. We recursively perform depth-search first on Helen, so the computer first adds Fred to the call stack:

We now begin depth-first search on Helen. She's the current vertex, so we mark her as visited:

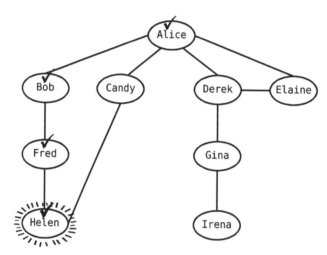

Helen has two adjacent vertices: Fred and Candy.

Step 7: We've already visited Fred, so we can ignore him.

Step 8: Candy has *not* yet been visited, so we recursively perform depth-search on Candy. First, though, Helen gets added to the call stack:

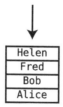

We perform depth-first search on Candy. She's now the current vertex, and we mark her as visited:

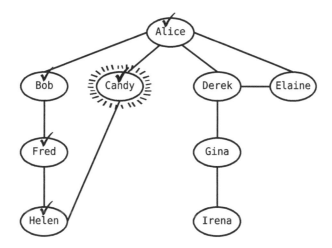

Candy has two adjacent vertices: Alice and Helen.

Step 9: We've already visited Alice, so we can ignore her.

Step 10: We've already visited Helen, so we can ignore her as well.

Since Candy has no other neighbors, we're done performing depth-first search on Candy. At this point, then, the computer begins to unwind the call stack.

First, it pops off Helen from the call stack. We've already iterated over all her neighbors, so the depth-first search on Helen is complete.

The computer pops off Fred. We've iterated over all his neighbors too, so we're done searching him as well.

The computer pops off Bob, but we're done with him as well.

The computer then pops Alice off the call stack. Within our search of Alice, we were in the middle of looping through all of Alice's neighbors. Now, this loop already iterated over Bob. (This was Step 2.) This leaves Candy, Derek, and Elaine.

Step 11: Candy has already been visited, so there's no need to perform search on her.

However, we've not yet visited Derek or Elaine.

Step 12: Let's proceed by recursively performing depth-first search on Derek. The computer adds Alice to the call stack once again:

The depth-first search of Derek now begins. Derek is the current vertex, so we mark him as visited:

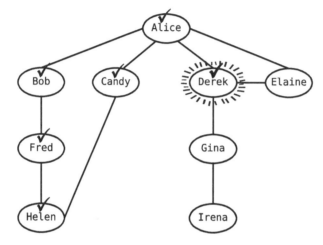

Derek has three adjacent vertices: Alice, Elaine, and Gina.

Step 13: Alice has already been visited, so we don't need to perform another search on her.

Step 14: Let's visit Elaine next, by recursively performing depth-first search on her vertex. Before we do, the computer adds Derek to the call stack:

We now perform depth-first search on Elaine. We mark Elaine as visited, as shown in the graph on page 343.

Elaine has two adjacent vertices: Alice and Derek.

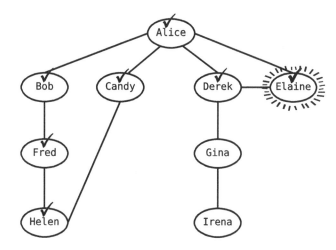

Step 15: Alice has already been visited, so there's no need to perform another search on her.

Step 16: Derek, too, has already been visited.

Since we iterated over all Elaine's neighbors, we're done searching Elaine. The computer now pops Derek from the call stack and loops over his remaining adjacent vertices. In this case, Gina is the final neighbor to visit.

Step 17: We've never visited Gina before, so we recursively perform depth-first search on her vertex. First, though, the computer adds Derek to the call stack again:

We begin our depth-first search of Gina, and mark her as visited, as shown in the graph on page 344.

Gina has two neighbors: Derek and Irena.

Step 18: Derek has already been visited.

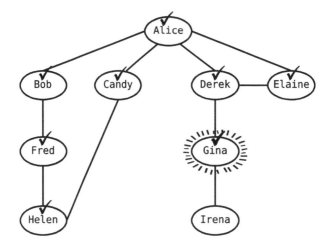

Step 19: Gina has one unvisited adjacent vertex—namely, Irena. Gina gets added to the call stack so that we can recursively perform depth-first search on Irena:

We begin search on Irena and mark her as visited:

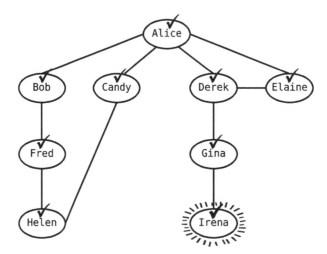

We iterate over Irena's neighbors. Irena has only one neighbor: Gina.

Step 20: Gina has already been visited.

The computer then unwinds the call stack, popping off each vertex one by one. However, since each vertex on the call stack has already iterated over all of its neighbors, there's nothing more for the computer to do with each vertex.

This means we're done!

Code Implementation: Depth-First Search

Here is an implementation of depth-first traversal:

```
def dfs_traverse(vertex, visited_vertices):
    visited_vertices[vertex.value] = True

    print(vertex.value)

    for adjacent_vertex in vertex.adjacent_vertices:
        if not visited_vertices.get(adjacent_vertex.value):
            dfs_traverse(adjacent_vertex, visited_vertices)
```

Our dfs_traverse method accepts a single vertex and a visited_vertices hash table. The first time we call this function, we pass in the empty hash table visited_vertices. For the above example, we'd perform a depth-first traversal starting with Alice, with the following:

```
dfs_traverse(alice, {})
```

As we visit vertices, though, we populate this hash table with the vertices we've visited and pass along the same hash table with each recursive call.

The first thing we do within the function is mark the current vertex as visited. We do this by adding the vertex's value to the hash:

```
visited_vertices[vertex.value] = True
```

We then optionally print the vertex's value just to get feedback that we've truly traversed it:

```
print(vertex.value)
```

Next, we iterate over all the adjacent vertices of the current vertex:

```
for adjacent_vertex in vertex.adjacent_vertices:
```

We check each adjacent vertex to see whether it has already been visited. If it has, we do nothing, but if it has never been visited, we recursively call dfs_traverse on that adjacent vertex:

```
if not visited_vertices.get(adjacent_vertex.value):
    dfs_traverse(adjacent_vertex, visited_vertices)
```

Again, we also pass in the visited_vertices hash table so the ensuing call has access to it.

If we want to use depth-first search to search for a particular vertex, we can use a modified version of the previous function:

```
def dfs(vertex, search_value, visited_vertices):
    visited_vertices[vertex.value] = True

    if vertex.value == search_value:
        return vertex

    for adjacent_vertex in vertex.adjacent_vertices:
        if adjacent_vertex.value == search_value:
            return adjacent_vertex

        if not visited_vertices.get(adjacent_vertex.value):
            vertex_we_are_searching_for = dfs(adjacent_vertex,
                                              search_value,
                                              visited_vertices)

            if vertex_we_are_searching_for:
                return vertex_we_are_searching_for

    return None
```

This implementation also recursively calls itself for each vertex, but returns the vertex_we_are_searching_for if it finds the correct vertex.

Breadth-First Search

Breadth-first search, often abbreviated BFS, is another way to search a graph. Unlike depth-first search, breadth-first search does *not* use recursion. Instead, the algorithm revolves around our old friend, the queue. As you'll recall, the queue is a FIFO data structure, and whatever goes in first, comes out first.

Let's look at the algorithm for breadth-first search. As with our walk-through of depth-first search, we're going to focus on graph *traversal* using breadth-first search; that is, we're going to visit each vertex from our example social network.

Here's the BFS traversal algorithm:

1. Start at any vertex within the graph. We'll call this the *starting vertex.*

2. Add the starting vertex to the hash table to mark it as having been visited.

3. Add the starting vertex to a queue.

4. Start a loop that runs while the queue isn't empty.

5. Within this loop, remove the first vertex from the queue. We'll call this the *current vertex.*

6. Iterate over all the adjacent vertices of current vertex.

7. If the adjacent vertex was already visited, ignore it.

8. If the adjacent vertex has *not* yet been visited, mark it as visited by adding it to a hash table, and add it to the queue.

9. Repeat this loop (starting from Step 4) until the queue is empty.

Breadth-First Search Walk-Through

This isn't as complex as it seems. Let's walk through the traversal step by step.

To set things up, let's work with Alice as our starting vertex. We'll mark her as visited and add her to the queue:

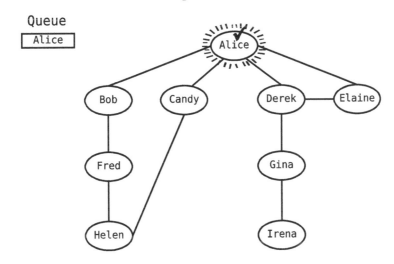

We now begin the core algorithm.

Step 1: We remove the first vertex from the queue and it make it the current vertex. This would be Alice, as she's currently the *only* item in the queue. So at this point, the queue is empty.

Since Alice is the current vertex, we proceed to iterate over Alice's adjacent vertices.

Step 2: We'll start with Bob. We'll mark him as visited and add him to the queue:

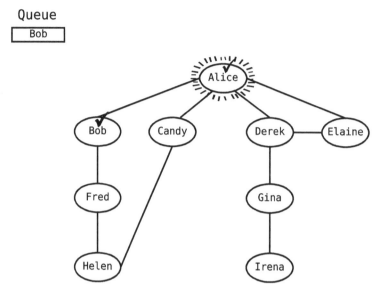

Note that Alice *is still the current vertex,* as indicated by the lines around her. However, we've still marked Bob as visited and added him to the queue.

Step 3: We move on to Alice's other adjacent vertices. Let's choose Candy; we'll mark her as visited and add her to the queue:

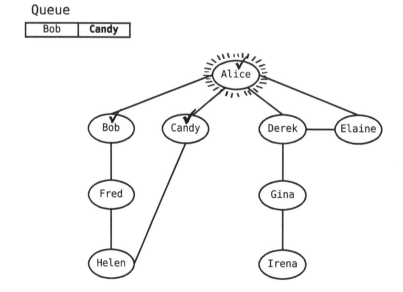

Step 4: We then mark Derek as visited and add him to the queue:

Queue

Bob	Candy	**Derek**

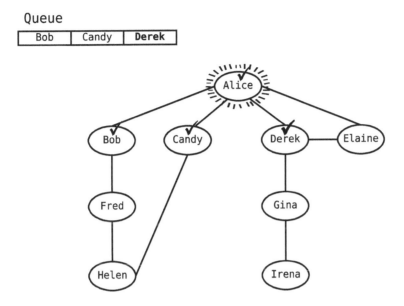

Step 5: We do the same with Elaine:

Queue

Bob	Candy	Derek	**Elaine**

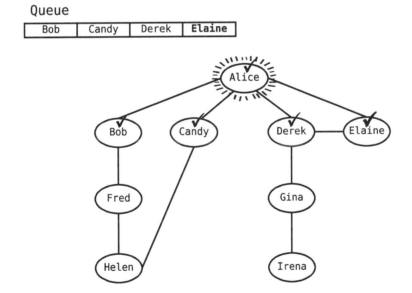

Step 6: Now that we've iterated through all the neighbors of the current vertex (Alice), we remove the first item from the queue and make it the current vertex. In our case, Bob is at the front of the queue, so we dequeue him and make him the current vertex, as shown in the graph on page 350.

Queue

Candy	Derek	Elaine

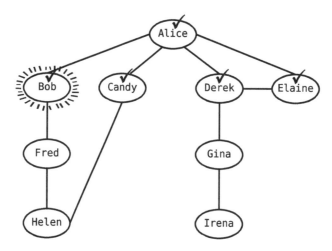

Since Bob is the current vertex, we iterate over all of his adjacent vertices.

Step 7: Alice has already been visited, so we ignore her.

Step 8: Fred has not yet been visited, so we mark him as visited and add him to the queue:

Queue

Candy	Derek	Elaine	**Fred**

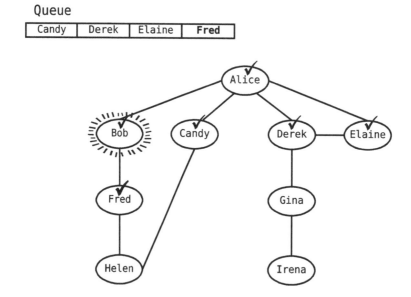

Step 9: Bob has no more adjacent vertices. This means we pull the first item out of the queue and make it the current vertex. This would be Candy:

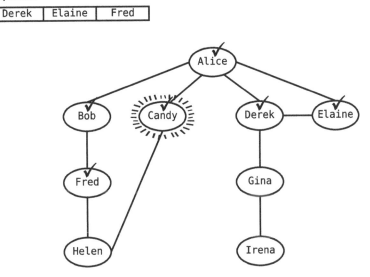

We iterate over Candy's adjacent vertices.

Step 10: Alice has already been visited, so we ignore her again.

Step 11: Helen, on the other hand, has not yet been visited. We mark Helen as visited and add her to the queue:

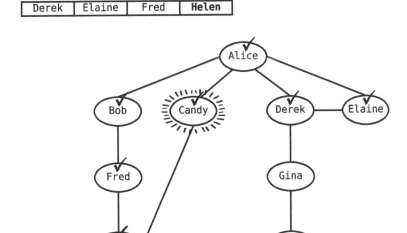

Step 12: We're done iterating over Candy's adjacent vertices, so we pull the first item from the queue (Derek), and make it the current vertex:

Queue

Elaine	Fred	Helen

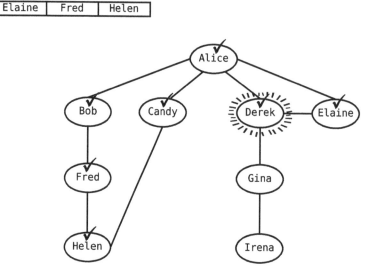

Derek has three adjacent vertices, so we iterate over them.

Step 13: Alice has already been visited, so we ignore her.

Step 14: The same goes for Elaine.

Step 15: This leaves Gina, so we mark her as visited and add her to the queue:

Queue

Elaine	Fred	Helen	**Gina**

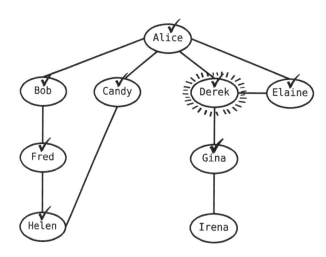

Step 16: We've visited all of Derek's immediate friends, so we take Elaine off the queue and designate her as the current vertex:

Queue

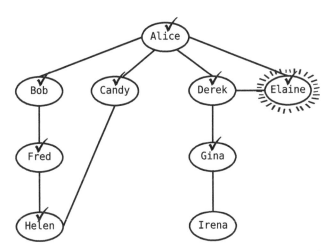

Step 17: We iterate over Elaine's adjacent vertices, starting with Alice. She's already been visited, though.

Step 18: We've already visited Derek too.

Step 19: We pull the next person off the queue (Fred), and turn him into the current vertex:

Queue

| Helen | Gina |

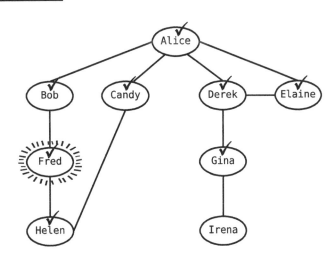

Step 20: We iterate over Fred's neighbors. Bob has already been visited.

Step 21: Helen also has already been visited.

Step 22: Since Helen is at the front of the queue, we dequeue Helen and make her the current vertex:

```
Queue
  Gina
```

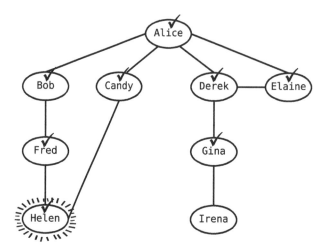

Step 23: Helen has two adjacent vertices. We've already visited Fred.

Step 24: We've also already visited Candy.

Step 25: We remove Gina from the queue and make her the current vertex:

```
Queue
(Empty)
```

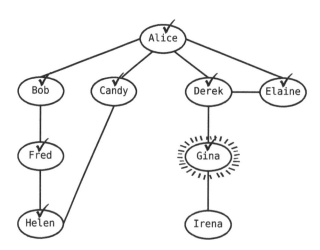

Step 26: We iterate over Gina's neighbors. Derek has already been visited.

Step 27: Gina has one unvisited adjacent friend, Irena, so we visit Irena and add her to the queue:

Queue

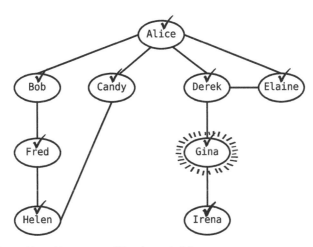

We're now done iterating over Gina's neighbors.

Step 28: We remove the first (and only) person from the queue, which is Irena. She becomes the current vertex:

Queue
(Empty)

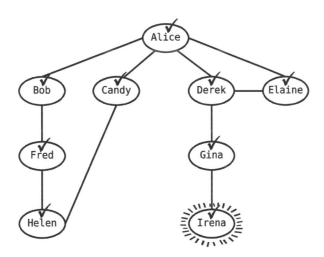

Step 29: Irena has just one adjacent vertex, Gina, but Gina has already been visited.

We should now remove the next item from the queue, but the queue is empty! This means our traversal is complete.

Code Implementation: Breadth-First Search

Here's our code for breadth-first traversal:

```
import queue_implementation

def bfs_traverse(starting_vertex):
    queue = queue_implementation.Queue()

    visited_vertices = {}
    visited_vertices[starting_vertex.value] = True
    queue.enqueue(starting_vertex)

    while queue.read():
        current_vertex = queue.dequeue()
        print(current_vertex.value)

        for adjacent_vertex in current_vertex.adjacent_vertices:

            if not visited_vertices.get(adjacent_vertex.value):
                visited_vertices[adjacent_vertex.value] = True
                queue.enqueue(adjacent_vertex)
```

We begin by importing a queue_implementation module. This is simply the same queue implementation we created back in Queue Implementation, on page 145.

The bfs_traverse method accepts a starting_vertex, which is the vertex we begin our search from.

We start by creating the queue that fuels our algorithm:

```
queue = queue_implementation.Queue()
```

We also create the visited_vertices hash table in which we keep track of which vertices we've already visited:

```
visited_vertices = {}
```

We then mark the starting_vertex as visited and add it to the queue:

```
visited_vertices[starting_vertex.value] = True
queue.enqueue(starting_vertex)
```

We begin a loop that runs as long as the queue isn't empty:

```
while queue.read():
```

We remove the first item from the queue and make it the current vertex:

```
current_vertex = queue.dequeue()
```

Next, we print the vertex's value just to see in our console that our traversal is working correctly:

```
print(current_vertex.value)
```

We then iterate over all the adjacent vertices of our current vertex:

```
for adjacent_vertex in current_vertex.adjacent_vertices:
```

For each adjacent vertex that hasn't been visited, we add it to the hash table to mark it as visited and then add it to the queue:

```
if not visited_vertices.get(adjacent_vertex.value):
    visited_vertices[adjacent_vertex.value] = True
    queue.enqueue(adjacent_vertex)
```

And that's the gist of it.

DFS vs. BFS

If you look carefully at the order of breadth-first search, you'll notice that we first traverse all of Alice's immediate connections. We then spiral outward and gradually move farther and farther from Alice. With depth-first search, though, we immediately move as far away from Alice as we possibly can until we're forced to return to her.

So we have two methods of searching a graph: depth-first and breadth-first. Is one approach better than the other?

As you've probably caught on by now, it depends on your situation. In some scenarios, depth-first may be faster, while in others, breadth-first might be the better choice.

Usually, one of the main factors in determining which algorithm to use is the nature of the graph you're searching and what you're searching for. The key here, as mentioned earlier, is that breadth-first search traverses all the vertices closest to the starting vertex before moving farther away. Depth-first search, on the other hand, immediately moves as far away from the starting vertex as it can. Only when the search hits a dead end does it return back to the starting vertex.

So let's say we want to find all the *direct* connections of a person in a social network. For example, we may want to find all of Alice's actual friends in our earlier example graph. We're not interested in who her friends' friends are—we only want a list of her direct connections.

If you look at the breadth-first approach, you'll see that we immediately find all of Alice's direct friends (Bob, Candy, Derek, and Elaine) before moving on to her "second-degree" connections.

However, when we traversed the graph with the depth-first algorithm, we ended up touching Fred and Helen (two people who aren't Alice's friends) before finding Alice's other friends. In a larger graph, we could waste even more time traversing many unnecessary vertices.

But let's take a different scenario. Say our graph represents a family tree, which may look as follows:

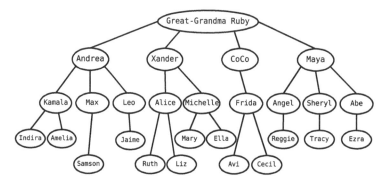

This family tree shows all the descendants of Great-Grandma Ruby, the proud matriarch of a wonderful family. Let's say we know that Ruth is a great-grandchild of Ruby, and we want to find Ruth in the graph.

Now, here's the thing. If we used breadth-first search, we'd end up traversing all of Ruby's children and grandchildren before reaching even the first great-grandchild.

However, if we use depth-first search, we'd move down the graph right away, reaching the first great-grandchild in just a few steps. While it's possible that we'd have to traverse the entire graph before finding Ruth, we at least have a shot at finding her quickly. With breadth-first search, though, we have no choice but to traverse all the non–great-grandchildren before we can start inspecting the great-grandchildren.

The question to always ask, then, is do we want to stay close to the starting vertex during our search, or do we specifically want to move far away. Breadth-first search is good for staying close, and depth-first search is ideal for moving far away quickly.

The Efficiency of Graph Search

Let's analyze the time complexity of graph search using Big O notation.

In both depth-first search and breadth-first search, we traverse all the vertices in a worst-case scenario. The worst-case scenario may be that we're intending to do a full-graph traversal, or we may be searching for a vertex that doesn't exist in the graph. Or, the vertex we're searching for may just happen to be the last vertex in the graph that we check.

In any case, we touch all vertices in the graph. At first glance, this would seem to be O(N), with N being the number of vertices.

However, in both search algorithms, for each vertex we traverse, *we also iterate over all of its adjacent vertices*. We may ignore an adjacent vertex if it has already been visited, but we still spend a step checking that vertex to see whether we've visited it.

So for each vertex we visit, we also spend steps checking each of the vertex's adjacent neighbors. This would seem tough to peg down using Big O notation, since each vertex may have a different number of adjacent vertices.

Let's analyze a simple graph to make this clear:

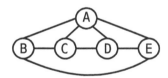

Here, Vertex A has four neighbors. By contrast, B, C, D, and E each have three neighbors. Let's count the number of steps it takes to search this graph.

At the very least, we have to visit each of the five vertices. This alone takes five steps.

Then, for *each* vertex, we iterate over each of its neighbors.

This would add the following steps:

A: 4 steps to iterate over 4 neighbors
B: 3 steps to iterate over 3 neighbors
C: 3 steps to iterate over 3 neighbors
D: 3 steps to iterate over 3 neighbors
E: 3 steps to iterate over 3 neighbors

This yields sixteen iterations.

So we have the visiting of the five vertices, plus sixteen iterations over adjacent neighbors. That's a total of twenty-one steps.

But here's another graph with five vertices:

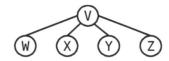

This graph has five vertices, but the count of iterations over adjacent neighbors is as follows:

V: 4 steps to iterate over 4 neighbors
W: 1 step to iterate over 1 neighbor
X: 1 step to iterate over 1 neighbor
Y: 1 step to iterate over 1 neighbor
Z: 1 step to iterate over 1 neighbor

This is a total of eight iterations.

We have the five vertices, plus eight iterations over adjacent neighbors. This is a total of thirteen steps.

So, we have two graphs, each containing five vertices. However, searching one takes twenty-one steps, while searching the other takes thirteen steps.

It emerges that we can't just count how many vertices are in the graph. Instead, *we also need to consider how many adjacent neighbors each vertex has.*

To effectively describe the efficiency of graph search, then, we're going to need to use *two* variables. We need one to represent the number of vertices in the graph and another to be the total number of adjacent neighbors each vertex has.

O(V + E)

Interestingly enough, Big O notation doesn't use the variable N to describe either of these things. Instead, it uses the variables V and E.

The V is the easier one. V stands for *vertex* and represents the number of vertices in the graph.

E, interestingly, stands for *edge*, meaning the number of edges in the graph.

Now, computer scientists describe the efficiency of graph search as O(V + E). This means that the number of steps is the number of vertices in the graph *plus* the number of edges in the graph. Let's see why this is the efficiency of graph search, as it's not immediately intuitive.

Specifically, if you look at our two earlier examples, you'll notice that V + E doesn't seem to be accurate.

In the A-B-C-D-E graph, there are five vertices and eight edges. This would be a total of thirteen steps. However, we noted that there's actually a total of twenty-one steps.

And in the V-W-X-Y-Z graph, there are five vertices and four edges. O(V + E) says that graph search would have nine steps. But we saw that there are actually thirteen.

The reason for this discrepancy is that while O(V + E) only counts the number of edges once, in reality, graph search touches each edge *more* than once.

In the V-W-X-Y-Z graph, for example, there are only four edges. However, the edge between V and W is used twice; that is, when V is the current vertex, we find its adjacent neighbor W using that edge. But when W is the current vertex, we find its adjacent vertex V using that same edge.

With this in mind, the most accurate way to describe the efficiency of graph search in the V-W-X-Y-Z graph would be to count the five vertices, plus:

2 * edge between V and W
2 * edge between V and X
2 * edge between V and Y
2 * edge between V and Z

So this comes out to be V + 2E, since we visit all the vertices once (that's the V) and use each edge twice (that's the 2E).

In this example, V is 5, as we visit 5 vertices. And since we use each of the four edges twice, 2E comes out to be 8. This is how V + 2E gives us a total of thirteen steps.

The answer, though, to why we just call this O(V + E), is because *Big O drops the constants*. While in reality the number of steps is V + 2E, we reduce this to O(V + E).

So while O(V + E) is ultimately just an approximation, it's good enough, as are all expressions of Big O.

What is definitely clear, though, is that increasing the number of edges *will* increase the number of steps. After all, both the A-B-C-D-E and V-W-X-Y-Z graphs have five vertices, but because the A-B-C-D-E graph has more edges, it takes considerably more steps.

At the end of the day, graph search is O(V + E) in a worst-case scenario, where the vertex we're searching for is the last one we find (or isn't present in the graph at all). And this is true for both breadth-first search and depth-first search.

However, we saw earlier that depending on the shape of the graph and the data we're searching for, our choice of breadth-first versus depth-first can optimize our search where we'd hope to find our vertex at some point *before* having to traverse the entire graph. The right method of search can help us increase the odds that we won't end up in a worst-case scenario and that we'll find the vertex early.

In the next section, you're going to learn about a specific type of graph that comes with its own set of search methods that can be used to solve some complex but useful problems.

Graph Databases

Because graphs are so efficient at working with data involving relationships (such as friends in a social network), special *graph databases* are often used to store this kind of data in real-world software applications. These databases use the concepts you're learning about in this chapter, as well as other elements of graph theory, to optimize efficiency of operations around this kind of data. Indeed, many social networking applications are powered by graph databases under the hood.

Some examples of graph databases include Neo4j[a] and ArangoDB[b]. These websites are a good place to start if you're interested in learning more about how graph databases work.

---

a. http://neo4j.com
b. https://www.arangodb.com

Weighted Graphs

We've already seen that graphs can come in a number of different flavors. Another useful type of graph, known as a *weighted graph*, adds additional information to the *edges* of the graph.

Here's a weighted graph that represents a basic map of several major cities in the United States:

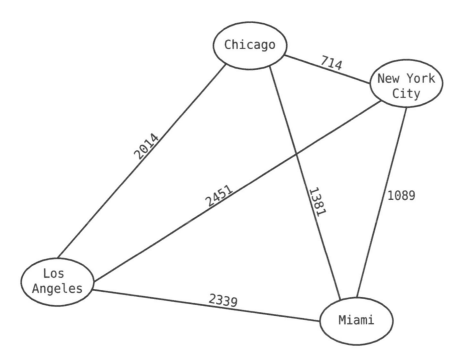

In this graph, each edge is accompanied by a number that represents the distance in miles between the cities the edge connects. For example, there are 714 miles between Chicago and New York City.

It's also possible to have weighted graphs that are also directional. In the following example, we can see that although a flight from Dallas to Toronto is $138, a flight from Toronto back to Dallas is $216:

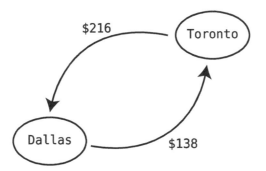

Weighted Graphs in Code

We need to make a slight modification to our code if we want to add weights to our graph. One way to do this is to use a hash table to represent the adjacent vertices rather than using an array:

```
class WeightedGraphVertex:

    def __init__(self, value):
        self.value = value
        self.adjacent_vertices = {}

    def add_adjacent_vertex(self, vertex, weight):
        self.adjacent_vertices[vertex] = weight
```

As you can see, self.adjacent_vertices is now a hash table instead of an array. The hash table will contain key-value pairs, where in each pair, the adjacent vertex is the key and the weight (of the edge from this vertex to the adjacent vertex) is the value.

When we use the add_adjacent_vertex method to add an adjacent vertex, we now pass in both the adjacent vertex as well as the weight.

Since we'll continue to deal with the example of a graph that depicts flight fares to and from various cities, we'll create a special class called City. This is the same implementation as the preceding WeightedGraphVertex but uses class and variable names appropriate to our use case:

```
class City:

    def __init__(self, name):
        self.name = name
        self.routes = {}

    def add_route(self, city, price):
        self.routes[city] = price
```

So if we want to create the Dallas–Toronto flight price graph from earlier, we can run the following code:

```
dallas = City("Dallas")
toronto = City("Toronto")

dallas.add_route(toronto, 138)
toronto.add_route(dallas, 216)
```

The Shortest Path Problem

Weighted graphs can be very useful in modeling all sorts of datasets, and they also come with some powerful algorithms that help us make the most out of that data.

Let's harness one of these algorithms to save us a bit of money.

Here's a graph that demonstrates the costs of available flights between five different cities:

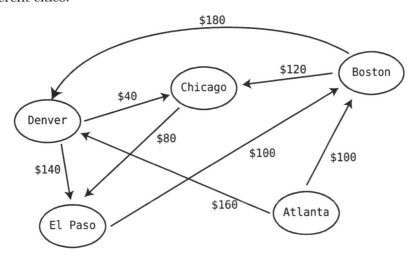

Now, say I'm in Atlanta and want to fly to El Paso. Unfortunately, we can see in this graph that there's no direct route from Atlanta to El Paso at this time. However, I can get there if I'm willing to stop over in other cities along the way. For example, I can fly from Atlanta to Denver and then from Denver to El Paso. But there are other paths as well, and each path has a different price. The Atlanta–Denver–El Paso path will set me back $300, but the Atlanta–Denver–Chicago–El Paso path only costs $280.

The puzzle, now, is this: how do we create an algorithm that finds the *cheapest* price I'd have to shell out to get to my destination? Let's assume we don't care about how many stops we have to make; we're just out to get the cheapest fare.

This kind of puzzle is known as the *shortest path problem*. This problem can take other forms as well. For example, if the graph showed us distances between cities, we might want to find the path that has the shortest distance. But here, the shortest path we're looking for is the cheapest one, since the weights represent flight prices.

Dijkstra's Algorithm

Numerous algorithms can solve the shortest path problem, and one of the most famous is one discovered by Edsger Dijkstra (pronounced "dike' struh") in 1959. Unsurprisingly, this algorithm is known as *Dijkstra's algorithm*.

In this section, we're going to use Dijkstra's algorithm to find the cheapest path in our city flights example.

Dijkstra's Algorithm Setup

The first thing to note is that Dijkstra's algorithm comes with a free bonus. By the time we're done, we're not just going to find the cheapest price from Atlanta to El Paso, but also we're going to find the cheapest prices from Atlanta to *all* known cities. As you'll see, the algorithm simply works this way; we end up gathering all of this data. So we'll know the cheapest price from Atlanta to Chicago, the cheapest price from Atlanta to Denver, and so on.

To set things up, we'll create a way to store the cheapest known prices from our starting city to all other known destinations. In our code that follows, we'll use a hash table for this. For our example walk-through, though, we'll use a visual table that looks like this:

From Atlanta To:	City #1	City #2	City #3	Etc.
	?	?	?	?

The algorithm will begin at the Atlanta vertex, as it's the only city we're currently aware of. As we discover new cities, we'll add them to our table and record the cheapest price from Atlanta to each of these cities.

By the time the algorithm is complete, the table will look like this:

Cheapest Price from Atlanta To:	Boston	Chicago	Denver	El Paso
	$100	$200	$160	$280

In code, this will be represented with a hash table that looks like so:

```
{"Atlanta": 0, "Boston": 100, "Chicago": 200,
"Denver": 160, "El Paso": 280}
```

(Note that Atlanta is in the hash table as well with a value of 0. We'll need this to get the algorithm to work, but it also makes sense, as it costs nothing to get to Atlanta from Atlanta, since you're already there!)

In our code and going forward, we'll call this table the cheapest_prices_table, as it stores all the cheapest prices from the starting city to all other destinations.

Now, if all we wanted to do is figure out the cheapest price to get to a particular destination, the cheapest_prices_table would contain all the data we need. But we probably also want to know the actual path that would get us the cheapest price. For instance, if we want to get from Atlanta to El Paso, we don't want to just know the cheapest price is $280; we also want to know that to get this price, we need to fly the specific path of Atlanta–Denver–Chicago–El Paso.

To achieve this, we'll also need *another* table, which we'll call the cheapest_previous_stopover_city_table. The purpose of this table will only become clear once we jump into the algorithm, so I'll hold off on the explanation until then. For now, though, it'll suffice to show what it'll look like by the end of the algorithm.

Cheapest Previous Stopover City from Atlanta:	Boston	Chicago	Denver	El Paso
	Atlanta	Denver	Atlanta	Chicago

(Note that this table, too, will be implemented using a hash table.)

Dijkstra's Algorithm Steps

Now that everything is set up, here are the steps for Dijkstra's algorithm. For clarity, I'm going to describe the algorithm in terms of cities, but you can replace the word "city" with "vertex" to make it work for any weighted graph. Also note that these steps will become clearer when we walk through an example. But for now, here we go:

1. We visit the starting city, making it our "current city."

2. We check the prices from the current city to each of its adjacent cities.

3. If the price to an adjacent city from the starting city is cheaper than the price currently in cheapest_prices_table (or the adjacent city isn't yet in the cheapest_prices_table at all):

    a. We update the cheapest_prices_table to reflect this cheaper price.

    b. We update the cheapest_previous_stopover_city_table, making the adjacent city the key and the current city the value.

4. We then visit whichever unvisited city has the cheapest price from the starting city, making it the current city.

5. We repeat the Steps 2 through 4 until we've visited every known city.

Again, this will all make more sense when we walk through an example.

Dijkstra's Algorithm Walk-Through

Let's walk through Dijkstra's algorithm step by step.

To start, our cheapest_prices_table only contains Atlanta:

From Atlanta To:
$0

At the start of the algorithm, Atlanta is the only city we have access to; we've not yet "discovered" the other cities.

Step 1: We officially visit Atlanta and make it the current_city.

To indicate that it's the current_city, we'll surround it with lines. And to add to the record that we've visited it, we'll add a check mark:

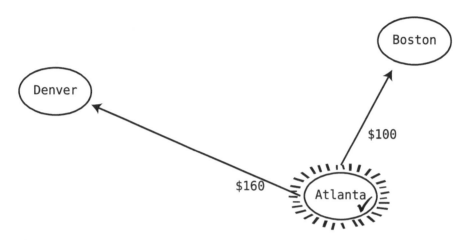

In the next steps, we'll proceed to inspect each of the current_city's adjacent cities. This is how we discover new cities; if a city we have access to has adjacent cities we weren't aware of before, we can add them to our map.

Step 2: One city adjacent to Atlanta is Boston. As we can see, the price from Atlanta to Boston is $100. We then check the cheapest_prices_table to see whether this is the cheapest known price from Atlanta to Boston, but it turns out we haven't recorded *any* prices from Atlanta to Boston yet. That means this is the cheapest *known* flight from Atlanta to Boston (as of now), so we add that to the cheapest_prices_table:

From Atlanta To:	*Boston*
$0	*$100*

Since we've made a change to the cheapest_prices_table, we now also need to modify the cheapest_previous_stopover_city_table, making the adjacent city (Boston) the key and the current_city the value:

Cheapest Previous Stopover City from Atlanta:	*Boston*
	Atlanta

Adding this data to this table means that to earn the cheapest known price from Atlanta to Boston ($100), the city we need to visit *immediately before Boston* is Atlanta. At this point, this is obvious, since Atlanta is the *only* way to get to Boston that we know of. However, as we proceed, we'll see why this second table becomes useful.

Step 3: We've checked out Boston, but Atlanta has another adjacent city, Denver. We check whether the price ($160) is the cheapest known route from Atlanta to Denver, but Denver isn't in the cheapest_prices_table at all yet, so we add it as the cheapest known flight:

From Atlanta To:	Boston	*Denver*
$0	$100	*$160*

We then also add Denver and Atlanta as a key-value pair to the cheapest_previous_stopover_city_table:

Cheapest Previous Stopover City from Atlanta:	Boston	*Denver*
	Atlanta	*Atlanta*

Step 4: By this point, we've inspected all of Atlanta's adjacent cities, so it's time to visit our next city. But we need to figure out which city to visit next.

Now, as stated in the algorithm steps earlier, we only proceed to visit cities we haven't yet visited. Furthermore, among the unvisited cities, we always choose to *first* visit the city that has the cheapest known route *from the starting city.* We can get this data from the cheapest_prices_table.

In our example, the only cities we know about that we haven't visited yet are Boston or Denver. By looking at the cheapest_prices_table, we can see that it's cheaper to get from Atlanta to Boston than it is to get from Atlanta to Denver, so we're going to visit Boston next.

Step 5: We visit Boston and designate it as the current_city:

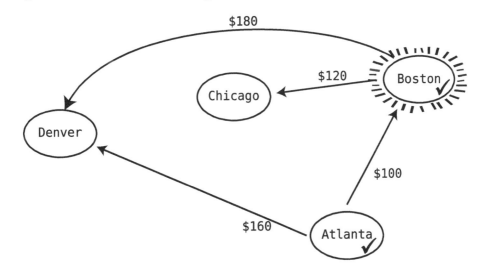

Next, we're going to inspect Boston's adjacent cities.

Step 6: Boston has two adjacent cities, Chicago and Denver. (Atlanta isn't considered adjacent, since we can't fly from Boston to Atlanta.)

Which city should we visit first—Chicago or Denver? Again, we want to first visit the city whose price is cheapest if we were flying to it *from Atlanta*. So let's do the math.

The price from Boston to Chicago alone is $120. When looking at the cheapest_prices_table, we can see that the cheapest route from Atlanta to Boston is $100. So this means that the cheapest flight from Atlanta to Chicago *with Boston as the previous stopover city* would be $220.

Since, at this point, this is the only known price from Atlanta to Chicago, we'll add it to the cheapest_prices_table. We'll insert it in the middle of the table to keep the cities alphabetized:

From Atlanta To:	Boston	*Chicago*	Denver
$0	$100	*$220*	$160

Again, because we made a change to that table, we'll also modify the cheapest_previous_stopover_city_table. The adjacent city always becomes the key, and the current_city always becomes the value, so the table becomes:

Cheapest Previous Stopover City from Atlanta:	Boston	*Chicago*	Denver
	Atlanta	*Boston*	Atlanta

In our quest to find the city to visit next, we analyzed Chicago. We'll inspect Denver next.

Step 7: Let's now look at the edge between Boston and Denver. We can see that the price is $180. Since the cheapest flight from Atlanta to Boston, again, is $100, that would mean the cheapest flight from Atlanta to Denver *through Boston as the previous stopover city* is $280.

This gets a little interesting, because when we inspect our cheapest_prices_table, we can see that the cheapest route from Atlanta to Denver is $160, *which is cheaper* than the Atlanta–Boston–Denver route. Accordingly, *we do not modify* either of our tables; we want to leave $160 as the cheapest known route from Atlanta to Denver.

We're done with this step, and since we've looked at all of Boston's adjacent cities, we can now visit our next city.

Step 8: The current known unvisited cities are Chicago and Denver. Again, the one we visit next—and pay careful attention to this—is the city with the cheapest known path *from our starting city* (Atlanta).

Looking at our cheapest_prices_table, we can see that it's cheaper to go from Atlanta to Denver ($160) than it is to go to from Atlanta to Chicago ($220), so that means that we visit Denver next:

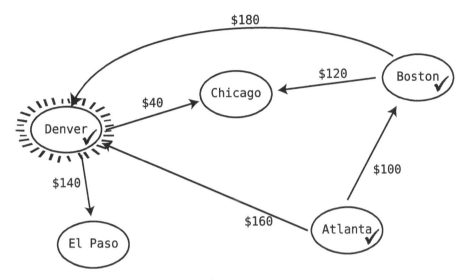

Next up, we'll look at Denver's adjacent cities.

Step 9: Denver has two adjacent cities, Chicago and El Paso. Which of these cities will we visit next? To find out, we need to analyze the prices to each city. Let's start with Chicago.

It costs just $40 to go from Denver to Chicago (a good deal!), which means the cheapest flight from Atlanta to Chicago *through Denver as the previous stopover city* would be $200, since the cheapest route from Atlanta to Denver is $160.

When looking at the cheapest_prices_table, we can see that the current cheapest price from Atlanta to Chicago is $220. That means this new route we just found to Chicago through Denver is even cheaper, so we can update the cheapest_prices_table accordingly:

From Atlanta To:	Boston	Chicago	Denver
$0	$100	*$200*	$160

Whenever we update the cheapest_prices_table, we also have to update the cheapest_previous_stopover_city_table. We set the adjacent city (Chicago) as the key and the current_city (Denver) as the value. Now, in this case, Chicago already exists as a key. This means we'll be overwriting its value from Boston to Denver:

Cheapest Previous Stopover City from Atlanta:	Boston	Chicago	Denver
	Atlanta	*Denver*	Atlanta

What this means is that to nab the cheapest flight path from Atlanta to Chicago, we need to stop over at Denver as the city immediately prior to Chicago; that is, Denver should be our second-to-last stop before we proceed to Chicago. Only then will we save the most money.

This information will be useful in determining the cheapest path from Atlanta to our destination city, as you'll see in a little bit. Hang on, we're almost there!

Step 10: Denver has another adjacent city, El Paso. The price from Denver to El Paso is $140. We can now construct our first known price from Atlanta to El Paso. The cheapest_prices_table tells us the cheapest price from Atlanta to Denver is $160. This means if we then go from Denver to El Paso, we incur another $140, making the total price from Atlanta to El Paso $300. We can add this to the cheapest_prices_table:

From Atlanta To:	Boston	Chicago	Denver	El Paso
$0	$100	$200	$160	$300

We must then also add the key-value pair of El Paso-Denver to our cheapest_previous_stopover_city_table:

Cheapest Previous Stopover City from Atlanta:	Boston	Chicago	Denver	El Paso
	Atlanta	Denver	Atlanta	Denver

Again, this means that to save the most money when flying from Atlanta to El Paso, our second-to-last stop should be Denver.

We've seen all our current_city's adjacent cities, so it's time to visit our next city.

Step 11: We have two known unvisited cities, Chicago and El Paso. Since it's cheaper to get from Atlanta to Chicago ($200) than it is to get from Atlanta to El Paso ($300), we visit Chicago next, as shown in the graph on page 373.

Step 12: Chicago has only one adjacent city, El Paso. The price from Chicago to El Paso is $80 (not bad). With this information, we can now calculate the cheapest price from Atlanta to El Paso when assuming that Chicago is our second-to-last stop.

The cheapest_prices_table shows us that the cheapest path from Atlanta to Chicago is $200. Adding the $80 to this means the cheapest price from Atlanta to El Paso *with Chicago as the second-to-last stop* would cost $280.

Wait! This is cheaper than the currently known cheapest path from Atlanta to El Paso. In our cheapest_prices_table, we see that the cheapest known price is $300. But when we fly through Chicago, the price is $280, which is cheaper.

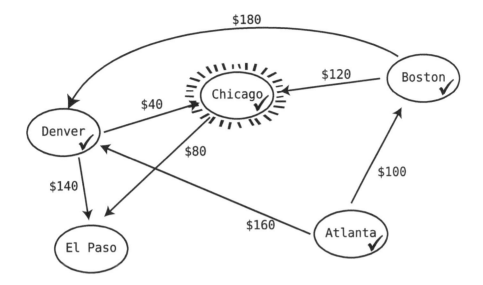

Accordingly, we need to update the cheapest_prices_table to indicate our newly found cheapest path to El Paso:

From Atlanta To:	Boston	Chicago	Denver	El Paso
$0	$100	$200	$160	*$280*

We also need to update the cheapest_previous_stopover_city_table, with El Paso as the key and Chicago as the value:

Cheapest Previous Stopover City from Atlanta:	Boston	Chicago	Denver	El Paso
	Atlanta	Denver	Atlanta	*Chicago*

Chicago has no more adjacent cities, so we can now visit our next city.

Step 13: El Paso is the only known unvisited city, so let's make it our current_city, as shown in the graph on page 374.

Step 14: El Paso has only one outbound flight, which is to Boston. That flight costs $100. Now, the cheapest_prices_table reveals that the cheapest price from Atlanta to El Paso is $280. So if we travel from Atlanta to Boston *with El Paso* as the second-to-last stop, our grand total will be $380. This is more expensive than the cheapest-known price from Atlanta to Boston ($100), so we don't update any of our tables.

Since we've visited every known city, we now have all the information we need to find the cheapest path from Atlanta to El Paso.

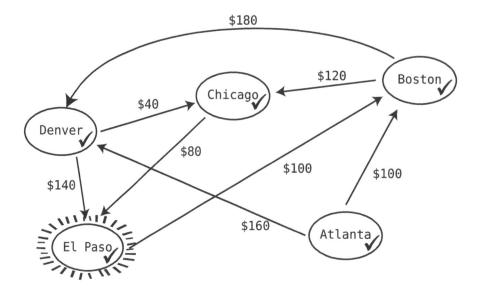

Finding the Shortest Path

If we just want to know the cheapest price from Atlanta to El Paso, we can look in our cheapest_prices_table and see that it's $280. But if we want to figure out the *exact* path to fly to snag that low price, we have one last thing to do.

Remember the cheapest_previous_stopover_city_table? It's now time to use that data.

Currently, the cheapest_previous_stopover_city_table looks like this:

Cheapest Previous Stopover City from Atlanta:	Boston	Chicago	Denver	El Paso
	Atlanta	Denver	Atlanta	Chicago

We can use this table to draw the shortest path from Atlanta to El Paso—if we go backward.

Let's look at El Paso. Its corresponding city is Chicago. This means the cheapest route from Atlanta to El Paso involves stopping over in Chicago as the *immediate step* before flying to El Paso. Let's write this down:

```
Chicago -> El Paso
```

Now, if we look up Chicago in the cheapest_previous_stopover_city_table, we can see that its corresponding value is Denver. This means the cheapest route from Atlanta to *Chicago* involves stopping in Denver right before Chicago. Let's add this to our figure:

```
Denver -> Chicago -> El Paso
```

If we then look up Denver in the cheapest_previous_stopover_city_table, we can see that the cheapest flight to get from Atlanta to Denver is to fly directly from Atlanta to Denver:

```
Atlanta -> Denver -> Chicago -> El Paso
```

Now, Atlanta happens to be our starting city, so this route is the exact path we'd take from Atlanta to El Paso to get the cheapest price.

Let's review the logic we're using to chain together the cheapest path.

Remember, the cheapest_previous_stopover_city_table contains, for each destination, the second-to-last stop before that destination to earn the cheapest price if you're flying from Atlanta.

So from the cheapest_previous_stopover_city_table, we can see that the cheapest price from Atlanta to El Paso means:

- We need to fly directly from Chicago to El Paso, and
- We need to fly directly from Denver to Chicago, and
- We need to fly directly from Atlanta to Denver.

This means that the following is our cheapest path:

```
Atlanta -> Denver -> Chicago -> El Paso
```

And…that's it. Whew!

Code Implementation: Dijkstra's Algorithm

Before we get to the actual algorithm, we can set up our example from earlier, using this code:

```
atlanta = City("Atlanta")
boston = City("Boston")
chicago = City("Chicago")
denver = City("Denver")
el_paso = City("El Paso")

atlanta.add_route(boston, 100)
atlanta.add_route(denver, 160)
boston.add_route(chicago, 120)
boston.add_route(denver, 180)
chicago.add_route(el_paso, 80)
denver.add_route(chicago, 40)
denver.add_route(el_paso, 140)
el_paso.add_route(boston, 100)
```

Finally, here's the code for Dijkstra's algorithm. It doesn't make for light reading, and it's probably the most complex piece of code in this book. However, if you're ready to study it carefully, read on.

In our implementation here, this method does not live inside the City class, but outside it. The method accepts two City instances and returns the shortest path between them:

```python
def dijkstra_shortest_path(starting_city, final_destination):
    cheapest_prices_table = {}
    cheapest_previous_stopover_city_table = {}
    unvisited_cities = [starting_city]
    visited_cities = {}

    cheapest_prices_table[starting_city.name] = 0
    current_city = starting_city

    while unvisited_cities:
        visited_cities[current_city.name] = True
        unvisited_cities.remove(current_city)

        for adjacent_city in current_city.routes:
            price = current_city.routes.get(adjacent_city)

            if (not visited_cities.get(adjacent_city.name)
                    and adjacent_city not in unvisited_cities):
                unvisited_cities.append(adjacent_city)

            price_through_current_city = \
                (cheapest_prices_table[current_city.name] + price)

            if (not cheapest_prices_table.get(adjacent_city.name) or
                (price_through_current_city
                    < cheapest_prices_table[adjacent_city.name])):

                cheapest_prices_table[adjacent_city.name] = \
                    price_through_current_city
                cheapest_previous_stopover_city_table[adjacent_city.name] = \
                    current_city.name

        cheapest_price = float('inf')
        for city in unvisited_cities:
            if cheapest_prices_table[city.name] < cheapest_price:
                current_city = city
                cheapest_price = cheapest_prices_table[city.name]

    shortest_path = []
    current_city_name = final_destination.name

    while current_city_name:
        shortest_path.insert(0, current_city_name)
        current_city_name = \
            cheapest_previous_stopover_city_table.get(current_city_name)

    return shortest_path
```

We have a decent amount of code here, so let's break it down.

The dijkstra_shortest_path function accepts two vertices, representing the starting_city and final_destination.

Eventually, our function will return an array of strings that represent the cheapest path. For our example, this function would return:

```
["Atlanta", "Denver", "Chicago", "El Paso"]
```

The first thing our function does is set up the two primary tables that fuel the entire algorithm:

```
cheapest_prices_table = {}
cheapest_previous_stopover_city_table = {}
```

We then set up ways to track which cities we've visited and the ones we have yet to visit:

```
unvisited_cities = [starting_city]
visited_cities = {}
```

Note that we prepopulate unvisited_cities with the starting_city as the only item in the array.

It may seem odd that unvisited_cities is an array, while visited_cities is a hash table. The reason we've made visited_cities a hash table is because in the code that follows we only use it for lookups, for which a hash table is an ideal choice in terms time complexity.

The choice of the best data structure for the unvisited_cities is less simple. In our code that follows, the next city we visit is always the cheapest unvisited city to reach from the starting city. Ideally, then, we always want immediate access to the cheapest option from among the unvisited cities. Our code that accesses this data is simpler if the data structure is an array.

In truth, a priority queue would be a perfect fit for this, as its whole function is to provide ready access to the least (or greatest) value from a collection of items. As you saw in Chapter 16, Keeping Your Priorities Straight with Heaps, on page 277, a heap is generally the best data structure for implementing a priority queue. However, I've instead chosen to use a simple array for this implementation only to keep the code as simple and small as possible, since Dijkstra's algorithm is complex enough on its own. But I encourage you to try replacing the array with a priority queue.

Next, we add the first key-value pair to the cheapest_prices_table with the starting_city as the key and 0 as the value. Again, this makes sense because it costs nothing to get to the starting_city as we're already there:

```
cheapest_prices_table[starting_city.name] = 0
```

As the last bit of setup, we designate the starting_city to be our current_city:

```
current_city = starting_city
```

We now begin the core of the algorithm, which takes the form of a loop that runs as long as unvisited_cities contains any cities. Within this loop, we mark the current_city as having been visited by adding its name to the visited_cities hash table.

```
while unvisited_cities:
    visited_cities[current_city.name] = True
```

And, by definition, since we've visited current_city, we need to remove it from the list of unvisited_cities:

```
unvisited_cities.remove(current_city)
```

Next, within the while loop we begin another loop, iterating over all of the adjacent cities of the current_city:

```
for adjacent_city in current_city.routes:
```

Within this inner loop, we first add each adjacent city to the array of unvisited_cities if it's a city we've never visited before. Additionally, we only add the adjacent city to unvisited_cities if it's not already there:

```
if (not visited_cities.get(adjacent_city.name)
    and adjacent_city not in unvisited_cities):
    unvisited_cities.append(adjacent_city)
```

Next, we calculate the cheapest possible price to get from the starting city to the adjacent city, assuming that the current_city is the second-to-last stop. We do this by using the cheapest_prices_table to look up the cheapest known route to the current_city and then adding that to the price of the route from the current_city to the adjacent city. This calculation then gets stored in a variable called price_through_current_city:

```
price_through_current_city = cheapest_prices_table[current_city.name] + price
```

Then we look within the cheapest_prices_table to see whether this price_through_current_city is now the cheapest known flight from the starting city to the adjacent city. If the adjacent city isn't yet in the cheapest_prices_table, this price is, by definition, the cheapest known price:

```
if (not cheapest_prices_table.get(adjacent_city.name) or
    (price_through_current_city
    < cheapest_prices_table[adjacent_city.name])):
```

If the price_through_current_city *is* now the cheapest route from the starting city to the adjacent city, we update the two main tables; that is, we store the new price for the adjacent city in the cheapest_prices_table. And we also update the cheapest_previous_stopover_city_table with the adjacent city's name as the key and the current_city's name as the value:

```
cheapest_prices_table[adjacent_city.name] = price_through_current_city
cheapest_previous_stopover_city_table[adjacent_city.name] = current_city.name
```

After iterating over all the adjacent cities of the current_city, it's time to visit the next city. We use the following snippet to find the cheapest unvisited city we can reach from the starting city and declare the cheapest city to be our new current_city:

```
cheapest_price = float('inf')
for city in unvisited_cities:
    if cheapest_prices_table[city.name] < cheapest_price:
        current_city = city
        cheapest_price = cheapest_prices_table[city.name]
```

The preceding code creates a cheapest_price variable and sets it to *infinity*. This is a little trick to ensure that each price we encounter will be lower than the initial value of cheapest_price. The loop then iterates over each of the unvisited_cities, checking each city against the cheapest_prices_table. Each time it finds a cheaper city, it sets current_city to that city. By the time the loop completes, current_city will indeed be pointing to the cheapest unvisited city.

The main while loop ends once the unvisited_cities array is empty. This means we visited all the cities in the graph!

At this point, the two tables have been fully populated with all the data we need. If we so chose, we could at this point simply return the cheapest_prices_table and see all the cheapest prices to all known cities from the starting_city.

Instead, though, we proceed to find the precise cheapest path to get to our final_destination.

To set things up for this, we create an array called shortest_path, which is what we'll return at the end of the function:

```
shortest_path = []
```

We also create a variable called current_city_name, which starts out as the name of the final_destination:

```
current_city_name = final_destination.name
```

We then begin a while loop that populates the shortest_path. This loop will insert all the cities in backward order, starting with the final_destination and working its way to the starting_city:

```
while current_city_name:
    shortest_path.insert(0, current_city_name)
```

We then use the cheapest_previous_stopover_city_table to find the city that should be the stop immediately preceding the current_city_name. This previous city now becomes the new current_city_name:

```
current_city_name = \
  cheapest_previous_stopover_city_table.get(current_city_name)
```

The shortest_path now contains the backward path from the final_destination to the starting_city, so that's what we finally return:

```
return shortest_path
```

Although our implementation deals with cities and prices, all the variable names can be changed to handle the shortest path for *any* weighted graph.

The Efficiency of Dijkstra's Algorithm

Dijkstra's algorithm is a general description of the approach for finding the shortest path within a weighted graph, but it doesn't specify the precise code implementation. In fact, a number of variations in how this algorithm can be written are out there.

In our code walk-through, for example, we used a simple array for the unvisited_cities data structure, but I noted that a priority queue could be used instead.

It turns out that the precise implementation has a considerable effect on the algorithm's time complexity. But let's at least analyze *our* implementation.

When we use a simple array for keeping track of the cities we haven't visited yet (unvisited_cities), our algorithm can take up to $O(V^2)$ steps. This is because the worst-case scenario for Dijkstra's algorithm is when each vertex has an edge leading to every other vertex within the graph. In this case, for every vertex we visit, we check the weight of the path from that vertex to every other vertex. This is V vertices multiplied by V vertices, which is $O(V^2)$.

Other implementations, such as using a priority queue instead of an array, lead to faster speeds. Again, there are several variations of Dijkstra's algorithm, and each variation needs its own analysis to determine its precise time complexity.

Whatever implementation of the algorithm you choose, though, is a big win over the alternative, which would be to find *every* possible path through the graph and then select the fastest one. Dijkstra's algorithm gives a sure way to proceed thoughtfully through the graph and zero in on the shortest path.

Wrapping Up

We're almost at the end of our journey, as this chapter represents the last significant data structure you'll encounter in this book. You've seen that graphs are extremely powerful tools for dealing with data involving relationships, and in addition to making our code fast, they can also help solve tricky problems.

In truth, I could fill a book just discussing graphs. So many interesting and useful algorithms surround this data structure, such as the minimum spanning tree, topological sort, bidirectional search, the Floyd–Warshall algorithm, the Bellman–Ford algorithm, and graph coloring, just to name a few. But this chapter should serve as the foundation for you to explore these additional topics.

Along our travels, our primary focus has been on how fast our code will run; that is, we've been measuring how efficient our code performs in terms of time, and we've been measuring that in terms of counting the number of steps our algorithms take.

However, efficiency can be measured in ways other than speed alone. In particular, we might care about how much *memory* a data structure or algorithm might consume. In the next chapter, you'll learn how to analyze the efficiency of our code in terms of *space*.

Exercises

The following exercises provide you with the opportunity to practice with graphs. The solutions to these exercises are found in the section Chapter 18, on page 455.

1. The first graph on page 382 powers an e-commerce store's recommendation engine. Each vertex represents a product available on the store's website. The edges connect each product to other "similar" products the site will recommend to the user when browsing a particular item.

    If the user is browsing "nails", what other products will be recommended to the user?

2. If we perform *depth*-first search on the second graph on page 382, starting with the A vertex, what is the order in which we'll traverse all the vertices? Assume that when given the choice to visit multiple adjacent vertices, we'll first visit the node that is earliest in the alphabet.

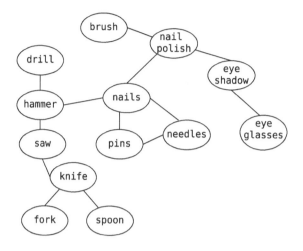

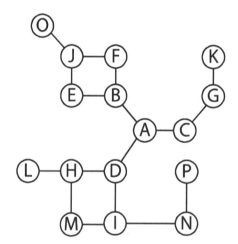

3. If we perform *breadth*-first search on the previous graph starting with the A vertex, what is the order in which we'll traverse all the vertices? Assume that when given the choice to visit multiple adjacent vertices, we'll first visit the node that is earliest in the alphabet.

4. In this chapter, I only provided the code for breadth-first *traversal*, as discussed in Breadth-First Search, on page 346; that is, the code simply printed the value of each vertex. Modify the code so that it performs an actual *search* for a vertex value provided to the function. (We did this for depth-first search.) In other words, if the function finds the vertex it's searching for, it should return that vertex's value. Otherwise, it should return None.

5. In Dijkstra's Algorithm, on page 365, we saw how Dijkstra's algorithm helped us find the shortest path within a weighted graph. However, the concept of a shortest path exists within an unweighted graph as well. How?

The shortest path in a classic (unweighted) graph is the path that takes the fewest number of vertices to get from one vertex to another.

This can be especially useful in social networking applications. Take the example network that follows:

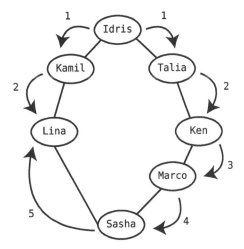

If we want to know how Idris is connected to Lina, we'd see that she's connected to her from two different directions; that is, Idris is a second-degree connection to Lina through Kamil, but she's also a fifth-degree connection through Talia. Now, we're probably interested in *how closely* Idris is connected to Lina, so the fact that she's a fifth-degree connection is unimportant given that they're also second-degree connections.

Write a function that accepts two vertices from a graph and returns the shortest path between them. The function should return an array containing the precise path, such as ["Idris", "Kamil", "Lina"].

Hint: The algorithm may contain elements of both breadth-first search and Dijkstra's algorithm.

CHAPTER 19

Dealing with Space Constraints

When analyzing the efficiency of various algorithms throughout this book, we've focused exclusively on how fast they run—that is, their time complexity. However, another measure of efficiency can be useful as well, which is how much *memory* an algorithm consumes. This measure is known as *space complexity*.

Space complexity becomes an important factor when memory is limited. If you have an enormous amount of data, or are programming for a small device with limited memory, space complexity can matter a lot.

In a perfect world, we'd always use algorithms that are both fast *and* memory-efficient. However, sometimes we can't have both, and we need to choose between the two. Each situation requires a careful analysis to know when we need to prioritize speed over memory, and memory over speed.

Big O of Space Complexity

Interestingly, computer scientists use Big O notation to describe space complexity just as they do for time complexity.

Back when I introduced Big O notation in Chapter 3, O Yes! Big O Notation, on page 35, I described Big O in terms of what I called the "key question." For time complexity, the key question was: *if there are N data elements, how many steps will the algorithm take?*

To use Big O for space complexity, we just need to reframe the key question. When it comes to memory consumption, the key question is: *if there are N data elements, how many units of memory will the algorithm consume?*

Here's a simple example.

Let's say we're writing a function that accepts an array of strings and returns an array of those strings in ALL CAPS. For example, the function would accept an array like ["tuvi", "leah", "shaya", "rami", "yechiel"] and return ["TUVI", "LEAH", "SHAYA", "RAMI", "YECHIEL"]. Here's one way we can write this function:

```
def make_uppercase(array):
    new_array = []

    for string in array:
        new_array.append(string.upper())

    return new_array
```

In this make_uppercase function, we accept an array. We then create a *brand-new array* called new_array and fill it with uppercase versions of each string from the original array.

By the time this function is complete, we'll have two arrays floating around in our computer's memory. We have the original array, which contains ["tuvi", "leah", "shaya", "rami", "yechiel"], and we have new_array, which contains ["TUVI", "LEAH", "SHAYA", "RAMI", "YECHIEL"].

When we analyze this function in terms of space complexity, we can see that this function *creates* a brand-new array that contains N elements. This is *in addition* to the original array which also holds N elements.

So let's return to our key question: *if there are N data elements, how many units of memory will the algorithm consume?*

Because our function generated an additional N data elements (in the form of new_array), we'd say that this function has a *space efficiency of O(N).*

The way this appears on the following graph should look familiar:

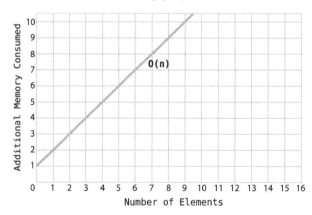

Note that this graph is identical to the way we've depicted O(N) in graphs in previous chapters, with the exception that the vertical axis now represents *memory consumed* rather than time.

Now, let's present an alternative make_uppercase function that is more memory-efficient:

```
def make_uppercase(array):
    for index in range(len(array)):
        array[index] = array[index].upper()

    return array
```

In this second version, we don't create any new arrays. Instead, we modify each value within the original array *in place,* replacing each string with an uppercase version of that string. We then return the modified array.

This is a drastic improvement in terms of memory consumption since our new function *doesn't consume any additional memory at all.*

How do we describe this in terms of Big O notation?

Recall that with time complexity, an O(1) algorithm was one whose speed remained constant no matter how large the data. Similarly, with space complexity, O(1) means that the memory consumed by an algorithm is constant no matter how large the data.

Our revised make_uppercase function consumes a constant amount of additional space (zero!) no matter whether the original array contains four elements or one hundred. Because of this, this function is said to have a space efficiency of O(1).

It's worth emphasizing that when using Big O to describe space complexity, we're only counting the *new data* the algorithm is generating. Even our second make_uppercase function deals with N elements of data in the form of the array passed into the function. However, we're not factoring those N elements into our Big O description, since the original array exists in any case, and we're only focused on the *extra* space the algorithm consumes. This extra space is more formally known as *auxiliary space.*

However, it's good to know that there are some references that include the original input when calculating the space complexity, and that's fine. We're not including it, and whenever you see space complexity described in another resource, you need to determine whether it's including the original input.

Let's now compare the two versions of make_uppercase in both time and space complexity:

Version	Time Complexity	Space Complexity
Version #1	O(N)	O(N)
Version #2	O(N)	O(1)

Both versions are O(N) in time complexity, since they take N steps for N data elements. However, the second version is more memory-efficient, as it is O(1) in space complexity compared to the first version's O(N).

It turns out that Version #2 is more efficient than Version #1 in terms of space while not sacrificing any speed, which is a nice win.

Trade-Offs Between Time and Space

Here's a function that accepts an array and returns whether it contains any duplicate values (you may recognize this function from Chapter 4, Speeding Up Your Code with Big O, on page 47:

```
def has_duplicate_value(array):
    for i in range(len(array)):
        for j in range(len(array)):
            if (i != j) and (array[i] == array[j]):
                return True

    return False
```

This algorithm uses nested loops and has a time complexity of O(N²). We'll call this implementation Version #1.

Here's a second implementation, Version #2, that employs a hash table and just a single loop:

```
def has_duplicate_value(array):
    existing_values = {}

    for value in array:
        if value not in existing_values:
            existing_values[value] = True
        else:
            return True

    return False
```

Version #2 starts out with an empty hash table called existing_values. We then iterate over each item from the array, and as we encounter each new item, we store it as a key in the existing_values hash table. (We set the value arbitrarily to True.) If, however, we encounter an item that's already a key in the hash table, we return True, as it means we found a duplicate value.

Now, which of these two algorithms is more efficient? Well, it all depends on whether you consider time or space. As far as time is concerned, Version #2 is much more efficient, as it's only O(N), compared with Version #1's O(N^2).

However, when it comes to *space*, Version #1 is actually more efficient than Version #2. Version #2 consumes up to O(N) space, as it creates a hash table that may end up containing all N values from the array passed to the function. Version #1, however, doesn't consume any additional memory beyond the original array, and therefore has a space complexity of O(1).

Let's look at the complete contrast between the two versions of has_duplicate_value:

Version	Time Complexity	Space Complexity
Version #1	O(N^2)	O(1)
Version #2	O(N)	O(N)

We can see that Version #1 more efficient when it comes to memory, but Version #2 is faster in terms of raw speed. So how do we decide which algorithm to choose?

The answer, of course, is that it depends on the situation. If we need our application to be blazing fast and we have enough memory to handle it, then Version #2 might be preferable. If, on the other hand, we're dealing with a hardware/data combination where we need to consume memory sparingly and speed isn't our biggest need, then Version #1 might be the right choice. Like all technology decisions, when there are trade-offs, we need to look at the big picture.

Let's look at a third version of this same function and see where it falls compared to the first two versions:

```python
def has_duplicate_value(array):
    array.sort()

    for i in range(len(array) - 1):
        if array[i] == array[i + 1]:
            return True

    return False
```

This implementation, which we'll call Version #3, begins by sorting the array. It then iterates over each value within the array and checks to see whether it's the same as the next value. If it is, we've found a duplicate value. However, if we get to the end of the array and there are no two consecutive values that are the same, we know that the array contains no duplicates.

Let's analyze the time and space efficiency of Version #3.

In terms of time complexity, this algorithm is O(N log N). We can assume that Python's sorting algorithm is one that takes O(N log N), as the fastest known sorting algorithms are known to do. The additional N steps of iterating over the array are trivial beside the sorting steps, so O(N log N) is the grand total when it comes to speed.

Space is a slightly more complex matter, as various sorting algorithms consume varying amounts of memory. Some of the earliest algorithms we've encountered in the book, like Bubble Sort and Selection Sort, consume no extra space because all the sorting happens in place. Interestingly, though, the faster sorts do take up some space for reasons you'll see shortly. Most implementations of Quicksort actually take up O(log N) space.

So let's see where Version #3 lands in comparison with the previous two versions:

Version	Time Complexity	Space Complexity
Version #1	$O(N^2)$	$O(1)$
Version #2	$O(N)$	$O(N)$
Version #3	$O(N \log N)$	$O(\log N)$

It turns out Version #3 strikes an interesting balance between time and space. In terms of time, Version #3 is faster than Version #1 but slower than Version #2. When it comes to space, it's more efficient than Version #2 but less efficient than Version #1.

So when may we want to use Version #3? Well, if we're concerned about both time *and* space, this might be our fix.

Ultimately, in each given situation, we need to know what our minimum acceptable speeds and bounds of memory are. Once we understand our constraints, we can then pick and choose from various algorithms so that we can eke out acceptable efficiency for our speed and memory needs.

Up until this point, you've seen how our algorithms can consume extra space when they create additional pieces of data, such as new arrays or hash tables. However, it's possible for an algorithm to consume space even if it's not doing any of those things. And this can come to bite us if we're not expecting it.

The Hidden Cost of Recursion

We've dealt quite a bit with recursive algorithms in this book. Let's look at a simple recursive function:

```
def recurse(n):
    if n < 0:
        return

    print(n)
    recurse(n - 1)
```

This function accepts a number n and counts down to 0, printing each decrementing number along the way.

It's a straightforward bit of recursion and seems harmless. Its speed is O(N), as the function will run as many times as the argument n. And it doesn't create any new data structures, so it doesn't seem to take up any additional space.

Or does it?

I explained how recursion works under the hood back in Chapter 10, Recursively Recurse with Recursion, on page 149. You learned that each time a function recursively calls itself, an item is added to the call stack so that the computer can come back to the outer function once the inner function is complete.

If we pass the number 100 into our recurse function, it would add recurse(100) before proceeding to execute recurse(99). And it would then add recurse(99) to the call stack before executing recurse(98).

The call stack would be at its peak when recurse(-1) is called, and there would be 101 items in the call stack, from recurse(100) down to recurse(0).

Now, even though the call stack will eventually get unwound, we do need enough memory to store these 101 items for *at least some period of time*. It emerges, then, that our recursive function *takes up O(N) space*. In this case, N is the number passed into the function; if we pass in the number 100, we need to temporarily store about 100 function calls in the call stack.

An important principle emerges from all of this: *a recursive function takes up a unit of space for each recursive call it makes*. This is the sneaky way recursion can gobble up memory; even if our function doesn't explicitly create new data, the recursion itself adds data to the call stack.

To properly calculate how much space a recursive function takes, we always need to figure out how big the call stack would be at its peak.

For our recurse function, the call stack will be about as large as whatever number n is.

At first, this may seem a bit trivial. After all, our modern computers can handle a few items on the call stack, right? Well, let's see.

When I pass in the number 20,000 into the recurse function on my sleek, up-to-date laptop, *my computer cannot process it.* Now, 20,000 doesn't seem like a very large number. But this is what happens when I run recurse(20000):

My computer prints the numbers from 20000 until 19005 and then terminates with the message:

```
RecursionError: maximum recursion depth exceeded while calling a Python object
```

Because the recursion lasted from 20000 until about 19000 (I'm rounding 19005 down), we can figure out that the call stack reached a size of about 1,000 when the computer ran out of memory. It turns out my computer will not tolerate a call stack that contains more than 1,000 items.

This is a *huge* limitation on recursion, as I can't use my beautiful recurse function on a number greater than 1,000!

Let's contrast this to a simple loop approach:

```
def loop(n):
    while n >= 0:
        print(n)
        n -= 1
```

This function accomplishes the same goal using a basic loop instead of recursion.

Because this function doesn't use recursion, and doesn't take up any additional memory, it can process a huge number without *ever* causing the computer to run out of space. The function may take some time on huge numbers, but it'll get the job done without giving up prematurely as the recursive function did.

With this in mind, we can now understand why Quicksort is said to take up O(log N) space. Quicksort makes O(log N) recursive calls, so at its peak has a call stack that is the size of log(N).

When we can implement a function using recursion, then, we need to weigh recursion's benefits against its drawbacks. Recursion allows us to use the "magical" top-down mindset, as you looked at in Chapter 11, Learning to Write in Recursive, on page 161, but we also need our function to get the job done. And if we're processing a lot of data, or even just a number like 20,000—or even 1,000—recursion may not cut it.

Again, this isn't to discredit recursion. It just means we need to weigh all the pros and cons of each algorithm in every situation.

Wrapping Up

We've now covered how to measure the efficiency of our algorithms from all angles, including time *and* space. You're now armed with the analytical abilities to weigh each algorithm against the next and make informed decisions on which approach to use for your own applications.

As you're now able to make your own decisions, it's time to move on to the final chapter of our journey. In it, I'm going to provide a few last pieces of advice on how to optimize your own code, while taking you through some realistic scenarios that we'll optimize together.

Exercises

The following exercises provide you with the opportunity to practice with space constraints. The solutions to these exercises are found in the section Chapter 19, on page 458.

1. Following is the word builder algorithm we encountered in Word Builder, on page 97. Describe its *space* complexity in terms of Big O:

```python
def word_builder(array):
    collection = []

    for index_i, i in enumerate(array):
        for index_j, j in enumerate(array):
            if index_i != index_j:
                collection.append(i + j)

    return collection
```

2. Following is a function that reverses an array. Describe its *space* complexity in terms of Big O:

```python
def reverse(array):
    new_array = []

    for value in array:
        new_array.insert(0, value)

    return new_array
```

3. Create a new function to reverse an array that takes up just O(1) extra space.

4. Following are three different implementations of a function that accepts an array of numbers and returns an array containing those numbers multiplied by 2. For example, if the input is [5, 4, 3, 2, 1], the output will be [10, 8, 6, 4, 2].

```
def double_array_1(array):
    new_array = []

    for value in array:
        new_array.append(value * 2)

    return new_array

def double_array_2(array):
    for i in range(len(array)):
        array[i] *= 2

    return array

def double_array_3(array, index=0):
    if index >= len(array):
        return

    array[index] *= 2
    double_array_3(array, index + 1)

    return array
```

Fill in the table that follows to describe the efficiency of these three versions in terms of both time and space:

Version	Time Complexity	Space Complexity
Version #1	?	?
Version #2	?	?
Version #3	?	?

CHAPTER 20

Techniques for Code Optimization

We've come a long way. You now have the tools to analyze the time and space complexity of algorithms across a wide variety of data structures. With these concepts, you're now able to write code that is fast, memory-efficient, and beautiful.

In this final chapter of our journey, I'd like to leave you with some additional techniques for optimizing code. Sometimes it's difficult to see how an algorithm can be improved. Over the years, I've found the following mental strategies help me see how I can make my code more efficient. I hope they'll be helpful to you as well.

Prerequisite: Determine Your Current Big O

Before we get into the optimization techniques, though, it's important to stress that there's something you need to do *before* you start optimizing your algorithm.

The prerequisite to optimization is *determining the efficiency of your current code.* After all, it's impossible to make an algorithm faster if you don't know how fast it is now.

By now, you have a thorough understanding of Big O notation and the various categories of Big O. Once you know what category of Big O your algorithm belongs to, you can begin optimizing.

Throughout the rest of this chapter, I'll refer to this step of determining your current algorithm's Big O as the "prereq."

Start Here: The Best-Imaginable Big O

While all the techniques in this chapter are useful, you'll find that some come in handy for certain scenarios, while others are effective for other scenarios.

This first technique, however, applies to *all* algorithms and should be the first step of your optimization process.

And here it is.

Once you've determined the efficiency of your current algorithm (the prereq), come up with what you believe to be what I call the "best-imaginable Big O." (I've seen others refer to this as the "best-conceivable runtime" when applied to speed.)

Essentially, the best-imaginable Big O is the absolute best Big O you could dream of for the problem at hand. This is the Big O you know is absolutely impossible to beat.

For example, if we were to write a function that prints every item from an array, we'd probably say that the best-imaginable Big O for this task is O(N). Given that we have to print each of the N items in the array, *we have no choice* but to process each of the N items. There's no way around this fact, as we need to "touch" each item to print it. Because of this, O(N) is the best-imaginable Big O we could imagine for this scenario.

When optimizing an algorithm, then, we need to determine *two* Big Os. We need to know the Big O our algorithm *currently* takes (the prereq), and we need to come up with the best-imaginable Big O the task could *possibly* take.

If these two Big Os are not the same, it means we have something to optimize. If, say, my current algorithm has a runtime of O(N^2), but the best-imaginable Big O is O(N), we now have an improvement to strive for. The gap between the two Big Os shows us the potential gains we can make through optimization.

Let's summarize these steps:

1. Determine the Big O category of your current algorithm. (This is the prereq.)

2. Determine the best-imaginable Big O you could dream of for the problem at hand.

3. If the best-imaginable Big O is faster than your current Big O, you can now try to optimize your code, with the goal of bringing your algorithm as close to the best-imaginable Big O as possible.

It's important to stress that it's *not always possible to achieve the best-imaginable Big O*. After all, just because you can dream of something doesn't mean it can become reality.

In fact, it might turn out that your current implementation cannot be optimized further. However, the best-imaginable Big O is still a tool for giving us a goal to shoot for with our optimization.

Often, I find that I can successfully optimize an algorithm to a speed that is *in between* my current Big O and the best-imaginable Big O.

For example, if my current implementation is $O(N^2)$, and my best-imaginable Big O is $O(\log N)$, I'll aim to optimize my algorithm to become $O(\log N)$. If, in the end, my optimizations speed up my code to "just" $O(N)$, that's still a great success, and the best-imaginable Big O will have served a useful purpose.

Stretching the Imagination

As you've seen, the benefit of coming up with the best-imaginable Big O is that it gives us an optimization goal to shoot for. To really make the most of this, it's worth stretching the imagination a bit to come up with a best-imaginable Big O that is *amazing*. In fact, I recommend making your best-imaginable Big O the fastest Big O you can think of that isn't outright impossible.

Here's another mental trick I use for stoking my imagination. I pick a *really* fast Big O for the problem at hand—let's call it "Amazing Big O." I then ask myself, "If someone told me that they know how to pull off the Amazing Big O for this problem, would I believe them?" If I'd believe someone who said that they figured out how to solve this problem with the efficiency of Amazing Big O, I then make the Amazing Big O my best-imaginable Big O.

Once we know the Big O of our current algorithm and the best-imaginable Big O that we're aiming for, we're primed for optimization.

In the remainder of this chapter, we are going to explore additional optimization techniques and mental strategies that can help us boost the efficiency of our code.

Magical Lookups

One of my favorite go-to optimization techniques is to ask myself, "If I could magically find a desired piece of information in $O(1)$ time, can I make my algorithm faster?" If the answer to this is yes, I then use a data structure (often a hash table) to make that magic happen. I call this technique "magical lookups."

Let me clarify this technique with an example.

Magically Looking Up Authors

Let's say we're writing library software and we have data about books and their authors contained in two separate arrays.

Specifically, the array of authors looks like this:

```
authors = [
  {"author_id": 1, "name": "Virginia Woolf"},
  {"author_id": 2, "name": "Leo Tolstoy"},
  {"author_id": 3, "name": "Dr. Seuss"},
  {"author_id": 4, "name": "J. K. Rowling"},
  {"author_id": 5, "name": "Mark Twain"}
]
```

As you can see, it's an array of hash tables, with each hash table containing an author's name and ID.

We also have a separate array containing data about books:

```
books = [
  {"author_id": 3, "title": "Hop on Pop"},
  {"author_id": 1, "title": "Mrs. Dalloway"},
  {"author_id": 4, "title": "Harry Potter and the Sorcerer's Stone"},
  {"author_id": 1, "title": "To the Lighthouse"},
  {"author_id": 2, "title": "Anna Karenina"},
  {"author_id": 5, "title": "The Adventures of Tom Sawyer"},
  {"author_id": 3, "title": "The Cat in the Hat"},
  {"author_id": 2, "title": "War and Peace"},
  {"author_id": 3, "title": "Green Eggs and Ham"},
  {"author_id": 5, "title": "The Adventures of Huckleberry Finn"}
]
```

Like the authors array, the books array contains a number of hash tables. Each hash table contains a book's title and the author_id, which can allow us to determine the book's author using the data from the authors array. "Hop on Pop", for example, has the author_id of 3. This means the author of "Hop on Pop" is Dr. Seuss, since he's the author whose ID is 3, as indicated in the authors array.

Now, let's say we want to write code that combined this information together to create an array in the following format:

```
books_with_authors = [
  {'author': 'Dr. Seuss', 'title': 'Hop on Pop'},
  {'author': 'Virginia Woolf', 'title': 'Mrs. Dalloway'},
  {'author': 'J. K. Rowling', 'title': "Harry Potter and the Sorcerer's Stone"},
  {'author': 'Virginia Woolf', 'title': 'To the Lighthouse'},
  {'author': 'Leo Tolstoy', 'title': 'Anna Karenina'},
  {'author': 'Mark Twain', 'title': 'The Adventures of Tom Sawyer'},
```

```
    {'author': 'Dr. Seuss', 'title': 'The Cat in the Hat'},
    {'author': 'Leo Tolstoy', 'title': 'War and Peace'},
    {'author': 'Dr. Seuss', 'title': 'Green Eggs and Ham'},
    {'author': 'Mark Twain', 'title': 'The Adventures of Huckleberry Finn'}
]
```

To do this, we'd probably need to iterate through the array of books and connect each book to its respective author. How would we go about this specifically?

One solution may be to use nested loops. The outer loop would iterate over each book, and for each book, we'd run an inner loop that would check each author until it found the one with the connecting ID. Here's an implementation of this approach:

```
def connect_books_with_authors(books, authors):
    books_with_authors = []

    for book in books:
        for author in authors:
            if book["author_id"] == author["author_id"]:
                books_with_authors.append({"title": book["title"],
                                           "author": author["name"]})

    return books_with_authors
```

Before we can optimize our code, we need to fulfill our prereq and determine our current algorithm's Big O.

This algorithm has a time complexity of O(N * M), since for each of the N books, we need to loop through M authors to find the book's author.

Now, let's see if we can do better.

Again, the first thing we need to do is come up with the best-imaginable Big O. In this case, we definitely need to iterate over all N books, so it would seem impossible to beat O(N). Since O(N) is the fastest speed I can think of that isn't downright impossible, we'll say that O(N) is our best-imaginable Big O.

We're now ready to use the new magical lookups technique. To do this, I'll ask myself the question mentioned at the start of this section: "If I could magically find a desired piece of information in O(1) time, can I make my algorithm faster?"

Let's apply this to our scenario. We currently run an outer loop that iterates over all the books. Currently, for each book, we run an inner loop that tries to find the book's author_id in the authors array.

But what if we had the magical ability to find an author *in just O(1) time?* What if we didn't have to loop through *all* the authors each time we wanted to look one up and we could instead find the author immediately? That would bring a huge speed boost to our algorithm, as we could potentially eliminate our inner loop and bring our code's speed up to the vaunted O(N).

Now that we've determined that this magical finding ability could help us, the next step is to try to make this magic come alive.

Bringing in the Extra Data Structure

One of the easiest ways we can achieve this magical lookup ability is to bring an additional data structure into our code. We'll use this data structure to specifically store data in such a way that allows us to look that data up quickly. In many cases, the hash table is the perfect data structure for this, since it has O(1) lookups, as you learned in Chapter 8, Blazing Fast Lookup with Hash Tables, on page 113.

Right now, because the author hash tables are stored in an array, it will always take us O(M) steps (M being the number of authors) to find any given author_id within that array. But if we store that same information in a hash table, we now gain our magical ability to find each author in just O(1) time.

Here's one possibility of what this hash table could look like:

```
author_hash_table =
{1: "Virginia Woolf", 2: "Leo Tolstoy", 3: "Dr. Seuss",
4: "J. K. Rowling", 5: "Mark Twain"}
```

In this hash table, each key is the author's ID, and the value of each key is the author's name.

So let's optimize our algorithm by first moving the authors data into this hash table and only then run our loop through the books:

```
def connect_books_with_authors(books, authors):
    books_with_authors = []
    author_hash_table = {}

    for author in authors:
        author_hash_table[author["author_id"]] = author["name"]

    for book in books:
        books_with_authors.append({"title": book["title"],
            "author": author_hash_table[book["author_id"]]})

    return books_with_authors
```

In this version, we first iterate through the authors array and use that data to create the author_hash_table. This takes M steps, with M being the number of authors.

We then iterate through the list of books and use the author_hash_table to "magically" find each author in a single step. This loop takes N steps, with N being the number of books.

This optimized algorithm takes a grand total of O(N + M) steps, since we run a single loop through the N books, and a single loop through the M authors. This is drastically faster than our original algorithm, which took O(N * M).

It's worth noting that by creating the extra hash table, we're using up an additional O(M) space, whereas our initial algorithm didn't take up any extra space at all. However, this is great optimization if we're willing to sacrifice the memory for the sake of speed.

We made this magic happen by first dreaming what magical O(1) lookups could do for us, and we then granted ourselves our own wish by using a hash table to store our data in an easy-to-find way.

The fact that we can look up hash table data in O(1) time isn't new, as we looked at this back in *Blazing Fast Lookup with Hash Tables*. The specific tip I'm sharing here, though, is to constantly *imagine* that you can perform O(1) lookups on any kind of data and notice whether that would speed up your code. Once you have the vision of how O(1) lookups would help you, you can then try to use a hash table or other data structure to turn that dream into reality.

The Two Sum Problem

Let's look at another scenario in which we can benefit from magical lookups. This is one my favorite optimization examples.

The *two sum problem* is a well-known coding exercise. The task is to write a function that accepts an array of numbers and return True or False depending on whether there are any two numbers in the array that add up to 10 (or another given number). For simplicity, let's assume there will never be duplicate numbers in the array.

Let's say this is our array:

```
[2, 0, 4, 1, 7, 9]
```

Our function would return True, since the 1 and 9 add up to 10.

But let's look at the following array:

```
[2, 0, 4, 5, 3, 9]
```

In this case, we return False. Even though the three numbers 2, 5, and 3 add up to 10, we specifically need *two* numbers to add up to 10.

The first solution that comes to mind is to use nested loops to compare each number to every other number and see if they add up to 10. Here's a Python implementation:

```python
def two_sum(array):
    for i in range(len(array)):
        for j in range(len(array)):
            if i != j and array[i] + array[j] == 10:
                return True

    return False
```

As always, before attempting an optimization, we need to satisfy our prereq and figure out the current Big O of our code.

As is typical in a nested-loop algorithm, this function has a runtime of $O(N^2)$.

Next, to see if our algorithm is worth optimizing, we need to see if the best-imaginable Big O would be any better.

In this case, it would seem that we absolutely have to visit each number in the array at least once. So, we couldn't beat O(N). And if someone told me that there's an O(N) solution to this problem, I suppose I'd believe them. So let's make O(N) our best-imaginable Big O.

Now, let's ask ourselves the magical lookup question: "If I could magically find a desired piece of information in O(1) time, can I make my algorithm faster?"

Sometimes it helps to begin walking through our current implementation while asking this question along the way, so let's do that.

Let's mentally walk through our outer loop with the example array of [2, 0, 4, 1, 7, 9]. This loop begins with the first number, which is the number 2.

Now, what piece of information might we desire to look up while we're looking at the 2? Again, we want to know if this 2 could be added to another number in the array to provide a sum of 10.

Thinking about it further, while looking at the 2, I'd want to know whether *there's an 8 somewhere* in this array. If we could, magically, do an O(1) lookup and know that there's an 8 in the array, we could immediately return True. Let's call the 8 the 2's *counterpart*, since the two numbers add up to 10.

Similarly, when we move on to the 0, we'd want to do an O(1) lookup to find its counterpart—a 10—in the array, and so on.

With this approach, we can iterate through the array just once and do magical O(1) lookups along the way to see whether each number's counterpart exists in the array. As soon as we find any number's counterpart, we return True, but if we get to the end of the array without finding any numerical counterparts, we return False.

Now that we've determined we'd benefit from these magical O(1) lookups, let's try to pull off our magic trick by bringing in an extra data structure. Again, the hash table is usually the default option for magical lookups because of its O(1) reads. (It's uncanny how often hash tables can be used to speed up algorithms.)

Since we want to be able to look up any number from the array in O(1) time, we'll store those numbers as keys in a hash table. The hash table may look like this:

```
{2: True, 0: True, 4: True, 1: True, 7: True, 9: True}
```

We can use any arbitrary item to serve as the values; let's decide to use True.

Now that we can look up any number in O(1) time, how do we look up a number's counterpart? Well, we noticed that when we iterated over the 2, we knew that the counterpart should be 8. We knew this because we know intuitively that $2 + 8 = 10$.

Essentially, then, we can calculate any number's counterpart by subtracting it from 10. Because $10 - 2 = 8$, that means 8 is the 2's counterpart.

We now have all the ingredients to create a really fast algorithm:

```python
def two_sum(array):
    hash_table = {}

    for value in array:
        if hash_table.get(10 - value):
            return True
        else:
            hash_table[value] = True

    return False
```

This algorithm iterates once through each number in the array.

As we visit each number, we check whether the hash table contains a key that is the counterpart of the current number. We calculate this as 10 - value. (For example, if value is 3, the counterpart would be 7, since $10 - 3 = 7$.)

If we find any number's counterpart, we immediately return True, as that means we've found two numbers that add up to 10.

Additionally, as we iterate over each number, we insert the number as a key into the hash table. This is how we populate the hash table with the numbers as we proceed through the array.

With this approach, we drastically increased the algorithm's speed to O(N). We pulled this off by storing all of the data elements in a hash table for the express purpose of being able to perform O(1) lookups throughout the loop.

Consider the hash table your magical wand, and become the programming wizard you were destined to be. (Okay, enough of that.)

Recognizing Patterns

One of the most helpful strategies for both code optimization and algorithm development in general is to find patterns within the problem at hand. Often, the discovery of a pattern can help you cut through all the complexity of a problem and develop an algorithm that is simple.

The Coin Game

Here's a great example. A game I call "the coin game" has two players who compete in the following way: they start with a pile of coins, and each player has the choice of removing either one or two coins from the pile. The player who removes the last coin *loses*. Fun, right?

It turns out that this isn't a game of random chance, and with the right strategy, you can *force* your opponent to take the last coin and lose the game. To make this clear, let's start with some really small coin piles and see how the game plays out.

If there's just one coin in the pile, the player whose turn it is loses, since they have no choice but to take the last coin.

If there are two coins left, the player whose turn it is can force a win. This is because they can take just one coin and thereby force their opponent to take the final coin.

When there are three coins remaining, the player whose turn it is can also force a win, since they can remove two coins, forcing their opponent to take the final coin.

Now, when there are four coins left, the current player is in trouble. If they remove one coin, the opponent is given a pile of three coins, which we established earlier can allow that player to force a win. Similarly, if the current player removes two coins, the opponent is left with two coins, which can also allow the opponent to force a win.

If we were to write a function that calculated whether you can win the game when presented with a coin pile of a given size, what approach should we take? If we think about this carefully, we may realize we can use subproblems to help calculate an accurate result for any number of coins. This would make top-down recursion a natural fit for solving this problem.

Here's a Python implementation of a recursive approach:

```python
def game_winner(number_of_coins, current_player="you"):
    if number_of_coins <= 0:
        return current_player

    if current_player == "you":
        next_player = "them"
    elif current_player == "them":
        next_player = "you"

    if (game_winner(number_of_coins - 1, next_player) == current_player or
            game_winner(number_of_coins - 2, next_player) == current_player):
        return current_player
    else:
        return next_player
```

This game_winner function is given a number of coins and the player whose turn it is (either "you" or "them"). The function then returns either "you" or "them" as the winner of the game. When the function is first called, the current_player is "you".

We define our base case as when the current_player is dealt 0 or fewer coins. This means the other player took the last coin and the current player, by default, won the game.

We then define a next_player variable, which keeps track of which player will go next.

Then we do our recursion. We recursively call our game_winner function on piles of coins that are both one and two coins smaller than the current pile, and see if the next player would win or lose in those scenarios. If the next_player loses in both scenarios, that means the current_player will win.

This isn't an easy algorithm, but we pulled it off. Now let's see if we can optimize it.

To satisfy our prereq, we first need to figure out our algorithm's current speed.

You may have noticed that this function makes multiple recursive calls. If alarm bells are going off in your head, that's for good reason. The time complexity of this function is a whopping $O(2^N)$, which can be unbearably slow.

We can improve this by using the memoization technique you learned about in Chapter 12, Dynamic Programming, on page 185, which could bring the speed up to $O(N)$, with N being the number of coins in the starting pile. That's a huge improvement.

But let's see if we can push our algorithm's speed even further.

To determine whether we can optimize our algorithm further, we need to ask ourselves what we think the best-imaginable Big O is.

Because N is just a single number, I could conceive that we can make an algorithm that takes just O(1) time. Since we don't actually have to touch N items in an array or anything like that, if someone told me they figured out an algorithm for the coin game that was just O(1), I'd believe them. So let's strive for O(1).

But how do we get there? This is where finding a pattern can help.

Generating Examples

While each problem has a unique pattern, I found a technique for finding patterns that helps across *all* problems—and that is to *generate numerous examples*. This means we should take a bunch of example inputs, calculate their respective outputs, and see if we can detect a pattern.

Let's apply this to our case.

If we map out who wins for coin piles of size 1 through 10, we get this table:

Number of Coins	Winner
1	Them
2	You
3	You
4	Them
5	You
6	You
7	Them
8	You
9	You
10	Them

The pattern becomes clear when we lay it out this way. Basically, starting with 1 coin, every third number gives victory to the opponent. Otherwise, you are the winner.

So if we take the number of coins and subtract 1, each "them" ends up at a number that is divisible by 3. At this point, then, we can determine who will win based on a single division calculation:

```
def game_winner(number_of_coins):
    if (number_of_coins - 1) % 3 == 0:
        return "them"
    else:
        return "you"
```

This code is saying that if after subtracting 1, the number_of_coins is divisible by 3, the winner is "them". Otherwise, "you" are the winner.

Because this algorithm consists of a single mathematical operation, it's O(1) in both time and space. It's also a lot simpler! This is a real win-win-win.

By generating many examples of coin piles (as inputs) and seeing who'd win the game (as outputs), we were able to identify a pattern in how the coin game works. We were then able to use this pattern to cut to the heart of the problem and turn a slow algorithm into an instantaneous one.

The Sum Swap Problem

Here's an example where we can use both pattern recognition and magical lookups *together* to optimize an algorithm.

The next problem, known as the *sum swap problem,* goes like this:

We want to write a function that accepts two arrays of integers. As an example, let's say these are our arrays:

$$array\_1 = [5, 3, 2, 9, 1] \quad \boxed{\text{Sum: } 20}$$

$$array\_2 = [1, 12, 5] \quad \boxed{\text{Sum: } 18}$$

Currently, the numbers in array_1 add up to 20, while the numbers in array_2 add up to 18.

Our function needs to find one number from each array that can be swapped to cause the two array sums to be equal.

In this example, if we swapped the 2 from array_1 and the 1 from array_2, we'd get:

$$array\_1 = [5, 3, 1, 9, 1] \quad \boxed{\text{Sum: } \mathbf{19}}$$

$$array\_2 = [2, 12, 5] \quad \boxed{\text{Sum: } \mathbf{19}}$$

And both arrays would now have the same sum—namely, 19.

To keep things simple, our function won't actually perform the swap but will return the two indexes that we'd have to swap. We can do this as an array containing the two indexes. So, in this case, we swapped index 2 of array_1 with index 0 of array_2, so we'll return an array of [2, 0]. In a case where there's no possible swap that makes the two arrays equal, we'll return None.

One way we can write this algorithm is to use nested loops; that is, as our outer loop points to each number from array_1, an inner loop can iterate over each number from array_2 and test the sums of each array if we were to swap the two numbers.

To begin optimizing this, we must first satisfy our prereq of knowing the Big O of our current algorithm.

Because our nested-loops approach visits M numbers from the second array for each of the N numbers of the first array, this algorithm is O(N * M). (I'm discussing N and M because the arrays may be two different sizes.)

Can we do better? To find out, let's determine what we think the best-imaginable Big O may be.

It would seem that we absolutely have to visit each number from the two arrays at least once, since we need to be aware of what all the numbers are. But it's possible that this may be *all* we need to do. If so, this would be O(N + M). Let's make this our best-imaginable Big O and aim for that.

Next, we need to try to dig up any patterns hidden within the problem. Again, the best technique to dig up patterns is to come up with numerous examples and look for patterns among them.

So let's look at a number of different examples where swapping numbers will cause the two arrays to have equal sums, as shown in the diagram on page 409.

In looking at these examples, a few patterns begin to emerge. Some of these patterns may seem obvious, but let's look at them anyway.

One pattern is that to achieve equal sums, the larger array needs to trade a larger number with a smaller number from the smaller array.

A second pattern is that with a single swap, each array's sum changes by the same amount. For example, when we swap a 7 with a 4, one array's sum *decreases* by 3, while the other array's sum *increases* by 3.

A third interesting pattern is that the swaps always cause the two array sums to fall out *exactly in the middle* of where the two array sums began.

In the first case, for example, array_1 was 18 and array_2 was 12. When making a correct swap, the two arrays land at 15, which is exactly in the middle between 18 and 12.

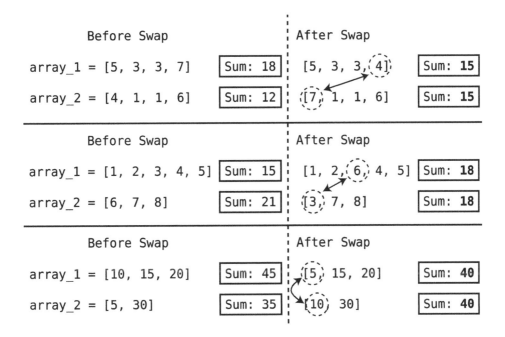

When we think about it further, this third pattern is a logical outgrowth of the other patterns. Since a swap causes the two arrays to shift their sums by the same amount, the *only* way to make their sums equal is to meet in the middle.

Based on this, if we know the sums of the two arrays, we should be able to look at any number in one of the arrays and calculate what number it should be swapped with.

Let's take this example again:

$$array\_1 = [5, 3, 3, 7] \quad \boxed{\text{Sum: } 18}$$

$$array\_2 = [4, 1, 1, 6] \quad \boxed{\text{Sum: } 12}$$

We know that for a swap to work successfully, we'll need the two arrays' sums to land in the middle. The exact middle between 18 and 12 is 15.

Let's look at different numbers from array_1 and figure out what number we'd want to swap it with. We can call this other number its counterpart. Let's start with the first number from array_1, which is the number 5.

What number would we want to swap the 5 with? Well, we know that we want array_1 to decrease by 3, and array_2 to increase by 3, so we'd need to swap the 5 with a number 2. It just so happens that array_2 doesn't contain a 2, so the 5 cannot be successfully swapped with any number from array_2.

If we look at the next number from array_1, it's a 3. We'd have to swap this with a 0 from array_2 to get the two sums to be equal. Alas, a 0 doesn't exist in array_2.

The last number from array_1, though, is a 7. We can calculate that we'd want to swap the 7 with a 4 to make the sums both land at 15. Luckily, array_2 does contain a 4, so we can make a successful swap.

So, how do we express this pattern in code?

Well, we can first determine how much an array sum needs to shift using this calculation:

```
shift_amount = (sum_1 - sum_2) // 2
```

Here, sum_1 is the sum of array_1, and sum_2 is the sum of array_2. If sum_1 is 18 and sum_2 is 12, we end up with a difference of 6. We then divide that by 2 to determine how much each array needs to shift. This is the shift_amount.

In this case, the shift_amount is 3, indicating that array_2 needs to increase by 3 to hit the target sum. (Likewise, array_1 needs to *decrease* by 3.)

So we can start building our algorithm by first calculating the sums of the two arrays. We can then loop through all the numbers in one of the arrays and look for the counterpart in the other.

If we were to iterate over each number in array_2, for example, we know that the current number would have to be swapped with its counterpart, which would be the current number plus the shift_amount. For example, if the current number is 4, to find its counterpart, we add the shift_amount(3) to it and get 7. This means we need to find a 7 in array_1 to swap with our current number.

So, we've figured out that we can look at any number in either array and know exactly what its counterpart from the other array should be. But how does this help? Don't we still need to use nested loops and have an algorithm that is O(N * M)? That means that for each number in one array, we have to search the entire other array for the counterpart.

This is where we can invoke magical lookups and ask ourselves, "If I could magically find a desired piece of information in O(1) time, can I make my algorithm faster?"

Indeed, if we could find a number's counterpart from the other array in just O(1) time, our algorithm would be much faster. And we can achieve those quick lookups by following the usual technique of bringing in our good ol' hash table.

If we first store the numbers from one array in a hash table, we can then immediately find any number from it in O(1) time as we iterate through the other array.

Here's the complete code:

```
def sum_swap(array_1, array_2):
    hash_table = {}
    sum_1 = 0
    sum_2 = 0

    for index, num in enumerate(array_1):
        sum_1 += num
        hash_table[num] = index

    for num in array_2:
        sum_2 += num

    # If the input consists of integers and the difference
    # between the two sums are odd, it's impossible to find
    # an integer smack in the middle, so no swap is possible:
    if (sum_1 - sum_2) % 2 == 1:
        return None

    shift_amount = (sum_1 - sum_2) // 2

    for index, num in enumerate(array_2):
        if num + shift_amount in hash_table:
            return [hash_table[num + shift_amount], index]

    return None
```

This approach is much faster than our original O(N * M) one. If we consider array_1 to be N and array_2 to be M, we could say that this algorithm runs in O(N + M) time. While we do iterate over array_2 twice and it is technically 2M, it becomes M since we drop the constants.

This approach takes up an extra O(N) space since we copy all N numbers from array_1 into the hash table. Again, we're sacrificing space to gain time, but this is a big win if speed is our primary concern.

In any case, this is another example of where discovering patterns allows us to cut to the heart of the problem and develop a simple and fast solution.

Greedy Algorithms

This next tactic can speed up some of the most stubborn algorithms. It doesn't work in every situation, but when it does, it can be a game changer.

Let's talk about writing greedy algorithms.

This may sound like a strange term, but here's what it means. A *greedy algorithm* is one that, in each step, chooses what appears to be the best option *at that moment in time*. This will make sense with a basic example.

Array Max

Let's write an algorithm that finds the greatest number in an array. One way we can do this is to use nested loops and check each number against every other number in the array. When we find the number that is greater than every other number in the array, it means we've found the greatest number in the array.

As is typical for such algorithms, this approach takes $O(N^2)$ time.

Another approach would be to sort the array in ascending order and return the final value from the array. If we use a fast sorting algorithm like Quicksort, this would take O(N log N) time.

A third option is the greedy algorithm:

```
def max(array):
    if not array:
        return None

    greatest_number = array[0]

    for number in array:
        if number > greatest_number:
            greatest_number = number

    return greatest_number
```

After ensuring the array isn't empty, we say the following:

```
greatest_number = array[0]
```

This line "assumes" that the first number in the array is the greatest_number. Now, this is a "greedy" assumption; that is, we're declaring the first number to be the greatest_number because it's the greatest number we've encountered so far. Of course, it's also the *only* number we've encountered so far! But that's what a greedy algorithm does—it chooses what appears to be the best option based on the information available at that moment in time.

Next, we iterate over all the numbers in the array. As we find any number that is greater than the greatest_number, we make this new number the greatest_number. Here too, we're being greedy; each step selects the best option based on what we know at that moment in time.

We're basically like a child in a candy shop grabbing the first candy we see, but as soon as we see a bigger candy, we drop the first one and grab the bigger one.

Yet, this seemingly naive greediness actually works. By the time we're done with the function, our greatest_number will indeed be the greatest number in the entire array.

And while being greedy isn't a virtue in a societal context, it can do wonders for algorithm speed. This algorithm takes just O(N) time, as we touch each number in the array just once.

Largest Subsection Sum

Let's see another example of how greed pays off.

We're going to write a function that accepts an array of numbers and returns the largest sum that could be computed from any "subsection" of the array.

Here's what I mean. Let's take the following array:

[3, -4, 4, -3, 5, -9]

If we computed the sum of all the numbers in this array, we'd get -4.

But we can also compute the sum of *subsections* of the array:

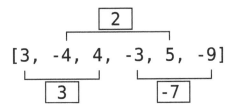

When I refer to subsections, I mean *contiguous subsections*; that is, a subsection is a section of the array that contains a series of numbers *in a row*.

The following is *not* a contiguous subsection, since the numbers are not in a row:

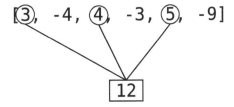

Our job is to find the largest sum that can be computed from *any* subsection within the array. In our example, the largest sum is 6, derived from the following subsection:

$$[3, \;\; \text{-}4, \;\; 4, \;\; \text{-}3, \;\; 5, \;\; \text{-}9]$$

$$\boxed{6}$$

To make the discussion simpler, let's assume the array contains at least one positive number.

Now, how can we write the code to calculate the largest subsection sum?

One approach would be to calculate the sum of every subsection within the array and pick out the greatest one. However, there are about $N^2 / 2$ subsections for N items in an array, so the mere generation of the different subsections would take $O(N^2)$ time.

Again, let's start by dreaming up the best-imaginable Big O. We definitely need to inspect each number at least once, so we can't beat O(N). So let's make O(N) our goal.

At first glance, O(N) seems beyond our reach. How can we add up multiple subsections by iterating over the array a single time?

Let's see what happens if we get a little greedy...

A greedy algorithm in this context would attempt to "grab" the greatest sum at each step as we iterate over the array. Here's what this might look like as we iterate over the earlier example array.

Starting at the front of the array, we encounter a 3. In perfect greedy fashion, we'll say that our greatest sum is 3:

greatest sum = 3

$$[3, \;\; \text{-}4, \;\; 4, \;\; \text{-}3, \;\; 5, \;\; \text{-}9]$$

$$\boxed{3}$$

Next, we reach the -4. When we add this to the previous number of 3, we get a current sum -1. So 3 is still our greatest sum:

greatest sum = 3

$$[3, \;\; \text{-}4, \;\; 4, \;\; \text{-}3, \;\; 5, \;\; \text{-}9]$$

$$\boxed{\text{-}1}$$

We then hit the 4. If we add this to our current sum, we get 3:

greatest sum = 3

$$[3, \ -4, \ 4, \ -3, \ 5, \ -9]$$

3

As of now, 3 is still the greatest sum.

The next number we reach is a -3. This puts our current sum at 0:

greatest sum = 3

$$[3, \ -4, \ 4, \ -3, \ 5, \ -9]$$

0

Again, while 0 is our *current* sum, 3 is still our *greatest* sum.

Next, we reach the 5. This makes our current sum 5. In our greed, we'll declare this to be the greatest sum, as it's the greatest sum we've encountered so far:

greatest sum = 5

$$[3, \ -4, \ 4, \ -3, \ 5, \ -9]$$

5

We then reach the last number, which is -9. This deflates our current sum to -4:

greatest sum = 5

$$[3, \ -4, \ 4, \ -3, \ 5, \ -9]$$

-4

By the time we get to the end of the array, our greatest sum is 5. So if we follow this pure-greed approach, it would appear that our algorithm should return 5.

However, 5 is *not* the greatest subsection sum. A subsection in the array yields a sum of 6:

$$[3, \ -4, \ 4, \ -3, \ 5, \ -9]$$

6

The problem with our algorithm is that we only calculated the largest sum based on subsections that always begin with the first number in the array. But other subsections begin with numbers later on in the array as well, and we haven't accounted for those.

Our greedy algorithm, then, didn't pan out as we'd hoped.

But we shouldn't give up yet! Often, we need to tweak greedy algorithms a bit to get them to work.

Let's see if finding a pattern may help. (It usually does.) As we've seen before, the best way to find a pattern is to generate lots of examples. So let's come up with some examples of arrays with their largest subsection sums and see if we discover anything interesting:

```
[1, 1, 0, -3, 5]       [5, -2, 3, -8, 4]
              └─┘       └────────────┘
               5              6

[2, -3, 1, 2, -1]       [5, -8, 2, 1, 0]
        └──────┘               └─┘
            3                   5
```

When analyzing these cases, an interesting question emerges: why is it that in some cases, the greatest sum comes from a subsection that starts at the beginning of the array, and in other cases it doesn't?

In looking at these cases, we can see that when the greatest subsection *doesn't* start at the beginning, it's because a negative number broke the streak:

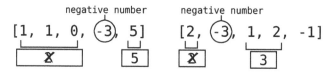

The greatest subsection *would've* been derived from the beginning of the array, but a negative number killed the streak, and the greatest subsection has to start later on in the array.

But wait a second. In some cases, the greatest subsection *includes* a negative number, and the negative number didn't break the streak:

```
            negative number
                 ↓
        [5, (-2) 3, -8, 4]
         └──────────┘
              6
```

So what's the difference?

The pattern is this: if the negative number causes the preceding subsection's sum to sink to a negative number, the streak is broken. But if the negative number simply lowers the current subsection's sum, and the sum remains a positive number, the streak isn't broken.

If we think about it, this makes sense. If, as we're iterating through the array, our current subsection's sum becomes less than 0, *we're best off just resetting the current sum to 0*. Otherwise, the current negative sum will just detract from the greatest sum we're trying to find.

So let's use this insight to tweak our greedy algorithm.

Again, let's start with the 3. The greatest sum is currently 3:

$$\text{greatest sum} = 3$$

$$[3, \ -4, \ 4, \ -3, \ 5, \ -9]$$

$$\boxed{3}$$

Next, we encounter the -4. This would make our current sum -1:

$$\text{greatest sum} = 3$$

$$[3, \ -4, \ 4, \ -3, \ 5, \ -9]$$

$$\boxed{-1}$$

Since we're trying to find the subsection with the greatest sum, and our current sum is a negative number, we need to reset the current sum to 0 before continuing on to the next number:

$$\text{greatest sum} = 3$$

$$[3, \ -4, \ 4, \ -3, \ 5, \ -9]$$

$$\boxed{0}$$

We'll also start a brand-new subsection beginning with the next number.

Again, the reasoning is that if the next number is positive, we may as well just start the next subsection from there, without letting the current negative number drag down the sum. Instead, we're going to perform a reset by setting the current sum to 0 and considering the next number to be the *beginning* of a new subsection.

So let's continue.

We now reach a 4. Again, this is the beginning of a new subsection, so the current sum is 4, which also becomes the greatest sum we've seen yet:

greatest sum = 4

[3, -4, **4**, -3, 5, -9]

4

Next, we encounter the -3. The current sum is now 1:

greatest sum = 4

[3, -4, **4**, **-3**, 5, -9]

1

We next come upon a 5. This makes the current sum 6, which is the greatest sum as well:

greatest sum = 6

[3, -4, **4**, **-3**, **5**, -9]

6

Finally, we reach the -9. This would make the current sum -3, in which case we'd reset it to 0. However, we've also reached the end of the array, and we can conclude the greatest sum is 6. And, indeed, that is the correct result.

Here's the code for this approach:

```python
def max_sum(array):
    current_sum = 0
    greatest_sum = 0

    for num in array:
        if current_sum + num < 0:
            current_sum = 0
        else:
            current_sum += num
            if current_sum > greatest_sum:
                greatest_sum = current_sum

    return greatest_sum
```

Using this greedy algorithm, we were able to solve this thorny problem in just O(N) time, as we loop through the array of numbers just once. That's a great improvement over our initial $O(N^2)$ approach. In terms of space, this algorithm is O(1), as we don't generate any extra data.

While the discovery of a pattern helped us discover the precise solution, by adopting the greedy mindset, we knew what kind of pattern we were looking for in the first place.

Greedy Stock Predictions

Let's look at one more greedy algorithm.

Say we're writing financial software that makes stock predictions. The particular algorithm we're working on now looks for a positive trend for a given stock.

Specifically, we're writing a function that accepts an array of stock prices and determines whether there are any *three* prices that create an upward trend.

For example, take this array of stock prices that represents the price of a given stock over time:

```
[22, 25, 21, 18, 19.6, 17, 16, 20.5]
```

Although it may be difficult to spot at first, there are three prices that form an upward trend:

$$[22, \ 25, \ 21, \ \boxed{18}, \ \boxed{19.6}, \ 17, \ 16, \ \boxed{20.5}]$$

As we go from left to right, there are three prices where a "right-hand" price is greater than a "middle" price, which in turn is greater than a "left-hand" price.

The following array, on the other hand, does not contain a three-point upward trend:

```
[50, 51.25, 48.4, 49, 47.2, 48, 46.9]
```

Our function should return True if the array contains an upward trend of three prices and False if it does not.

So how do we go about this?

One way we can do this is with three nested loops. As one loop iterates over each stock price, a second loop iterates over all the stock prices that follow. And for each round of the second loop, a third nested loop checks all the prices that follow the second price. As we point to each set of three stock prices, we check whether they're in ascending order. As soon as we find such a set, we return True. But if we complete the loops without finding any such trend, we return False.

The time complexity of this algorithm is $O(N^3)$. That's pretty slow! Is there any way we can optimize this?

Let's first think about the best-imaginable Big O. We definitely need to inspect each stock price to find a trend, so we know that our algorithm cannot be faster than $O(N)$. Let's see if we can optimize for such a speed.

Once again, it's time to get greedy.

To apply the greedy mentality to our case, we'd want to somehow keep grabbing what we think is the lowest point of our three-price upward trend. It would also be cool if we can use the same greedy approach to constantly grab what we think are the middle and highest points of that trend.

Here's what we'll do:

We'll assume the first price from the array is the lowest point in the three-price upward trend.

As far as the middle price, we'll initialize it to a number that's guaranteed to be greater than even the highest stock price in the array. To do this, we'll set it to infinity. This particular step might be the least intuitive at first glance, but you'll see shortly why we need to do this.

We'll then make a single pass through the entire array, according to the following steps:

1. If the current price is lower than the lowest price we've encountered so far, this price becomes the new lowest price.

2. If the current price is higher than the lowest price, but lower than the middle price, we update the middle price to be the current price.

3. If the current price is higher than the middle price, it means we've found a three-price upward trend!

Let's see this in action. First, we'll start with a simple example, working with this array of stock prices:

$$[5, 2, 8, 4, 3, 7]$$

We begin iterating through the array, starting with the 5. We start out of the gates with pure greed, and assume that this 5 is the smallest price in the three-point trend as shown in the following array on page 421.

$$[\overset{\downarrow}{\underset{\text{low}}{(5)}}\ 2,\ 8,\ 4,\ 3,\ 7]$$

Next, we proceed to the 2. Because the 2 is lower than the 5, we get even greedier and assume that the 2 is now the lowest price in the trend:

$$[5,\ \overset{\downarrow}{\underset{\text{low}}{(2)}}\ 8,\ 4,\ 3,\ 7]$$

We arrive at the next number in the array, which is 8. This is higher than our lowest point, so we keep the lowest point at 2. However, it's less than the current middle price, which is infinity, so we now greedily assign the 8 to be our *middle* point in the three-point trend:

$$[5,\ \underset{\text{low}}{(2)}\ \overset{\downarrow}{\underset{\text{medium}}{(8)}}\ 4,\ 3,\ 7]$$

Next up, we reach the 4. This is higher than the 2, so we continue to assume that the 2 is the lowest point in our trend. However, because the 4 is less than the 8, we make the 4 our middle point instead of the 8. This, too, is out of greed, as by making our middle point lower, we increase our chances of finding a higher price later on, forming the trend that we're seeking. So the 4 is our new middle point:

$$[5,\ \underset{\text{low}}{(2)}\ 8,\ \overset{\downarrow}{\underset{\text{medium}}{(4)}}\ 3,\ 7]$$

The next number in the array is the 3. We'll leave our lowest price at 2, since the 3 is greater than it. But we will make it our new middle point, since it's less than the 4:

$$[5,\ \underset{\text{low}}{(2)}\ 8,\ 4,\ \overset{\downarrow}{\underset{\text{medium}}{(3)}}\ 7]$$

Finally, we reach the 7, which is the last value in the array. Because the 7 is greater than our middle price (which is 3), this means the array contains an upward three-point trend, and our function can return True:

Note that two such trends exist in the array. There's 2-3-7, but there's also 2-4-7. Ultimately, though, this doesn't matter to us, since we're just trying to determine whether this array contains *any* upward trend; so finding a single instance is enough to return True.

Here's an implementation of this algorithm:

```python
def is_increasing_triplet(array):
    lowest_price = array[0]
    middle_price = float('inf')

    for price in array:
        if price <= lowest_price:
            lowest_price = price
        elif price <= middle_price:
            middle_price = price
        else:
            return True

    return False
```

One counterintuitive aspect of this algorithm is worth pointing out. Specifically, in some scenarios, it would appear this algorithm wouldn't work, yet it does.

Let's take a look at this scenario:

$$[8, 9, 7, 10]$$

Let's see what happens when we apply our algorithm to this array.

At first, the 8 becomes our lowest point:

Then the 9 becomes our middle point:

$$(8) \quad (9) \quad 7, \quad 10]$$

low medium

Next, we reach the 7. Because this is lower than our lowest point, we update the lowest point to be 7:

$$[8, \quad (9) \quad (7) \quad 10]$$

medium low

We then reach the 10:

$$[8, \quad (9) \quad (7) \quad 10]$$

medium low

Because the 10 is greater than the current middle point (9) our function returns True. Now, this is the correct response, since our array indeed contains the trend of 8-9-10. However, by the time our function is done, our lowest point variable is pointing to the 7. But the 7 is not part of the upward trend!

Despite this being the case, our function still returned the correct response. And this is because all our function needs to do is reach a number that is higher than the middle point. Because the middle point was only established once we already found a lower point before it, as soon as we reach a number higher than the middle point, it still means an upward trend is present in the array. This is true even though we ended up overwriting the lower point to be some other number later on.

In any case, our greedy approach paid off, as we only iterated over our array a single time. This is an astounding improvement, as we turned an algorithm that ran at $O(N^3)$ into one of $O(N)$.

Of course, a greedy approach doesn't *always* work. But it's another tool you can try out when optimizing your algorithms.

Change the Data Structure

Another helpful optimization technique is to imagine what would happen if we stored our given data in an alternative data structure.

For example, we may be working on a problem where the data is given to us in the form of an array. However, reimagining that same data stored as a hash table, tree, or other data structure can sometimes reveal clever optimization opportunities.

Our use of a hash table for the magical lookup technique earlier is a specific example of this. And we're about to see that changing the data structure can be useful for other scenarios as well.

The Anagram Checker

Here's one example. Let's say we're writing a function that determines whether two given strings are anagrams of one another. We encountered an anagram function before in Anagram Generation, on page 177, but there we dealt with a function that produced every anagram of a string. Here, we're just going to compare two strings side by side. We'll return True if they're anagrams of each other and False if they're not.

Now, we could use the anagram-generating function to solve this problem; that is, we can produce all the anagrams of the first string and see if the second string matches any of those anagrams. However, since for N characters in the string there will always be N! anagrams, our algorithm will take at least O(N!) time. This is disastrously slow.

You know the drill. Before we proceed to optimize our code, we need to come up with our best-imaginable Big O.

Now, we certainly need to visit each character from both strings at least once. And since the input strings may be of different sizes, touching each character just once would be O(N + M). As I couldn't imagine a faster speed for the task at hand, this is what we'll aim for.

In theory, we could put some code at the beginning of the function that immediately returns False if the two strings have different sizes, since it's impossible for strings of different sizes to be anagrams. In that case, the speed we'd aim for is 2N since the algorithm will only be working with strings that are the same size. This reduces to O(N).

However, for the sake of this discussion, we'll allow someone to input two strings that may be of different sizes, and so we'll aim for O(N + M).

Let's work our way there.

A second possible approach to our problem is to run nested loops to compare the two strings. Specifically, as an outer loop iterates over each character from the first string, we compare that character to every character of the second string. Each time we find a match, we delete a character from the second string. The idea here is that if every character from the first string is also present in the second string, we'd end up deleting every character from the second string by the time we complete our outer loop.

So, if by the time we finish looping, characters still remain from the second string, it means the strings aren't anagrams. Also, if we're still iterating over the first word, but we've already deleted the entire second string, it also means the strings aren't anagrams. But if we make it to the end of the loop and the second string has been completely deleted, we can conclude that the two strings are indeed anagrams.

Here's a Python implementation of this:

```python
def are_anagrams(first_string, second_string):
    second_string_array = list(second_string)

    for i in range(len(first_string)):
        if len(second_string_array) == 0:
            return False

        for j in range(len(second_string_array)):
            if first_string[i] == second_string_array[j]:
                del second_string_array[j]
                break

    return len(second_string_array) == 0
```

Now, it just so happens that deleting items from an array while you're looping through it can be error prone; if you don't do it right, it's like sawing off the tree branch you're sitting on. But even though we've handled that correctly, our algorithm runs at O(N * M). This is way faster than O(N!) but much slower than the O(N + M) we're shooting for.

An even faster approach would be to sort the two strings. If after sorting the two strings they're exactly the same, it means they're anagrams; otherwise, they're not.

This approach will take O(N log N) for each string using a fast sorting algorithm like Quicksort. Since we may have two strings of different sizes, this adds up to be O(N log N + M log M). This is a nice improvement over O(N * M), but let's not stop now—we're aiming for O(N + M), remember?

This is where using an alternative data structure can be extremely helpful. We're dealing with strings, but let's imagine that we'd store the string data in other types of data structures.

We *could* store a string as an array of single characters. But this doesn't help us.

Let's next imagine the string as a hash table. What would that even look like?

One possibility is to create a hash table where each character is a key, and the value is the number of occurrences of that character within the word. For example, the string "balloon" would look like so:

```
{"b": 1, "a": 1, "l": 2, "o": 2, "n": 1}
```

This hash table indicates that the string has one "b", one "a", two "l"s, two "o"s, and one "n".

Now, this doesn't tell us *everything* about the string. Namely, we couldn't tell from the hash table the *order* of characters within the string. So there's a bit of data loss in this regard.

However, that data loss is *exactly* what we need to help us determine whether the two strings are anagrams: two strings turn out to be anagrams if they have the same number of each character, no matter what the order is.

Take the words "rattles", "startle", and "starlet". They all have two "t"s, one "a", one "l", one "e", and one "s"—and that's what allows them to be anagrams and easily reordered to become each other.

We can now write an algorithm that converts each string into a hash table that tallies the count of each type of character. Once we've converted the two strings into two hash tables, all that's left is to compare the two hash tables. If they're equal, it means the two strings are anagrams.

Here's an implementation:

```python
def are_anagrams(first_string, second_string):
    first_word_hash_table = {}
    second_word_hash_table = {}

    for char in first_string:
        if char in first_word_hash_table:
            first_word_hash_table[char] += 1
        else:
            first_word_hash_table[char] = 1

    for char in second_string:
        if char in second_word_hash_table:
            second_word_hash_table[char] += 1
        else:
            second_word_hash_table[char] = 1

    return first_word_hash_table == second_word_hash_table
```

In this algorithm, we iterate over each character from both strings just once, which is N + M steps.

When checking whether the hash tables are equal with return first_word_hash_table == second_word_hash_table, Python under the hood probably takes up to another N + M steps. This is because Python has to iterate over each of the key-value pairs in the hash tables to make sure the pairs exist in both hash tables. However, this still totals just 2(N + M) steps, which reduces to O(N + M). This is much faster than any of our previous approaches.

To be fair, we're taking up some extra space with the creation of these hash tables. Our previous suggestion of sorting the two strings and comparing them would take up no extra space if we did the sorting in place. But if speed is what we're after, we can't beat the hash table approach, as we touch each character from the strings *just once*.

By converting the strings into another data structure (in this case, hash tables), we were able to access the original data in such a way that allowed our algorithm to become blazing fast.

It's not always obvious what new data structure to use, so it's good to imagine how the current data may look if it were converted into a variety of formats, and see if that reveals any optimizations. That being said, hash tables turn out very often to be a great choice, so that's a good place to start.

Group Sorting

Here's another example of how changing the data structure can allow us to optimize our code. Let's say we have an array containing several different values and we want to reorder the data so that the same values are grouped together. However, we don't necessarily care what order the *groups* are in.

For example, let's say we have the following array:

```
["a", "c", "d", "b", "b", "c", "a", "d", "c", "b", "a", "d"]
```

Our goal is to sort this into groups, like so:

```
["c", "c", "c", "a", "a", "a", "d", "d", "d", "b", "b", "b"]
```

Again, we don't care about the order of the groups, so these results would also be acceptable:

```
["d", "d", "d", "c", "c", "c", "a", "a", "a", "b", "b", "b"]
["b", "b", "b", "c", "c", "c", "a", "a", "a", "d", "d", "d"]
```

Now, any classic sorting algorithm would accomplish our task, since we'd end up with this:

```
["a", "a", "a", "b", "b", "b", "c", "c", "c", "d", "d", "d"]
```

As you know, the fastest sorting algorithms clock in at O(N log N). But can we do better?

Let's begin by coming up with the best-imaginable Big O. Since we know that there generally aren't sorting algorithms faster than O(N log N), it may be difficult to imagine how we can sort something in a faster time.

But since we're not doing a precise sort, if someone told me that our task can be done in O(N) time, I suppose I'd believe them. We certainly can't beat O(N), since we need to visit each value at least once. So let's aim for O(N).

Let's employ the technique we've been discussing and imagine our data in the form of another data structure.

We may as well start with a hash table. What would our array of strings look like if it were a hash table?

If we took a similar approach to what we did with the anagrams, we could represent our array in the following way:

```
{"a": 3, "c": 3, "d": 3, "b": 3}
```

As with our previous example, there's some data loss: we couldn't convert this hash table back into our original array, as we wouldn't know the original order of all the strings.

However, for our purposes of grouping, this data loss doesn't matter. In fact, the hash table contains all the data we need to create the grouped array we're looking for.

Specifically, we can iterate over each key-value pair within the hash table and use that data to populate an array with the correct number of each string. Here's the code for this:

```
def group_sort(array):
    hash_table = {}
    new_array = []

    for value in array:
        if value in hash_table:
            hash_table[value] += 1
        else:
            hash_table[value] = 1

    for key in hash_table:
        count = hash_table[key]
        for i in range(count):
            new_array.append(key)

    return new_array
```

Our group_array function accepts an array and then begins by creating an empty hash_table and an empty new_array.

We first collect the tallies of each string and store them in the hash table:

```
for value in array:
    if hash_table.get(value):
        hash_table[value] += 1
    else:
        hash_table[value] = 1
```

This creates the hash table that looks like this:

```
{"a": 3, "c": 3, "d": 3, "b": 3}
```

Then we proceed to iterate over each key-value pair and use this data to populate the new_array:

```
for key in hash_table:
    count = hash_table[key]
    for i in range(0, count):
        new_array.append(key)
```

So when we reach the pair "a": 3, we add three "a"s to the new_array. And when we reach "c": 3, we add three "c"s to the new_array, and so on. By the time we're done, our new_array will contain all the strings organized in groups.

This algorithm takes just O(N) time, which is a significant optimization over the O(N log N) that sorting would have taken. We do use up O(N) space with the extra hash table and new_array, although we could choose to overwrite the original array to save additional memory. That being said, the space taken up by the hash table would still be O(N) in the worst case, where each string in the array is different.

But again, if speed is our goal, we achieved our best-imaginable Big O, which is a fantastic win.

Wrapping Up

The techniques presented here can be useful in optimizing your code. Again, you'll always want to start by determining your current Big O and the best-imaginable Big O. After that, you have all the other techniques at your disposal.

You'll find that some techniques work better than others in certain situations, but they're all worth thinking about in a given situation to see if they may be the right tool for the job.

With experience, you'll hone your optimization sense and probably develop additional techniques of your own!

Parting Thoughts

You've learned a lot in this journey, but your journey is only just beginning. (Cue dramatic music.)

You've learned that the right choices in algorithm design and data structures can dramatically affect the performance of your code.

You've learned how to determine the efficiency of your code.

You've learned how to optimize your code to make it faster, more memory-efficient, and more elegant.

What you can take away from this book is a framework for making educated technology decisions. Creating great software involves evaluating the trade-offs of the available options, and you're now armed with the ability to see the pros and cons of each option and make the best choice for the task at hand. And you also have the ability to think of *new* options that may not have been immediately obvious at first glance.

I hope you also take away from this book the knowledge that topics like these—which seem so complex and esoteric—are just a combination of simpler, easier concepts that are within your grasp. Don't be intimidated by resources that make a concept seem difficult simply because they don't explain it well—a concept can always be broken down in a way it can be understood.

With the foundation you've built, more advanced topics and techniques are now within your reach. I invite you to continue your data structures and algorithms journey with me *in Volume 2 of this book*, which is expected to be published next. Keep your eye out for it.

In Volume 2 you'll discover additional data structures, algorithms, and concepts that are fascinating, powerful, and *practical*. I dare say that they'll transform you into an even better software engineer than you are now. Most importantly, Volume 2 will continue to *change the way you think*.

And of course, we'll also have a lot of fun along the way. See you on the other side!

(Oh, but don't forget to do your exercises first.)

Exercises

The following exercises provide you with the opportunity to practice with optimizing your code. The solutions to these exercises are found in the section Chapter 20, on page 459.

1. You're working on software that analyzes sports players. Following are two arrays of players of different sports:

```
basketball_players = [
  {first_name: "Jill", last_name: "Huang", team: "Gators"},
  {first_name: "Janko", last_name: "Barton", team: "Sharks"},
  {first_name: "Wanda", last_name: "Vakulskas", team: "Sharks"},
  {first_name: "Jill", last_name: "Moloney", team: "Gators"},
  {first_name: "Luuk", last_name: "Watkins", team: "Gators"}
]

football_players = [
  {first_name: "Hanzla", last_name: "Radosti", team: "32ers"},
  {first_name: "Tina", last_name: "Watkins", team: "Barleycorns"},
  {first_name: "Alex", last_name: "Patel", team: "32ers"},
  {first_name: "Jill", last_name: "Huang", team: "Barleycorns"},
  {first_name: "Wanda", last_name: "Vakulskas", team: "Barleycorns"}
]
```

If you look carefully, you'll see that there are some players who participate in more than one kind of sport. Jill Huang and Wanda Vakulskas play both basketball *and* football.

You are to write a function that accepts two arrays of players and returns an array of the players who play in *both* sports. In this case, that would be the following:

```
["Jill Huang", "Wanda Vakulskas"]
```

While there are players who share first names and players who share last names, we can assume there's only one person who has a particular *full* name (meaning first *and* last name).

We can use a nested-loops approach, comparing each player from one array against each player from the other array, but this would have a runtime of O(N * M). Your job is to optimize the function so that it can run in just O(N + M).

2. You're writing a function that accepts an array of distinct integers from 0, 1, 2, 3…up to N. However, the array will be missing one integer, and your function is to *return the missing one*.

For example, this array has all the integers from 0 to 6 but is missing the 4:

```
[2, 3, 0, 6, 1, 5]
```

Therefore, the function should return 4.

The next example has all the integers from 0 to 9 but is missing the 1:

```
[8, 2, 3, 9, 4, 7, 5, 0, 6]
```

In this case, the function should return the 1.

Using a nested-loops approach would take up to $O(N^2)$. Your job is to optimize the code so that it has a runtime of $O(N)$.

3. You're working on some more stock-prediction software. The function you're writing accepts an array of predicted prices for a particular stock over the course of time.

For example, look at this array of seven prices:

```
[10, 7, 5, 8, 11, 2, 6]
```

It predicts that a given stock will have these prices over the next seven days. (On Day 1, the stock will close at $10; on Day 2, the stock will close at $7; and so on.)

Your function should calculate the greatest profit that could be made from a single "buy" transaction followed by a single "sell" transaction.

In this example, the most money could be made if we bought the stock when it was worth $5 and sold it when it was worth $11. This yields a profit of $6 per share.

Note that we could make even more money if we buy and sell multiple times, but for now, this function focuses on the most profit that could be made from just *one* purchase followed by *one* sale.

Now, we could use nested loops to find the profit of every possible buy-and-sell combination. However, this would be $O(N^2)$ and too slow for our hotshot trading platform. Your job is to optimize the code so that the function clocks in at just $O(N)$.

4. You're writing a function that accepts an array of numbers and computes the highest product of any two numbers in the array. At first glance, this is easy, as we can just find the two greatest numbers and multiply them. However, our array can contain negative numbers and look like this:

```
[5, -10, -6, 9, 4]
```

In this case, it's actually the product of the two *lowest* numbers, -10 and -6 that yield the highest product of 60.

We could use nested loops to multiply every possible pair of numbers, but this would take $O(N^2)$ time. Your job is to optimize the function so that it's a speedy $O(N)$.

5. You're creating software that analyzes the data of body temperature readings taken from hundreds of human beings. These readings are taken from both healthy and sick people and range from 95 to 105 degrees Fahrenheit.

Here's a sample array of temperature readings:

```
[98, 99, 95, 105, 104, 98, 101, 99, 100, 97]
```

You are to write a function that sorts these readings from lowest to highest.

If you used a classic sorting algorithm such as Quicksort, this would take O(N log N). *However, in this case, it's possible to write a faster sorting algorithm.*

Yes, that's right. Even though you've learned that the fastest sorts are O(N log N), this case is different. Why? In this case, there's a *limited number of possibilities* of what the readings will be. In such a case, we can sort these values in O(N). It may be N multiplied by a constant, but that's still considered O(N).

6. You're writing a function that accepts an array of unsorted integers and returns the length of the *longest consecutive sequence* among them. The sequence is formed by integers that increase by 1. For example, have a look at this array:

```
[10, 5, 12, 3, 55, 30, 4, 11, 2]
```

The longest consecutive sequence is 2-3-4-5. These four integers form an increasing sequence because each integer is one greater than the previous one. While there's also a sequence of 10-11-12, it's only a sequence of three integers. In this case, the function should return 4, since that's the length of the *longest* consecutive sequence that can be formed from this array.

Here's one more example:

```
[19, 13, 15, 12, 18, 14, 17, 11]
```

This array's longest sequence is 11-12-13-14-15, so the function would return 5.

If we sorted the array, we can then traverse the array just once to find the longest consecutive sequence. However, the sorting itself would take O(N log N). Your job is to optimize the function so that it takes O(N) time.

Exercise Solutions

Chapter 1

These are the solutions to the exercises found in the section Exercises, on page 19.

1. Let's break down each of the cases:

    a. Reading from an array always takes just one step.

    b. Searching for a nonexistent element within an array of size 100 will take 100 steps, as the computer needs to inspect each element of the array before determining the element cannot be found.

    c. The insertion will take 101 steps: 100 shifts of each element to the right, and one step to insert the new element at the front of the array.

    d. Insertion at the end of an array always takes one step.

    e. The deletion will take 100 steps: first the computer deletes the first element and then shifts the remaining 99 elements to the left, one at a time.

    f. Deletion at the end of an array always takes one step.

2. Let's break down each of the cases:

    a. Like the array, reading from the array-based set will take just one step.

    b. Like the array, searching the array-based set will take 100 steps, as we inspect each element before concluding that the element isn't there.

    c. To insert into the set, we first need to conduct a full search to make sure the value doesn't already exist within the set. This search will take 100 steps. Then we need to shift all 100 elements to the right to make room for the new value. Finally, we drop the new value at the beginning of the set. This is a total of 201 steps.

d. This insertion takes 101 steps. Again, we need to conduct a full search before inserting, which takes 100 steps. We then conclude with the final step of inserting the new value at the end of the set.

e. The deletion will take 100 steps, just like a classic array.

f. The deletion will take one step, just like a classic array.

3. If the array contains N elements, searching for all instances of the string "apple" in an array will take N steps. When searching for just one instance, we can cut our search short as soon as we find it. But if we need to find all instances, we have no choice but inspect each element of the entire array.

Chapter 2

These are the solutions to the exercises found in the section Exercises, on page 34.

1. Linear search on this array would take four steps. We start at the beginning of the array and check each element from left to right. Because the 8 is the fourth number, we'll find it in four steps.

2. Binary search would take just one step in this case. We start the binary search at the middlemost element, and the 8 just happens to be the middlemost element!

3. To solve this, we need to count how many times we halve 100,000 until we get down to 1. If we keep dividing 100,000 by 2, we see that it takes us sixteen times until we get down to about 1.53. If we halve this a seventeenth time, we get roughly 0.76, which is already below 1. This suggests that in a worst-case scenario, it takes either sixteen or seventeen steps to perform binary search on 100,000 elements. If your answer is either sixteen or seventeen, it means you understand this concept well. Nice job!

In practice, binary search takes *sixteen* steps. We can see this if we (tediously) walk through each step.

Let's start with 100,000 elements. When dealing with an even number of elements, there isn't an exact item in the center. Instead, there are *two* central elements, and we arbitrarily search one of them. By searching this element, we've essentially taken it out of the picture, leaving behind 50,000 elements on one side of it and 49,999 on the other side. In the worst-case scenario, the value we're searching for is among the 50,000 elements.

Let's perform a few more searches. Our second search leaves us with 25,000 elements. Our third search leaves 12,500 elements remaining. Our fourth search whittles down the elements to 6,250. The fifth search leaves us with 3,125 elements.

Now, this is the first time we're encountering an odd number of elements. Here, there's a single central element, and when we search it, each side will have 1,562 elements. Therefore, when doing the math for our next search, we can subtract 1 from 3,125 (since we've removed the central element from the picture) and divide 3,124 by 2. This, as we noted, gives us 1,562.

When we continue this pattern, it emerges that it takes sixteen steps to halve 100,000 until we find the value we're searching for.

Chapter 3

These are the solutions to the exercises found in the section Exercises, on page 45.

1. This is O(1). We can consider N to be the year passed into the function. But no matter what the year is, the algorithm doesn't vary in how many steps it takes.

2. This is O(N). For N elements in the array, the loop will run N times.

3. This is O(log N). In this case, N is the number number_of_grains, which is passed into the function. The loop runs as long as placed_grains < number_of_grains, but placed_grains starts at 1 and *doubles* each time the loop runs. If, for example, number_of_grains was 256, we'd keep doubling the placed_grains nine times until we reach 256, meaning that our loop would run eight times for an N of 256. If number_of_grains was 512, our loop would run nine times, and if number_of_grains was 1024, the loop would run ten times. Since our loop runs only one more time each time N is doubled, this is considered O(log N).

4. This is O(N). N is the number of strings within the array, and the loop will take N steps.

5. This is O(1). We can consider N to be the size of the array, but the algorithm takes a fixed number of steps no matter what N is. The algorithm does account for whether N is even or odd, but in either case, it takes the same number of steps.

Chapter 4

These are the solutions to the exercises found in the section Exercises, on page 60.

1. Here is the completed table:

N Elements	O(N)	O(log N)	$O(N^2)$
100	100	About 7	10,000
2000	2000	About 11	4,000,000

2. The array would have sixteen elements, since 16^2 is 256. (Another way of saying this is that the square root of 256 is 16.)

3. The algorithm has a time complexity of $O(N^2)$. N, in this case, is the size of the array. We have an outer loop that iterates over the array N times, and for each of those times, an inner loop iterates over the same array N times. This results in N^2 steps.

4. The following version is O(N), as we only iterate through the array once:

```python
def greatest_number(array):
    if not array:
        return None

    greatest_number_so_far = array[0]

    for i in array:
        if i > greatest_number_so_far:
            greatest_number_so_far = i

    return greatest_number_so_far
```

Chapter 5

These are the solutions to the exercises found in the section Exercises, on page 76.

1. After dropping the constants, we can reduce the expression to O(N).

2. After dropping the constant, we can reduce the expression to $O(N^2)$.

3. This algorithm is one of O(N), with N being the size of the array. While there are two distinct loops that process the N elements, this is simply 2N, which is reduced to O(N) after dropping the constants.

4. This algorithm is one of O(N), with N being the size of the array. Within the loop, we run three steps, which means our algorithm takes 3N steps. However, this is reduced to O(N) when we eliminate the constants.

5. This algorithm is one of $O(N^2)$, with N being the size of the array. While we only run the inner loop half of the time, this simply means that the algorithm runs for N^2 / 2 steps. However, the division by 2 is a constant, so we express this simply as $O(N^2)$.

Chapter 6

These are the solutions to the exercises found in the section Exercises, on page 93.

1. In Big O notation, $2N^2$ + 2N + 1 gets reduced to $O(N^2)$. After getting rid of all the constants, we're left with N^2 + N, but we also drop the N since it's a lower order than N^2.

2. Since log N is a lower order than N, it's simply reduced to O(N).

3. The important thing to note here is that the function ends as soon as we find a pair that sums to 10. The best-case scenario, then, is when the first two numbers add up to 10, since we can end the function before the loops even get underway. An average-case scenario may be when the two numbers are somewhere in the middle of the array. The worst-case scenarios are when there aren't any two numbers that add up to 10, in which case we must exhaust both loops completely. This worst-case scenario is $O(N^2)$, where N is the size of the array.

4. This algorithm has an efficiency of O(N), as the size of the array is N, and the loop iterates through all N elements.

    This algorithm continues the loop even if it finds an "X" before the end of the array. We can make the code more efficient if we return True as soon as we find an "X":

```
def contains_X(string):
    for char in string:
        if char == "X":
            return True

    return False
```

Chapter 7

These are the solutions to the exercises found in the section Exercises, on page 108.

1. Here, N is the size of the array. Our loop runs for N / 2 times, as it processes two values each round of the loop. However, this is expressed as O(N) because we drop the constant.

2. It's slightly tricky to define N in this case, since we're dealing with two distinct arrays. The algorithm only processes each value once, so we could decide to call N the total number of values between both arrays, and the time complexity would be O(N). If we want to be more literal and call one array N and the other M, we could alternatively express the efficiency as O(N + M). However, because we're simply adding N and M together, it's simpler to just use N to refer to the total number of data elements across both arrays and call it O(N).

3. In a worst-case scenario, this algorithm runs (approximately) as many times as the number of characters in the needle multiplied by the number of characters in the haystack. Imagine, for example, that we're searching for the needle ab within the haystack aaaaaaaaaaab. Every time our outer loop reaches a new a, we run an inner loop looking for ab.

    Since the needle and haystack may have different numbers of characters, this is O(N * M).

4. N is the size of the array, and the time complexity is $O(N^3)$, as it's processed through triply-nested loops. Really, the middle loop runs N / 2 times, and the innermost loop runs N / 4 times, so this is N * (N / 2) * (N / 4), which is N^3 / 8 steps. But we drop the constant, leaving us with $O(N^3)$.

5. N is the size of the resumes array. Since in each round of the loop we eliminate half of the resumes, we have an algorithm of O(log N).

Chapter 8

These are the solutions to the exercises found in the section Exercises, on page 131.

1. The following implementation first stores the values of the first array in a hash table and then checks each value of the second array against that hash table:

```
def get_intersection(array1, array2):
    intersection = []
```

```
hash_table = {}

for value in array1:
    hash_table[value] = True

for value in array2:
    if hash_table.get(value):
        intersection.append(value)

return intersection
```

This algorithm has an efficiency of O(N).

2. The following implementation checks each string in the array. If the string isn't yet in the hash table, the string gets added. If the string *is* in the hash table, that means it's been added before, which means it's a duplicate! This algorithm has a time complexity of O(N):

```
def find_duplicate(array):
    hash_table = {}

    for value in array:
        if hash_table.get(value):
            return value
        else:
            hash_table[value] = True

    return None
```

3. The following implementation begins by creating a hash table out of all the characters we encounter in the string. Next, we iterate over each character of the alphabet and check to see whether the character is contained within our hash table. If it isn't, it means the character is missing from the string, so we return it:

```
def find_missing_letter(string):
    hash_table = {}

    for char in string:
        hash_table[char] = True

    alphabet = "abcdefghijklmnopqrstuvwxyz"

    for char in alphabet:
        if not hash_table.get(char):
            return char

    return None
```

4. The following implementation begins by iterating over each character in the string. If the character doesn't yet exist in the hash table, the character is added to the hash table as a key with the value of 1, indicating the character has been found once so far. If the character is already in the hash

table, we simply increment the value by 1. So if the character "e" has the value of 3, it means the "e" exists three times within the string.

Then we iterate over the characters again and return the first character that only exists once within the string. This algorithm is O(N):

```python
def first_non_duplicate(string):
    hash_table = {}

    for char in string:
        if hash_table.get(char):
            hash_table[char] += 1
        else:
            hash_table[char] = 1

    for char in string:
        if hash_table.get(char) == 1:
            return char

    return None
```

Chapter 9

These are the solutions to the exercises found in the section Exercises, on page 147.

1. Presumably, we'd want to be nice to the callers and answer their phone calls in the order in which they were received. For this, we'd use a queue, which processes data FIFO (first in, first out).

2. We'd be able to read the 4, which is now the top element in the stack. This is because we'll have popped the 6 and the 5, which were previously sitting on top of the 4.

3. We'd be able to read the 3, which is now at the front of the queue, after having dequeued the 1 and the 2.

4. We can take advantage of the stack because of the fact that we pop each item in the reverse order of which they were pushed onto the stack. So we'll first push each character of the string onto the stack. Then we'll pop each one off while adding them to the end of a new string:

```python
import stack as stack_module

def reverse(string):
    stack = stack_module.Stack()
    new_string = ""

    for char in string:
        stack.push(char)
```

```
while stack.read():
    new_string += stack.pop()
return new_string
```

The stack_module referred to here is simply our homegrown Stack implementation from Chapter 9, which we've saved in a file called stack.py.

Chapter 10

These are the solutions to the exercises found in the section Exercises, on page 159.

1. The base case is if low > high:—that is, we want to stop the recursion once low has exceeded high. Otherwise, we'd end up printing numbers even greater than the high number, and onto infinity.

2. We'd have infinite recursion! factorial(10) calls factorial(8), which calls factorial(6), which calls factorial(4), which calls factorial(2), which calls factorial(0). Since our base case is if number == 1:, we never end up with number ever being 1, so the recursion continues. factorial(0) calls factorial(-2), and so on.

3. Let's say low is 1 and high is 10. When we call sum(1, 10), that in turn returns 10 + sum(1, 9). That is, we return the sum of 10 plus whatever the sum of 1 through 9 is. sum(1, 9) ends up calling sum(1, 8), which in turn calls sum(1, 7), and so on.

   We want the last call to be sum(1, 1), in which we simply want to return the number 1. This becomes our base case:

```
def sum(low, high):
    # Base case:
    if high == low:
        return low

    return high + sum(low, high - 1)
```

4. This approach is similar to the file directory example from the text:

```
def print_all_items(array):
    for value in array:
        # If the current value is a Python "list", in other words, an array:
        if isinstance(value, list):
            print_all_items(value)
        else:
            print(value)
```

We iterate over each item within the outer array. If the value is itself another array, we recursively call the function on that subarray. Otherwise, it's the base case where we simply print the value to the screen.

Chapter 11

These are the solutions to the exercises found in the section Exercises, on page 181.

1. Let's call our function character_count. The first step is to pretend that the character_count function has already been implemented.

   Next, we need to identify the subproblem. If our problem is the array ["ab", "c", "def", "ghij"], then our subproblem can be the same array missing one string. Let's specifically say that our subproblem is the array minus the *first* string, which would be ["c", "def", "ghij"].

   Now, let's see what happens when we apply the "already-implemented" function on the subproblem. If we were to call character_count(["c", "def", "ghij"]), we'd get a return value of 8, since there are eight characters in total.

   So to solve our original problem, all we have to do is add the length of the first string ("ab") to the result of calling the character_count function on the subproblem.

   Here's one possible implementation:

   ```
   def character_count(array):
       # Base case: when the array is empty:
       if not array:
           return 0

       return len(array[0]) + character_count(array[1:])
   ```

   Note that our base case is an empty array, in which case there are zero characters to count.

2. First, let's pretend the select_even function already works. Next, let's identify the subproblem. If we try to select all the even numbers in the example array [1, 2, 3, 4, 5], we could say that the subproblem is all the numbers in the array besides the first one. So let's imagine select_even([2, 3, 4, 5]) already works and returns [2, 4].

   Since the first number in the array is 1, we don't want to do anything other than return the [2, 4]. However, if the first number in the array was a 0, we'd want to return the [2, 4] with the 0 added to it.

Our base case is an empty array.

Here's one possible implementation:

```
def select_even(array):
    if not array:
        return []

    if array[0] % 2 == 0:
        return [array[0]] + select_even(array[1:])
    else:
        return select_even(array[1:])
```

3. The definition of a triangular number is n plus the previous number from the sequence, with n referring to the place where the number falls in the pattern. (For example, if we're computing the sequence's seventh number, then n is 7.) If the name of our function is triangle, we can express this simply as n + triangle(n - 1). The base case is when n is 1.

```
def triangle(n):
    if n == 1:
        return 1

    return n + triangle(n - 1)
```

4. Let's pretend that our function, index_of_x, has already been implemented. Next, let's say the subproblem is our string minus its first character. For example, if our input string is "hex", the subproblem is "ex".

Now, index_of_x("ex") would return 1. To calculate the index of the "x" for the original string, we would add 1 to this since the additional "h" at the front of the string moves the "x" down one index. Here's our code:

```
def index_of_x(string):
    if string[0] == "x":
        return 0

    return index_of_x(string[1:]) + 1
```

5. This exercise is similar to the staircase problem. Let's break this down:

From the starting position, we have only two choices of movement. We can either move one space to the right or one space downward.

What this means is that the total number of unique shortest paths will be the number of paths from the space to the right of S + the number of paths from the space below S.

The number of paths from the space to the right of S is the same as calculating the paths in a grid of six columns and three rows, as you can see here:

The number of paths from the space below the S is the equivalent of the paths in a grid of seven columns and two rows:

Recursion allows us to express this beautifully:

```
return unique_paths(rows - 1, columns) + unique_paths(rows, columns - 1)
```

All we need to do now is add the base case. Possible base cases include when we have just one row or one column, since in such cases, there's only one path available to us.

Here's the complete function:

```
def unique_paths(rows, columns):
    if rows == 1 or columns == 1:
        return 1

    return unique_paths(rows - 1, columns) + unique_paths(rows, columns - 1)
```

Chapter 12

These are the solutions to the exercises found in the section Exercises, on page 198.

1. The problem here is the function recursively calls itself *twice* each time it runs. Let's make it so that it only calls itself once each time:

```
def add_until_100(array):
    if not array:
        return 0

    sum_of_remaining_numbers = add_until_100(array[1:])

    if array[0] + sum_of_remaining_numbers > 100:
        return sum_of_remaining_numbers
```

```
    else:
        return array[0] + sum_of_remaining_numbers
```

2. Here is the memoized version:

```
def golomb(n, memo):
    if n == 1:
        return 1

    if n not in memo:
        memo[n] = 1 + golomb(n - golomb(golomb(n - 1, memo), memo), memo)

    return memo[n]
```

3. To accomplish memoization here, we need to make a key that takes into account both the number of rows and the number of columns. To this end, we can make our key be based on the row and column together.

```
def unique_paths(rows, columns, memo):
    if rows == 1 or columns == 1:
        return 1

    if (rows, columns) not in memo:
        memo[(rows, columns)] = (unique_paths(rows - 1, columns, memo)
                                 + unique_paths(rows, columns - 1, memo))

    return memo[(rows, columns)]
```

Note that we use a Python tuple of (rows, columns) as our key instead of an array [rows, columns]. This is because Python doesn't allow arrays to be used as hash table keys. We didn't cover tuples in this book, but in short, they are immutable arrays. In other words, once a tuple is created, it can never be changed.

Chapter 13

These are the solutions to the exercises found in the section Exercises, on page 224.

1. If we sort the numbers, we know that the three greatest numbers will be at the end of the array, and we can just multiply them together. The sorting will take O(N log N):

```
def greatest_product_of_3(array):
    array.sort()

    return array[-1] * array[-2] * array[-3]
```

(This code takes for granted that there are at least three values in the array. You can add code to handle arrays where this is not the case.)

2. If we presort the array, we can then expect each number to be at its own index. That is, the 0 should be at index 0, the 1 should be at index 1, and so on. We can then iterate through the array looking for a number that doesn't equal the index. Once we find it, we know that we just skipped over the missing number:

```python
def find_missing_number(array):
    array.sort()

    for index, num in enumerate(array):
        if num != index:
            return index

    return None
```

The sorting takes N log N steps, and the loop afterward takes N steps. However, we reduce the expression (N log N) + N to O(N log N) since the added N is a lower order compared to N log N.

3. This implementation uses nested loops and is $O(N^2)$:

```python
def max(array):
    if not array:
        return None

    for i in array:
        i_is_greatest_number = True

        for j in array:
            if j > i:
                i_is_greatest_number = False

        if i_is_greatest_number:
            return i
```

The next implementation simply sorts the array and returns the last number. The sorting is O(N log N):

```python
def max(array):
    if not array:
        return None

    array.sort()

    return array[-1]
```

Our next and final implementation is O(N), since we iterate just once over the array:

```python
def max(array):
    if not array:
        return None

    greatest_number_so_far = array[0]
```

```
    for number in array:
        if number > greatest_number_so_far:
            greatest_number_so_far = number

    return greatest_number_so_far
```

Chapter 14

These are the solutions to the exercises found in the section Exercises, on page 245.

1. One way we can do this is with a simple while loop:

```
def print_list(self):
    current_node = self.first_node

    while current_node:
        print(current_node.data)
        current_node = current_node.next_node
```

2. With a doubly linked list, we have immediate access to the last nodes and can follow their "previous node" links to access the previous nodes. This code is basically the inverse of the previous exercise:

```
def reverse_print(self):
    current_node = self.last_node

    while current_node:
        print(current_node.data)
        current_node = current_node.previous_node
```

3. Here, we use a while loop to move through each node. However, before we move forward, we check ahead using the node's link to ensure that there *is* a next node:

```
def last(self):
    current_node = self.first_node

    while current_node.next_node:
        current_node = current_node.next_node

    return current_node.data
```

For fun, here's an alternative implementation that uses recursion:

```
def recursive_last(self, current_node=None):
    if not current_node:
        current_node = self.first_node

    if current_node.next_node:
        return self.recursive_last(current_node.next_node)
    else:
        return current_node.data
```

4. One way to reverse a classic linked list is to iterate through the list while keeping track of three variables.

    The primary variable is the current_node, which is the primary node we're iterating over. We also keep track of the next_node, which is the node immediately after the current_node. And we also keep track of the previous_node, which is the node immediately before the current_node. See the following diagram:

    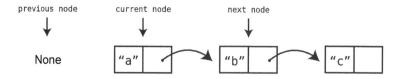

    Note that when we first begin and the current_node is the first node, the previous_node points to None; there are no nodes before the first node.

    Once we have our three variables set up, we proceed with our algorithm, which begins a loop.

    Inside the loop, we first change the current_node's link to point to the previous_node:

    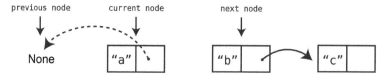

    Then we shift all our variables to the right:

    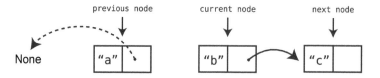

    We begin the loop again, repeating this process of changing the current_node's link to point to the previous_node, until we reach the end of the list. Once we reach the end, the list will have been fully reversed.

    Here's the implementation for this algorithm:

    ```python
    def reverse(self):
        previous_node = None
        current_node = self.first_node
    ```

```
while current_node:
    next_node = current_node.next_node
    current_node.next_node = previous_node

    previous_node = current_node
    current_node = next_node

self.first_node = previous_node
```

5. Believe it or not, we can delete a middle node without having access to any of the nodes that precede it.

   Following is a diagram of an example situation. We have four nodes, but we only have access to node "b". This means we don't have access to node "a", since links only point *forward* in a classic linked list. We've indicated this using a dashed line; that is, we don't have access to any node to the left of the dashed line:

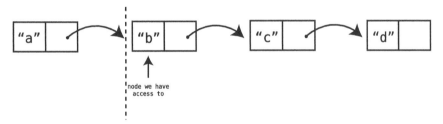

   Now, here's how we can delete node "b" (even though we don't have access to node "a"). For the sake of clarity, we're going to call this node the "access node," since it's the first node we have access to.

   First, we take the *next* node beyond the access node and copy its data into the access node, overwriting the access node's data. In our example, this means copying the string "c" into our access node:

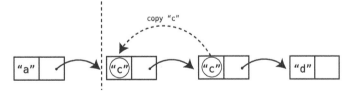

   We then change the link of the access node and have it point to the node that is *two* nodes to the right of it. This effectively deletes the original "c" node:

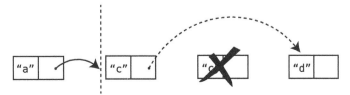

The code for this is short and sweet:

```
def delete_node(node):
    node.data = node.next_node.data
    node.next_node = node.next_node.next_node
```

Chapter 15

These are the solutions to the exercises found in the section Exercises, on page 275.

1. The tree should look like this. Note that it's not well balanced, as the root node only has a right subtree and no left one:

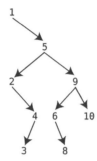

2. Search within a balanced binary search tree takes a maximum of about log(N) steps. So, if N is 1,000, search should take a maximum of about 10 steps.

3. The greatest value within a binary search tree will always be the bottom rightmost node. We can find it by recursively following each node's right child until we hit the bottom:

```
def max(node):
    if node.right_child:
        return max(node.right_child)
    else:
        return node.value
```

4. Here's the order for preorder traversal:

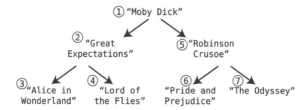

5. Here is the order for postorder traversal:

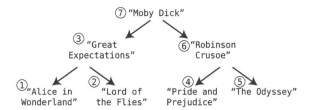

Chapter 16

These are the solutions to the exercises found in the section Exercises, on page 300.

1. After inserting an 11, the heap would look like this:

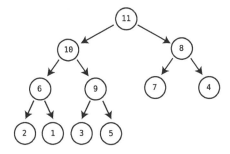

2. After deleting the root node, the heap would look like this:

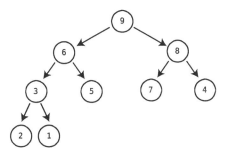

3. The numbers would be in perfect descending order. (This is for a max-heap. For a min-heap, they'd be in *ascending* order.)

   Do you realize what this means? It means you've just discovered another sorting algorithm!

   Heapsort is a sorting algorithm that inserts all the values into a heap and then pops each one. As you can see from this exercise, the values always end up in sorted order.

Like Quicksort, Heapsort is O(N log N). This is because we need to insert N values into the heap, and each insertion takes log N steps.

While there are fancier versions of Heapsort that try to maximize its efficiency, this is the basic idea.

Chapter 17

These are the solutions to the exercises found in the section Exercises, on page 326.

1. This trie stores the words: "tag", "tan", "tank", "tap", "today", "total", "we", "well", and "went".

2. Here is a trie that stores the words "get", "go", "got", "gotten", "hall", "ham", "hammer", "hill", and "zebra":

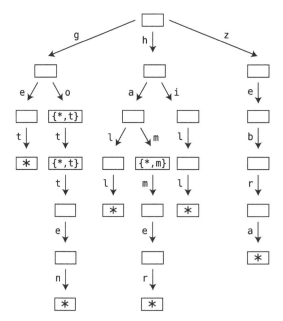

3. The following code starts at the trie's node and iterates over each of its children. For each child, it prints the key and then recursively calls itself on the child node:

```
def traverse(self, node=None):
    current_node = node or self.root

    for key, child_node in current_node.children.items():
        print(key)

        if key != "*":
            self.traverse(child_node)
```

4. Our autocorrect implementation is a combination of the search and collect_all_words functions:

```
def autocorrect(self, word):
    current_node = self.root
    word_found_so_far = ""

    for char in word:
        if current_node.children.get(char):
            word_found_so_far += char
            current_node = current_node.children.get(char)
        else:
            return word_found_so_far + \
                self.collect_all_words([], current_node)[0]

    return word
```

The basic approach is that we first search the trie to find as much of the prefix as we can. When we hit a dead end, instead of just returning None (as the search function does), we call collect_all_words on the current node to collect all the suffixes that stem from that node. We then use the first suffix of the array and concatenate it with the prefix to suggest a new word to the user.

Chapter 18

These are the solutions to the exercises found in the section Exercises, on page 381.

1. If a user is browsing "nails", the website will recommend "nail polish", "needles", "pins", and "hammer".

2. The order of depth-first search would be A-B-E-J-F-O-C-G-K-D-H-L-M-I-N-P, as seen in the following image:

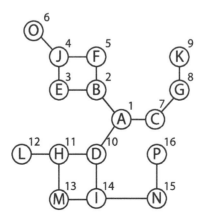

3. The order of breadth-first search would be A-B-C-D-E-F-G-H-I-J-K-L-M-N-O-P, as seen in the following image:

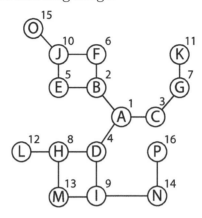

4. Following is an implementation of breadth-first search:

```
import queue_implementation

def bfs(starting_vertex, search_value):
    queue = queue_implementation.Queue()
    visited_vertices = {}
    visited_vertices[starting_vertex.value] = True
    queue.enqueue(starting_vertex)

    while queue.read():
        current_vertex = queue.dequeue()
        if current_vertex.value == search_value:
            return current_vertex

        for adjacent_vertex in current_vertex.adjacent_vertices:

            if not visited_vertices.get(adjacent_vertex.value):
                visited_vertices[adjacent_vertex.value] = True
                queue.enqueue(adjacent_vertex)

    return None
```

5. To find the shortest path in an *unweighted* graph, we're going to use breadth-first search. The main feature of breadth-first search is that it stays close to the starting vertex as long as possible. This feature will serve as the key to finding the shortest path.

Let's apply this to our social-networking example. Because breadth-first search stays close to Idris as long as possible, we'll end up finding Lina first through the shortest possible path. Only later on in the search would we end up finding Lina through longer paths. In fact, we can even stop the search as soon we as find Lina. (Our implementation that follows doesn't end early, but you can modify it to do so.)

As we visit each vertex for the first time, then, we know that the *current* vertex is *always* part of the shortest path from the *starting* vertex to the *vertex* we're visiting. (Remember, with BFS, the current vertex and the vertex we're visiting aren't necessarily the same.)

For example, when we visit Lina for the first time, Kamil will be the current vertex. This is because in BFS, we'll get to Lisa first through Kamil before we get to her through Sasha. When we do visit Lina (through Kamil), we can store in a table that the shortest path from Idris to Lina will be through Kamil. This table is similar to the cheapest_previous_stopover_city_table from Dijkstra's algorithm.

In fact, whenever we visit *any* vertex, the shortest path from Idris to that vertex will be through the current vertex. We'll store *all* of this data in a table called previous_vertex_table.

Finally, we can then use this data to work backward from Lina to Idris to build the precise shortest path between the two of them.

Here's our implementation:

```
import queue_implementation

def shortest_path(first_vertex, second_vertex, visited_vertices):
    queue = queue_implementation.Queue()
    previous_vertex_table = {}

    visited_vertices[first_vertex.value] = True
    queue.enqueue(first_vertex)

    while queue.read():
        current_vertex = queue.dequeue()

        for adjacent_vertex in current_vertex.adjacent_vertices:
            if not visited_vertices.get(adjacent_vertex.value):
                visited_vertices[adjacent_vertex.value] = True
                queue.enqueue(adjacent_vertex)
                previous_vertex_table[adjacent_vertex.value] = \
                    current_vertex.value

    shortest_path = []
    current_vertex_value = second_vertex.value

    while current_vertex_value != first_vertex.value:
        shortest_path.insert(0, current_vertex_value)
        current_vertex_value = \
            previous_vertex_table.get(current_vertex_value)

    shortest_path.insert(0, first_vertex.value)

    return shortest_path
```

Chapter 19

These are the solutions to the exercises found in the section Exercises, on page 393.

1. The space complexity is $O(N^2)$. This is because the function creates the array called collection, which will end up holding N^2 strings.

2. This implementation takes up $O(N)$ space, as we create a new_array containing N items.

3. The following implementation uses this algorithm: we swap the first item with the last item in place. Then we swap the second item with the second-to-last item in place. We then proceed to swap the third item with the third-to-last item in place, and so on. Since everything is done in place and we don't create any new data, this has a space complexity of $O(1)$.

```
def reverse(array):
    i = 0

    while i < len(array) // 2:
        mirror_of_i = len(array) - 1 - i
        array[i], array[mirror_of_i] = array[mirror_of_i], array[i]

        i += 1

    return array
```

(While Python may, under the hood, be creating a temporary variable to accomplish each swap, we never have more than that one piece of data stored at any time during the algorithm's execution.)

4. Here's the completed table:

Version	Time Complexity	Space Complexity
Version #1	O(N)	O(N)
Version #2	O(N)	O(1)
Version #3	O(N)	O(N)

All three versions run for as many steps as there are numbers in the array, so the time complexity is $O(N)$ for all of them.

Version #1 creates a brand-new array to store the doubled numbers. This array will have the same length as the original array, so takes up $O(N)$ space.

Version #2 modifies the original array in place, so takes up zero extra space. This is expressed as $O(1)$.

Version #3 also modifies the original array in place. However, since the function is recursive, the call stack at its peak will have N calls on it, taking up O(N) space.

Chapter 20

These are the solutions to the exercises found in the section Exercises, on page 430.

1. We can optimize this algorithm if we ask ourselves, "If I could magically find a desired piece of information in O(1) time, can I make my algorithm faster?"

   Specifically, as we iterate over one array, we'd want to "magically" look up that athlete from the other array in O(1) time. To accomplish this, we can first transform one of the arrays into a hash table. We'll use the full name (that is, the first *and* last name) as the key, and True (or any arbitrary item) as the value.

   Once we've turned one array into this hash table, we then iterate over the other array. As we encounter each athlete, we do an O(1) lookup in the hash table to see if that athlete already plays the other sport. If they do, we add that athlete to our multisport_athletes array, which we return at the end of the function.

   Here's the code for this approach:

```
def find_multisport_athletes(array_1, array_2):
    hash_table = {}
    multisport_athletes = []

    for athlete in array_1:
        hash_table[athlete["first_name"]
                   + " "
                   + athlete["last_name"]] = True

    for athlete in array_2:
        if hash_table.get(athlete["first_name"]
                          + " "
                          + athlete["last_name"]):
            multisport_athletes.append(athlete["first_name"]
                                       + " "
                                       + athlete["last_name"])

    return multisport_athletes
```

   This algorithm is O(N + M) since we iterate through each set of players just once.

2. For this algorithm, generating examples to find a pattern will be immensely helpful.

Let's take an array that has six integers and see what would happen if we removed a different integer each time:

```
[1, 2, 3, 4, 5, 6] : missing 0: sum = 21
[0, 2, 3, 4, 5, 6] : missing 1: sum = 20
[0, 1, 3, 4, 5, 6] : missing 2: sum = 19
[0, 1, 2, 4, 5, 6] : missing 3: sum = 18
[0, 1, 2, 3, 5, 6] : missing 4: sum = 17
[0, 1, 2, 3, 4, 6] : missing 5: sum = 16
```

Hmm. When we remove the 0, the sum is 21. When we remove the 1, the sum is 20. And when we remove the 2, the sum is 19, and so on. This definitely seems like a pattern!

Before we go further, let's call the 21 in this case the "full sum." This is the sum of the array when it's just missing the 0.

If we analyze these cases carefully, we'll see that the sum of any array is less than the full sum by the *amount of the missing number*. For example, when we're missing the 4, the sum is 17, which is four less than 21. And when we're missing the 1, the sum is 20, which is one less than 21.

So we can begin our algorithm by calculating what the full sum is. We can then subtract the actual sum from the full sum, and that will be our missing number.

Here's the code for this:

```python
def find_missing_number(array):
    full_sum = 0

    for num in range(1, len(array) + 1):
        full_sum += num

    current_sum = 0

    for num in array:
        current_sum += num

    return full_sum - current_sum
```

This algorithm is O(N). It takes N steps to calculate the full sum and then another N steps to calculate the actual sum. This is 2N steps, which reduces to O(N).

3. We can make this function much faster if we use a greedy algorithm. (Perhaps this shouldn't be a surprise given that our code is trying to make the greatest possible profit on stocks.)

To make the most profit, we want to buy as low as possible and sell as high as possible. Our greedy algorithm begins by assigning the very first price to be the buy_price. We then iterate over all the prices, and as soon as we find a lower price, we make it the new buy_price.

Similarly, as we iterate over the prices, we check how much profit we'd make if we sold at that price. This is calculated by subtracting the buy_price from the current price. In good greedy fashion, we save this profit in a variable called greatest_profit. As we iterate through all the prices, whenever we find a *greater* profit, we turn that into the greatest_profit.

By the time we're done looping through the prices, the greatest_profit will hold the greatest possible profit we can make by buying and selling the stock one time.

Here's the code for our algorithm:

```
def find_greatest_profit(array):
    buy_price = array[0]
    greatest_profit = 0

    for price in array:
        potential_profit = price - buy_price

        if price < buy_price:
            buy_price = price
        elif potential_profit > greatest_profit:
            greatest_profit = potential_profit

    return greatest_profit
```

Because we iterate over the N prices just once, our function takes O(N) time. We not only made a lot of money, but we made it fast.

4. This is another algorithm where generating examples to find a pattern will be the key to optimizing it.

As stated in the exercise, it's possible for the greatest product to be a result of negative numbers. Let's look at various examples of arrays and their greatest products formed by two numbers:

```
[-5, -4, -3, 0, 3, 4] -> Greatest product: 20 (-5 * -4)
[-9, -2, -1, 2, 3, 7] -> Greatest product: 21 (3 * 7)
[-7, -4, -3, 0, 4, 6] -> Greatest product: 28 (-7 * -4)
[-6, -5, -1, 2, 3, 9] -> Greatest product: 30 (-6 * -5)
[-9, -4, -3, 0, 6, 7] -> Greatest product: 42 (6 * 7)
```

Seeing all these cases may help us realize that the greatest product can only be formed by either the greatest two numbers or the *lowest* two (negative) numbers.

With this in mind, we should design our algorithm to keep track of these four numbers:

- The greatest number
- The second-to-greatest number
- The lowest number
- The second-to-lowest number

We can then compare the product of the two greatest numbers versus the product of the two lowest numbers. And whichever product is greater is the greatest product in the array.

Now, how do we find the greatest two numbers and the lowest two numbers? If we sorted the array, that would be easy. But that's still O(N log N), and the instructions say that we can achieve O(N).

In fact, we can find all four numbers in *a single pass* through the array. It's time to get greedy again.

Here's the code, followed by its explanation:

```python
def greatest_product(array):
    greatest_number = float("-inf")
    second_to_greatest_number = float("-inf")

    lowest_number = float("inf")
    second_to_lowest_number = float("inf")

    for number in array:
        if number >= greatest_number:
            second_to_greatest_number = greatest_number
            greatest_number = number
        elif number > second_to_greatest_number:
            second_to_greatest_number = number

        if number <= lowest_number:
            second_to_lowest_number = lowest_number
            lowest_number = number
        elif number < second_to_lowest_number:
            second_to_lowest_number = number

    greatest_product_from_two_highest = (greatest_number
                            * second_to_greatest_number)

    greatest_product_from_two_lowest = (lowest_number
                            * second_to_lowest_number)

    if (greatest_product_from_two_highest
            > greatest_product_from_two_lowest):
        return greatest_product_from_two_highest
    else:
        return greatest_product_from_two_lowest
```

Before we begin our loop, we set the greatest_number and second_to_greatest_number to be *negative* infinity. This ensures they start out *lower* than any number currently in the array.

We then iterate over each number. If the current number is greater than the greatest_number, we greedily turn the current number into the new greatest_number. If we've already found a second_to_greatest_number, we reassign the second_to_greatest_number to be whatever the greatest_number was before we reached the current number. This ensures the second_to_greatest_number will indeed be the second-to-greatest number.

If the current number we're iterating over is less than the greatest_number but greater than the second_to_greatest_number, we update the second_to_greatest_number to be the current number.

We follow this same process to find the lowest_number and the second_to_lowest_number.

Once we've found all four numbers, we compute the products from the two highest numbers and the products of the two lowest numbers and return whichever product is greater.

5. The key to optimizing this algorithm is the fact that we're sorting a finite number of values. Specifically, there are only eleven types of temperature readings that we may find in this array, namely:

   95, 96, 97, 98, 99, 100, 101, 102, 103, 104, 105

   Let's assume our input array is:

   [98, 99, 95, 105, 104, 99, 101, 99, 101, 97]

   If we imagine our array of temperatures as a *hash table*, we can store each temperature as a key and the number of occurrences as the value. This would look something like this:

   {98: 1, 99: 3, 95: 1, 105: 1, 104: 1, 101: 2, 97:1}

   With this in mind, we can run a loop that runs from 95 up through 105 and *checks the hash table* for how many occurrences of that temperature there are. Each of these lookups take just O(1) time.

   Then we use that number of occurrences to populate a new array. Because our loop is set to go up from 95 through 105, our array will end up in perfect ascending order.

Here's the code for this:

```python
def sort_temperatures(array):
    hash_table = {}

    for temperature in array:
        if temperature in hash_table:
            hash_table[temperature] += 1
        else:
            hash_table[temperature] = 1

    sorted_temperatures = []
    temperature = 95

    while temperature <= 105:
        if temperature in hash_table:
            for i in range(hash_table[temperature]):
                sorted_temperatures.append(temperature)

        temperature += 1

    return sorted_temperatures
```

Let's now analyze the efficiency of this algorithm. We take N steps to create the hash table. We then run a loop eleven times for all possible temperatures from 95 up to 105.

In each round of this loop, we run a nested loop to populate the sorted_temperatures with the temperatures. However, this inner loop will *never end up running more times than the N temperatures* from the input array. This is because the inner loop only runs one time for each temperature in the original array.

Thus, we have N steps to create the hash table, eleven steps for the outer loop, and N steps for the inner loop. This is 2N + 11, which is reduced to a beautiful O(N).

This algorithm is a classic sorting algorithm called *counting sort*. It's useful any time we're dealing with a relatively small range of possible input values, such as our case where there are only eleven possible values.

6. This optimization employs the most brilliant use of magical lookups that I've ever seen.

    Imagine we're iterating over the array of numbers and we encounter a 5. Let's ask ourselves the magical lookup question: "If I could magically find a desired piece of information in O(1) time, can I make my algorithm faster?"

Well, to determine whether the 5 is part of the longest consecutive sequence, we'd want to know whether there's a 6 in the array. We'd also want to know if there's a 7, and an 8, and so on.

We can achieve each of those lookups in O(1) time if we first store all the numbers from our array in a hash table; that is, the array [10, 5, 12, 3, 55, 30, 4, 11, 2] could look like this if we moved the data to a hash table:

```
{10: True, 5: True, 12: True, 3: True, 55: True,
 30: True, 4: True, 11: True, 2: True}
```

In this case, if we encounter the 2, we can then run a loop that keeps checking for the next number in the hash table. If it finds it, we increase the length of the current sequence by one. The loop repeats this process until it can't find the next number in the sequence. Each of these lookups takes just one step.

But, you may ask, how does this help? Imagine our array is [6, 5, 4, 3, 2, 1]. When we iterate over the 6, we'll find that there isn't a sequence that builds up from there. When we reach the 5, we'll find the sequence 5-6. When we reach the 4, we'll find the sequence 4-5-6. When we reach the 3, we'll find the sequence 3-4-5-6, and so on. We'll still end up going through about $N^2 / 2$ steps finding all those sequences.

The answer is that we'll only start building a sequence if the current number is the *bottom number* of the sequence. So we won't build 4-5-6 when there's a 3 in the array.

But how do we know if the current number is the bottom of a sequence? By doing a magical lookup!

How? Before running a loop to find a sequence, we'll do an O(1) lookup of the hash table to check whether there's a number *that's 1 less than current number*. So if the current number is 4, we'll first check to see whether there's a 3 in the array. If there is, we won't bother to build a sequence. We only want to build a sequence starting from the bottom number of that sequence; otherwise we have redundant steps.

Here's the code for this:

```
def longest_sequence_length(array):
    hash_table = {}
    greatest_sequence_length = 0

    for number in array:
        hash_table[number] = True

    for number in array:
```

```
        if not hash_table.get(number - 1):
            current_sequence_length = 1
            current_number = number

            while hash_table.get(current_number + 1):
                current_number += 1
                current_sequence_length += 1

                if current_sequence_length > greatest_sequence_length:
                    greatest_sequence_length = current_sequence_length

    return greatest_sequence_length
```

In this algorithm, we take N steps to build the hash table. We take another N steps to iterate through the array. And we take about another N steps looking up numbers in the hash table to build the different sequences. All in all, this is about 3N, which is reduced to O(N).

Index

Thank you!

We hope you enjoyed this book and that you're already thinking about what you want to learn next. To help make that decision easier, we're offering you this gift.

Head on over to https://pragprog.com right now, and use the coupon code BUYANOTHER2023 to save 30% on your next ebook. Offer is void where prohibited or restricted. This offer does not apply to any edition of the *The Pragmatic Programmer* ebook.

And if you'd like to share your own expertise with the world, why not propose a writing idea to us? After all, many of our best authors started off as our readers, just like you. With up to a 50% royalty, world-class editorial services, and a name you trust, there's nothing to lose. Visit https://pragprog.com/become-an-author/ today to learn more and to get started.

We thank you for your continued support, and we hope to hear from you again soon!

The Pragmatic Bookshelf

Pragmatic Bookshelf

SAVE 30%!
Use coupon code
BUYANOTHER2023

A Common-Sense Guide to Data Structures and Algorithms, Second Edition

If you thought that data structures and algorithms were all just theory, you're missing out on what they can do for your code. Learn to use Big O notation to make your code run faster by orders of magnitude. Choose from data structures such as hash tables, trees, and graphs to increase your code's efficiency exponentially. With simple language and clear diagrams, this book makes this complex topic accessible, no matter your background. This new edition features practice exercises in every chapter, and new chapters on topics such as dynamic programming and heaps and tries. Get the hands-on info you need to master data structures and algorithms for your day-to-day work.

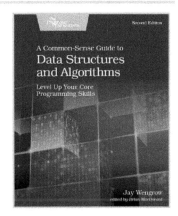

Jay Wengrow
(506 pages) ISBN: 9781680507225. $45.95
https://pragprog.com/book/jwdsal2

Exercises for Programmers

When you write software, you need to be at the top of your game. Great programmers practice to keep their skills sharp. Get sharp and stay sharp with more than fifty practice exercises rooted in real-world scenarios. If you're a new programmer, these challenges will help you learn what you need to break into the field, and if you're a seasoned pro, you can use these exercises to learn that hot new language for your next gig.

Brian P. Hogan
(118 pages) ISBN: 9781680501223. $24
https://pragprog.com/book/bhwb

From Objects to Functions

Build applications quicker and with less effort using functional programming and Kotlin. Learn by building a complete application, from gathering requirements to delivering a microservice architecture following functional programming principles. Learn how to implement CQRS and EventSourcing in a functional way to map the domain into code better and to keep the cost of change low for the whole application life cycle.

If you're curious about functional programming or you are struggling with how to put it into practice, this guide will help you increase your productivity composing small functions together instead of creating fat objects.

Uberto Barbini
(468 pages) ISBN: 9781680508451. $47.95
https://pragprog.com/book/uboop

Effective Haskell

Put the power of Haskell to work in your programs, learning from an engineer who uses Haskell daily to get practical work done efficiently. Leverage powerful features like Monad Transformers and Type Families to build useful applications. Realize the benefits of a pure functional language, like protecting your code from side effects. Manage concurrent processes fearlessly. Apply functional techniques to working with databases and building RESTful services. Don't get bogged down in theory, but learn to employ advanced programming concepts to solve real-world problems. Don't just learn the syntax, but dive deeply into Haskell as you build efficient, well-tested programs.

Rebecca Skinner
(668 pages) ISBN: 9781680509342. $57.95
https://pragprog.com/book/rshaskell

Functional Programming in Java, Second Edition

Imagine writing Java code that reads like the problem statement, code that's highly expressive, concise, easy to read and modify, and has reduced complexity. With the functional programming capabilities in Java, that's not a fantasy. This book will guide you from the familiar imperative style through the practical aspects of functional programming, using plenty of examples. Apply the techniques you learn to turn highly complex imperative code into elegant and easy-to-understand functional-style code. Updated to the latest version of Java, this edition has four new chapters on error handling, refactoring to functional style, transforming data, and idioms of functional programming.

Venkat Subramaniam
(274 pages) ISBN: 9781680509793. $53.95
https://pragprog.com/book/vsjava2e

Programming Kotlin

Programmers don't just use Kotlin, they love it. Even Google has adopted it as a first-class language for Android development. With Kotlin, you can intermix imperative, functional, and object-oriented styles of programming and benefit from the approach that's most suitable for the problem at hand. Learn to use the many features of this highly concise, fluent, elegant, and expressive statically typed language with easy-to-understand examples. Learn to write maintainable, high-performing JVM and Android applications, create DSLs, program asynchronously, and much more.

Venkat Subramaniam
(460 pages) ISBN: 9781680506358. $51.95
https://pragprog.com/book/vskotlin

Agile Web Development with Rails 7

Rails 7 completely redefines what it means to produce fantastic user experiences and provides a way to achieve all the benefits of single-page applications – at a fraction of the complexity. Rails 7 integrates the Hotwire frameworks of Stimulus and Turbo directly as the new defaults, together with that hot newness of import maps. The result is a toolkit so powerful that it allows a single individual to create modern applications upon which they can build a competitive business. The way it used to be.

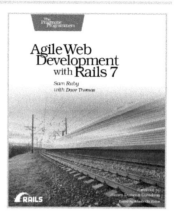

Sam Ruby
(474 pages) ISBN: 9781680509298. $59.95
https://pragprog.com/book/rails7

Creating Software with Modern Diagramming Techniques

Diagrams communicate relationships more directly and clearly than words ever can. Using only text-based markup, create meaningful and attractive diagrams to document your domain, visualize user flows, reveal system architecture at any desired level, or refactor your code. With the tools and techniques this book will give you, you'll create a wide variety of diagrams in minutes, share them with others, and revise and update them immediately on the basis of feedback. Adding diagrams to your professional vocabulary will enable you to work through your ideas quickly when working on your own code or discussing a proposal with colleagues.

Ashley Peacock
(156 pages) ISBN: 9781680509830. $29.95
https://pragprog.com/book/apdiag

Designing Data Governance from the Ground Up

Businesses own more data than ever before, but it's of no value if you don't know how to use it. Data governance manages the people, processes, and strategy needed for deploying data projects to production. But doing it well is far from easy: Less than one fourth of business leaders say their organizations are data driven. In *Designing Data Governance from the Ground Up*, you'll build a cross-functional strategy to create roadmaps and stewardship for data-focused projects, embed data governance into your engineering practice, and put processes in place to monitor data after deployment.

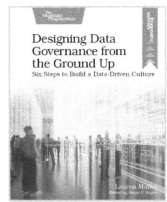

Lauren Maffeo
(100 pages) ISBN: 9781680509809. $29.95
https://pragprog.com/book/lmmlops

Concurrent Data Processing in Elixir

Learn different ways of writing concurrent code in Elixir and increase your application's performance, without sacrificing scalability or fault-tolerance. Most projects benefit from running background tasks and processing data concurrently, but the world of OTP and various libraries can be challenging. Which Supervisor and what strategy to use? What about GenServer? Maybe you need back-pressure, but is GenStage, Flow, or Broadway a better choice? You will learn everything you need to know to answer these questions, start building highly concurrent applications in no time, and write code that's not only fast, but also resilient to errors and easy to scale.

Svilen Gospodinov
(174 pages) ISBN: 9781680508192. $39.95
https://pragprog.com/book/sgdpelixir

The Pragmatic Bookshelf

The Pragmatic Bookshelf features books written by professional developers for professional developers. The titles continue the well-known Pragmatic Programmer style and continue to garner awards and rave reviews. As development gets more and more difficult, the Pragmatic Programmers will be there with more titles and products to help you stay on top of your game.

Visit Us Online

This Book's Home Page
https://pragprog.com/book/jwpython
Source code from this book, errata, and other resources. Come give us feedback, too!

Keep Up-to-Date
https://pragprog.com
Join our announcement mailing list (low volume) or follow us on Twitter @pragprog for new titles, sales, coupons, hot tips, and more.

New and Noteworthy
https://pragprog.com/news
Check out the latest Pragmatic developments, new titles, and other offerings.

Save on the ebook

Save on the ebook versions of this title. Owning the paper version of this book entitles you to purchase the electronic versions at a terrific discount.

PDFs are great for carrying around on your laptop—they are hyperlinked, have color, and are fully searchable. Most titles are also available for the iPhone and iPod touch, Amazon Kindle, and other popular e-book readers.

Send a copy of your receipt to support@pragprog.com and we'll provide you with a discount coupon.

Contact Us

Online Orders:	*https://pragprog.com/catalog*
Customer Service:	*support@pragprog.com*
International Rights:	*translations@pragprog.com*
Academic Use:	*academic@pragprog.com*
Write for Us:	*http://write-for-us.pragprog.com*

Milton Keynes UK
Ingram Content Group UK Ltd.
UKHW021509170324
439539UK00002B/6